STUDYING LEADERSHIP

Praise for *Studying Leadership*

'This book has the potential of being a core text for academics, research students (MSc, PhD, DBA) and academic-consultants.'
Javier Marcos, Cranfield University

'The chapters set out some of the key issues in leadership studies at the current time. They successfully combine a review of the theoretical position in leadership and give a critical assessment of these theories in the current leadership climate.'
Dr Claire Collins, Henley Business School, University of Reading

'This book is well constructed and very well researched. It has a clearly thought out logical flow with enough material to inform and challenge both undergraduate and postgraduate students.'
Lise Georgeson, Academic Director, St Mary's University College

'A distinctive book written in an eloquent style and manner that captures the readers' imagination of the past, present and future perception of leadership. It highlights and draws together the main concepts covered in each chapter and provides a very good basis for understanding leadership. This book is readable, credible and avoids jargon. Thus, it helps both UG and PG students to conceptualize leadership at a higher level.'
David Hyams-Ssekas, University Campus Oldham

STUDYING
LEADERSHIP

TRADITIONAL & CRITICAL APPROACHES

Doris Schedlitzki & Gareth Edwards

Los Angeles | London | New Delhi
Singapore | Washington DC

Los Angeles | London | New Delhi
Singapore | Washington DC

SAGE Publications Ltd
1 Oliver's Yard
55 City Road
London EC1Y 1SP

SAGE Publications Inc.
2455 Teller Road
Thousand Oaks, California 91320

SAGE Publications India Pvt Ltd
B 1/I 1 Mohan Cooperative Industrial Area
Mathura Road
New Delhi 110 044

SAGE Publications Asia-Pacific Pte Ltd
3 Church Street
#10-04 Samsung Hub
Singapore 049483

Editor: Kirsty Smy
Development editor: Robin Lupton
Assistant editor: Nina Smith
Production editor: Sarah Cooke
Marketing manager: Alison Borg
Cover design: Francis Kenney
Typeset by: C&M Digitals (P) Ltd, Chennai, India
Printed and bound in Great Britain by Ashford
Colour Press Ltd

Library of Congress Control Number: 2013941887

British Library Cataloguing in Publication data

A catalogue record for this book is available from
the British Library

MIX
Paper from
responsible sources
FSC® C011748

ISBN 978-1-4462-0796-3
ISBN 978-1-4462-0797-0 (pbk)

We would like to dedicate this book to those who inspire us most:
Julian, Iris and Ellie Rose.

Summary of Contents

Contents

List of Tables

List of Figures

Acknowledgements

We would like to thank our colleagues Anita Gulati, Roger Williams, Tony Nelson and Laura Riches for sharing their experiences with us in the form of six fascinating case studies. We hope the readers will enjoy these as much as we do. We would also like to thank our publisher Sage – and particularly Robin Lupton and Kirsty Smy – for their patience and trust. Finally, we would like to acknowledge the contributions of our colleagues in the wider leadership community, whose work has informed the writing of this book and whose comments on the future of leadership studies have inspired the epilogue.

About the Authors

Doris Schedlitzki

Doris has worked within the field of leadership studies for over 10 years, starting with the completion of her DPhil at the University of Oxford on *Critical Approaches to Cross-cultural Leadership Studies*. Her current research focus on leadership and leadership development explores the areas of cross-cultural studies of leadership, discourse and leadership, leadership as identity, psychoanalytic approaches to leadership and the role of national language within cultural leadership studies. Doris is involved in several projects and collaborations related to these different areas with UK and international colleagues in leadership and management studies, history and linguistics. She has published her work in the form of academic journal articles on leadership and leadership development in *Leadership*, *Management Learning*, the *Scandinavian Journal of Management*, the *Leadership and Organization Development Journal* and the *International Journal of Management Education*. Doris's book publications include, for example, book chapters on leadership and national language, leadership in departments and the link between authentic leadership and emotional labour. She has also co-edited the Palgrave book *Worldly Leadership*. In her current academic role in the field of Organisation Studies at the University of the West of England, Doris teaches leadership studies at both undergraduate and postgraduate level and supervises MSc dissertations and Doctoral theses on leadership. Her approach to teaching leadership studies embraces experiential and reflective methods as well as the use of arts-based methods such as imagery, mythology and story-telling. Doris has enjoyed sharing her conceptual and pedagogical experience with leadership studies and leadership development through the writing of this book and particularly the contrasting of traditional, current and critical perspectives.

Gareth Edwards

Gareth has worked within the field of leadership studies for over 15 years which was also initiated by the completion of his PhD at the University of Strathclyde on

Leadership Effectiveness across Hierarchical Levels in Organisations. His current research on leadership and leadership development explores aspects of distributed leadership and in particular explores community perspectives, such as belonging, symbolism, networks, language and liminality. Gareth is involved in a number of research projects and collaborations related to these different areas with UK and international colleagues in leadership and management studies, strategic management and history. He has published his work on leadership and leadership development through journal articles and special issues in the *International Journal of Management Reviews, Management Learning, Advances in Developing Human Resources*, the *Leadership and Organization Development Journal* and *Organisations and People*. Gareth's book publications include, for example, book chapters on leadership for sustainable development, the changing face of leadership and evaluating leadership development. He is also co-editor of the Palgrave book *Worldly Leadership*. Gareth brings his conceptual and leadership development experience into his current academic role in the field of Organisation Studies at the University of the West of England, and his teaching of Undergraduate, MSc and MBA students. He also supervises MSc dissertations and Doctoral theses on leadership and leadership development. Gareth's approach to teaching leadership studies is fundamentally based on experiential and reflective methods as well as the use of arts-based methods such as film, photographs and collage. Gareth has enjoyed sharing his conceptual and training and development experience within the field of leadership studies and leadership development through the writing of this book and particularly the contrasting of academic and training and development perspectives.

Guided Tour

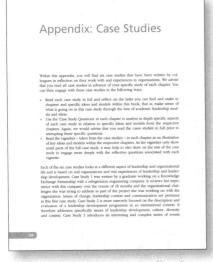

Six long integrative **Case Studies** in an Appendix at the back of the book may be read in advance and applied to the models and ideas covered in each chapter, highlighting links between topics.

Vignette boxes introduce you to an extract from one of the six case studies. Drawing on real-life examples, they ask you to apply a particular theory or idea introduced in this chapter to the example.

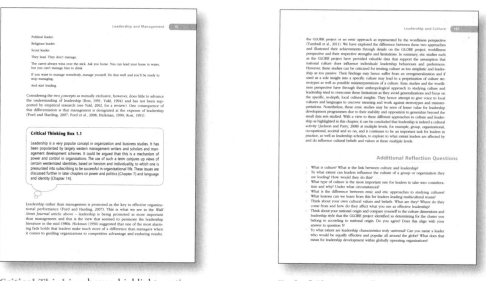

Critical Thinking boxes highlight particular limitations or current critical debates in relation to a particular theory or idea discussed in the chapter.

End of Chapter Reflection Questions are provided at the end of the chapter and challenge you to reflect on key theories and ideas discussed in the chapter and how they relate to your own knowledge and view on leadership.

In-chapter Reflective Questions are provided throughout the chapters to challenge you to reflect on key theories and ideas discussed in the chapter and how they relate to your own knowledge and view on leadership.

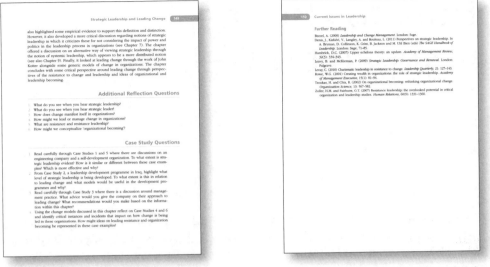

Case Study Questions are provided at the end of the chapter and ask you to apply particular theories or ideas from this chapter to case studies included in the Appendix of the book.

Further Reading lists at the end of each chapter contain brief outlines of key books and academic journal articles.

How to Use the Companion Website

Schedlitzki and Edwards' *Studying Leadership: Traditional and Critical Approaches* is supported by a companion website. Visit **www.sagepub.co.uk/studyleadership** to take advantage of the additional learning resources for students and lecturers.

For Students

- **Video Links** highlight real life examples and illustrations of leadership issues
- **Free selected SAGE journal articles** from each chapter are available to further develop your understanding

For Lecturers

- **Instructor Manual** containing tutor notes for each chapter to support your teaching.
- **Experiential Exercises with Tutor Notes** provide you with specific examples for exercises to use in class.
- **PowerPoint Slides** featuring learning objectives and key concepts from each chapter.

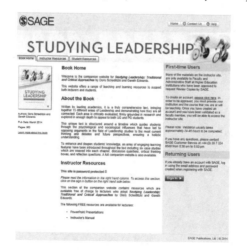

Introduction

Mapping Different Approaches to Studying Leadership

In this book, we aim to introduce you to models, theories and topics of leadership and highlight the existence of wider debates in research and key developments within the field of leadership studies over time. Our motivation to provide such a comprehensive and critical overview of leadership studies stems partly from the difficulties we have encountered with introducing our students to, and asking them to engage deeply, with the wider field of leadership research. A key reason for this struggle has been the predominant focus of existing textbooks on presenting leadership theories, models and research ideas in a topical fashion and without recognition of wider epistemological, philosophical and geographical debates. Such textbooks have further tended to either focus on mainstream leadership theories and topics or alternatively to focus only on critical and alternative approaches to leadership. A second aim of this book has therefore been to give voice to different methodologies, epistemological and geographical approaches to the study of leadership that have formed leadership studies into the complex and exciting field that it is today. In the remainder of this introductory chapter, we will give you an overview of the different parts and chapters of this book as well as briefly introduce the key debates and developments in the field of leadership studies.

Overview of the Book

This book will enrich your modular study of leadership through a comprehensive outline of key leadership theories, topics and trends in the wider field of leadership studies. This outline will be enhanced through recognition and giving attention to wider debates within the topical field as well as leadership studies in general. Chapters will hence not only outline theories and ideas but also introduce and discuss timelines and different geographically-based debates, and recognise equally psychological and sociological contributions where appropriate. The latter element has been either ignored in many textbooks or these have taken a predominantly psychological or sociological stance on leadership. This has usually been to the disadvantage of students of leadership studies as it has silenced the origins and underlying assumptions of specific theories and ideas and possibly limited their ability to explore critical questions around such theories and ideas and to contextualise these appropriately. This book gives also voice to topics that have so far been neglected in mainstream leadership textbooks such as the perceptions and context of leadership, power and politics, distributed leadership, followership, toxicity, authenticity, language, identity, arts and aesthetics.

We have divided the book into three main parts to highlight and group historical developments in leadership theory as well as current debates and topics. The first part of the book will therefore introduce you to key theories that are often associated with traditional, mainstream views of leadership that are largely driven by psychological perspectives. In Chapter 1 we revisit the long-standing debate on differences and similarities in leadership and management and we do so through recognition of some of the key views voiced over the decades on this subject as well as through highlighting issues of language and change. Chapter 2 discusses the origins and current contributions, strengths and weaknesses of leadership traits, skills, intelligences and styles approaches to leadership, carefully selecting key theories to represent each of these areas of leadership studies and link these to wider and recurring debates on leadership. Chapter 3 then considers the context and relationship with followers further by critically evaluating early contingency and Leader-Member-Exchange (LMX) theories of leadership. The relational and contextual nature of leadership will be discussed in relation to these studies and picked up again in Part II of the book in Chapters 5 and 6. Chapter 4, the final chapter of Part I, then completes this review of traditional approaches to leadership through a critical discussion of the origins and currency of the transformational and charismatic theories of leadership.

Part II of this book introduces you to some of the main topics and perspectives currently explored within the wider remit of leadership studies and will link these again to historical developments as well as critical debates in leadership research. Chapter 5 picks up the idea of context of leadership from the psychologically informed studies of leadership to look more closely at the importance of different contexts and the conceptualisation of leadership as a contextual phenomenon from a sociological perspective. A bridge will be formed in this chapter between the social constructivist view of the contextual phenomenon of leadership and a more psychological perspective of its construction through the eye of followers in light of the implicit leadership theory and the relevance of social identity theory. In recognition of the limitations of focussing on the leader only, Chapter 6 gives voice to the important field of studies on followership. We highlight the main contributions and explore in greater depth psychoanalytic and relational approaches to leadership. Chapter 7 focuses on the relevance of power and politics for leadership and particularly highlights critical views on the role of power within the concept and practice of leadership. Chapter 8 then looks closely at the role of leadership in change and linked to this considers issues of strategic leadership. Chapter 9 shifts the focus of our review of leadership studies from the individual to the group level and explores the increasingly popular field of distributed leadership. In Chapter 10, we critically discuss the benefits of etic and emic approaches to studying leadership across culture. We make reference here to a diverse set of cultures such as the organisational, occupational, regional and national one. At the national level we evaluate the strengths and weaknesses of large-scale, cross-cultural studies compared to worldly and inter-cultural leadership studies. The final chapter of this second part of the book is then dedicated to a wider review of the leadership development field and aims to cover a broad introduction to different development approaches and notions of self-leadership, as well as draw the reader's attention to current situational, socially constructed and aesthetic approaches to leadership development.

In Part III of the book, we look more closely at the most recent trends within leadership studies and cover the areas of gender and diversity, toxicity and authenticity, ethics and sustainability, language and identity and finally arts and aesthetics. These chapters build on the more established ideas presented in Part II and aim to stretch your understanding of the more socially constructed, critical approaches to understanding and studying leadership. An epilogue follows at the end of the book that builds especially on Part III and aims not only to reflect on the key themes running through the book but also to consider what may be the key debates and research strands around leadership in the future. This epilogue draws on a series of statements from leadership scholars to investigate the breadth of these possible future avenues of leadership studies.

In the next two sections, we will introduce you to some of the key developments and debates within leadership studies that have occurred over the last century and conclude this introductory chapter with information on key learning features in this book.

Leadership Studies – A Changing Landscape

Upon opening any textbook on leadership, you will usually encounter a reference to the vast and fuzzy nature of leadership studies and be alerted to the ongoing yet so far unlucky attempt to agree on a definition of leadership. In 1985 Bennis and Nanus argued that 'no clear unequivocal understanding exists as to what distinguishes leaders from non-leaders ... Never have so many laboured so long to say so little' (1985: 4). This statement is as true today as it was then or even more so in light of diversification of the focus in leadership studies away from the individual and towards the social process. One of the definitions we use most often in our teaching is the following by Northouse:

> Leadership is a process whereby an individual influences a group of individuals to achieve a common goal. (2006: 3)

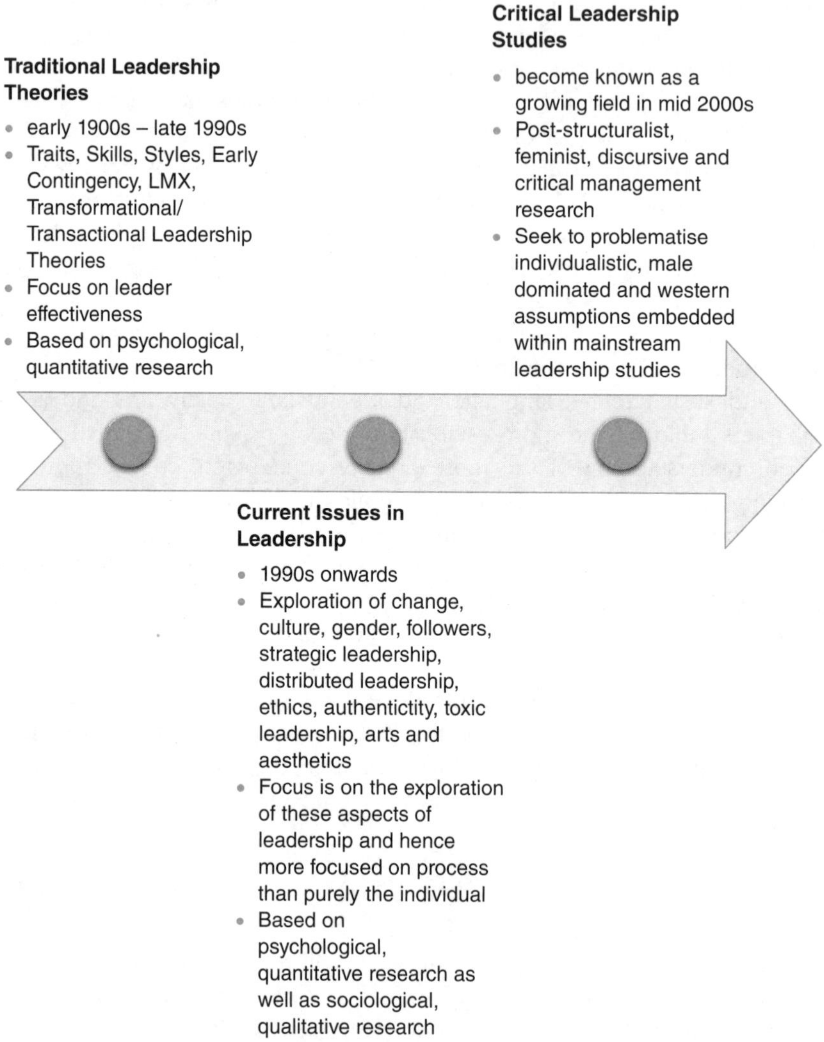

Traditional Leadership Theories

- early 1900s – late 1990s
- Traits, Skills, Styles, Early Contingency, LMX, Transformational/ Transactional Leadership Theories
- Focus on leader effectiveness
- Based on psychological, quantitative research

Critical Leadership Studies

- become known as a growing field in mid 2000s
- Post-structuralist, feminist, discursive and critical management research
- Seek to problematise individualistic, male dominated and western assumptions embedded within mainstream leadership studies

Current Issues in Leadership

- 1990s onwards
- Exploration of change, culture, gender, followers, strategic leadership, distributed leadership, ethics, authentictity, toxic leadership, arts and aesthetics
- Focus is on the exploration of these aspects of leadership and hence more focused on process than purely the individual
- Based on psychological, quantitative research as well as sociological, qualitative research

Figure 1.1   **A Timeline of Leadership Studies**

This definition highlights the shift we have seen over the last century towards seeing leadership as a process that occurs within a wider group context and that involves some form of purpose and the presence of some form of influencing and power to move towards that purpose. We will explore this basic definition further throughout the book and highlight differences in approaches to seeing, conceptualising and studying leadership. This will include the study of assigned vs. emergent leadership, leadership as a person or a process (Grint, 2005a) and the relationship between leadership and management as well as the role of followers. We will further explore the context of leadership and the role that power, change, culture, diversity and identity play. Figure 1.1 opposite aims to summarise the most significant changes within the field of leadership studies.

Grint's (2011) insightful historical overview of the major developments in leadership studies since 1840 stresses the cyclical nature of rational and normative patterns in leadership models and theories, linking these further to changes in the wider political field. Whilst recognising these binary or cyclical patterns in leadership studies, we should also recognise gradual linear movements and developments from a philosophical, methodological and geographical perspective that have occurred over the last century. Initially dominated by large-scale quantitative survey research (Bryman, 2011), based predominantly within US academic universities and by and large situated within a psychological perspective, leadership studies and leadership development were for the greater part of the 20th century predominantly concerned with the individual leader. Subsequently, we have seen a plethora of theories and models on the traits and behaviours of a leader and the relationship between leader and follower.

It was towards the end of the 20th century that research and scholarly contributions on leadership started to see an increasing impact from the European continent and with it increasingly a shift towards sociologically influenced, qualitative studies and conceptualisations of leadership. Subsequently we have seen a shift towards relational, social constructivist views of leadership and a distinct move away from the individual leader towards leadership as a social process. These movements involved further shifts in the wider literature from heroic to post-heroic, distributed forms of leadership and followership studies. The last decade has further seen the rise of what Collinson (2011) has termed 'Critical Leadership Studies', including post-structuralist, feminist, discursive and critical management research that has critically reviewed and problematised the still heavily individualistic, white, male dominated and western assumptions embedded within mainstream leadership studies.

On the global front, we have also seen a shift from cross-cultural leadership studies towards worldly (e.g. Turnbull et al., 2011) and inter- and intra-cultural leadership studies. These approaches are increasingly questioning the colonial approach that leadership studies and leadership development have often taken and imposed western models on other countries. In response, the worldly and inter- and intra-cultural approaches attempt to strengthen the voice of individual native languages and cultures. Within leadership development practices, we have seen similar significant shifts over the last century both within university settings and independent training companies. What was traditionally a practice oriented area is now increasingly being supported and supplemented through rigorous and critical research on current and future practice, including traditional cognitive as well as situated, co-constructed learning and aesthetic approaches to leadership development. Areas that remain under-developed are those of ethics in leadership, diversity, toxicity, identity, relational approaches, aesthetic approaches and psychoanalytic approaches to leadership, creating exciting future avenues for leadership studies.

Key Debate – Psychological and Sociological Perspectives

A key part of this development of leadership theories – as highlighted in Figure 1.1 – has been the establishment of two main streams: psychologically driven studies and sociologically driven studies, as well as associated preferences for and outcomes of quantitative and qualitative research methods. These two main streams will be addressed throughout this book and voice will be given within most chapters to views, ideas and challenges of leadership from each of these streams. We hope to give you a more balanced view of leadership studies through this recognition of different streams and approaches to studying leadership and the advantages and limitations either approach brings.

Psychologically driven approaches to leadership are often associated with the 'dominant' or 'mainstream' paradigm within leadership studies and focus 'primarily on individuals and on their internal dynamics' (Collinson, 2011: 183). Collinson (2011:182) further stresses that models and theories associated with this approach (e.g. trait, situational, contingency, path-goal, leader-member exchange, social identity, emotional intelligence, charismatic and transformational leadership theories) focus primarily on the 'question of what makes an effective leader' and tend to embrace quantitative, large-scale, standardised questionnaire methods of enquiry to underpin their abstract models/theories of reality. Critical views of this dominant, mainstream psychological, individualist approach to leadership studies have increased in terms of frequency and dominance within the wider leadership literature and have been especially nurtured by European based journals such as *Leadership*. Critical writers (e.g. Fairhurst, 2007; Jackson and Parry, 2008) have been particularly concerned with the leader-centric, essentialist view of leaders and leadership that sees followers as passive recipients or mere moderators in the predictive, effective leadership equation. The success and nature of leadership have been treated as a top-down influence process (Collinson, 2011) where leaders change followers' vision and values to attain a predefined goal. This emphasis on the individual leader and with it the dualist approach to leaders and followers has in the view of these critical writers led to an unrealistic, romanticised view of leaders and a neglect of followers.

Fairhurst (2007) and Grint (1997) have been especially influential through their writings in offering alternative views of leadership: those of the 'socially and discursively constructed nature of leadership dynamics' (Collinson, 2011: 183). This alternative, sociologically driven approach to leadership has been gaining in voice and momentum over the last two decades, especially within a European scholarly context, and is slowly but steadily gaining in importance alongside the mainstream one. This critical or sociologically driven approach is drawing predominantly on qualitative, interpretive methods of enquiry that aim to explore and uncover 'the shifting possible constructions of leadership located within their complex conditions, processes and consequences' (Collinson, 2011: 183).

It is important for the reader and student of leadership studies to be aware of these two streams of or approaches to leadership research and theory as they have fundamentally different foci and assumptions on leadership, and hence, are able to explore and address very different aspects of leadership. Gaining an understanding of the strengths and limitations of either approach may enable a deeper understanding of the different views on and conceptualisations of leadership. For example, whilst one of the key strengths of psychologically driven theories of leadership is to offer researchers and practitioners a means to exploring the 'essence' of leaders and predict their effectiveness within their contexts, hence informing selection and career progression processes in organisations, this focus on the individual and his/her essence could also be seen as a key limitation from a sociologically driven perspective. Grint (1997) has criticised this focus on essence for its ignorance of the socially constructed, dynamic nature of both 'leadership' and 'context' (Collinson, 2011).

From a sociological, critical perspective, all forms of leadership are subjective, socially and discursively constructed and dynamic. Hence, all accounts of leadership are interpretive and tied to the social encounters of those involved in them – a collective product that is stable and 'real' only at that moment in time and in the views of those involved in it. Accounts of leadership are hence re-interpreted and re-constructed over time, stressing the very dynamic nature of leadership. The key strength of this approach to leadership is its emphasis on the 'intrinsically relational' (Ospina and Sorenson, 2007, cited in Collinson, 2011: 183) that stresses the equally important role of leaders and followers and predominantly explores the interactional process between all social actors involved rather than the individuals as such. This sociologically driven approach to leadership with its qualitative research methods and its recognition of the significance of context and the dynamic, multiple forms of leadership context is then also able to explore in greater depth differences in leadership conceptualisation in light of the multiple identities and value sets that leaders and followers may have. The latter strength could on the other hand be seen to be a key limitation from a psychological perspective as qualitative research is so deeply rooted in the local meaning that it does not allow for generalisations and predictive theories of effective leadership.

Additional Features

In order to maximise the potential of this book's contribution to your study of leadership, we would strongly recommend making the most use of the pedagogic features of each chapter as well as the online companion website. In each chapter you will find diagrams and summary tables that will give you a snapshot summary of key theories or issues. In order to give you a clearer indication of developments in the field of leadership studies as well as introduce you to key ongoing debates, there will be critical thinking boxes highlighting current and critical ideas in the individual chapters. There will further be reflective questions and case study vignettes illustrating theory in action and asking you to engage in active reflection on how theories and ideas relate to your own experiences and practice. At the end of each chapter you will find summaries of the chapter as well as additional reflective and self-test questions, case study specific questions and sources for further reading. In the appendix of the book you will also find six case studies based on real organisations and organisational experiences that the vignettes and chapter specific, case study related questions are linked to. We strongly advise that you read all six case studies in advance of your study of individual chapters as this will help you to put both vignettes and the case study specific questions in the further context of each case study.

The online companion supplements these elements through presentation slides summarising each chapter as well as exercises to explore and apply your knowledge on a specific chapter. We hope that you will find the book and its companion a useful guide through your modular study of leadership or as a companion during leadership development programmes.

Part I
Traditional Approaches to Leadership

1

Leadership and Management

In this chapter we explore the meanings derived from two closely connected concepts – leadership and management. We discuss differing views of whether these concepts are the same, different or interconnected. We also link the views around leadership and management to theoretical perspectives such as transformational and transactional leadership (discussed further in Chapter 4). We conclude the chapter with a brief discussion linking conceptualizations of leadership and management with the broad notion of change in organizations and suggest that a critical perspective on the question of leadership, management and change is useful in making sense of the interconnections and relationships between concepts.

Chapter Aims

- Introduce and critically discuss the link between leadership and management
- Explore the differences and similarities between the two concepts
- Critically discuss the link between leadership, management and change
- Introduce a debate around the enactment of leadership and management within organizations

Leadership and Management: Are They the Same?

> Leadership is one of the most observed and least understood phenomena on earth. (Burns, 1978: 2)

> Management is a mysterious thing in so far as the more research that is undertaken the less we seem to be able to understand. (Grint, 1995: 3)

These opinions indicate a similarity, evident over the years, in the ambiguity surrounding the concepts of leadership and management, that is, the large amount of research devoted to each phenomenon, yet the uncertainty about their conceptual underpinnings. The question of whether leadership is different from or similar to management is a well-worn path in the leadership literature. Most, if not all textbooks on leadership will have a section of the debates that continue to run up to the present day. We summarize and critically consider these viewpoints which enables us to develop our thinking around other concepts such as leading change in organizations (see Chapter 8).

First, the chapter is framed in the contemporary debate about the shortcomings of current leadership (and management) theory. The study of leadership was described in the early part of the 21st century as fragmented, internally inconsistent and confusing (Gill, 2003) and disconnected and directionless (Zaccaro and Klimoski, 2001). For example, Gill (2003) suggested that nothing had changed much since the early 1980s, when Quinn (1984) had suggested that researchers on leadership were increasingly becoming frustrated with the field owing to the apparent continual stream of unconnected empirical studies despite a large investment in the research topic. A similar view is also evident in the management literature (Hales, 1986, 1999). Hales (1986), about the same time as Quinn, expressed a similar view in relation to management, whereby he critiques management studies along the same lines:

> Anyone seeking to build a consistent body of knowledge from the different research studies by a process of contrast and comparison finds the task difficult. Moving from one study to another invariably brings both a change in focus and in the categories employed to describe the phenomenon (management). The whole is a disconnected area of research with little sense of a sustained, systematic accretion of knowledge. (1986: 105)

Hales (1999) later suggested that an adequate account of the generic features of managerial work must be attentive to the influence of context. In essence he suggests how a manager's location within different institutional and organizational systems both generates and shapes their work. A similar argument has emerged in the literature concerning leadership:

> ... the various parts of [the empirical and conceptual leadership] literature still appear disconnected and directionless. In our opinion, a major cause of the state of the field is that many studies of leadership are context free; that is, low consideration is given to

organizational variables that influence the nature and impact of leadership. Such research … tends to focus on interpersonal processes between individuals, nominally leaders and followers. (Zaccaro and Klimoski, 2001: 3)

In addition, Ghoshal (2005) suggested that currently influential theories of management span diverse academic disciplines, including psychology, sociology and economics. Similarly Gill (2006) suggested the same of leadership, which is researched under a number of different perspectives – psychology, sociology, philosophy, anthropology, military and business strategy, political science, history, theology, sport, the arts and mythology. The similarity of these separate comments about leadership and management raises the question: are these scholars discussing one and the same concept? These comments certainly suggest that we have been investigating the same concept but referring to them differently in name. As we will see there has been a number of differing perspectives on the distinction between leadership and management.

Reflective Question 1.1

Think about your experiences in organizations. What would you define as leadership and management? Are these definitions the same, similar or different?

One issue concerning the concepts of leadership and management is which one is the overriding concept. Four views appear to permeate the leadership and management literature (Hunt, 1991).

1. Leadership is a broader concept than management (Hersey and Blanchard, 1988).
2. Leadership and management cannot be differentiated (a manager is by definition the same as a leader).
3. Leadership is one of the many roles of a manager (Bass, 1985a; Mintzberg, 1980).
4. Leadership and management can be sharply differentiated to the extent of calling some people leaders and some people managers (Bennis and Nanus, 1985; Korukonda and Hunt, 1987; Kotter, 1990; Schneider, 1989; Zaleznik, 1977).

As we shall see these views appear to overlap and are interwoven in the discussion on whether leadership is the same as or different from management. From here we will go on to highlight the differing views on whether leadership and management are the same or different, whether management is being downplayed in favour of leadership and whether using the concept of change alongside leadership and management helps us make sense of the confusion that surrounds attempts to define the two concepts.

Leadership Versus Management or Leadership not Management

The words 'leadership' and 'management' do appear to have a different origin (sometimes referred to as etymological background). For example, the word 'management' comes from the Latin word *manus* and has a meaning of handling things (objects, machinery and so on). The word 'management' appears to have grown in stature during the industrial revolution when it had a link to the handling of machinery in particular. The word 'leadership', on the other hand, comes from the Anglo-Saxon word *laeder*, which appears to have a meaning around 'a road' or 'a path', suggesting some form of direction giving. It is these etymological differences that appear to have marked out the way scholars have tried to distinguish the two concepts – leadership and management. Some scholars (Bennis, 1989; Bennis and Nanus, 1985; Hickman, 1990; Kotter, 1988, 1990; Rost, 1991; Zaleznik, 1977) have had serious conceptual concerns in regarding leadership and management as synonymous (Rost, 1991). These scholars, therefore, have tried to differentiate the two concepts; in some cases conceptualizing them as mutually exclusive (Bennis and Nanus, 1985; Zaleznik, 1977). In other words, some people are viewed as managers and others are viewed as leaders (Yukl, 2002). Some distinctions between leadership and management and leaders and managers have been:

> We manage things, but we lead people. (Attributed to John Adair)
>
> Managers have subordinates – leaders have followers. (Attributed to Murray Johannsen)
>
> Management is about arranging and telling. Leadership is about nurturing and enhancing. (Attributed to Tom Peters)
>
> The manager administers, the leader innovates; the manager is a copy, the leader is an original; the manager maintains, the leader develops. (Bennis, 1989: 45)
>
> Managers are people who do things right. Leaders are people who do the right things. (Bennis and Nanus, 1985).

Another example comes from an article in the *Wall Street Journal* in 1984, entitled 'Let's Get Rid of Management', and reads:

> People don't want to be managed. They want to be led. Whoever heard of a world manager?
>
> World leader.
>
> Yes.
>
> Educational leader.

Political leader.

Religious leader.

Scout leader.

They lead. They don't manage.

The carrot always wins over the stick. Ask you horse. You can lead your horse to water, but you can't manage him to drink.

If you want to manage somebody, manage yourself. Do that well and you'll be ready to stop managing.

And start leading.

Considering the two concepts as mutually exclusive, however, does little to advance the understanding of leadership (Rost, 1991; Yukl, 1994) and has not been supported by empirical research (see Yukl, 2002, for a review). One consequence of this differentiation is that management is denigrated at the expense of leadership (Ford and Harding, 2007; Ford et al., 2008; Hickman, 1990; Rost, 1991).

Critical Thinking Box 1.1

Leadership is a very popular concept in organization and business studies. It has been popularized by largely western management writers and scholars and management development schemes. It could be argued that this is a mechanism of power and control in organizations. The use of such a term conjures up views of certain westernized identities, based on heroism and individuality, to which one is pressurized into subscribing to be successful in organizational life. These issues are discussed further in later chapters on power and politics (Chapter 7) and language and identity (Chapter 14).

Leadership rather than management is promoted as the key to effective organizational performance (Ford and Harding, 2007). This is what we see in the *Wall Street Journal* article above – leadership is being promoted as more important than management and this is the view that seemed to permeate the leadership literature in the mid-1980s. Hickman (1990) suggested that one of the most alarming fads holds that leaders make much more of a difference than managers when it comes to guiding organizations to competitive advantage and enduring results.

He goes on to suggest that this wrongheaded notion has given too distorted a picture of managers as dull, impersonal, plodding, tedious, unimaginative and stagnant souls. Rost (1991) defends management against these unfavourable connotations. He suggests management is what the industrial age was all about and that much of it is not going to change in the post-industrial era. Furthermore, he suggests civilization is so complex that it has to be 'managed'. People do not fall neatly into these two stereotypes, which imply that managers are always ineffective and which denigrate them at the expense of the more fashionable 'leadership' (Hickman, 1990; Rost, 1991; Yukl, 2002). Gronn (2003) further explains the limitations of this view:

> While they canonize individualist leadership, the proponents of exceptional leadership downplay or demonize management. Typical here is Bennis and Nanus's (1985: 21) notorious dismissal of managers as 'people who do things right' compared with leaders, who 'do the right thing'. But this contrast between 'things right' and 'the right thing' is both epistemologically and empirically unsound. Epistemologically, it is an attempt to resurrect the traditional distinction between facts and values. Thus, 'things right' reduces to competence or technical mastery, whereas 'the right thing' implies desirable ends, purposes or values. (2003: 281–282)

More recently Ford and colleagues have also observed that leadership is promoted at the expense of management:

> Many texts and organisational practices have merely replaced the term 'manager' with the term 'leader', but post-structuralist perspectives show that this is no 'mere' substitution, no mere sleight of hand or semantic inflation, but one that can bring about construction of different identities (Burrell, 1992). (2008: 3)

Ford and her colleagues go on to discuss the implications this has on identity in the workplace. However, while in a sense the change from 'leader' to 'manager' appears on the surface just a simple semantic change, they go on to suggest that this change does have an impact on people's identities in organizations and has caused the pressure to succumb to such demands as 'you must now be a leader'. Ford and Harding (2007) explain that this construction of subject positions or identities is seen by some scholars (for example, Alvesson and Willmott, 2002) as manipulative and exploitative. This is particularly poignant for females in organizations who can feel particularly pressurized by this masculine interpretation of leadership and indeed the very masculine nature of the debate – 'leadership not management' – in the first place. So while the literature pushed for leadership over management in the 1980s in search of something new, more flexible, more attuned to the contemporary organizational need to respond to change (discussed further later in this chapter), this push also raised issues concerning changes in identity in organizations and the denigration of management.

VIGNETTE 1.1

Extract from Case Study 3 highlighting conceptualizations of leadership and management

The Procurement Department of a large utility company, Lowe Power, had evolved pretty successfully from the old rule-bound model of the corporate policeman to a leaner, more commercial model of supply chain management. Even though relationships internally could be difficult and fractious, the department had scored some big wins and was operating with roughly two-thirds of the staff from the previous year. However, Frank Illingworth, the Finance Director, to whom Procurement reported, was pretty sure that re-organizing the department into market facing teams would yield a step-change in Procurement performance, not just in cost improvement, but also in enhanced service to the operations.

1. What would you describe as management and what would you describe as leadership within this excerpt?

Leadership and Management

A more balanced view is proposed by scholars such as Bass (1985a, 1990), Hickman (1990), Kotter (1988), Mintzberg (1980) and Rost (1991), who conceive leading and managing as distinct processes but do not assume that leaders and managers are different types of people. Yukl (2002), however, also criticizes this view because, he says, it can obscure more than it reveals, especially if it encourages simplistic theories of effective leadership. He does concede, however, that most scholars agree that success as a manager involves leading (Yukl, 2002). So a sensible view may be, as Bass (1985a) points out, that leadership is a managerial skill and that managers need to know what leadership is expected of them in their role. This view that leadership and management are not synonymous and that both are needed in organizations is poorly defined and even here there is a tendency to separate and differentiate the concepts of leadership and management (Cammock et al. 1995). For example, a contemporary view relates to the 'full range leadership' model (Avolio, 1999; Avolio and Bass, 1993, 2002). The transactional/transformational model of leadership (discussed further in Chapter 4) has been criticized in light of the seemingly closer relationship that transactional leadership has with 'management' rather than 'leadership' (Alimo-Metcalfe, 1998; Bryman, 1992; Gill, 2006; Sadler, 1997). Similarly, Antonakis and House (2002) suggest that transactional leadership is typical of management in its use of setting objectives and monitoring outcomes. This view is supported in part by empirical evidence from studies looking at the factor structure of the questionnaire, whereby the active management-by-exception factor has been found to stand alone in comparison to transformational factors and contingent reward (Edwards et al., 2012).

In addition, this distinction between transactional and transformational leadership as the distinction between management and leadership, respectively, has been related to culture. It has been suggested that the transactional leader works within the organizational culture as it exists, whereas the transformational leader changes the organizational culture (Bass, 1985a). This is corroborated by Schein (1992) who suggests that the unique function of leadership, that which distinguishes it from management and administration, is a concern for culture. Leaders, he says, create, manage and change culture (see Chapter 10 for a broader discussion of leadership and culture). An identity perspective has also been suggested (Carroll and Levy, 2008), whereby management is seen as a 'default identity', whereas leadership is seen as an 'emergent or desirable identity' (see Chapter 14 for a broader discussion on leadership and identity).

Related to the transformational/transactional distinction is a recent empirical piece that suggests leadership and management are distinct based on emotionality (Young and Dulewicz, 2008). Leadership is seen as more intense and emotional, reflecting human drives and desires, whereas management is seen as more impersonal, reflecting order and consistency. Although this research is restricted to the British Royal Navy it does indicate the beginnings of addressing the leadership and management question on an empirical basis as opposed to uninformed definitions (Yukl, 1994). Further empirical investigation would be useful in making the distinction between leadership and management. As can be seen from the discussion above this area of deliberation has largely been built on defining these concepts without a foundation of research findings.

Leadership, Management and Change

One of the most popular distinctions regarding leadership is that linked to the notion of change. Kotter (1990) for example suggests that:

- *management* produces orderly results which keep things working efficiently;
- *leadership* creates useful change;
- we need both if organizations and nations are to prosper.

Some recent, more critical articles, however, would suggest that leadership is as much about the resistance to change as it is about the creation of change (Zoller and Fairhurst, 2007; Levay, 2010). This contention, therefore, again puts forward the idea of change being the distinguishing factor between the two concepts as moot. Further discussion regarding leadership and change can be found in Chapter 8. Finally, however, another recent contribution to the debate beds the discussion within change itself and based on the issue of problem-solving activity (Grint, 2005b, 2008). The division between leadership and management in this conceptualization is based on whether problems have been seen before – *déjà vu* – linked to management or whether they have not been seen before – *vu jàdé* – linked to leadership (Weick, 1993). Management, therefore, is about coping with problems that reoccur (tame problems) and leadership deals with new complex problems (wicked problems) that do not have certain answers or endpoints and are largely ambiguous in nature (Grint, 2005b, 2008). This differentiation could mark a new approach by which to discuss these concepts in relation to each other, however, as noted above, further empirical support for this distinction is needed.

Reflective Question 1.2

Think about your experiences of change in organizations. How would you see the relationship between leadership and management based on your involvement with change?

Summary

This chapter has explored the variety of opinion reading the conceptual relationship between leadership and management. First, the chapter highlighted the possibility that we are discussing the same concept but using different words. This was done by exploring similar discussions and debates within both the leadership and management literature. Second, it has highlighted the original push to try to differentiate leadership from management, and the problems associated with this notion – the denigration of management and the potential for manipulation and exploitation with regard to creating identities of leadership in organizations. This included some critical comments regarding the very use of the word 'leadership' in an organizational context. Third, the chapter has also highlighted other notions that connect the two concepts in organizational practice, but still mark out differences through issues such as change, culture and emotion. The chapter finally highlights more critical comments that challenge our thinking around leadership as the creator of change and highlight that resistance to change is led too. The debate regarding leadership and management will no doubt continue, but at least in this chapter we have been able to start to reflect on the concept of leadership that will engage us over the ensuing chapters.

Additional Reflection Questions

1. What is management in relation to leadership?
2. How do we practice management and leadership in organizations?

3. Why might the promotion of leadership be controlling, manipulative or exploitative in organizations?
4. How might leadership be enacted in the resistance to change?
5. What wicked and tame problems have you experienced in you working life?
6. How might we research the relationship between leadership and management and what issues might that raise?

Case Study Questions

1. Look at either Case Study 1 or Case Study 3 and explore different perspectives on leadership and management. Discuss your conclusions in relation to the ideas put forward by Ford and Harding (2007) in the further reading list.
2. In Case Study 2 there is a discussion around leadership development in Iraq. Review this case study and critically discuss the extent to which concepts of leadership and management can be culturally bound. Compare this to the leadership and management discussed in Case Study 6. What similarities and differences can you highlight and why might they be important?
3. Reflect on Case Studies 4 and 5. To what extent is there leadership and to what extent is there management? Critically examine the case studies through perspectives of change, culture and emotion.
4. Reflect on Case Studies 1, 3 and 4. To what extent can you identify 'tame' and 'wicked' problems (see Grint, 2005b, 2008)?

Further Reading

Carroll, B. and Levy, L. (2008) Defaulting to management: Leadership defined by what it is not. *Organization*, 15(1): 75–96.

Ford, J. and Harding, N. (2007) Move over management: We are all leaders now. *Management Learning*, 38(5): 475–493.

Gill, R. (2011) *Theory and Practice of Leadership*, second edition. London: Sage.

Grint, K. (2005) Problems, problems, problems: The social construction of leadership. *Human Relations*, 58 (11): 1467–1494.

Weick, K.E. (1993) The collapse of sensemaking in organizations: The Mann Gulch Disaster. *Administrative Science Quarterly*, 38: 628–652.

Zoller, H.M. and Fairhurst, G. T. (2007) Resistance leadership: The overlooked potential in critical organization and leadership studies. *Human Relations*, 60(9): 1331–1360.

2

Leadership Competencies: Traits, Personality, Skills, Styles and Intelligences

In this chapter we explore the competencies of an individual as a leader. This reflects some of the more traditional approaches to theorizing about leadership. We start by looking at the research on what characteristics make a leader with links to trait theory and personality studies. From trait theory and personality we examine frameworks of leadership skills and leadership styles, detailing more about what a leader should do and how they should do it. We finish the chapter looking at the more recent idea of the intelligences of leadership, which includes discussions of emotional intelligence and other forms of intelligence. A key part of this chapter is to consider the differences between these approaches, which, on the surface, seem similar but have distinct variations in their approach.

Chapter Aims

- Introduce and critically discuss traditional approaches to leadership that look at the traits, characteristics and personality of leaders
- Introduce and critically discuss the notion of leadership style
- Introduce and critically discuss the notion of intelligence or intelligences and the link to leadership
- Explore the difference between traits, skills, styles and intelligences of leadership

What are Traits, Skills, Styles and Intelligences? What is Personality?

Before we explore the underlying theories in this area further, it is worth reflecting on their differences first. This can be done quite easily by looking at their dictionary (*Oxford English Dictionary*) definitions:

Trait – a distinguishing feature in character, appearance, habit or portrayal.

Personality – a distinctive character or qualities of a person, personal existence or identity, being a person.

Skill – expertness, a practised ability, facility in an action.

Style – a kind or sort, a manner of writing, speaking or doing, a distinctive manner of a person.

Intelligence – understanding, a quickness of understanding.

Keep these definitions in mind as progression is made through the chapter to help you distinguish one approach from the other. While these elements are largely derived from psychological research (please see general psychology texts for further information, such as Gross, 2010) they also reflect some of the areas considered in later chapters of this book, such as facility in an action, which suggests notions of context and leadership (discussed in Chapter 5). Also there is reference to identity and being a person (explored further in Chapter 14) and the idea of traits or characteristics as a portrayal has resonances of the aesthetic or artist representation of the leader and leadership (explored in Chapter 15). So while we might recognize these theories of leadership as traditional they also have links to the areas of leadership studies we will investigate later in the book.

Traits, Characteristics, Personality and Leadership

Traditionally we think of leadership studies starting with the ideal of the 'great man' theories (Carlyle, 1866), in which the idea of a leader was seen through the lens of what it takes to achieve a position of responsibility in society. Whether it be a military officer or upstanding gentleman, the view was that a person was born into a leader role in society. From this view research developed along the lines of identifying characteristics of these born leaders and hence the trait theory approach was developed (Stogdill, 1948). From the late 1940s until the 1990s trait research was ongoing and found a number of characteristics that appear to be linked to leadership. Table 2.1 shows some of the key pieces of research over this time and the traits they identified.

Table 2.1   **Key Trait Research Studies and Findings**

Stogdill (1948)	Mann (1959)	Stogdill (1974)	Lord et al. (1984)	Kirkpatrick and Locke (1991)
Intelligence	Intelligence	Achievement	Intelligence	Drive
Alertness	Masculinity	Persistence	Masculinity	Motivation
Insight	Adjustment	Insight	Dominance	Integrity
Responsibility	Dominance	Self-confidence		Confidence
Initiative	Extroversion	Responsibility		Cognitive ability
Persistence	Conservatism	Cooperativeness		Task knowledge
Self-confidence		Tolerance		
Sociability		Influence		
		Sociability		

Source: Northouse, P.G. (2007) *Leadership: Theory and Practice.* Thousand Oaks, CA: Sage p. 18.

From this summary, Northouse (2007) goes on to conclude that the following are major leadership traits:

- intelligence (Zaccaro et al., 2004) (a further exploration of intelligence and leadership is developed later in this chapter);
- self-confidence;
- determination;
- integrity;
- sociability.

These traits appear to relate to the research on linking leadership to personality and particularly to research that finds a strong link between the big five personality factors (neuroticism, extraversion, openness, agreeableness and conscientiousness) (Judge et al., 2002). Despite these findings and over a century of research on trait theory that provides us with benchmarks when looking for or at leaders (Northouse, 2007), the trait approach does not account for situational variances (which we will explore in Chapter 3). Nor does it actually provide us with a definitive list of which traits make leaders and there is no consideration of the relationship with leadership outcomes (Northouse, 2007). A wider view, where the behaviours of a leader are developed, is put forward by the styles approach, which is discussed in the next section.

Reflective Question 2.1

Think of a leader from your past experience. Which traits, characteristics and personality factors did they exhibit?

Leadership Styles

Similar to the trait and skills approach, the styles approach to leadership has been around since the late 1930s, and like the trait and skills approaches, represents one of the foundations of modern leadership research and theory. The styles approach was developed initially through the now famous Boys Club Experiments (Lewin et al., 1939), and the Ohio (Halpin and Winer, 1957; Stogdill and Coons, 1957) and Michigan (Katz and Kahn, 1951; Likert, 1961) State Studies, and led to the development of the Managerial Grid (Blake and Mouton, 1964, 1978) and Action Centred Leadership (Adair, 1973). Excepting John Adair's work, style theories tend to orientate towards two paradigms – people versus task and directive versus participative styles (Wright, 1996). These styles are described below.

- *Concern for task* – the extent to which the leader emphasizes the task objectives.
- *Concern for people* – the extent to which the leader emphasizes the needs, interests and so on of the group.
- *Directive leadership* – the extent to which the leader makes all the decisions regarding group activity.
- *Participative leadership* – the extent to which the leader shares decision making concerning group activity.

The model of Action Centred Leadership (Adair, 1973), however, takes into consideration three elements – the task, the team and the individual. The application and discourse surrounding the styles approach are still prominent in organizational discussions to date and have stood the test of time. This could be because they help provide a language with which to describe leadership in a generic way. This has led to some useful leadership assessment tools such as the Leader Behaviour Description Questionnaire (LBDQ) (Hemphill and Coons, 1957). The main disadvantage of the styles approach, however, was the lack of situational variance in the theory, tending toward a single best way of leading approach. This then led on to the idea of situational and contingency leadership approaches, discussed in Chapter 3. At this point, however, it is also worth reflecting on research conducted to look at leadership styles across an organization, similar to the suggestions made by the skills approach above.

Critical Thinking Box 2.1

Compare the discussions on transformational and transactional leadership from Chapter 4 with the discussion on style in this chapter. To what extent have we

(Continued)

(Continued)

moved on in theoretical terms? It could be argued that transformational and trans-actional leadership are different labels for largely the same concepts as concern for people and concern for task.

Leadership Styles across Hierarchical Levels[1]

There is mounting empirical evidence for differences in leadership styles across hierarchical levels. One study (Kabacoff, 1999), for example, found differences in the leadership styles and practices of individuals representing seven management levels and nine job functions within North American organizations (cited by Oshagbemi and Gill, 2004). A recent study provides further evidence that the use of leadership styles (directive, consultative, participative and delegative) varies across hierarchical levels in organizations (Oshagbemi and Gill, 2004) (see Table 2.2 for definitions of these styles). It found that leadership style appears to vary across three levels in organizations: senior-level, middle-level and lower-level management. Senior-level managers appear to use more delegative and participative styles and less directive styles than lower-level managers. Middle-level managers appear to use a delegative style more than lower-level managers do and to use a delegative style less than senior-level managers do. It also appears that the use of a consultative style remains constant across the various hierarchical levels in organizations.

Oshagbemi and Gill (2004) suggest the reason why senior-level managers use delegative and participative styles more than managers lower in the organization is hierarchical in nature. For example, they suggest that the opportunity to participate in policy formulation and decision making and to delegate tasks is more prevalent at senior management levels than at lower management levels. This view supports the models previously reviewed in this chapter (Brown and Jaques, 1965; Jacobs and Jaques, 1987; Jaques, 1976, 1989, 1990; Jaques and Clement, 1991; Katz and Kahn, 1966, 1978; Mintzberg, 1980).

An earlier study referring to Chinese and Japanese organizations, however, has reported no differences in the use of leadership styles across hierarchical levels (Ming-Wang and Satow, 1994). The results concerning leadership style across hierarchical levels, therefore, are mixed. National culture is a factor that differs between these two studies and thus may account for the differences in findings. For example, differences in the use

---

[1]Parts of this section were originally written for the unpublished doctoral thesis of one of the authors (Edwards, 2005).

Table 2.2   **Operational Definitions of Leadership Styles**

Leadership style	Definition
Directive	The leader tells followers what to do and how to do it, what is expected of them, specifying standards of performance and setting deadlines for completion of work, initiates action, and exercises firm rule to ensure followers follow prescribed ways of doing things. The leader also ensures followers are working to capacity, reassigning tasks to balance the workload.
Consultative	The leader tells followers what to do, but only after discussing matters with them first and hearing their opinions, feelings, ideas and suggestions.
Participative	The leader discusses and analyses problems with followers to reach a consensus on what to do and how to do it. The group makes decisions as a whole and followers have as much responsibility for decisions as the leader. They participate as equals in decision making.
Delegative	The leader describes the problem or need and the conditions that have to be met, and makes suggestions, but leaves it to followers to decide what to do and how to do it.

Source: Adapted from Gill, R.W.T. (1997) Cross-cultural similarities and differences in leadership styles and behaviour: A comparison between UK and Southeast Asian managers. Working Paper No. LT-RG-97-8. Ross-on-Wye, Herefordshire: The Leadership Trust Foundation. (Originally published in Bass, B.M. et al. (1975) Management styles associated with organizational, task, personal and interpersonal contingencies. *Journal of Applied Psychology*, 60(6): 720–729.)

of leadership styles between UK and Southeast Asian managers have been found in previous research (Gill, 1985, 1999). Gill found that Southeast Asian managers see themselves as more directive and less delegative than western managers do. This may also be the case between UK managers and their Chinese and Japanese counterparts. Further research, however, is needed to test this hypothesis, as Chinese and Japanese cultures may differ from Southeast Asian cultures, which are more heterogeneous.

The styles approach has a number of strengths associated with it: for example, it marked a major shift in leadership research, there is a wide range of studies that support the general principles it promotes and therefore it provides us with a broad conceptual map from which to draw and discuss leadership (Northouse, 2007). However, the approach also has some criticisms – for example, there is a lack of empirical evidence for a direct relationship between styles and performance outcomes and there is a lack of a universal style for all situations, therefore bringing into question its situational applicability (Northouse, 2007). A similar perspective to the styles approach is posited in the skills approach to leadership, discussed in the next section.

VIGNETTE 2.1

Extract from Case Study 1 illustrating leadership styles

The second quartile at Space Engineering Services focused on designing the new system. This included the performance review form, guidelines for use for both

(Continued)

(Continued)

management and employees, core competencies which all employees are to be measured on, and the policy and procedures behind the appraisals. Once the design was completed, I had started to focus on the pilot. With this in mind, I created a training package for the managers to understand performance management, as well as use the performance reviews. I trained 16 managers in performance management, interviewing skills, and how to conduct appraisals.

1. What would you recommend as an effective leadership style to help in this situation?

Skills Approaches to Leadership[2]

There are a number of differing models and frameworks that make up the skills approach. We will discuss these over the next few pages.

Three Skills Model of a Leader's Work

A popular model of skills of a manager or leader in an organization suggests three distinct skill sets: conceptual, human and technical (Argyris, 1964; Burns, 1957; Katz,1974; Mackenzie, 1969, Mann, 1965; Shiba, 1998). Technical skill is described as an understanding of, and proficiency in, a specific kind of activity, particularly one involving methods, processes, procedures or techniques (Katz, 1974). A later development of this model added that technical skill can be dichotomized into functional and problem-solving skills (Shiba, 1998). Human skill is portrayed as the ability to work effectively as a group member and to build cooperative effort within a team. Furthermore, the skill has been subdivided into (a) leadership ability within a manager's own unit and (b) skill in inter-group relationships (Katz, 1974). Finally, conceptual skill involves the ability to see the enterprise as a whole. It includes recognizing how the various functions of the organization depend on one another, and how changes in any one part affect all others. It also extends to visualizing the relationship of the individual business with the industrial sector, the community, and the political, social and economic forces of the nation as a whole (Katz, 1974). The value of this model is that it demonstrates a shift in the relevant importance of technical, human and conceptual

---

[2]Parts of this section were originally written for the unpublished doctoral thesis of one of the authors (Edwards, 2005).

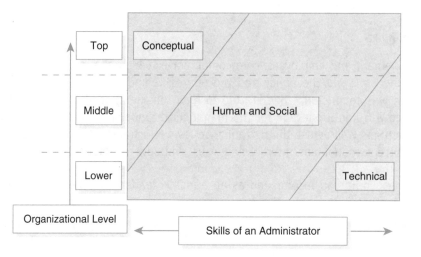

Figure 2.1   The Skills of an Effective Administrator

Source: Katz, R.L. (1974) Skills of an effective administrator. *Harvard Business Review*, 52(5): 90–102.

skills throughout organizational levels. Human and social skills remain consistently important throughout all organizational levels, while conceptual skills increase in importance and technical skills decrease in importance as one ascends organizational levels (see Figure 2.1). (The word 'administrator' is equivalent here to the word 'manager' or 'leader'.)

The results of research also provide some empirical support for this model (Guest, 1955–6; Howard and Bray, 1988; Mahoney, 1961; Mahoney et al., 1965; Pavett and Lau, 1983; Stamp, 1988; Thomason, 1966, 1967). For example, Guest (1955–6) conducted some 500 interviews with foremen from an automobile industry plant. Each task highlighted in this study can be attributed to one of Katz's skill sets. Furthermore, Mahoney (1961) concluded from a review of several studies that the higher the level of a manager the more time they spent on planning and organizing rather than on the technical work of the organization. This was confirmed by Mahoney et al. (1965), who found that, while supervising was the main activity of 51% of lower-level managers, it was the main activity of only 36% of middle-level managers and 22% of top-level managers. Top-level managers, they suggested, were more likely to be generalists and planners than were lower-level managers. Around the same time, Thomason (1966, 1967) concluded:

> Relative time spent on activities relating to current production problems decreases as one moves up the hierarchy; that spent on general management policy increases as one moves upwards. (1967: 28)

More recent research has also produced support for the importance of the need for increasing the use of conceptual skills higher up an organizational hierarchy and the need for human and social skills to remain constant (Pavett and Lau, 1983). A study of conceptual skills in an assessment centre also predicted advancement to higher levels of management 20 years later (Howard and Bray, 1988). One particular conceptual skill, cognitive complexity (the organization of constructs and their similarity: see Bieri, 1955), has also been identified as predicting managerial advancement remarkably well (Stamp, 1988). It seems that there has been no research investigating this model for nearly 20 years. It would be worthwhile for future research to investigate whether this model is still relevant to contemporary organizations. Some scholars, however, do view the model as useful (Bass, 1990; Hunt, 1991; Yukl, 1994). As Hunt suggests:

> Its [Katz's model's] wide usage and underlying face validity makes it a useful conceptual anchor point to discussing different leader skill mixes. (1991: 159)

These skills focused models of leadership, managerial and administrative work help us start to think about the mix of competencies needed in organizations. However, they are limited as they do not make clear the difference between management, administration and leadership.

Mintzberg's Model of the Nature of Managerial Work

A similar model to the one above was developed directly from observing five chief executive officers at work (Mintzberg,1980). The model describes 10 roles that managers carry out. The roles are categorized by Mintzberg as interpersonal, informational and decisional. The model also uses a three-category approach to understanding management but, differing from Katz's model (described above), it incorporates the roles for each category (see Figure 2.2). A criticism of Mintzberg's model is that it has been generalized from interviews with five chief executive officers. There is a great deal of research that relates to Mintzberg's work (Alexander, 1979; Carlson, 1951; Chapple and Sayles, 1961; Kurke and Aldrich, 1983; Lau et al., 1980; Leduc and Block, 1985; Martin, 1956, 1959; McCall and Segrist, 1980; Nilakant, 1991; Paolillo, 1981; Pavett and Lau, 1983; Sayles, 1964; Stieglitz, 1969; Whitely, 1978). It has been suggested, however, that the results of this research are inconsistent and do not add much to our conceptual understanding of what managers actually do (Hunt, 1991). In general, the theories, frameworks and models reviewed in this section so far suffer from mixed empirical support and are antiquated (all were developed between 1950 and 1980). Since that initial development, organizational philosophies have changed and flattened hierarchies and team-based work have been introduced (London and Tornow, 1998). This development has had an impact on management and

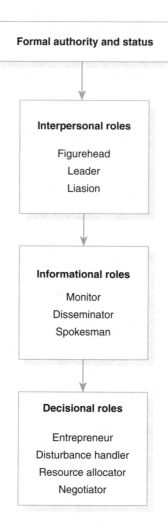

Figure 2.2   Mintzberg's Categories and Roles of a Manager

Source: Mintzberg, H. (1980) *The Nature of Managerial Work*. Englewood Cliffs, NJ: Prentice-Hall, p. 59.

leadership (Bartlett and Ghoshal, 1997). Operating-level managers have had to evolve from their traditional role as front-line implementers to become innovative entrepreneurs. Senior-level managers have had to redefine their primary role from administrative controllers to developmental coaches. And top-level executives have been forced to see themselves less as strategic architects and more as organizational leaders (Bartlett and Ghoshal, 1997). This brings about the question of the focus of leadership, which is discussed in the next section.

'Leadership *of* Organizations' versus 'Leadership *in* Organizations'

A distinction has been drawn in the literature between 'leadership *of* organizations' and 'leadership *in* organizations' (Dubin, 1979; Storey, 2005). Leadership *of* organizations essentially focuses on leadership of the organization overall. It involves human actors in interaction with the organization in its entirety. This is similar to Katz's (1974) description of 'conceptual skills' considered earlier in the chapter. Leadership *in* organizations, on the other hand, involves team leadership and face-to-face interaction at various levels. An estimated 90% of the current leadership literature focuses on the latter kind of leadership (Hunt, 1991; Hunt and Ropo, 1998; Phillips and Hunt, 1992). A similar estimation (Zaccaro and Horn, 2003) suggests only 5% of the leadership literature has focused on executive leadership or 'leadership *of* organizations' (Storey, 2005). This has led to a recent call by Storey (2005) for more research into organizational leadership. This thesis, by investigating leadership throughout an organization, provides data concerning both forms of leadership.

The dichotomy provided by Dubin (1979) and reiterated later by Storey (2005) has been criticized, however, for being too simplistic. Leadership at the top-level of an organization also involves face-to-face interaction, and leadership at lower levels of the organization sometimes involves strategic business units, which may operate as complex semi-autonomous 'mini-organizations'. Despite this fuzziness, the classification has been described as useful enabling of a differentiation between types of leadership research (Hunt and Ropo, 1998). Hunt and Ropo (1998) also suggest that 'leadership of organizations' includes a more comprehensive set of activities than does 'leadership in organizations'. Furthermore, there has been recent empirical evidence that suggested a differentiation in the identity of an organizational unit based on hierarchical level (Corley, 2004). Corley suggests that at the top level of an organization identity is seen in light of the organization's strategy based on its purpose and mission. Conversely, at the bottom of the organization's hierarchy identity is seen in relation to culture based on shared values and beliefs. There are other models that can aid a more detailed understanding of the leadership skills needed across organizations.

A Systems Model of Leadership Across Organizations

Likely differences in leadership behaviour across hierarchical level were pointed out long ago (Selznick, 1957). In accordance with Selznick's work, Gill (2011) proposes that top-level leaders are responsible for the vision and mission of the organization, the development of appropriate strategies, and the identification and promotion of supportive shared values throughout the organization. Lower-level leaders, in contrast, Gill says, are responsible for implementing strategies, performing routine tasks, and encouraging individual involvement and team working. The systems model of leadership is helpful to elaborate this theory. The so-called systems model of leadership

(Katz and Kahn, 1966, 1978) has been widely regarded as a conceptually elegant framework (Hunt, 1991). Katz and Kahn's model suggests that at lower levels little 'leadership' is required. This is because the focus is on the administration of effective operations. At middle levels administrative procedures are developed and implemented, and human relations skills are important. At the top levels of an organization, administrative procedures are initiated to reflect new policy (see Table 2.3).

The model also suggests that the skills appropriate at one level of the organization are inappropriate or even dysfunctional at another (Katz and Kahn, 1966, 1978). However, Sinha (1995) argues that the leadership functions and skills proposed in Katz and Kahn's model are relevant to an extent at all levels. Gill (2006) adds that the suggestion of there being little leadership at the lower levels of an organization is contentious. For example, he suggests that leadership is needed wherever there are subordinates or followers. Furthermore, research has found charismatic leadership at all levels in organizations, though most frequently at the top level of the hierarchy (Bass, 1992). This has provided some, albeit equivocal, support for systems theory (Katz and Kahn, 1966, 1978).

Table 2.3   The Systems Model of Leadership

Level	Leadership function	Cognitive skills	Affective skills
Top	Change, creation and elimination of organizational structure	System perspective	To create charisma
Middle	Supplementing, piecing and improvising for the structural inadequacies	Subsystem perspective	Human relations skills
Lower	Utilization of existing structure	Technical knowledge	Concern for equity in the use of rewards and sanctions (i.e. being fair)

Source: Adapted from Sinha, J.B.P. (1995) *The Cultural Context of Leadership and Power.* New Delhi: Sage, pp. 39–40. (Originally published in Katz, D. and Kahn, R.L. (1966) *The Social Psychology of Organizations.* New York: John Wiley.)

Stratified Systems Theory and 'Time Span of Discretion'

Stratified-systems theory (SST) (Brown and Jaques, 1965; Jacobs and Jaques, 1987; Jaques, 1976, 1989, 1990; Jaques and Clement, 1991) is a prescriptive model of organizational structure based on defining the hierarchical level according to the task complexity involved at each level. SST suggests a general model of organizational functioning such that tasks or requirements increase in complexity with ascending organizational levels. Increasing task complexity is a function of the uncertainties created by the necessity to deal with a more encompassing and a more turbulent environment as a manager is promoted up the organizational hierarchy (Hunt, 1991).

'Time span of discretion' is defined as the maximum time for completing critical tasks within organizations (Brown and Jaques, 1965; Jacobs and Jaques, 1987; Jaques,

Table 2.4   **Domains and Levels in Stratified-Systems Theory**

Time span	Level	Domain
20 years and over	VII – Corporation	Systems
10–20 years	VI – Group	Systems
5–10 years	V – Company	Organizational
2–5 years	IV – Division (general management)	Organizational
1–2 years	III – Department	Direct
Over 3 months and under 1 year	II – Section	Direct
Up to 3 months	I – Shop floor (direct employee)	Direct

Source: Hunt, J.G. (1991) *Leadership: A New Synthesis.* Newbury Park, CA: Sage, p. 17.

1976, 1989, 1990; Jaques and Clement, 1991). The model shows seven levels of time span grouped into three domains. These domains are systems, organizational and direct leadership. Time span is defined as the longest target completion time for the leader's critical tasks at each hierarchical level (Hunt, 1991; Jaques and Clement, 1991) (see Table 2.4).

As Waldman et al. (2004) stress, SST focuses on the cognitive aspects of leadership where effective and ineffective leaders can be distinguished in terms of their level of conceptual capacity (Jaques and Clement, 1991; Lewis and Jacobs, 1992). Conceptual capacity is defined as the ability to think abstractly and integrate complex information, providing an antecedent to leadership action (Waldman et al., 2004). SST, however, has been criticized for being too rigid and mechanistic (Kleiner, 2001) and therefore it may not be attuned to contemporary organizations.

SST relates to the previous leadership models reviewed. There appears to be a relationship between 'organizational leadership' and 'leadership *of* organizations'. Similarly there appears to be a relationship between 'direct leadership' and 'leadership *in* organizations'. SST goes further, conceptually, by suggesting 'systems leadership'. When compared to the systems model of leadership (Katz and Kahn, 1966, 1978) one might expect a difference between top-level leadership, which represents 'organizational leadership', and middle-level and lower-level leadership, which represent 'direct leadership'.

Similar distinctions have been suggested in the past (Barnard, 1950; Etzioni, 1961; Katz and Kahn, 1966, 1978; Niles, 1949, 1958; Pfiffner and Sherwood, 1960). Indeed, the relationship that SST has with systems theory (Katz and Kahn, 1966, 1978) has been highlighted by Hunt (1991). Both theories, he asserts, conceptualize different and increasingly complex leadership requirements as one moves higher up the organization and that both theories have break points where the requirements become qualitatively different. However, the empirical support for SST is mixed. Some studies show support for the theory (Derossi, 1974, 1978; Martin, 1956, 1959), while others have found little support (Goodman, 1967; Nilakant, 1991).

In general, the skills approach has a number of strengths: it is quite vast in its theoretical and research orientation with a number of frameworks being proposed, it stresses the importance of leadership being seen as a skill, it is intuitively appealing and it provides a useful framework for leadership development programmes (Northouse, 2007). It does, however, have a number of disadvantages, such as it seems to be discussing concepts outside the leadership domain (Northouse, 2007). Indeed, it could be argued that it is actually discussing the management or administration of organizations (see the discussion in Chapter 1). The skills approach also appears to have limited predictive value, and it could be argued that it is very trait-like; to what extent are these models discussing skills or traits and characteristics? Finally, the frameworks and models are probably unwieldy when considering differing contexts (Northouse, 2007). A more contemporary approach to leadership that seems to resonate with some of the discussion in this chapter so far is the work on intelligences of leadership, discussed next.

Reflective Question 2.2

Again, thinking of a leader from your past experience, what skills did they exhibit? Relate these skills to the theories and frameworks discussed above.

The Intelligences of Leadership

A contemporary concern regarding leadership studies appears to be the relationship leadership has with intelligence. Traditionally, as we see above from the trait approach, intelligence has been defined as that derived from IQ tests, but more recently intelligence has been widened to include emotional intelligence (Goleman, 1995; Salovey and Mayer, 1990) and spiritual intelligence (Zohar and Marshall, 2001) and as far as Howard Gardner's (2000) ideas reading multiple intelligences. This section discusses each of these approaches and discovers a more critical theme developing, particularly around the popular idea of emotional intelligence.

Gill (2006) has developed an intelligence-based approach to leadership that suggests a general model of leadership would include cognitive intelligence, spiritual intelligence, emotional intelligence and moral intelligence alongside behavioural ability. He describes each as the following:

Cognitive intelligence – The ability to perceive and understand information, reason with it, imagine possibilities, use intuition and imagination, make judgements, solve problems and make decisions.

Spiritual intelligence – The ability to understand that human beings have an animating need for meaning, value and a sense of worth in what they seek and do and to respond to that need.

Emotional intelligence – The ability to understand oneself and the feelings and needs of other people, exercise self-control and respond to other people in appropriate ways in order to influence, motivate and inspire them.

Moral intelligence – The ability to differentiate right from wrong according to universal moral principles.

Behavioural ability – Using and responding to emotion (for example, body language), communicating in other ways (writing, speaking and active listening), using personal power and using different leadership styles according to the situation.

Spiritual intelligence has been discussed within business discourse since the turn of the millennia, at least, and has been described as:

> … the intelligence with which we address and solve problems of meaning and value. (Zohar and Marshall, 2001: 3).

However, the emotional intelligence theme has been developed more rigorously by the likes of Daniel Goleman (1995) and Salovey and Mayer (1990). The work of Goleman, especially, is keen to merit emotional intelligence over and above normal IQ as fundamentally important for leaders, whereas Salovey and Mayer take a more empirical approach and identify five aspects to emotional intelligence:

- knowing one's emotions;
- managing emotions;
- motivating oneself;
- recognizing emotions in others;
- handling relationships.

Recent research, however, has challenged some of the ideas regarding emotional intelligence and the seemingly fundamental link it has to leadership. This research suggests that it is not as applicable as first thought, especially when investigating certain cultures and context, such as the construction industry (Lindebaum and Cartwright, 2010; Lindebaum and Cassell, 2012). These concerns regarding emotional intelligence have almost come full circle from the trait and personality research especially when one reads the debate in *Leadership Quarterly* in 2009, which shows John Antonakis and colleagues (2009) arguing that emotional intelligence appears to be not related to leadership when controlling for the big five personality structure, whereas Neal Ashkanasy and Marie Dasborough argue that emotional intelligence and emotionality are still important factors in the leadership process. Finally, the expansion of our theoretical knowledge reading intelligence could develop this field even further, especially when we highlight Howard Gardner's (1999) ideas on multiple intelligence. He identifies seven intelligences (linguistic, logical-mathematic, musical, bodily kinesthetic, spatial, interpersonal and intrapersonal) and alludes to the three others (naturalist, spiritual, existential). This could see the expansion of this discussion and debate.

Summary

At the beginning of this chapter we started by defining the concepts discussed – traits, skills, styles, intelligence and personality – and developed some distinction between these differing leadership competencies. The chapter then reviewed the literature and research around the area of leadership and traits, characteristics and personality, discussing both early trait theories and the more modern trait and personality, theories. We then went on to look at the various research on leadership styles. Here we concluded that there were two generic areas of leadership style theory and research – those connected with decision making and those connected with orientation, either towards people or the task. The chapter has also reviewed recent research that has tried to take a distributed (see Chapter 9) notion on leadership and investigated styles and skills across organizations. The chapter also reiterated the distinction between leadership 'of' the organization where some might suggest the idea of strategic leadership (see Chapter 8) and leadership 'in' the organization. Finally, the chapter has reviewed contemporary ideas that link the importance of intelligence to leadership and concluded that intelligences are of a multiple nature but there are some that appear to be explicitly linked to leadership such as emotional intelligence, spiritual intelligence and moral intelligence.

Additional Reflection Questions

1. What are leadership traits? What is the link between traits and leadership?
2. To what extent do we characterize a leader?
3. What skills are needed to be a leader? How might these differ across organizations?
4. What is the difference between a directive style of leadership and a participative one? Use examples from your work experience to explain these differences.
5. Has leadership really moved on from leadership style or are we stuck with these general descriptive terms?
6. Think about your own intelligences. How might they contribute to you taking a leadership role?

Case Study Questions

1. Read carefully through Case Study 1 and Case Study 6. From your review of these case studies highlight the leadership traits that may be seen as effective in each of the scenarios discussed.

2. From Case Study 2, a leadership development programme in Iraq, highlight which skills are being developed for leadership. To what extent are these appropriate to the context?

3. Read carefully through Case Study 3 where there is a discussion around management practice. Reflect back on the styles highlighted in the chapter and identify where they occur in the case study.

4. Read Case Studies 4 and 5. Critically reflect on the extent to which you can identify intelligences, emotional, spiritual, moral or otherwise. What evidence can you gather for the importance of these intelligences to leadership?

Further Reading

Corley, K.G. (2004) Defined by our strategy or our culture? Hierarchical differences in perceptions of organizational identity and change. *Human Relations*, 57(9): 1145–1177.

Gill, R. (2011) *Theory and Practice of Leadership*, second edition. London: Sage.

Goodman, P.S. (1967) An empirical examination of Elliot Jaques' concept of time span. *Human Relations*, 20: 155–170.

Northouse, P.G. (2007) *Leadership: Theory and Practice*. Thousand Oaks, CA: Sage.

Storey, J. (2005) What next for strategic-level leadership research? *Leadership*, 1(1): 89–104.

Zaccaro, S.J., Kemp. C. and Bader, P. (2004) Leader traits and attributes. In J. Antonakis, A.T. Cianciolo and R.J. Sternberg (eds), *The Nature of Leadership*. Thousand Oaks, CA: Sage. pp. 101–124.

3

Contingency and LMX Theories of Leadership

Following our review of traits, skills and styles approaches to leadership in Chapter 2, we will introduce and critically evaluate a number of contingency theories that followed these approaches and intended to enrich existing theories of effective leadership at the time through the incorporation of contextual variables as a key mediator of leader effectiveness. We will, as part of this, also highlight the relatively passive role that followers continue to be placed in within these theories and move on to discuss Leader–Member Exchange (LMX) theories of leadership that attempt to move the leader–follower relationship to centre stage. Throughout the chapter we will evaluate these theories to draw out strengths, limitations and practical applications.

Chapter Aims

- Introduce common characteristics and aims of contingency theories of leadership
- Present and critically evaluate situational leadership theory, least preferred co-worker (LPC) theory and path-goal theory
- Discuss and critically review other relevant early contingency theories
- Introduce and critically evaluate LMX theories

General Characteristics of Early Contingency Theories of Leadership

Thoughout the 1960s–1980s, leadership scholars continued on the quest of the early leadership theories, introduced in the previous chapter, to establish a model of effective leadership. This quest was pursued through a new wave of theories and models of leadership throughout the 1960s, 1970s and 1980s that explored the role and importance of contextual variables in leadership. These theories argued that there was not one 'right' or effective leadership style and trait but rather that different situations required different types of leadership (Yukl, 2011). This step away from a universal success formula for leadership was a significant development in our understanding of leadership as well as our approach to developing leaders. These early contingency theories also raised the wider question of to what extent successful leadership is solely dependent on the individual leader. Instead, it was recognized that different aspects of the leadership situation have a significant impact on which behaviours and traits are required from a leader. In his recent review of these early contingency theories Yukl (2011) draws out the following common characteristics/meta categories summarized in Figure 3.1.

Most contingency theories treat these situational variables as 'conditions the leader cannot change in the short term' (Yukl, 2011: 286) and which therefore affect, influence or moderate the extent to which a specific leadership behaviour gives rise to

Individual leadership behaviours, e.g.:

- Task-oriented behaviour
- Relations-oriented behaviour
- Participative behaviour
- Contingent reward behaviour

Leadership effectiveness, e.g. subordinate/team satisfaction or performance

Situational variables, e.g.:

- Characteristics of the work (e.g. task structure, role interdependence)
- Characteristics of the subordinates (e.g. needs, values)
- Characteristics of the leader (e.g. expertise, interpersonal stress)
- Characteristics of the leadership position (e.g. leader authority, formal policies)

Figure 3.1   Common Characteristics of the Early Contingency Theories

leader effectiveness. Yukl (2011) adds that the subordinate characteristics can act as mediators between leader behaviours and leader effectiveness at both individual subordinate and group/team level. In later years, research into contingency theories of leadership increasingly blurred the boundaries between contextually bound models of leadership and universal models of leadership (Yukl, 2011). This reflects the need for universal theories to be contextualized and an equally a desire for contextually bound models to be universally applicable.

To give readers a succinct insight into the nature and purpose of the early contingency theories, we have chosen to outline in detail three of the most well-known contingency theories: situational leadership theory, the LPC contingency model and the path-goal theory. We then briefly introduce other developments in this field of leadership studies since the 1960s and highlight common strengths and weaknesses in a final section of the first part of this chapter.

Reflective Question 3.1

Think about your own experiences with leadership – which aspects of the situation and context in which leadership takes place are most important? Why? Is this always the case?

Situational Leadership Theory

Hersey and Blanchard's (1971) situational leadership theory examines appropriate leadership behaviours for different situations. To be effective, a leader must therefore match his/her behaviour to the situation he/she faces. More specifically, this establishes the right mix of directive and supportive leader behaviours in relation to a subordinate's maturity, that is, competence and confidence in completing the assigned task. A leader therefore needs to analyse each subordinate's maturity and assess the right mix of supportive and directive behaviours required. The situational leadership theory recognizes that the subordinate's maturity may change over time depending on the wider context. A leader is therefore expected to adjust the mix of directive and supportive leadership behaviours to match these changes.

This theory has been very popular and extensively used in organizational leadership development settings. Recognizing later developments of this model (Blanchard et al., 1993; Graeff, 1997) that include decision procedures, we will focus our discussion of the situational model here on Hersey and Blanchard's (1971) original ideas. Figure 3.2 below outlines a refinement of this original model by Blanchard et al. (1985) as is used widely in leadership development contexts:

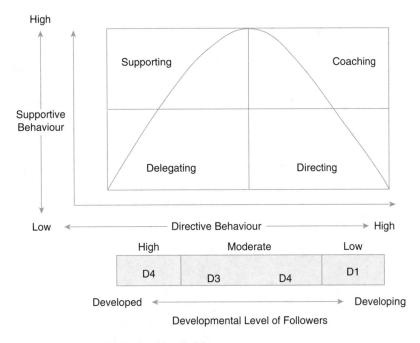

Figure 3.2   **The Situational Leadership Model**

Source: Adapted from Blanchard et al. (1985).

Leadership Behaviour Styles

As shown in Figure 3.2, the situational leadership theory includes four main leadership behaviour styles:

- Directing (S1) – The leader exhibits mainly directive behaviours, providing subordinates with clarity and instructions on the task and goal that need to be achieved. This leadership style may be particularly observed in work settings in which the completion of the task is of utmost importance or the task may have risks associated with it, for example, a firefighter or police officer in action; a complex production setting.
- Coaching (S2) – The leader employs both directive and supportive behaviours to focus on both the task and the subordinates' needs. Although the leader focuses more on providing encouragement and support than in S1, the leader is still expected to give guidance on the how and what of tasks and goals. This leadership style therefore acknowledges that a focus on the subordinate's needs and motivation is as important as a focus on task completion. This may be particularly important in a situation where the task is complex or in which subordinates face challenges in completing the task.

- Supporting (S3) – The leader is predominantly focusing on supporting and encouraging the subordinates to ensure that they apply their skills effectively to achieve the set task. The supportive behaviours include listening, motivating, praising, giving feedback and consulting subordinates. This leadership style may be observed when subordinates' knowledge or skills are central to achieving a task and where the completion of the task is not of the utmost importance.
- Delegating (S4) – The leader shows the least involvement in the subordinates' daily work and therefore shows little directive or supportive behaviours. The subordinate is expected to have high confidence and competence in the given task and to take the initiative and responsibilities for completing the task.

In addition, the appropriateness and effectiveness of each of these four leadership styles are then linked to subordinates' development levels (as a moderating situational variable). Hence the model argues that a leader should display any of the above four leadership styles depending on the subordinates' development level.

Subordinate Development Levels

The model in Figure 3.2 displays the different development or maturity levels of subordinates. According to Blanchard et al. (1985), the development level of subordinates reflects the extent to which they have the competence, confidence and commitment to complete the task given. The continuum displayed at the bottom of the model reflects the different mix of degrees of competence, confidence and commitment of subordinates in relation to a task. Similar to the four categories of leadership behaviours, Blanchard et al. (1985) identified four main development levels:

- D1 – Subordinates are likely to be new to the task as they have low levels of competence (do not know how to do the task) but are highly excited by and committed to the task.
- D2 – Subordinates start to acquire relevant skills and learn how to do the task, their competence levels rise but their initial motivation and excitement have gone down slightly.
- D3 – Subordinates feel quite competent to do the task but may lack the commitment and motivation as they are unsure whether they can complete the task on their own.
- D4 – Subordinates develop their skills as far as possible and show both high levels of competence and commitment to complete the task.

Effective Leadership

As highlighted above, effective leadership requires the leader to engage in on-going analyses of subordinates' situations and to re-evaluate their own behaviours in relation to the needs of each individual subordinate. When a subordinate is new to a task, he/she is likely to need the leader to be relatively directive. As the subordinate's developmental level in relation to this task increases, the leader is required to move from directive, to coaching, supportive and delegating behaviours. Over time subordinates move forwards and backwards along the development continuum and a leader has to adjust their behaviour to match their developmental level in order to be effective. In the short term, a leader needs to then match their behaviour to the subordinate's level of maturity. This requires significant flexibility from the leader to be effective as subordinates' contexts, tasks and with it developmental levels may change quickly in a short period.

Key Critique

A key limitation often highlighted is the lack of robust empirical evidence for the validity of this model (Vecchio and Boatwright, 2002). How reliable and applicable is this model in different contexts? Vecchio's (1987) research has, for example, shown that the suggested style/subordinate developmental level match may not be applicable across all types of work settings. Vecchio and Boatwright (2002) have further criticized the lack of acknowledgement of different demographic characteristics of subordinates and show through research how differences in age, gender and so on may significantly affect subordinates' developmental level. Graeff (1997) has further noted the lack of clarity around the notions of commitment and competence in determining a subordinate's developmental level, that is, how are they defined and measured in relation to each other and across individuals? Finally, Northouse (2009) draws on research that has criticised the questionnaire associated with this model to favour situational leadership and hence to be a biased measurement.

Critical Thinking Box 3.1

Models such as the situational leadership theory assume that there is a 'right' way of leading in a specific situation and that this 'right' way can be determined, learned and changed. They have therefore been very popular in leadership development practice. Given these strong, positive assumptions, how might these models get used or abused in organizations and particularly in the development of leaders?

LPC Contingency Theory

In contrast to the situational leadership theory, Fiedler's (1964, 1967; Fiedler and Garcia, 1987) contingency theory assumes that leaders cannot change their behaviour. It therefore aims to match leaders based on their preferred leadership style to specific situations and contexts. Leader effectiveness is hence said to be contingent on the right match of a leader's style to an appropriate situation.

The LPC contingency theory is based on extensive empirical work conducted in predominantly military organizations, where Fiedler and colleagues studied and assessed leaders' styles in different contexts. They used the patterns that started to emerge to formulate generalizations about best-fit between specific styles and specific situations/contexts. The theory based on these generalizations should therefore enable organizations to pick the right leader with the right style for a specific situation.

Critical Thinking Box 3.2

Many of the early 20th-century leadership theories are based on research conducted within a military context. Furthermore, the majority of leadership theories from the 20th century are based on research conducted within the USA. This has had a profound influence on the nature and focus of these theories as it reflects the particular situational context of the military and the US-centric value system embedded in these theories. Other organizational and cultural contexts have hence been largely mute in leadership theory and Chapter 10 discusses the wider implications of this in greater detail.

Leadership Behaviours

Leadership behaviour in this theory is described as being either task motivated or relationship motivated:

- Task motivated – The leader has a primary concern for the given task and its completion.
- Relationship motivated – The leader is predominantly focused on the interrelationship with co-workers and followers.

Leader styles are measured based on the LPC score as developed by Fiedler (1967), where leaders with a higher LPC score are described as relationship motivated and those with a low LPC score are categorized as task motivated. This LPC score itself is determined by asking leaders to reflect on all their past and current co-workers and to pick the co-worker with whom they could work least well, that is, the least preferred co-worker, and to rate this co-worker on a number of bipolar scales. The sum of these individual ratings then creates the LPC score for a specific leader:

- overall critical rating leads to a low LPC score and the leader is identified as task motivated;
- overall lenient rating leads to a high LPC score and the leader is identified as relationship motivated.

Situational Variables

The LPC contingency theory has identified three main situational variables.

- Leader–member relations – the degree to which the group atmosphere is positive and the level of subordinate confidence, trust and loyalty in the leader.
- Task structure – the degree to which operational procedures are existent and clear, the final product is defined and the completion of the task certain.
- Position power – the degree to which the leader has the authority and control to evaluate subordinates' performance and issue rewards or punishments.

A respective mix of these situational variables determines what Fiedler called situational favourability. This means to what extent a situation enables a leader to take control over the subordinates and of the situation and hence be effective. A favourable situation is one where there are good leader–member relations, where tasks are clearly defined and the leader has strong position power. In contrast, poor leader–member relations, complex or unclear tasks and weak position power of the leader make for unfavourable situations. Moderately favourable situations are in between these two extremes. Figure 3.3 outlines the main propositions of this theory for leader effectiveness.

Leader–member relations	GOOD				POOR			
Task structure	High structure		Low structure		High structure		Low structure	
Position power	Strong power	Weak power	Strong power	Weak power	Strong power	Weak power	Strong power	Weak power
Preferred leadership style	1 Low LPCs		3		4 High LPCs		6 7 Low LPCs	
	Middle LPCs							

Figure 3.3 **Least Preferred Co-Worker (LPC) Model**

Source: Adapted from Fiedler (1967).

According to the LPC theory, task motivated leaders (low LPC score) are more effective in extreme situations, that is, either favourable or unfavourable situations. In contrast, relationship motivated leaders (high LPC score) are more effective in moderately favourable situations, that is, situations that are neither completely under control nor out of control. Fiedler (1995) clarified later that the right match between LPC score and type of situation is crucial as otherwise a wrong match may lead to enhanced stress for the leader and a reversion to less developed leadership behaviours and skills resulting in poor subordinate performance. This additional explanation still leaves open, however, an explanation of why the matches suggested above are the 'right ones'.

Reflective Question 3.2

Think of a leader you know and discuss their style in relation to the LPC model. In relation to this example also reflect on the assumption that a leader cannot change his/her style but has to be assigned to the 'right' situation. In your experience, is this always the case?

Effective Leadership

In order to be an effective leader, your style has to be a good match to the situation you are facing. The theory suggests strongly that if your style does not match well with the situation, you are likely to fail. The model above outlines what is deemed a good match for a low LPC leader and for a high LPC leader. It shows eight situational categories that manifest a different mix of the three situational variables outlined earlier. It states that leaders with a low LPC score are effective in categories 1, 2, 3 and 8 whereas leaders with a high LPC score are effective in categories 4, 5, 6 and 7. Leaders with a middle LPC score are said to be effective in categories 1, 2 and 3. An organization therefore has to analyse the situation using the three situational variables to determine the situational category and then match a leader with the right LPC score to this situation to engender effective leadership.

Key Critique

There are a few criticisms that have been voiced over the years in relation to the validity and reliability of the LPC theory. Northouse (2009) stresses that the LPC theory fails to fully explain why each leadership category is most effective in the

(Continued)

(Continued)

situations specified. This has neither been conceptually explained in depth nor has it been empirically explored. Another key criticism is in relation to the focus of the LPC theory and its associated measure on evaluating least preferred co-workers. Arguably, asking somebody to evaluate their own leadership behaviour by focussing on somebody else's behaviour may lead to projection of the self onto that other person and hence lead to a biased outcome. Amongst other criticisms relating to the reliability of the LPC measure is the problematic notion of medium LPC scores. Compared to the high and low LPC scores it seems relatively unclear what this behaviour may look like/mean in a work setting as it seems to cover a very broad and vague behavioural category. Finally, the LPC model makes the strong claim that leaders cannot change their preferred style and hence need to be matched to an appropriate situation. Northouse (2009) quite rightly criticizes how the theory fails to explore how this may practically happen in organizations and to what extent the organization has control over a leader's context, as well as the leaders available with the 'right' styles to match certain situations.

Path-Goal Theory

Path-goal theory (Evans, 1970, 1974; House, 1971, 1996; House and Dessler, 1974; House and Mitchell, 1974) explores how leaders can motivate followers to achieve set goals and improve their own and the organization's performance. The theory is linked to research on how to motivate employees and embraces the assumptions of expectancy theory of motivation that employees are more likely to perform well if they are confident that they are capable of doing a task, that they will achieve an expected outcome and if the reward for achieving this outcome is valued by the employees. A leader's job here is to ensure that there are no obstacles in the employee's 'path' to achieving the set outcomes, that he/she adapts their leadership behaviour to match the employee's needs and that he/she understand the employee's motivational process.

Path-goal theory is seen as different from the situational leadership theory and Fiedler's LPC model, as it goes beyond the mere matching of leadership style and situation and instead tries to explain the relationship between leader behaviour, subordinate characteristics and work context (Northouse, 2009). It is this ambitious focus on the relationship that makes this theory relatively complex compared to other contingency theories. Figure 3.4 summarizes its fundamental elements.

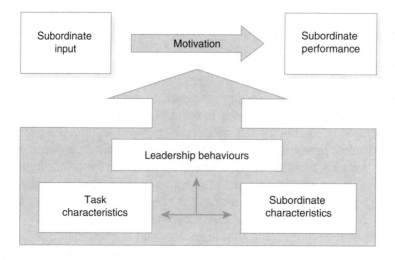

Figure 3.4 **Path-Goal Theory**

Leadership Behaviours

Drawing on House (1996), we can define the leadership behaviours used within the above model as follows.

- **Directive** – Behaviour directed toward providing a psychological structure for subordinates: letting subordinates know what they are expected to do, scheduling and coordinating work, giving specific guidance, and clarifying policies, rules, and procedures.
- **Supportive** – Behaviour directed toward the satisfaction of subordinates' needs and preferences, such as displaying concern for subordinates' welfare and creating a friendly and psychologically supportive work environment.
- **Participative** – Behaviour directed toward the encouragement of subordinate influence on decision making and work unit operations: consulting with subordinates and taking their opinions and suggestions into account when making decisions.
- **Achievement-oriented** – Behaviour directed toward encouraging performance excellence: setting challenging goals, seeking improvement, emphasizing excellence in performance, and showing confidence that subordinates will attain high standards of performance.

Each of these behaviours is, according to House and Mitchell's (1974) development of the theory, supposed to address specific subordinate needs and provide specific support and/or alleviate certain stressors within the subordinate's work context. House and Mitchell (1974) further argued that a leader is not fixed on one leadership behaviour but may adopt any or all of these behaviours towards different subordinates in different situations. House (1996) further clarified later that leaders can exhibit a mix of these behaviours towards one subordinate in a given situation or over time. With a view to leadership development, this theory encourages leaders to develop their ability to adapt their behaviour to the needs and context of their subordinates.

Situational Variables

In order to decide which leadership behaviour is the most appropriate one to motivate a subordinate, the leader must evaluate a subordinate's situation according to the following subordinate characteristics and task characteristics.

Subordinate Characteristics:

- Need for affiliation
- Preferences for structure
- Desires for control
- Self-perceived level of task ability

Task Characteristics:

- Nature and design of subordinate's task
- Formal authority system of the organization

Effective Leadership

In accordance with the above model each leader behaviour is suited to a specific situation and leaders are encouraged to adjust their behaviours to meet situational demands. Several key propositions were formulated by House and Mitchell (1974) outlining which leader behaviour was likely to be most appropriate for specific situations. For example, directive leader behaviour that provides guidance on tasks, roles, structures and procedures is predicted to be best suited for situations where the task is demanding, structures are unclear and subordinates lack experience and self-efficacy. Supportive leader behaviour that focuses on nurturing subordinate needs and welfare is suggested to be most effective where the task is tedious, repetitive, dangerous or stressful and subordinates are unsatisfied or frustrated. Participative leader behaviour that aims to be inclusive in decision making is predicted to be best suited for subordinates who like to be in control and autonomous and are faced by an ambiguous task and structure. Finally, achievement-oriented leader behaviour that provides challenges for subordinates is especially welcome by subordinates with ambiguous and complex tasks as it improves their level of self efficacy ad expectations to succeed. House (1996) has since provided a review and revision of these propositions in light of research (Yukl, 1994) challenging the validity of some of these propositions.

Key Critique

The path-goal theory has one of the most complex sets of situational variables linked to leadership styles across all early contingency theories. This is a conceptual strength but also a practical weakness. It certainly reduces the prescriptive value of this theory in comparison to other contingency theories. Furthermore, although this theory has attracted much empirical research, the findings have not been able to support consistently its validity and the reliability of effective leadership with regard to all different leadership styles and situational variables (Yukl, 2011). Finally, Northouse (2009) criticizes path-goal theory for not conceptually and empirically exploring the link between leadership behaviour and motivation in enough detail and depth. A more detailed exploration of the role of the follower in this relationship and in relation to motivation seems warranted.

Critical Thinking Box 3.3

The early contingency theories' focus on effectiveness as a measure of success of leadership is somewhat problematic. It does not include detailed considerations of what we mean by effectiveness and the extent to which the meaning of this term is contextually and culturally determined. These theories further lack an adequate ethical exploration of effectiveness and we therefore need to question to what extent this is always a desirable outcome of leadership.

Other Contingency Theories

While the above outlined three contingency theories are the most frequently cited in textbooks, there are four other theories and models associated with this stream of early contingency theories of effective leadership. We briefly introduce each theory in turn below and summarize the key characteristics and aims of these other contingency theories in Table 3.1.

- Kerr and Jermier's (1978) leadership substitutes theory explores situational variables (contextual aspects of the task, subordinates, organization) that make a leader employing either instrumental or supportive leadership behaviour ineffective or redundant.

- Vroom and Yetton (1973) in their normative decision model look further at decision-making procedures of participative leaders and their effectiveness. They explore a mix of situational variables and mediating variables that influences how appropriate and effective the different types of decision-making procedures of leaders are.
- Fiedler and Garcia's (1987) cognitive resources theory looks at the interaction of different sources of stress and a leader's cognitive abilities and leadership behaviours and their impact on group performance.
- Yukl's (1971) multiple-linkage model examines in detail how situational variables moderate the influence of a leader's behaviour on individual and group performance. It includes a complex list of leader behaviours, mediators and situational variables in an effort to provide a detailed insight into the complexity of the link between leader behaviour, context and performance.

(For a more detailed reading, we advise readers to consult Yukl's (2011) critical review of early contingency theories of leadership.)

Table 3.1   Further Early Contingency Theories

Contingency theory	Authors	Leadership behaviours	Situational variables	Theory Aims
Leadership substitutes theory	Kerr and Jermier (1978) (revised by Howell et al., 1990; Podsakoff et al., 1993)	Instrumental and supportive leadership	Attributes of task, group and organization	Exploring situational variables that make instrumental or supportive leadership behaviour ineffective or redundant
Normative decision model	Vroom and Yetton (1973); later revision by Vroom and Jago (1988)	Participative leadership behaviour and specific decision procedures	Leader/follower knowledge, goal congruence Mediators: decision quality and acceptance of decisions	Exploring decision-making procedures of participative leaders and their impact on group performance
Cognitive resources theory	Fiedler and Garcia (1987)	Participative leadership, leader IQ and experience	Interpersonal stress and member knowledge	Exploring interaction of different sources of stress and leader's cognitive abilities, behaviours and impact on group performance
Multiple-linkage model	Yukl (1971, 1981, 1989)	Multiple leader behaviours	Attributes of task, group and organization	Exploring how situational variables moderate the influence of a leader's behaviour on individual and group performance

Source: Adapted from Yukl (2011).

VIGNETTE 3.1

Extract from Case Study 3 illustrating the analysis of a leadership situation

One day in May, ... Frank ... welcome(d) Michael Langer, the new Head of Procurement. ... Frank's brief to Mike had been simple and direct. 'Shake 'em up, Mike. A lot of them have been here a long time, and have got very used to the comfortable life.'

Mike was energized. In the interviews he had been able to demonstrate some pretty leading edge thinking about modern procurement techniques ... He was keen to put them to work. He had guessed Lowe Power would be a long way behind best practice and what little information he had picked up from the head-hunter and other contacts in the know had confirmed this. He could see an opportunity to transform the department, deliver significant gains for the business and make a name for himself in short order ...

Mike spent the first week on formalities, meeting the people, and getting an idea of who did what. He booked meetings with the Operations Directors as well as other Divisional heads. What he heard did not surprise him. There were a lot of complaints about the Procurement Department. 'Too bureaucratic', 'Hide-bound by process', 'Not sufficiently focused on value' were just some of the criticisms. He also carried out his own assessment. He quickly came to the view that, apart from learning the vocabulary of strategic procurement, not so much progress had been made in this direction. He also observed that the workload was unevenly distributed across the new department. The stationery contract and corporate travel for example were getting a lot more resources and attention than some business critical engineering requirements.

1. Reflect on Mike's analysis of the leadership situation that he is facing in the procurement department. Select two of the contingency theories introduced in this chapter to analyse and evaluate which leadership style Mike should adopt in the short and long term.

Critical Evaluation of Early Contingency Theories

In this critical evaluation section we will first of all highlight the key strengths of the contingency theories discussed above. We will then draw again on Yukl's (2011) very detailed critique of both the conceptual as well as methodological problems of these theories to summarize the key weaknesses. Additional limitations are highlighted in relation to Meindl et al. (1985) and Collinson's (2006, 2008) work in the area of followership. Finally, we will outline avenues for future contingency theories and the practical and conceptual use of contingency theories.

Strengths

In comparison to the early traits and styles approaches to leadership, the early contingency theories have added significantly to our understanding of leadership and especially our evaluation of the effectiveness of leaders through the introduction of situational variables. They showed that not every leader will be equally effective in every context and that leader effectiveness is instead dependent or contingent upon various situational factors. The range of contingency theories introduced in this chapter offers a range of situational factors, several different foci in leadership behaviours and alternative ways in which the two are linked to determine leader effectiveness. The contingency theories also vary in their approach to leader or situational adaptability. While most of the contingency theories, such as the situational leadership theory and the path-goal theory, argue that leaders can develop to adapt to different situations, Fiedler's contingency theory sees preferred leader styles as difficult to change and looks therefore at matching leaders to appropriate situations.

Apart from having developed our understanding of leaders and leadership conceptually, these early contingency theories have also been very appealing to practitioners. Northouse, for example, lists as one of the key strengths for situational leadership theory that 'it has stood the test of time in the marketplace. Situational leadership is well known and frequently used for training leaders in organizations' (2009: 96). Other strengths listed for situational leadership are its simplicity that makes it very practical and easy for organizations to use, its ability to predict effective leadership, its emphasis on leader flexibility (Northouse, 2009; Yukl, 1989) and its focus on subordinates (Yukl, 1989). Fiedler's contingency theory, conversely, is praised as having stood the test of empirical research (Peters et al., 1985) that has supported the theory's validity and reliability in explaining effective leadership. Similar to the situational leadership theory, its predictive value has been useful to our conceptual understanding and the use of organizations in developing leaders. In contrast to the situational leadership theory, Fiedler's contingency theory has usefully questioned the extent to which leaders can change. This may have helped to shift the blame for organizational failure away from the individual leader. A key strength of other contingency theories such as the path-goal theory or the multiple linkage model is the complex theoretical frameworks they provide and the extent to which this has added to our understanding of the links between leader behaviour, situation and group performance. These conceptually more complex models have further drawn on other concepts, such as motivation theory (path-goal theory) or decision-making process (normative decision model) to enrich our understanding of these complex links.

Weaknesses

There are specific conceptual weaknesses and methodological limitations for all of the contingency theories listed above. The extent of these weaknesses has over time led to the declining popularity of these theories among academics and practitioners. Yukl (2011) has drawn up a comprehensive list of such weaknesses and limitations that run across most of these theories.

- A key conceptual concern is that broad leadership behaviour categories leave too much room for interpretation and are inevitably too vague to allow for exact analyses of how they interact with situational variables.
- Another conceptual weakness is the overly simplified description of the relationship between leader behaviours and situational variables. It does not take into account variations within each leader behaviour category and how these may interact differently with changing situational variables.
- Not all contingency theories explain well enough the causal effects underlying the relationships they draw. This inevitably treats leaders or situational variables (including subordinates) as passive and focuses on unidirectional actions rather than interactional processes.
- Empirical studies and meta-analyses of relevant research studies have explored the validity and reliability of the various contingency theories and drawn up an overall weak and inconsistent picture.
- Two key methodological limitations are the use of convenience samples in field survey studies and behaviour description questionnaires as the main research instrument. The sampling method does not allow for a rigorous testing of the variability of dependent and independent variables and questionnaires tend to be riddled with potential respondent biases, making results less comparable.
- Studies testing a specific contingency theory have further tended to employ different criteria for measuring effective leadership, weakening the comparability of results across studies.
- Other methodological limitations are a lack of exploration of the interactional nature of the relationships between leader behaviour, moderating variables and situational variables as well as a lack of observation of longitudinal aspects of these relationships and the longitudinal affects of leader behaviours and decisions.
- A final concern is the lack of clarity on the level of analysis that the contingency theories and related empirical studies are taking, that is, whether they are looking at the dyadic or group or organizational level.

Further Critical Views and Future Research

Early contingency theories have failed to fully account for subordinate behaviours, the interactional nature of leadership processes, emotions, multiple or dispersed notions of leadership and a recognition of change-oriented and strategic leadership, as well as the dark side of leadership. These areas have been explored by other researchers and will be addressed in subsequent chapters. The very notion of context and situation has been further explored differently since these early contingency theories and Chapter 5 will discuss these recent avenues further, including theories around perceptions of leadership, multiple levels of analysis studies and qualitative approaches to exploring contexts.

Also, while Yukl's (2011) critique examines in great detail conceptual and methodological weaknesses, it does not address explicitly enough the extent to which followers are treated as passive in these theories and the implications this has for our understanding and practice of leadership. Since the 1980s, scholars have increasingly critiqued mainstream leadership theory – such as the contingency theories – for focusing too much on the leader and his/her unidirectional influence on followers. Meindl et al. (1985) have highlighted how this downplaying of the role of followers and the mutual interaction of the leader and follower in the leadership process has led to a romancing of the leader's impact on organizational performance. Collinson (2006, 2008) has further argued that another implication of the passive treatment of followers has been the acceptance of the privileged position of leaders over those of followers. This has subsequently given rise to a deeply embedded asymmetrical power relationship between leader and followers in organizations and modern society. These and other issues with regard to followers and power will be discussed further in Chapters 6 and 7.

In his critical review, Yukl (2011) stresses that for contingency theories to regain their popularity and academic robustness, they need to employ comparative field research looking into the variations in leader effectiveness in different situations. There is also a need for longitudinal studies exploring how and whether leaders adapt to situational changes over time, including experimental field and laboratory studies observing leaders diagnosing situations and interacting with their teams. More creative methods should include observations, diaries, critical incidents and interviews to move away from the bias ridden behavioural questionnaires employed by these early contingency theories. This may further help to capture the interrelatedness and fluidity of the complex mix of variables that make up a leader's context and the leadership process. Finally, Yukl (2011) highlights the need for studies into ineffective leadership behaviours to add to our understanding of the dark side of leadership.

Leader-Member Exchange (LMX) Theory

LMX theory marked a distinct shift in leadership studies as it moved the focus onto the individual follower and the dyadic relationship between leader and follower. This was in stark contrast to the traits, styles and early contingency approaches to leadership that treated followers as passive recipients of leadership as exerted by the leader.

Although recognized by some early contingency theories as a situational variable, leadership studies had up until then ignored the individual follower and their active engagement with leaders in a reciprocal process of leadership.

The earliest descriptions of what is now known as LMX theory can be found in works by Dansereau et al. (1975), Graen and Cashman (1975) and Graen (1976). It was then called the vertical dyad linkage (VDL) theory and focused predominantly on the vertical links between the individual leader and follower. The theory has since undergone many revisions and developments and is still an active field of research into leadership processes. Anand et al.'s (2011) most recent review of LMX research studies reports a total of 130 studies having been conducted between 2002 and 2009, where 70% of these studies focused on exploring further antecedents and consequences of LMX.

Vertical Dyads

Early work on the VDL theory treated the leadership process within a work group as a series of vertical dyads between a leader and every single follower. Each vertical dyad represents an individualized working relationship between a leader and a follower including exchanges and processes specific to each dyad. These early writings on vertical dyads further distinguished between two different types of working relationships: in-group and out-group. In-group relationships are characterized by expanded, enriched and individually negotiated role responsibilities whereas out-group relationships are based predominantly on the formal employment contract and hence the defined role. A follower's membership of the in- or out-group depends on how well the follower and leader work together. According to Dansereau et al. (1975) and Graen (1976) this depends on personality, personal characteristics and the follower's own initiative to work on their work and role relationship with the leader. How many role negotiations and exchanges there are between leader and follower are hence of importance as are reciprocal offers between leader and manager to go beyond the contracted role they have. Dansereau et al. (1975) have argued that in-group followers are likely to receive more information from the leader and tend to have more influence and confidence in and from their leader compared to those in the out-group.

Later studies (Graen and Uhl-Bien, 1995; Liden et al., 1993) expanded the focus of LMX theory to link the dyadic relationships to organizational effectiveness, the principal argument being that the quality of exchanges and working relationships is positively related to the effectiveness of leaders, followers and the wider organization. Graen and Uhl-Bien's (1995) review of LMX research studies showed that high quality (in-group) leader–member exchanges were linked to a higher performance, lower employee turnover, greater organizational commitment, more frequent promotions, higher job satisfaction and better work opportunities for followers including greater participation in decision making.

VIGNETTE 3.2

Extract from Case Study 5 illustrating a leader's attempts to strive for a company-wide in-group

June sees the development of human relationships and treating people as equally significant and part of a team as fundamental to leadership and living, whether it be the cleaner, the taxi driver, the bank manager or the Queen. June put it this way: 'Nobody was just a bank manager. It was a relationship and an integral part of the whole thing working, so he [the bank manager] was part of the team as far as I was concerned. And he gave advice and suggestions and he engaged with things and came to events and I am quite sure that it had an impact on him. I hope it gets passed on to other businesses in some way!'

June saw her bank manager and her suppliers such as cab drivers, florists and caterers as part of the same team: 'I refused to call people our suppliers. I called them our external partners ... that hierarchical thing of people coming to the back door and if they are lucky they get a box of chocolates at Christmas because they've been so good! So for me, I didn't often get angry, but there was somebody on duty one day and someone came to order a cab and they rang the cab company and the way they spoke to the woman they were ordering the cab from was as though she was a servant. I don't get irate often, but it was "how dare you talk to the people, who drop people off and help them out with their baggage ... that is the last memory they have of the Pierian Centre, they are so important and they are part of our team, we don't pay them on the books, but my God they are important, they are part of the service we offer!".'

1. This quote illustrates June's belief that everybody in and outside the company ought to be treated equally and as part of the in-group. Critically explore the advantages and challenges that this may bring for individual leader-follower relationships.

Leadership Making

A further development of the LMX theory has been the exploration of the process of leadership making (Graen and Uhl-Bien, 1991), which prescribes that, in light of the research listed above, it is vital for leaders to develop as many high-quality exchanges and work relationship as possible. Certainly within their own work group, leaders should strive to have high-quality exchanges with every subordinate so as to increase job satisfaction, performance and avoid the negative implications of out-group existence. In addition to the immediate work group, leaders should also strive to create networks of high-quality exchanges throughout the organization to ensure group and organizational effectiveness as well as impact positively on their own careers.

Graen and Uhl-Bien's (1991) work on leadership making suggests three phases in the high-quality exchange development process:

- Stranger phase – As leader and follower get to know each other, exchanges are largely rule bound and based on a mainly contractual relationship. Exchanges are of lower quality and leader–follower relations are predominantly influenced by the formal roles they have in the organization. Followers comply with rather than pro-actively engage with the leader and their interests are more likely to be focused on the self rather than the group.
- Acquaintance phase – Over time leaders and followers will test the extent to which either is interested in engaging in the information exchange, roles and responsibilities that go beyond the follower's contractually defined role. Trust and respect are being developed between leader and follower and their dyad is starting to move away from the pure contractual relationship to a more social, career-oriented one.
- Mature partnership phase – High level of reciprocal interactions, trust and respect leading to high-quality exchanges. Leader and follower have developed a more egalitarian relationship in which influence and control are balanced. This further means that leader and follower have come to rely on each other for specific favours, support, encouragement and advice. This has a positive impact on the working relations between leader and follower as well as positive outcomes for the wider organizational performance. Links can be drawn here between leader behaviours in mature partnerships and transformational leadership as discussed in the next chapter.

These phases can also be interpreted as a life-cycle model of leader–follower relationships over time and revolving around trust, respect and obligations.

Reflective Question 3.33

In your previous or current employment, have you experienced all aspects your the life-cycle model of the leader–follower relationship as suggested by LMX? How did this affect your work? Did you experience any positive or negative outcomes as a result of any of these phases?

Effective Leadership

Recognizing that leaders tend to establish mature partnerships with only a small number of trusted subordinates, LMX theory helps leaders become aware of the limitations of such an approach for group and organizational effectiveness and develop instead a greater number of mature partnerships. It helps leaders to realize the benefits of these mature partnerships for both follower and leader, as well as fully understand the obligations and long-term focus of these relationships.

Questionnaires have been developed alongside LMX theory to aid the analysis of a leader's current dyadic relationships. Leaders and their followers fill these in to assess the nature and effectiveness of their current working relationships in relation to such issues as trust, respect and responsibility. Once the current dyadic relationships have been analysed, LMX theory then encourages leaders to understand the possible problems of too many out-group relationships and to develop more high-quality exchanges leading to mature partnerships in the immediate work group and throughout the wider organization. Leaders can do so by considering each follower individually and tailoring their advice and support to provide opportunities for new roles and responsibilities that aid followers' development, job performance and satisfaction.

Critical Evaluation of LMX Theories

Strengths

LMX theory has added to our conceptual understanding of leadership processes significantly through its unique focus on the dyadic individual leader–follower relationships. As such it is the only approach to leadership that reminds leaders of how easy it is to build and perpetuate in-groups and out-groups and how important it is to develop better relationships with a wider range of subordinates over time. LMX theory also brings to the forefront the importance of communication and the relational nature of this as a key aspect of leadership. Although it started off as describing dyadic relationships in leadership, it has moved on to having prescriptive value in relation to leadership making and its positive outcomes for group and organizational performance. LMX theory continues to receive considerable attention from leadership scholars and is hence in contrast to styles and contingency approaches to leadership benefitting from current research and development. Over time research into LMX theory has, for example, taken into consideration aspects of context such as national culture and its impact on dyadic relationships. It has also further studied LMX at different levels (for example, individual, group and multi-level) and explored leader and follower behaviours within the dyadic relationship. Links have also been investigated between LMX and other areas of leadership studies such as transformational and servant leadership.

Weaknesses

Yet despite the many revisions, developments and research studies conducted over the last 27 years, the LMX theory of leadership still has a number of conceptual weaknesses. For example, despite attempts to revise and develop the theory, LMX still remains unclear in its explanation of how dyadic relationships develop over time. It is also not clear how single dyads affect each other and how inequality in dyadic relationships affects the overall performance of the work group. There is further still conceptual ambiguity concerning the nature of exchange relationships and again a lack of empirical insight into how these change over time and how role negotiation occurs.

An additional limitation to LMX theory is its sole focus on vertical dyads in assigned leader positions rather than lateral dyads in emergent leadership situations. Anand et al. (2011) further criticize the to-date limited exploration of context and particularly organizational culture and its impact on dyadic relationships. The predominant use of questionnaires in research studies is also limiting our ability to explore these aspects of LMX fully and Yukl (2010) suggests further use of longitudinal studies and qualitative research methods to overcome these problems. Finally, the very focus of LMX on in-groups and out-groups may have the negative side effect of increasing leaders' focus on group memberships. Consideration of other notions of attribution, fairness and equality is therefore necessary.

VIGNETTE 3.3

Extract from Case Study 1 highlighting issues of geographical distance for the leader–follower relationship

Another management challenge has developed via the new structure within the organization. This means that while employees worked under one single contract, rather than for multiple contracts, the management structure under this new regime would potentially result in managers and employees not being in the same geographical remit – making people management even harder, along with a severe lack of visible leadership.

1. The LMX theories do not explicitly consider leader-follower relationships where the leader is not visible or geographically remote. What implications could such remoteness have in relation to the development of high level exchanges?

Summary

In this chapter we have introduced you to the field of early contingency theories and the LMX theories. We have outlined and critically evaluated in detail the situational leadership theory, the least preferred co-worker theory and the path-goal theory. These three early contingency theories exemplify the aim of this field of leadership studies to create universally applicable models that link leadership behaviours and situational variables in an effort to predict successful, effective leadership. While these theories have proven very popular with practitioners, we have highlighted the common conceptual and methodological limitations of these early contingency theories and particularly the lack of empirical evidence for the relationships they propose. An additional key weakness of these theories is the treatment of followers as passive and the interaction between leader and follower as unidirectional. In response to this weakness, we have introduced the LMX theories that have the leader–follower relationship and hence the interactional nature of the leadership process at heart. In the critical evaluation of the LMX theories we focus the your attention on the limited exploration of time and context and the need for LMX theories to explore the influence of these on the leader–follower relationship further.

Additional Reflection Questions

1. What do you see as the shared principles of early contingency theories?
2. What is situational leadership theory and what are its implications for leader effectiveness?
3. Fiedler suggests that leaders cannot change their behaviour but have to be matched with the right situation. Critically discuss and compare to other contingency theories.
4. What are the links between path-goal theory and motivation theory?
5. Critically evaluate the merits and limitations of the contingency approach to leadership.
6. How relevant are these contingency theories for our understanding of leadership today? What could be done to increase their relevance?
7. What is the key contribution of LMX theories to our understanding of leadership and what are its implications for leader effectiveness?
8. How can LMX theory help today's organizations to improve their leadership structures and processes?

Case Study Questions

1. Case Study 1 highlights the problems that managers are facing in this organization due to their limited leadership training. With reference to the early contingency theories introduced in this chapter, which model would you recommend

the company uses to develop their managers further and evoke effective leadership? What may be the limitations of the model that you are proposing?

2. In Case Study 3, the new procurement department manager Mike is facing continuing resistance from his team to the new initiatives he is introducing. Using path-goal theory and situational leadership theory, evaluate the fit of Mike's leadership style to the follower and task characteristics of his team. What advice would you give to Mike to improve this situation? What other issues – not covered by these two theories – would you advise Mike to take into consideration?

3. Case Studies 4 and 5 introduce two female leaders (Lucy Hurst Brown and June Burrough) whose leadership is particularly rooted in specific beliefs and values about their organization and relationships with employees and stakeholders. Using the approach to leader–follower relationships offered by the LMX theories, compare these two leaders with a view to in-group and out-groups as well as the development phase of their relationships with employees and other stakeholders. Use your analysis to critically reflect on their effectiveness as leaders.

4. In light of the culturally specific views on leadership highlighted in Case Study 2, critically evaluate the extent to which LMX theories are applicable in an Iraqi context: for example, does the leader–follower relationship look different in this context from what it would in a UK context? Does it develop differently?

Further Reading

Anand, S., Hu, J., Liden, R.C. and P.R. Vidyarthi (2011) Leader-member exchange: Recent research findings and prospects for the future. In A. Bryman, D. Collinson, K. Grint, B. Jackson and M. Uhl-Bien (eds) *The SAGE Handbook of Leadership*. London: Sage, 311–325.

Blanchard, K., Zigarmi, D. and Nelson, R. (1993) Situational leadership after 25 years: A retrospective. *Journal of Leadership Studies*, 1(1): 22–36.

Graen, G.B. and Uhl-Bien, M. (1995) Relationship-based approach to leadership: Development of leader–member exchange (LMX) theory of leadership over 25 years: Applying a multi-level multi-domain perspective. *The Leadership Quarterly*, 6(2): 219–247.

House, R.J. (1996) Path-goal theory of leadership: Lessons, legacy and a reformulated theory. *Leadership Quarterly*, 7(3): 323–352.

Yukl, G. (2011) Contingency theories of effective leadership. In A. Bryman, D. Collinson, K. Grint, B. Jackson and M. Uhl-Bien (eds) *The SAGE Handbook of Leadership*. London: Sage, 286–298.

Charismatic and Transformational Leadership

Within this chapter we will explore theory concerning leadership that is sometimes referred to as the 'new approach' or the 'neo-charismatic approach'. The title 'new leadership approach' is rather misleading now as the theories involved – transformational leadership, charismatic leadership and visionary leadership – in some cases date back to the mid-1970s. These titles, however, describe a shift, a movement in leadership thinking, seemingly away from style and situational approaches. We explore the initial development of these approaches through ideas of charismatic leadership and then discuss aspects of transformational leadership, which, much of the time, incorporate charismatic and visionary elements. We will look at one such model of transformational leadership – 'The Full Range Leadership Model' (FRLM) – and the constituent dimensions that make up transformational, transactional leadership. We will also explore some of the limitations with transformational and charismatic approaches and consider the future for these ideas.

Chapter Aims

- Introduce and critically discuss charismatic and transformational approaches to leadership
- Present and critically evaluate notions of charisma, vision, inspiring, motivation and their link to leadership

- Discuss and critically examine the notion of transactional leadership
- Explore the difference between transactional and transformational leadership
- Highlight the downsides of charismatic, transformational and transactional leadership

Charismatic Leadership

The origins of theories such as transformational leadership are evident in early literature on charisma (Weber, 1947). The notion of charisma is semantically linked to the Greek work *karis* meaning 'gift of grace': a donation by the Holy Spirit to all believers (Marturano and Arsenault, 2008). In the apostolic writings we find several 'charismas', such as the ability to make prophecies, the power to perform miracles, discernments of spirits and some particular capacities to lead a society (Marturano and Arsenault, 2008). Weber (1947) also highlighted the nature of charisma as a special gift of divine origin and goes on to suggest that charisma occurs in social crises, when leaders emerge with a radical view or vision that then in turn attracts followers (Yukl, 2010). This aura-like perspective was developed into an organizational context in the mid-1970s through to the mid-1990s by researchers and writers such as Beyer (1999), Beyer and Browning (1999), Bryman (1992), Conger (1989), Conger and Kanungo (1987, 1998), House (1977) and Shamir et al. (1993; 1994). Some writers and researchers have suggested a behavioural view of charisma whereby one can identify what a charismatic leader does or how they behave (similar to those highlighted below in theories of transformational leadership), such as being a great orator (Bryman, 1992). Others, however, see charisma as a attribution from followers (Conger and Kanungo, 1987, 1998) and a third set of scholars acknowledge a more relational psychological process (House, 1977; Shamir et al., 1993; 1994).

Davis and Gardner (2012) summarize aspects of this discussion by suggesting that there have been various necessary conditions posited to the rise of charismatic leadership (Trice and Beyer, 1986; Weber, 1947, 1968; Willner, 1984):

1. a person who possesses extraordinary gifts;
2. a crisis or time of distress;
3. a revolutionary solution to the crisis;
4. followers who believe in the person and who are attracted to the miraculous qualities of the person;
5. validation of the person's gifts through repeated successes.

Davis and Gardner (2012) pick up on one of these aspects and go on to describe the continued discussion regarding the link charisma has with crisis. While highlighting empirical research that supports the link between a crisis and the emergence of charismatic leadership (Bligh et al., 2004a, 2004b; House et al., 1991; Pillai, 1996), they also point to other scholars who provide evidence that crisis is a facilitating but unnecessary requirement for charismatic leadership to emerge (Boal and Bryson, 1988; Halverston et al., 2004; Hunt et al., 1999; Pillai and Meindl, 1998). Furthermore they highlight research that suggests a negative relationship between charismatic leadership and crisis situations (Bligh et al., 2005; Pillai and Meindl, 1998; Williams et al., 2009).

In their study Davis and Gardner (2012) research the emergence of crisis and the use of charismatic rhetoric. Charismatic rhetoric refers to eight constructs used by Davis and Gardner – collective focus, temporal orientation, followers' worth, similarity to followers, values and moral justifications, tangibility, action and adversity. They use these constructs to investigate the speeches and radio addresses made by the former US president – George W. Bush. They conclude that the president's charismatic rhetoric was crisis responsive, which supports views above that crisis acts as a precursor for charismatic leadership. Similarly, Takala et al. (2013) have also found that crisis is important for the emergence of charisma. Takala and colleagues, however, discuss the media's role in developing the charismatic. They examine the representation of Barack Obama in the Finnish media and suggest that his charisma is developed and reinforced by the media being enthusiastic about his personality, life story and behaviour. They go on to suggest that this supports the notion that there is not just one form of charismatic leadership but many various ways that it can manifest itself. They show particular support for the framework developed by Streyer (1998) suggesting different types of charismatic leadership exist dependent on social context, that is, the paternalistic, heroic, missionary and majestic. Finally, they also suggest that ethics is also constructed as a crucial part of charismatic leadership. The link between ethics and leadership is discussed further in Chapter 13.

These aspects of charismatic leadership, such as the emergence during a crisis and the behavioural/attributional mix, have been the key tensions in understanding the charismatic paradigm. These issues also cross over into the transformational leadership paradigm and will, among others, be explored in the next section.

Critical Thinking Box 4.1

Often when we describe toxic leaders (see Chapter 13), these characters are charismatic figures. Therefore, we can be critical of the notion of charismatic leadership for lacking an ethical or moral aspect of leadership.

The Development of Transformational Leadership Theory[1]

Transformational leadership as a concept was first developed through consideration of accounts of revolution and revolt in society by Downton (1973). From here the concept was compared to a more transactional form of behaviour by the political scientist James MacGregor Burns (1978). In Burns' view the concept of transactional leadership was defined as a transaction or exchange between leader and followers, such as providing a material or psychological reward for followers' compliance with the leader's wishes. Transforming leadership, in contrast, Burns suggested, is linked to psychological fulfilment and moves people up the 'hierarchy of needs' (Maslow, 1954, 1968) and addresses people's higher-order 'needs' for achievement, self-esteem and self-actualization – for self-fulfilment. Bass (1985a) develops these ideas into a deeper appreciation of transformational leadership and goes on to suggest that it is a process of changing how people feel about themselves which in turn raises their motivation and enables them to achieve a performance beyond normal expectations.

Several theorists (Alban-Metcalfe and Alimo-Metcalfe, 2000; Alimo-Metcalfe and Alban-Metcalfe, 2001; Bass, 1985a, 1998; Bennis and Nanus, 1985; Podaskoff et al., 1990; Saskin, 1988; Tichy and Devanna, 1986, 1990) have proposed versions of trans-formational leadership that include and extend these ideas (Yukl, 1999). One of the most important versions that has generated the most research is the 'Full Range Leadership' model (Avolio, 1999; Avolio and Bass, 1993, 2002; Yukl, 1999). This comprises the dimensions *laissez-faire*, transactional and transformational leadership. According to this model, transformational leadership encourages people to look beyond self-interest for the common good (Bass, 1985a, 1990; Bass and Avolio, 1994).

FRLM

The FRLM was developed by Bernard Bass and Bruce Avolio (Avolio, 1999; Avolio and Bass, 1993, 2002) and comprises three component dimensions – transformational leadership, transactional leadership and *laissez-faire* or non-leadership. These three component parts include sub-dimensions. Definitions from Bass (1998) of each of these component sub-dimensions are given below. For transformational leadership these are attributed charisma/idealized influence, inspirational motivation, intellectual stimulation and individualized consideration (Bass, 1998; Bass and Riggio, 2006).

- *Attributed charisma/idealized influence* – Leaders behave or are attributed with characteristics that result in their being role models for their followers. Leaders are

---

[1]Parts of this section were originally written for the unpublished doctoral thesis of one of the authors (Edwards, 2005).

admired, respected and trusted. Followers identify with the leaders and want to emulate them. Leaders are perceived by their followers as having extraordinary capabilities, persistence and determination. Leaders are willing to take risks and are consistent rather than arbitrary. They can be counted on to do the right thing, demonstrating high standards of ethical and moral conduct.

- *Inspirational motivation* – Leaders behave in ways that motivate and inspire those around them by providing meaning and challenge to their followers' work. Team spirit is aroused. Enthusiasm and optimism are displayed. Leaders involve followers in envisioning attractive future states. Leaders clearly communicate expectations that followers want to meet. And they demonstrate commitment to goals and the shared vision.

- *Intellectual stimulation* – Leaders stimulate their followers' efforts to be innovative and creative by questioning assumptions, reframing problems and approaching old situations in new ways. They encourage creativity. There is no public criticism of individual members' mistakes. New ideas and creative problem solutions are solicited from followers, who are included in the process of addressing problems and finding solutions. Followers are encouraged to try new approaches, and their ideas are not criticized even if they differ from the leaders' ideas.

- *Individualized consideration* – Leaders pay special attention to each follower's needs for achievement and growth by acting as a coach or mentor. Followers and colleagues are developed to successively higher levels of potential. Individualized consideration is practised when new learning opportunities are created, along with a supportive climate. Individual differences in needs and desires are recognized and accepted by the leader. A two-way exchange in communication is encouraged, and 'management by walking around' is practised. Interactions with followers are personalized. The leader listens effectively and delegates tasks as a means of developing followers. Delegated tasks are monitored to discover whether followers need additional direction or support and to assess progress, but followers do not feel they are being checked on.

Transactional leadership behaviour, however, has the following constitutive sub-dimensions – contingent reward, active management-by-exception and passive management-by-exception. Again definitions from Bass (1998) are given below:

- *Contingent reward* – The leader assigns or gets agreement on what needs to be done and promises rewards or actually rewards others in exchange for satisfactorily carrying out the assignment.

- *Management-by-exception (active and passive)* – The leader actively monitors deviations from performance standards, mistakes and errors in followers' assignments and takes corrective action as necessary or waits passively for deviations, mistakes and errors to occur and then takes corrective action.

Finally, *laissez-faire* or non-leadership is defined by Bass (1998) as:

- *Laissez-faire* leadership – The leader avoids taking a stand, ignores problems, does not follow up and refrains from intervening.

The level of effectiveness of these behaviours is linked to the level of passivity, and therefore the dimensions associated with transformational leadership are seen as the most effective followed by those associated with transactional leadership, with *laissez-faire* behaviours being seen as the least effect and indeed, as ineffective (see Figure 4.1).

VIGNETTE 4.1

Extract from Case Study 6 highlighting transformational and transactional leadership

In Mike's view it was 'all about the psychology of change, about creating a different physiology even, and an atmosphere of thinking differently'. In Mike's view 'you should never be a victim of your own environment' and under his leadership the service was transformed and achieved 30% savings through the life of the PFI making itself financing, turning around abandoned call rates from frustrated customers as high as 40%. Now, under the current economic environment, the team are being asked to dig deep, and work even smarter and have now achieved a further 25% savings.

The team that head up the service have a strong gallows sense of humour, and work in a relaxed, mutually supportive but focused way. Mike's openness to new ideas, his view and confidence that his management team and staff are highly capable, his investment in them through management development, and their capacity in finding solutions, his own sense of humour, together with a 'hardnosed' focus on the role of data intelligence and integrated technology to target areas of the business and new ways of working in creating streamlined services, are critical factors in his team's success. Challenging existing systems and ways of working whilst using ideas and methods not traditionally associated with the UK public sector culture have set them apart as a high performing resilient team able to deliver more with less.

1. To what extent is transformational leadership exhibited here and to what extent is transactional leadership exhibited? How are they related?

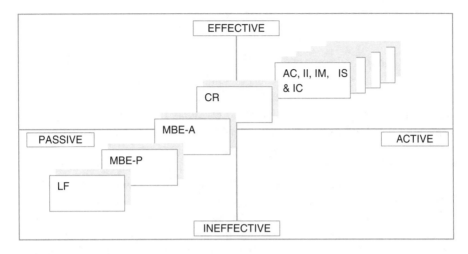

Figure 4.1   The 'Full Range Leadership' Model

Source: Adapted from Bass, B.M. and Avolio, B.J. (1994) 'Introduction'. In B.M. Bass and B.J. Avolio (eds) *Improving Organizational Effectiveness through Transformational Leadership*. Thousands Oaks, CA: Sage, pages 5–6.

Reflective Question 4.1

Think of a leader from your past experiences. What behaviours from those high-lighted above do they exhibit? Do these change in differing circumstances and why?

VIGNETTE 4.2

Extract from Case Study 3 highlighting the importance of understanding the dimensions of transformational leadership

Mike spent the first week on formalities, meeting the people, and getting an idea of who did what. He booked meetings with the Operations Directors as well as other Divisional heads. What he heard did not surprise him. There were a lot of complaints about the Procurement Department. 'Too bureaucratic', 'Hide-bound by process', 'Not sufficiently focused on value' were just some of the criticisms. He also carried out his own assessment. He quickly came to the view that, apart from learning the vocabulary of strategic procurement, not so much progress had been made in this direction. He also observed that workload was unevenly distributed across the new department. The

(Continued)

(Continued)

stationery contract and corporate travel for example were getting a lot more resource and attention than some business critical engineering requirements.

Inspired by a strong sense of purpose, Mike set a blistering pace. Alarmed that he couldn't find them, he asked for contracting calendars from each of the buying area managers. Unable to make sense of the different monthly reports from the market teams, he set about creating a standard report format with a lot more detail. This was necessarily an iterative exercise, and caused a deal of moaning and groaning, but at the end of May he was able to present the report in full to the monthly executive meeting. Mike noted, with some satisfaction, that his submission passed without remark.

Meanwhile, Mike was dismayed at the apparent lack of enthusiasm from his management team. They were sullen and uncommunicative in the weekly meeting. He'd talk, they'd listen, but it didn't feel right. Next steps would get recorded but rarely completed on time. A month after the request for contracting calendars, he still hadn't seen one. Once he had got the department on an even keel, he resolved to take time out to figure out what made them tick. In the meantime, there was a lot to do and a pressing need to get on. Determined to get to grips with the fundamentals, he called for detailed market and contract reviews from each buying group.

1. What dimensions of transactional and transformational leadership are evident in this extract? Look at the dimensions of transformational leadership, how might each of them help or hinder in this situation?

Developments of the FRLM

There have been concerns regarding the factor structure (the way a model or framework is developed from statistical analysis of questionnaire based data) of the FRLM. Since the original structure of the model was published (Bass, 1985a), subsequent studies have continued to produce empirical support for it (Hater and Bass, 1988; Hoover, 1987; Koh, 1990; Waldman et al., 1987). One modification that has been made is to include 'active' and 'passive' forms of management-by-exception (Hater and Bass, 1988; Yammarino and Bass, 1990). However, conflicting factor structures in more recent research using the Multifactor Leadership Questionnaire (MLQ) have led some scholars to suggest different conceptualizations of the Full Range Leadership Model (Antonakis et al., 2003; Avolio et al., 1999; Bycio et al., 1995; Carless, 1998; Den Hartog et al., 1997; Edwards et al., 2012; Goodwin et al., 2001; Hinkin and Schriesheim, 2008; Hinkin and Tracy, 1999; Howell and Avolio, 1993; Kanste et al., 2007; Rafferty and Griffin, 2004; Tejeda et al., 2001; Tepper and Percy, 1994; Yammarino and Dubinsky, 1994). Some alternative conceptualizations are listed in Table 4.1.

It has been pointed out, however, that the research discussed above has in some instances tested the FRLM across a variety of industrial and cultural settings and hierarchical levels and with non-homogeneous groups, which may lead to different factor structures (Antonakis et al., 2003; Edwards et al., 2012). One example is a study (Bycio et al., 1995) which found that leader gender and pooled ratings from people who reported to leaders at different hierarchical levels may have affected the patterns of factor correlations of the MLQ (Antonakis et al., 2003). In addition, Avolio et al. (1999) point out that Bycio et al. (1995) excluded from their data collection the *laissez-faire* scale, potentially affecting the pattern of results reported by them. Taking these considerations into account, a recent analysis of the MLQ (Antonakis et al., 2003) concluded that:

- the nine-factor model best represents the factor structure underlying the MLQ (Form 5X) instrument;

Table 4.1 Different Models of Transformational and Transactional Leadership Components and Behaviours

Model	Description
Null model	There is no systematic variance associated with the MLQ and no consistent factor structure can be produced (Avolio et al., 1999)
One-factor model	All items on the MLQ load onto a 'general or global' leadership factor (Avolio et al., 1999)
Two-factor model	Active and passive leadership behaviours (Bycio et al., 1995; Den Hartog et al., 1997). This two-factor model, however, has been discounted by Den Hartog et al. (1997) owing to the theoretical importance of the three factors and the differential effects of the two active types of leadership (transformational and transactional) found in many studies (Den Hartog et al. [1997] suggest Bryman [1992] as a good review source for these studies).
Alternative two factor model	Active constructive (transformational leadership and contingent reward) and passive corrective leadership (management-by-exception [active and passive] and *laissez-faire*) (Avolio et al., 1999)
Three-factor model	Transformational, transactional (contingent reward and management-by-exception [active]), and passive-avoidant leadership (management-by-exception [passive] and laissez-faire) (Avolio et al., 1999)
Alternative three-factor model	Transformational leadership (charismatic/inspirational and intellectual stimulation), developmental/transactional leadership (individualised consideration and contingent reward), passive corrective leadership (management-by-exception and *laissez-faire)* (Avolio et al., 1999)
A second alternative three-factor model	Active constructive leadership (transformational leadership and contingent reward), active management-by-exception and passive avoidant leadership (Edwards et al., 2012; Kantse et al., 2007)
Four-factor model	Transformational leadership, contingent reward, management-by-exception (active) and passive-avoidant leadership
Five-factor model	Transformational leadership, contingent reward, management-by-exception (active), management-by-exception (passive), *laissez-faire* leadership (Howell and Avolio, 1993)
Six-factor model	Charismatic/inspirational leadership, intellectual stimulation, individualised, contingent reward, management-by-exception (active), passive-avoidant leadership (Avolio et al., 1999)
Seven-factor model	Charismatic/inspirational leadership, intellectual stimulation, individualised consideration, contingent reward, management-by-exception (active), management-by-exception (passive), laissez-faire leadership (Avolio et al., 1999)

- the MLQ can be satisfactorily used to measure 'full range leadership' in relation to its underlying theory;
- the findings of this research indicate that it is premature to collapse factors in this model before exploring the context in which the survey ratings are collected.

Critical Thinking Box 4.2

The differing models of transformational and transactional leadership seem to suggest situational differences. The theory, however, seems to suggest one best way of leading – being transformational. Taking a cultural view (see Chapter 10) on transformational leadership behaviours and leadership in general would be useful here in exploring differing views of leadership in differing contexts.

VIGNETTE 4.3

Extract from Case Study 1 illustrating transformational leadership

There were difficulties with getting managers to submit the reviews. There seemed to be a lack of commitment and leadership from the directors, which may have affected the buy in from managers. With this in mind the overall completion rate was slightly lower than expected (76%).

After another round of employee opinion surveys in February 2012, the results reflected a drop in morale. There were some results that were below the baseline level of morale taken in December 2010, especially relating to items on management and training. These items were mainly in the service and compliance department. The items showed employees in this area were dissatisfied by the level of communication, support, and leadership displayed by their managers. They also were dissatisfied by the amount of training opportunities available to employees. A key management challenge in an organization without a clear communications strategy – how do you maintain regular communication with your employees?

1. Describe which transformational leadership behaviours may be helpful in this situation.
2. Compare this to the impact of transactional leadership behaviours.

Other Perspectives on Transformational Leadership

While the FRLM has dominated the literature and empirical research on transformational leadership it is worth noting that other models of transformational leadership are used in empirical research. Two popular models are those developed by Podaskoff et al. (1990) and Alban-Metcalfe and Alimo-Metcalfe (2000)/Alimo-Metcalfe and Alban-Metcalfe (2001). Podaskoff and colleagues, for example, developed a slightly different framework of transformational leadership that included the dimensions – articulating a vision, providing an appropriate model, fostering the acceptance of group goals, high performance expectations, individualized support and intellectual stimulation. Some dimensions are the same as those for the FRLM, however, there are some dimensions that provide a slightly different view of transformational leadership, for example being a role model and fostering the acceptance of group goals. In addition to this model, Alban-Metcalfe and Alimo-Metcalfe (2000) and Alimo-Metcalfe and Alban-Metcalfe (2001) developed a model of transformational leadership that was based more on a UK public sector context. They produced a nine factor model that included the dimensions:

- genuine concern for others;
- political sensitivity and skills;
- decisiveness, determination and self-confidence;
- integrity, trustworthy, honest and open;
- empowers, develops potential;
- inspirational networker and promoter;
- accessible and approachable;
- clarifies boundaries, involves others in decisions;
- encourages critical and strategic thinking.

As eluded to earlier these models have been hidden to some extent by the popularity of the FRLM and need to be appreciated alongside and in comparison to the FRLM. They certainly provide a wider appreciation of what might constitute transformational leadership but at the same time they may be diluting the concept into a catch-all for seemingly positive behaviours linked to leadership.

The Impact of Transformational Leadership

There is evidence from research that shows transformational leadership is exhibited by people in many diverse roles in society, business and politics (Avolio, 1999; Bass, 1998). For example, there is evidence of transformational leadership being exhibited by housewives active in the community (Avolio and Bass, 1994), chief executive officers (Yokochi, 1989), army colonels (Bass, 1985), world class leaders of movements (Bass, 1985), Methodist ministers (Onmen, 1987), school administrators (Koh, 1990;

Leithwood and Jantzi, 1990), Roman Catholic brothers and sisters (Druskat, 1994) and presidents of the USA (House et al., 1991).

Theories of transformational leadership can be credited with giving a clearer understanding of the reasons why some leaders fail, some survive and some transform the groups, organizations and societies they lead to new heights of achievement perhaps previously only imagined (Gill et al., 1998). Furthermore, transformational leadership describes what leaders do when they raise motivation and achievement beyond previous expectations and when they develop and motivate people to their fullest potential and contribution (Gill et al., 1998).

Indeed, research shows (Avolio, 1999) that transformational leadership increases: commitment (Pitman, 1993); the motivation (Masi, 1994) and loyalty (Kelloway and Barling, 1993) of followers; project quality and innovation (Keller, 1992); sales performance (Garcia, 1995); group/team performance (Carless et al., 1995; Sivasubramaniam et al., 1997; Thite, 1997); church attendance (Onmen, 1987); and organizational commitment and job satisfaction (Walumbwa et al., 2004). Transformational leadership has also been shown to increase the likelihood (Arnold et al., 2001; Avolio, 1999; Kelloway and Barling, 2000) of:

- managers championing projects (Howell and Higgins, 1990);
- the financial success of teams and departments (Avolio et al., 1988; Howell and Avolio, 1993);
- managers gaining a better performance appraisal (Hater and Bass, 1988; Waldman et al., 1987);
- promotion (Waldman et al., 1990; Yammarino and Bass, 1990);
- reaching long-term performance objectives in banks (Geyer and Steyrer, 1998);
- creating collaborative cultures in schools (Leithwood and Jantzi, 1990);
- commitment to the organization and related citizenship behaviour and job satisfaction in schools in Singapore (Koh, 1990);
- commitment to the organization/group (Arnold et al., 2001; Barling et al., 1996; Bycio et al., 1995; Koh et al., 1995);
- a sense of fairness within the organization (Pillai et al., 1995);
- trust in the leader/group (Arnold et al., 2001; Pillai et al., 1995; Podsakoff et al., 1996);
- enhanced satisfaction with both the job (Hater and Bass, 1988) and the leader (Hater and Bass, 1988; Koh et al., 1995);
- lower levels of both job stress (Sosik and Godshalk, 2000) and role stress (Podaskoff et al., 1996);
- subordinates' self-efficacy beliefs (Kirkpatrick and Locke, 1996) and team efficacy (Arnold et al., 2001);
- group potency and performance (Sosik et al., 1997).

Furthermore, there is research evidence that shows transformational leadership is positively related to work group reputation, cooperation and warmth (Weierter,

1994), friendliness (Krishnan, 2004; Weierter, 1994), reasoning (Krishnan, 2004), voting preferences and actual voting behaviour in US presidential elections (Pillai and Williams, 1998; Pillai et al., 2003) and higher levels of moral reasoning (Turner et al., 2002). Recent research also suggests that remote transformational leadership (for example, using transformational leadership in e-mail messages) still has the same positive effects on performance and attitudes that occur within face-to-face interaction (Kelloway et al., 2003). Importantly, the association between transformational leadership and organizational outcomes has been substantiated in both laboratory studies (Howell and Frost, 1989; Kirkpatrick and Locke, 1996) and field studies (Barling et al., 1996; Howell and Avolio, 1993) that go beyond traditional correlational findings (Kelloway and Barling, 2000). Empirical studies, therefore, appear to consistently show that the theory of transformational and transactional leadership is adequately descriptive of leadership behaviour in all facets of society (Atwater and Yammarino, 1992; Avolio et al., 1988; Bass, 1985a; Bass et al., 1987; Hater and Bass, 1988; Sosik, 1997; Yammarino et al., 1993).

However, some studies would challenge some of the research findings above. For example, Sivanathan and Fekken (2002) did not find a relationship between transformational leadership and moral reasoning. Indeed, despite the evidence highlighted above concerning the effectiveness of transformational leadership there is other evidence that suggests *both* active transactional and transformational leadership can be effective. For example, recent research found that both active transactional and transformational leadership behaviours were positively correlated with potency, cohesion and performance in 72 US Army platoons (Bass et al., 2003). Previous research supports this finding, suggesting that the most effective leaders typically display both transformational and transactional leadership (Avolio and Bass, 1998; Avolio et al., 1999; Bass and Avolio, 1993; Curphy, 1992; Hater and Bass, 1988; Howell and Avolio, 1993; Kane and Tremble, 1998). There is also evidence that transformational leadership augments transactional leadership, predicting levels of extra effort, job motivation and moral commitment (Gill, et al., 1998; Kane and Tremble, 1998). In addition, the magnitude of the augmentation effect has been shown to be greater at higher officer-levels, as opposed to lower officer-levels, in the US Army (Kane and Tremble, 1998).

The FRLM (Avolio and Bass, 1993) has been hailed as the leadership development solution for all managers regardless of organizational and national boundaries (Avolio, 1999; Bass, 1997). Indeed, research has shown that the Full Range Leadership Programme, which focuses on developing transformational leadership, has positive results in many applications (Avolio and Bass, 1998; Barling et al., 1996; Bass, 1998; Dvir, 1998). These improvements, however, tend to be accompanied by a reduction in the use of managing-by-exception (Bass, 1998; Bass and Avolio, 1990; 1994). Yet, as is discussed above, active transactional behaviours, especially contingent reward, but also active management-by-exception, have also been found to be effective alongside transformational leadership behaviours. A reduction in the use of active management-by-exception, therefore, is expected to be detrimental in some circumstances.

> **Reflective Question 4.2**
>
> Which situational influences may have an impact on when and how charismatic, transformational and transactional behaviours are exhibited by leaders? What situational factors may have an impact on how charismatic, transformational; and transactional behaviours are seen as effective?

Limitations of Transformational Leadership

There is no doubt that the concept of transformational leadership (including the FRLM) adds immensely to the understanding of leadership and to leadership development programmes. Transformational leadership, it seems, has rejuvenated leadership research in the past 25 years (Hunt, 1999). It adds visionary aspects of leadership and the emotional involvement of followers or employees to the previously well-established dimensions of leadership – consideration and initiation of structure (Koene et al., 2002). A number of limitations in the research into transformational leadership and especially the FRLM, however, are cited in the literature (Bryman, 1992; Gill, 2006; Yukl, 1999).

The potential dysfunctionality of transformational leadership, for example, has been insufficiently examined. Transformational leadership has the potential to move organizations in destructive directions. For example, while John F. Kennedy can be described as a transformational leader, so can Adolf Hitler, Vladimir Lenin and other totalitarian leaders (Tourish and Pinnington, 2002). In addition, the FRLM does not explain dysfunctional charisma, for example, where a leader's values are highly questionable or where followers are led into disaster and perdition (Gill, 2006). This has led to researchers from this field investigating areas such as authentic leadership (Avolio and Gardner, 2005). This area of theory and research will be discussed in more detail in Chapter 13.

Furthermore, Wright (1996) has suggested that contingent reward may be effective if the promise of reward for achievement is fulfilled but will be ineffective if the reward is not produced. Furthermore, he suggests that *laissez-faire* leadership, which is viewed in the model as ineffective, may actually be effective with groups such as highly competent and motivated researchers (Wright, 1996). In addition, Eisenbeiß and Boerner (2013), whilst finding transformational leadership linked to increased creativity in followers, they also identified a negative side effect; transformational leadership also increases followers' dependency which reduces their creativity. They go on to suggest that this negative effect attenuates the positive influence of transformational leadership. This suggests a short termism inherent in this form of leadership.

Also, the use of the 'full range leadership' label for the model invites critical evaluation of its completeness (Yukl, 1999). Gill (2006), for example, suggests that the model does not explain the nature of effective visioning and organizational mission, or the place of values, culture and strategy in leadership. There has been a call for the need to study the nature of contextual influences on the transformational leadership process (Antonakis et al., 2003; Pawar and Eastman, 1997). It has been suggested that the FRLM has ignored situational contingencies, for example hierarchical level in organizations (for example, Edwards and Gill, 2012), and pertains to a return to the 'one best way of leading' approach (Bryman, 1992; Gill, 2006). For example, the model has been criticized by Gill (2006) for common method variance (Podaskoff and Organ, 1986; Podaskoff et al., 2003): its dependence upon research data that were collected from the same people, possibly inflating correlation scores. Antonakis (2001) has also found through his research that because of the homogeneous samples used in the original research (Bass and Avolio, 1994) and non-homogeneous samples used by confirmatory samples, moderators were at play. Such moderators that were hypothesized were the level of risk, stability and bureaucratic conditions, as well as gender and, of particular relevance to this chapter, hierarchical level of the leader.

Finally, and more generally, transformational and charismatic approaches to leadership have been criticized for concentrating too much on the top of the organization and reflecting on top level leaders – researching and theorizing too much on the leadership *of* the organization (see Chapter 2) as opposed to looking at leadership within the organization (Jackson and Parry, 2011). It has also been criticized in perpetuating the obsession with the individual leader and the dualistic notion of leader and follower (Jackson and Parry, 2011), an issue we will develop further when we look at aspects of distributed leadership in Chapter 9.

The Future of the 'New Approach'

To look over the current peaks of knowledge concerning leadership, we must stand on sturdy theoretical scaffolding. We believe that this scaffolding is the Full Range Leadership Theory (FRLT), to which other theories of leadership should be compared and attached, so that the lacunae in the FRLT are identified and filled. In this way, a more complete full-range theory will emerge. (Antonakis and House, 2002: 19)

From this quote by Antonakis and House one could take the view, as they do, that the FRLM provides a useful scaffold to further develop leadership knowledge. On the surface, however, there appears to be a wealth of research concerning this aspect of leadership studies and this suggests that scholars would only find a futile engagement in attempting to add to the area around transformational leadership and allied theories. However, in many ways the FRLM has overridden other aspects discussed in the 'new approach'. Therefore ideas regarding vision in particular, but also charisma, may bear fruit if they can be divorced from the vice-like grip of transformational leadership. In addition, this area of leadership scholarship has also suffered from a concentration of quantitative and psychological focus. Further research could develop a more qualitative outlook on the themes discussed in this chapter alongside a sociological interpretation.

Summary

This chapter started by exploring the origins of charisma and the link it has with leadership. It has reviewed a variety of differing perspectives on charismatic leadership and highlighted the need for scholars to be sensitive to the tension in the literature between seeing charismatic leadership as an attribution process and seeing charismatic leadership as a set of behaviours. The chapter then went on to highlight the concept of transformational leadership. It reviewed the development of this concept in leadership studies from the early foundations in writing about revolution and political science towards more psychologically and behaviourally orientated models which represent modern interpretations of the concept. The chapter, in this review, explored the FRLM in more detail, highlighting the dimensions – such as notions of vision, inspiration and motivation – that make up ideas around transformational and transactional leadership. Within this discussion the chapter has highlighted a number of ways that these dimensions and concepts can be modelled and reviewed the wealth of research that highlights the impact transformational leadership can have on individuals, groups and organizations. The chapter then highlighted the limitations concepts such as charismatic and transformational leadership hold. Finally, the chapter offered some thoughts on how this area of research might be developed in the future.

Additional Reflection Questions

1. To what extent do charismatic and/or transformational leaders emerge in times of crisis?
2. What behaviours can we link with charismatic individuals?
3. Who do we attribute with charisma? And why?
4. How are transformational leadership behaviours effective and what outcomes might be expected?
5. How might we be critical of the 'new leadership approach'?
6. What does the future hold for the 'new leadership approach'?

Case Study Questions

1. Read carefully through Case Study 1 and Case Study 5 where there are discussions about an engineering company and a self-development organization. To what extent is charismatic leadership evident in these case studies and how are they similar or different?
2. From Case Study 2, a leadership development programme in Iraq, what advice would you give to the programme if it needs to develop charismatic, transformational and transactional behaviours?

3. Following on from Vignette 4.1, read carefully through Case Study 3 where there is a discussion around management practice. Highlight throughout where different dimensions of transformational (attributed charisma, idealized influence, inspirational motivation, intellectual stimulation and individualized consideration) and transactional leadership (contingent reward, active management-by-exception and passive management-by-exception) are exhibited and reflect on the likely outcomes from the use of these behaviours.

4. Read carefully through Case Study 4 where there is a discussion on a healthcare organization. Identify and critically evaluate behaviours that might be seen as transformational and/or transactional. Compare these behaviours to those found in Case Study 6: to what extant are they similar or different? Which is likely to be the most effective and impactful?

Further Reading

Bass, B.M. and Riggio, R.E. (2006) *Transformational Leadership*, second edition. New York: Psychology Press.

Conger, J.A. (2011) Charismatic leadership. In A. Bryman, D. Collinson, K. Grint, B. Jackson and M. Uhl Bien (eds) *The SAGE Handbook of Leadership*. London: Sage, 86–102.

Davis, K.M. and Gardner, W.L. (2012) Charisma under crisis revisited: presidential leadership, perceived leader effectiveness, and contextual influences. *Leadership Quarterly*, 23: 918–933.

Diaz-Saenz, H.R. (2011) Transformational leadership. In A. Bryman, D. Collinson, K. Grint, B. Jackson and M. Uhl Bien (eds) *The SAGE Handbook of Leadership*. London: Sage, 299–310.

Gill, R.W.T. (2011) *Theory and Practice of Leadership*, second edition. London: Sage.

Streyer, J. (1998) Charisma and the archetypes of leadership. *Organisation Studies*, 19(5): 807–828.

Tourish, D. and Pinnington, A. (2002) Transformational leadership, corporate cultism and the spirituality paradigm: An unholy trinity in the workplace? *Human Relations*, 55(2): 147–172.

Part II
Current Issues in Leadership

5

Perspectives on Leadership Context

Leadership context is both an important and highly ambiguous issue and although the importance of context has been recognized (Andrews and Field, 1998; Fairhurst, 2009; Liden and Antonakis, 2009; Osborn et al., 2002; see also special issue in *Human Relations* November 2009 Vol. 62(11)) it remains empirically and conceptually under-explored (Jepson, 2009a). Depending on which view or perspective we take, we may define and study leadership context differently. For example, leadership context is often viewed as the specific setting that leadership takes place in. Our study of leadership context from this point of view may focus on the conditions and circumstances that enable or influence leadership to happen and leaders to be effective. This view is most commonly focused on in textbooks and has been introduced in Chapter 2 through the early contingency theories of leadership and their focus on situational variables.

In addition to context as physical space, leadership context can also be explored as the symbolic space that sets the meaning of the phenomenon of leadership – that is, what leadership means and looks like is relational, time specific and related to common frames of reference within groups and societies. We argue that it is very important to consider this view of leadership context in depth as it helps to unpack the complexity of leadership processes as well as explore the meaning-making of individuals within this process and locate the constraints and possibilities that context as a symbolic space places on them. In this chapter, we therefore explore this view of leadership context in depth from a psychological perspective and a sociological perspective. We start with two theories from the psychological perspective – implicit leadership theory and social identity theory – highlighting specific foci and their roots within the US, psychology-centred research tradition. We then move on to introduce the notion of social constructivism as it is rooted in a sociologically informed and European-based research tradition, and finally conclude by introducing critically focused approaches to our understanding of leadership context. Other notions of context such as culture, gender and diversity will be picked up further in (Chapters 9 and 12).

Chapter Aims

- Introduce implicit leadership theory and social identity theory
- Critically evaluate US, psychology-centred research on leadership context
- Introduce and critically evaluate European, sociology-centred research on leadership context

Critical Thinking Box 5.1

As highlighted in Chapter 3, the majority of leadership theories of the 20th century were based on research conducted in a US context and focused on the individual leader and theory engagement with individual followers. This focus has silenced other cultural and organizational contexts as well as failed to explore in detail what the leadership context is, how different contextual factors interplay and affect and are affected by leadership.

A Psychological Perspective on Context – Implicit Leadership Theory

The earliest research into implicit leadership theory was led by Lord and colleagues (Lord and Maher, 1993; Lord et al., 1984; Phillips and Lord, 1986), drawing on Rosch's (1978) cognitive categorization theory. This research defined implicit theories as cognitive models or schema of real life phenomena that help individuals interpret, explain and predict actions and behaviours of the self and others every day.

In light of this definition of implicit theories, we can then define implicit *leadership* theories to be the cognitive schema of leadership that individuals have developed over time and hold, and that drive their evaluation and understanding of their own and others' leadership behaviour. Kenney et al. (1996) associate with a cognitive schema related to an individual's implicit leadership theory, the specific traits and behaviours that he/she classifies as being those of a leader. According to Schyns and Schilling (2011) followers especially draw on their implicit leadership theory to explain and predict their leader's behaviours. As followers are likely to have a range of different implicit leadership theories, the same leader behaviour may be interpreted and understood quite differently across followers and at different points in time. Furthermore, a follower's implicit leadership theories will influence not only what this individual sees as leadership behaviour as such but also what he/she classifies as good or bad, effective or ineffective leader behaviour.

Key Research Findings

Research into implicit leadership theories has since the 1980s been focused on several areas: examining the social construction of leadership through the lens of implicit leadership theories (Lord and Maher, 1993), that is, what affects the forming of implicit leadership theories; content of implicit leadership theories (Offermann et al., 1994), that is, what aspects of leadership are defined by an implicit leadership theory; the impact of implicit leadership theories on followers' perception of a specific leader (Ensaria and Murphy, 2003); and the fit between such theories and actual leader behaviour (Epitropaki and Martin, 2005).

The wider research around content of implicit leadership theories has been particularly active in terms of the exploration of content, that is, which aspects of leadership fall within an implicit leadership theory and what does this means for effective leadership. A large proportion of studies have focused their research into implicit leadership theories on the positive prototypes of effective leaders (for example, Gardner and Avolio, 1998; Kenney et al., 1996) while others have explored the gender related characteristics of ideal leader images in implicit leadership theories (Schein, 1975; Sczesny, 2003). These latter studies have particularly explored the think-manager-think-male stereotype and its implications for leadership. We will explore the field of gender and leadership further in Chapter 12.

Finally, and in relation to culture, the GLOBE project (House et al., 2004) has contributed significantly to this area of implicit leadership theories research with findings suggesting that perceptions of ideal and exceptional leader behaviour tend to be shared by individuals from the same country and these perceptions differ across different countries. They have therefore drawn the explicit link between cultural values and implicit leadership theories. We will explore the insights gained through the GLOBE project further in Chapter 10.

Critical View on Implicit Leadership Theories

Schyns and Schilling's (2011) research into content of implicit leadership theories has, however, highlighted a flaw in the conclusions drawn from some of the above research studies. This flaw is the relatively firm assumption of many studies that cognitive schema of leaders in general are positive and particularly so for effective leaders. Schyns and Schilling's (2011) research, however, shows that negative and ineffective leader characteristics are also part of general implicit leadership theories of individuals. This finding therefore calls for greater care regarding the extent to which we can at all draw generalizations about implicit leadership theories across a group of people and our ability to account for the different aspects of context of individuals that will influence their implicit leadership theories.

Implicit Leadership Theories in Leadership Development

Insights gained from this research into perceptions of leadership and implicit leadership theories are of further importance for the practice of 360-degree leader assessment and evaluation. Figure 5.1 illustrates the most prominent form of leader assessment and evaluation as adopted in practice in many public and private sector organizations. It is very popular as it enables organizations to evaluate leadership as a group process and take into consideration the views and perceptions of all the individuals involved in this process.

Research has indeed shown in relation to this tool that the aspects of leader behaviour deemed to be important by one individual may differ quite significantly from

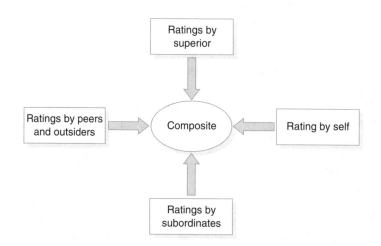

Figure 5.1   360-Degree Leader Assessment

those regarded as important by others (Alimo-Metcalfe, 1996; Borman, 1974; Bradley, 1978; Colvin, 2001; Ilgen and Feldman, 1983; Salam et al., 1997). These differences in perceptions can be linked to implicit leadership theories as well as social identity theories as discussed below.

Reflective Question 5.1

What do you see as good leadership? Reflect on your own cognitive schema influencing this view, for example, cultural influences, education, social background. Reflect on how your own cognitive schema may be influencing your view of good leadership. Has this view changed over time? Why?

A Psychological Perspective on Context – Social Identity Theory and Leadership

Another approach to understanding existing cognitive and value-based models of effective leadership is one that is focused on the group: social identity theory. Linked to social categorization theory (Turner, 1985), social identity theory is concerned with how individuals 'self-categorize themselves into different social categories, reflecting different levels of self-perception and belonging to social groups that dynamically relate to each other' (Jepson, 2009a: 47). Each social category, and by extension each social group, has its own set of prototypical behaviours, attitudes (Hogg, 2001; Tajfel, 1978; Von Cranach, 1986) and identity – 'who we are' – that are embodied by the members of this group during the process of social categorization and used actively to differentiate between in- and out-group members. These prototypical behaviours, traits and the social identity shared by a group then have a fundamental influence on who is a leader and what is effective leadership. According to Tajfel (1978) and Haslam (2004), an accepted and effective leader is the most prototypical member of a group with considerable power to set the agenda, mobilize members and influence the identity of the group.

The Prototypical Leader

Ellemers et al. (2004) and Haslam (2004) further elaborate on this link between leadership and social identity theory and posit that followers think more positively about their leader if the leader is able to share and create a common identity with a group. This positive link between a leader's prototypicality of the shared identity and its associated behaviour and traits is evolving and changing over time. Leader prototypicality itself can be seen as a constant process of influencing the social identity and being influenced by it.

This bears important implications for the formal appointment of managers to existing organizational groups as it suggest that leaders who are not in-group members will find it more difficult to be accepted and effective in this group compared to somebody who emerges as a leader from within the group (Hogg and van Knippenberg, 2003). It would also suggest that new leaders should focus on understanding the existing shared identity of the group they are entering and reflect on the extent to which their actions and behaviours are congruent with the expectations shared regarding effective leadership.

Influences on Leader Effectiveness

Linked to preferences for prototypical leaders is the concept of self-uncertainty. Uncertainty and especially self-uncertainty enhance an individual's drive to self-categorize into social groups. This drive is particularly evident in the forming of cults, where individuals can be seen to voluntarily sacrifice their personal freedom and may even accept physical or emotional harm for the benefit of feeling secure within the group and seeking certainty from the prototypical strong leader (for example, the Manson Family, Scientology, Jonestown). We can also observe these dynamics in times of radical change in organizations, where uncertainty leads to a drive to form cliques and networks and to seek security and certainty through these group memberships. Self-uncertainty also enhances an individual's seeking of information on the shared group behaviours and identity to resolve self-uncertainty. Leaders as the most prototypical in-group members may then be seen as a reliable source of such information and hence as helping to resolve self-uncertainty (Rast et al., 2012). The obvious conclusion we can draw from this is that there is a positive link between self-uncertainty and the success of prototypical leaders.

VIGNETTE 5.1

Extract from Case Study 3 illustrating the difficulties of a non-prototypical leader

The Procurement Department of a large utility company, Lowe Power, had evolved pretty successfully from the old rule-bound model of the corporate policeman to a leaner, more commercial model of supply chain management ... However, Frank Illingworth, the Finance Director, to whom Procurement reported, was pretty sure that re-organizing the department into market facing teams would yield a step-change in Procurement performance, not just in cost improvement, but also in enhanced service to the operations. The sudden departure of the Head of Procurement in September, 2008, provided Frank with his opportunity. While pursuing the external recruitment of a new Head of Procurement, he assumed direct responsibility for the department,

(Continued)

(Continued)

giving the task of drawing up new designs to Ken Tweedy, a relatively new member of the Procurement management team. Ken was thrilled to be asked. He had some misgivings about the existing structure, and was keen to make an impression. Who knew, this might even position him as the most likely second-in-command to the new Head of Procurement when he arrived. Ken set steadily about creating and evaluating alternative organizational models for the department. He found the design work interesting and rewarding, but really didn't like what happened after that. His colleagues seemed to be able to give him endless reasons why a particular proposal would not work, but also seemed very short on alternatives. Equally, presenting options to Frank (his boss) was frustrating. Not only would Frank refuse to hear a proposal out before interrogating it, he also seemed to have an inexhaustible fund of new criteria for assessing what the new organization should do.

1. The quote above highlights the difficulties Ken is facing as an assigned change leader. Critically evaluate these difficulties with reference to social identity theory and particularly the concept of prototypicality of an assigned leader.

Yet, there are some exceptions to this as more recent research (Abrams et al., 2008) has shown. When a group's leader is not established but the group perceives there to be a number of potential or prospective leaders, self-uncertainty may cause the group to search for a viable leader irrespective of prototypicality (Rast et al., 2012). The need for uncertainty reduction by the emergent leader is hence in these situations more important to followers than the prototypicality of such a leader. Again, times of radical change and uncertainty in organizations may lead to a greater propensity to accept a strong, visionary leader who offers certainty in his/her grand vision. In Chapter 13, we will explore how these strong leaders may turn out to be toxic and delve in more depth into the dynamics that allow such a leader to gain strength and acceptance in a group. We will also explore the role of followers in relation to social identity theory and the construction of leadership in Chapter 6.

Reflective Question 5.2

To which social groups do you belong? Choose two of these groups. Does your view on leadership change depending on which of these two groups you belong to? If yes, what does this tell you about the identity of each group and the likely prototypical leader?

Limitations

In connection to implicit leadership theories, it is also important to point out that individuals' perceptions of leaders and effective leadership are not only affected by the shared social identity of the social group they self-categorize themselves into at a specific point in time, but may also be influenced by their individual implicit leadership theories that again may be affected by other social group memberships and impressions of leadership gained over time in different contexts (Jackson and Parry, 2011). This increasing complexity demands that we are cautious in attributing leader perceptions and preferences too simplistically to either individual or social group structures. Avolio and Yammarino (2002), Dansereau et al. (1999) and Yammarino et al. (2005) have voiced concerns and called for greater clarity and accuracy of leadership research in identifying the level of analysis that is being studied and its relation to other levels of analysis, that is, individual, dyad and group.

Yet despite these calls and reviews of existing leadership research clarifying the actual levels of analysis of various traditional leadership theories (see Yammarino et al., 2005), there is still little conceptual and empirical advance in our understanding of the interaction of levels of analysis and the complexity of context from within this psychologically based field of leadership studies. In recognition of these limitations, we move our discussion of context on and into the sociologically informed field of leadership studies in the last section of this chapter. We discuss particularly the idea of social construction of leadership processes and its implications for our understanding of the complexity of context and the idea of leadership discourse as a contextual factor.

A Sociological Perspective on Context – Social Construction and Critical Approaches

In response to the continuing call for sound empirical research into the complexity of how context shapes leadership practice (Barker, 2001; Berry and Cartwright, 2000), Edwards and Jepson (2008) have empirically explored the importance of different contexts in organizations, drawing on both qualitative and quantitative research methods and data sets from two different industries in Germany and the UK. Their research reveals different contexts as important but also suggests that the immediate social context of the department in which an individual is based tends to have the most significant impact on that individual's understanding and practice of leadership.

In connection with this finding, Jepson (2009a) further explored the complex and interactional nature of different contexts affecting leadership practice. In reflection on existing research into leadership context and in light of her own qualitative research findings, she proposed three dominant contextual levels: the immediate social (for example, job, department, organization, industry), the general cultural (for example, organizational, regional, national culture – see also Chapter 10) and the historical,

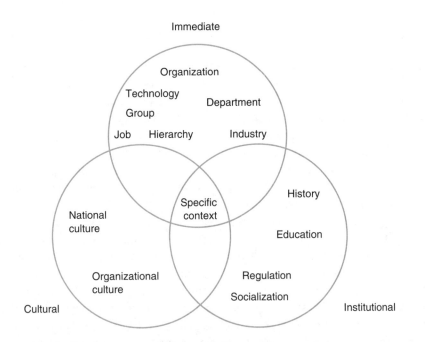

Figure 5.2   Dynamic Interaction of Different Levels and Types of Context

Source: Jepson, D. (2009) Leadership context: the importance of departments. *Leadership and Organization Development Journal*, 30(1): 36–52.

institutional context (for example, education, legal). Rather than looking at these contextual levels separately, Jepson suggested that these levels 'exist alongside and in relation to each other for a specific individual and can therefore be assumed to be interactional and dynamic in nature' (2009a: 39). Contextual levels should then be seen as fluid in their meaning and importance and can be said to be competing for importance in an individual's understanding and practice of leadership over a life-time. Figure 5.2 taken from Jepson (2009a: 39) illustrates this dynamic interaction.

VIGNETTE 5.2

Extract from Case Study 2 illustrating the interaction of Jepson's (2009a) contextual levels

The Iraqi Foundation for Technical Education (FTE) wanted a world-class development programme for its College Deans. It drew from the UK's acclaimed leadership

(Continued)

(Continued)

development programme which was adapted to become the Dean's Qualifying Programme (DQP).

I talked to anyone I could find with experience of leadership development in the Middle East. There is a paucity of published material on leadership in an Arab, let alone Iraqi context. I attended the Leadership Trust Foundation's first Worldly Leadership Conference on non-western forms of leadership wisdom.

Dr Mahmood wanted a programme which was robust and externally accredited. I initially used assessors from the UK programme to validate the written assignment from each participant. I established a partnership with the Chartered Management Institute so that successful graduates of DQP would be assessed to become Chartered Managers. This was the first time this external accreditation had happened in Iraq.

The content of the 16-month programme included taught elements on high performance working; change leadership; engaging with external stakeholders; innovation culture; motivation; and coaching skills. It included an experiential learning workshop to stimulate peer feedback and self-awareness. Participants were also required to undertake a 360-degree feedback process. They had to prepare a personal leadership development plan and also manage a change project in the workplace.

Almost all of this approach was new to the Iraqi culture in terms of content. In order to be a source of useful learning for Deans every aspect of the programme needed to be contextualized for a Middle East, Arab group. This contextualization took place beforehand when possible but in the pilot often occurred as a 'work in progress' in the classroom. Deans had been raised on didactic teaching methods. An informal style of learner-centred delivery was ground breaking for them.

1. Use Jepson's (2009a) three contextual levels to unpack different influences on the leadership development programme outlined in Case Study 2.

Interpretivist epistemology: a researcher assumes that reality is relative and multiple, that is, an individual's experience of reality is subjective.

This empirical exploration of the dynamic, interactional nature of context and especially the use of qualitative research methods is further linked to a wider movement within the field of leadership studies. Over the last 20 years, European scholars have become increasingly vocal and united in their call for an alternative to the dominant approach adopted by leadership models and theories focused on effective leadership as outlined above and in Chapters 1–3. Bolden et al. have captured the essence of this movement in leadership studies when claiming that 'many authors are now calling for a more qualitative approach grounded in an interpretivist epistemology and constructivist ontology (e.g., Conger, 1998;

Collinson, 2005; Grinta, 2005; Sinclair, 2007a) that recognizes the contextual and discursive nature of leadership practice (e.g., Alvesson, 1996; Fairhurst, 2007)' (2011: 15). Through this approach leadership can not only be seen as a fundamentally contextual process but it also helps to unravel the complexity of its contextual nature further. We will draw on several key contributions such as Grint (2001), Alvesson and Sveningsson (2003a) and Ford et al. (2008) to explore this approach further.

The Social Construction of Leadership

First, we must establish what we mean by interpretivist, constructivist and leadership as contextual. To do so we introduce the shared theoretical foundation of this alternative approach: social constructionism. Social constructionism challenges the conventional perspective on knowledge as an unbiased and objective view of the world and instead assumes knowledge to be a product of culture and history (Burr, 1995). From this perspective, individuals are seen to create their own reality on a daily basis via their interaction with other individuals. Hence, knowledge is a product of social activity and bears the imprint of the social context within which it is constructed (Gillespie, 1991). Research embedded in this perspective is primarily interested in studying 'the processes by which people come to describe, explain or otherwise account for the world they live in' (Gergen, 1985: 266). In other words, the reality an individual sees is truly subjective and fluid and it is continuously co-constructed through that individual's interaction with the self and context.

Key contributions by Alvesson and Sveningsson (2003a) and Grint (2001) have influenced significantly the adoption of a socially constructed approach to leadership research. According to Alvesson and Sveningsson, the definition and existence of leadership are subject to an infinite number of factors such as 'tasks, organisations, kinds of people, and societal and organisational cultures' (2003a: 377). What constitutes a leader is seen to be a social construct of all individuals involved and it is truly fluid and changing in its meaning and existence. Grint (2001) further argues that what constitutes context, a leadership situation and by extension appropriate or effective leadership behaviour is subjective and contestable. Therefore, whatever aspects of context come to shape or define leadership and effective leadership these are changing and affected by time, space, culture and power structures. Context of leadership is hence complex, multi-dimensional and socially constructed, and thus fluid and subjective. This perspective on leadership challenges the focus of mainstream leadership studies either on finding a universal model of leadership or defining the contextual variables influencing effective leadership behaviour. Further, who is recognized as a leader, what is seen as effective leadership behaviour and how, when and why leadership as a process takes place are not under the control of specific individuals. Instead leadership and the specific roles of leader and follower within this process are products of the interaction of all actors involved and within a physical and symbolic space, time and conversation. As such they are always changing and subjective.

Social constructionism: a theory of knowledge that suggests all knowledge is the outcome of and influenced by social interactions between individuals and their context.

VIGNETTE 5.3

Extract from Case Study 4 in relation to the multitude of physical and symbolic contextual influences on leadership

Through a period of high turbulence, taking on staff from the statutory sector, renegotiating terms downwards to match that of the charitable sector where pay is in some cases up to a third lower, the Brandon Trust has achieved a high trust brand and growing visibility. This in a world rocked by shocking scandals and abuse against adults with learning disabilities ... the Brandon Trust was one of the first charities to speak out against institutional 'care' of people with learning disabilities. So how have the Brandon Trust achieved growth, a trustworthy brand and a transformation of services in such a tough climate? ... For Lucy, values form the bedrock of both leadership and strategy ... 'In Winterbourne View, adults with learning disabilities were locked up in large groups and despite charging high fees, the company took the money and failed to deliver personalised support. As the recession began to bite, we had a discussion with our Board in relation to our values given the financial squeeze from government and commissioners. We upheld the fact that we are wholly against the institutional large scale warehousing of vulnerable people, no matter how financially attractive this may be. We are clear that this is against our values. But there is a tension between the amount of money available and the quality of care we want to provide. Despite this our solution cannot be to pile 'em high! Instead we have gone down the line of focusing on developing a service journey that provides highly creative models of individual support, adopting assistive technology where possible and taking on-going action to increase efficiencies and reduce overheads. Our strategy is quite broad based but it has clear principles. We also know that the bottom line for our survival depends on growth and increasing our market share.'

1. Carefully analyse the above abstract in relation to physical and symbolic contextual influences on the existence/meaning of leadership at the Brandon Trust.

Wood and Ladkin (2008) have explored leadership and its context through the medium of photography, which has helped to illustrate the importance of a research focus on the physical, symbolic, relational and emotional context of leadership. Their elaborations on what they term 'the leaderful moment', that is, the caption of a leadership process in a specific space, move the focus on leadership away from the specific individuals involved and puts the very space and symbolic context centre stage. Indeed through this lens it is the leaderful moment, that is, what we would otherwise describe as context, that is leadership. A useful example of such a leaderful moment and its subject construction as well as interpretation may be a case of a newspaper photograph we see that captures a particular event of conflict. While we may focus on the image portrayed and perceive it to carry an objective meaning in relation to conflict, power and leadership, it is really the subjective representation of the conflict as captured by the photographer. Our engagement with and interpretation of the photographer's image of this conflict then create a new subjective meaning. This process of sense-making is on-going and illustrates the never ending process of social construction and hence subjective meaning-making of reality and phenomena like leadership. We discuss the leaderful moment and other important aspects of context further in Chapters 9 and 11 in relation to distributed leadership and leadership development respectively.

Discourse and Context

Taking a more discursive lens on leadership (Fairhurst, 2007; Ford et al., 2008), we come to focus on language and text as a key aspect of context and also influential factors in the process of social construction. Through this lens, we explore the extent to which the concept of leaders and leadership as we know it is a social construct of the dominant discourse on leadership in academia, media and management consultancy. Dachler, for example, argues that leadership definitions are 'a reflection of what leadership research as a discipline in the context of western cultures has constructed as its reality, which is but one of many possible leadership realities that could be imagined' (1988: 265). Through its popularity, we have taken for granted that leadership exists and have been influenced in the way and when we see it by the dominant discourse on it. This has at times suppressed other possible realities in which leadership may take place and in the way it may take place (Ford, 2010). Alvesson and Sveningsson (2003a) go so far as to argue that our assumption that leadership is an organizationally important phenomenon stems from an academic and consultancy discourse rather than practice. It is hence in the frequent naming of it, that we have co-constructed leadership to be existent and of importance in organizations.

Ford et al. (2008: 5) support this argument and stress the performative effect of the wider leadership literature and discourse as 'it is through acts of speaking and writing that things come into existence'. Chia equally suggests that research can actively construct 'the very reality [it] is intending to investigate' (1996: 42). We will explore notions of discursive leadership and its link to an identity approach to leadership further in Chapter 14.

Critical Thinking Box 5.2

Scholars who have argued that the leadership literature has a performative effect explore the influence of writing and talk about leadership on our understanding and practice of leadership. According to this view, anything that we read, hear or talk about leadership will have a lasting impact on how we view leadership and lead ourselves. This extends to the media and television programmes such as *The Apprentice* (the BBC programme on a competition for a lucrative employment position with a successful CEO) – and our individual reactions to leadership on the programme will have a lasting impact on our views on leadership. Please see Chapter 14 for further details.

Power and Context

Bolden et al. (2011: 97) draw our attention to one final criticism of the dominant contextual theories outlined at the beginning of this chapter and in Chapter 3: its neglect of taking account of the role of power or 'how power shapes the context out of which leadership emerges'. In their elaboration of the link between power, context and leadership, they make reference to works by Goethals and Sorenson (2006) as well as Fairhurst (2009). Goethals and Sorenson (2006) have argued that context seen through a power perspective provides a 'framework for action that offers both opportunities and constraints for individual action. Context is linked to power because it allows room for individual agency yet shapes what is most likely to be successful; it both shapes and is shaped by individual actors; and combines elements of subjective perception and more concrete, observable features' (Bolden et al., 2011: 98).

What we see as a 'relevant' or 'important' context is hence shaped by the power structures we live in and the norms and values we take for granted as well as the interactions we are involved in. These interactions and our sense-making of them then shape the power structures, norms and values around us. Hence, what we see as situation or context influencing leadership is socially constructed and an outcome of power structures rather than determined by the individual. Drawing on Fairhurst (2009), Bolden et al. (2011) also highlight the temporal nature of what we see as context and therefore what influences leadership and how current experiences of leadership become context of leadership in the future.

Summary

In this chapter, we have continued our journey through the myriad writings on context of leadership and have particularly demonstrated the relative divide in the focus between US-centric, psychology-driven approaches to context and the recent more critically infused European-centric, sociologically driven approaches to studying leadership context. We have introduced the implicit leadership theories and social identity theory as examples of psychology-based approaches and highlighted the need to explore different, interacting levels of analysis of leadership and context, for example, individual, dyad, group. We have recognized the limitations of these psychologically focused approaches to fully account for the complexity of such interactions of contextual influences and subsequently introduced notions of social constructionism as characteristic of the sociologically driven approaches to studying leadership context. These suggest that what is context – and hence how leadership emerges – and what counts as effective leadership is an interactive, dynamic process that is subjective, contested in its very nature and affected by dominant discourses on leadership. In Table 5.1, we summarize and contrast the psychological and sociological perspectives on leadership context as discussed in this chapter and highlight implications for our understanding and study of leadership.

Table 5.1   Psychological and Sociological Perspectives on Leadership Context

	Psychological perspective on leadership context	Sociological perspective on leadership context
Dominant focus	Followers' perceptions (cognitive schema) of leadership – implicit leadership theory Shared assumptions/identity in a group and hence influencing what leadership should look like – social identity theory	Both leadership and context are a product of social interaction between all the individuals involved – social constructionism Stresses the changing, relational and symbolic nature of context and explores the role of power and discourse within this
Implications for leadership	Effective leadership depends on individual and shared assumptions held by those involved in a leadership process or relationship. If leaders understand or adapt to this, they will be accepted and successful in the group.	Effective leadership is not within the control of any one individual. What it is, whether, how and when it happens is a product of the social interaction of all the individuals involved and their interaction with context (which is equally co-constructed and fluid)

Additional Reflection Questions

1. What is an implicit leadership theory? How does it affect leadership practice?
2. How can implicit leadership theory help us to determine effective leadership? What are the limitations?

3. What is prototypicality? What role does it play in social identity theory?
4. Who determines a social identity?
5. What is the link between leadership and social identity theory?
6. What is the link between implicit leadership theory and social identity theory?
7. Grint argues that what constitutes leadership context is subjective and contested. What does this mean?
8. What other understanding of context can we gain through a discursive lens on leadership?
9. What is the link between power and leadership context?

Case Study Questions

1. Drawing on implicit leadership theory and social identity theory, analyse the resistance that managers in Case Study 1 are facing by the group of engineers. What should senior management do to improve leadership in the organization?
2. Following the argument put forward in this chapter that leadership is a social construct, discuss some of the possible variables influencing the existence and meaning of leadership in Case Study 4.
3. In Case Study 3 Mike, the new procurement manager, is facing a complex leadership situation where his team resists his 'leadership' and his boss, Frank, first supports and then turns on him. With reference to the power and context section, analyse how Mike's leadership situation changes over the course of his time described in the case study. How and by whom is he given power and how does he lose power? How does this influence his ability to lead?
4. Case Study 5 provides an in-depth picture of the unique approach to leadership and organizations held by June Burrough, founder of a social enterprise. Read carefully through the conversation with June to reflect critically on whether and how physical and symbolic context are interlinked and produce a strong discourse on effective leadership of a social enterprise.

Further Reading

Alvesson, M. and Sveningsson, S. (2003) The great disappearing act: difficulties in doing 'leadership'. *The Leadership Quarterly*, 14(6): 359–381.

Barker, R.A. (2001) The nature of leadership. *Human Relations*, 54(4): 469–494.

Ellemers, N., de Gilder, D. and Haslam, S.A. (2004) Motivating individuals and groups at work: a social identity perspective on leadership and group performance. *Academy of Management Reviews*, 29(3): 459–478.

Grint, K. (2005) Problems, problems, problems: the social construction of 'leadership'. *Human Relations*, 58(11): 1467–1494.

Jepson, D. (2009) Leadership context: the importance of departments. *Leadership and Organization Development Journal*, 30(1): 36–52.

Osborn, R.N., Hunt, J.G. and Jauch, L.R. (2002) Toward a contextual theory of leadership. *Leadership Quarterly,* 13(6): 797–837.

Schyns, B. and Schilling, J. (2011) Implicit leadership theories: think leader, think effective? *Journal of Management Inquiry*, 20(2): 141–150.

Wood, M. and Ladkin, D. (2008) The event's the thing: brief encounters with the leaderful moment. In K. Turnbull-James and J. Collins (eds) *Leadership Perspectives: Knowledge into Action*. Basingstoke: Palgrave Macmillan.

6

Followership, Psychoanalytic and Relational Approaches to Leadership

For most of the 20th century, leadership studies as a field was highly leader-centric and predominantly focused on the effectiveness of the leader as a person and leadership as a process in which followers were treated either as passive or reactive to the leader's actions. Early attempts to move the focus onto the relationship between leaders and followers – such as the LMX theory discussed in Chapter 3 – were still marked by their continuing focus on the individual leader and the leader's influence on this relationship. It is only over the last 15 years that we have seen significant movement in the focus of leadership studies on the role of followers and followership as the main thrust of research. This chapter is devoted to an exploration of the different follower-centric approaches to leadership. We will as part of this take a closer look at psychoanalytic and relational approaches to leadership that have significantly changed the way we study and view the leader–follower relationship.

Chapter Aims

- Highlight the limitations of leader-centric research and theories
- Introduce follower-centric approaches to leadership
- Highlight the benefits of follower-centric approaches to our understanding of leadership and the leader–follower relationship

- Discuss psychodynamic approaches and relational approaches to leadership and their relevance for our understanding of followership

Follower-centric Approaches to Leadership

The relative lack of focus on followers within the wider remit of leadership studies is something that has been highlighted repeatedly throughout the last 30 years by scholars such as Meindl et al. (1985) and Hollander (1995). These early contributions have helped to problematize the often overly romantic view of leaders in organizations and the treatment of followers as passive, reactive and compliant. Jackson and Parry (2011) stress that the very word 'follower' often carries with it notions of inferiority to the leader and hence is an outcome of and reinforces the accepted power imbalance in the leader–follower relationship as further discussed in Chapter 7. We therefore see contributions of followership as part of the critical movement within leadership studies that has evolved alongside the mainstream leadership literature (Bligh, 2011).

Notable contributions, particularly over the last 10 years (see edited volumes by Shamir et al., 2007 and Riggio et al., 2008), have worked towards the exploration of leadership as a socially constructed process where followers play an equally important role as leaders as well as in the closer exploration of different types of followers and their role in leadership and organizations. This trend has also helped to question the dominant individualistic and heroic model of leadership omnipresent in popular and mainstream academic literature. We will now introduce some of these important contributions and current trends within follower-centric approaches to leadership.

Effective Leaders or the Organization's Romance of Leadership

A key driver of the increasing focus on followers and followership was Meindl and colleagues' (1985) work on the romance of leadership. This body of work significantly helped to highlight the limitations and problems of the dominant focus of leadership studies and organizations in the 20th century. It particularly demonstrated the lack of evidence or 'proof' of the importance and the significance of single, heroic leaders in the leadership process (Bligh, 2011) and organizational success. Criticizing the taking-for-granted assumption that leadership is something inherently good and important and that individual leaders can be made responsible for all the positive and negative outcomes in organizations, Meindl et al. (1985) proposed that the organizational success attributed to leaders may be no more than a halo effect. They suggested that success may not be directly linked to the actions of a leader but may instead reflect the belief of followers in these leaders that drives the positive actions of those followers leading to organizational success. This may especially be true if a leader has been associated with organizational success previously. His/her arrival in a team or organization may trigger positive engagement by the followers that on its own creates future organizational success. Yet, the exaggerated belief in the leader as hero can evoke an overreliance and dependence of followers on their leader and/or lead to legitimization and acceptance of an imbalanced leader with 'inflated status and power' (Shamir, 2007: xi). The importance of power and the asymmetrical relationship between leader and follower is further discussed in Chapter 7.

Critical Thinking Box 6.1

A key criticism of the existing leadership literature has been its predominant focus on the individual leader and its relative ignorance of the follower. Grint (2010) has argued that this deep-set desire for individual leaders stems from our anxieties in the face of uncertainty and constant change in modern society. What other reasons may explain this desire?

Jackson and Guthey (2007) have explored the persistence of images of great leaders and the association of success and failure with these images. Their analysis shows the continuation of such exaggerated beliefs and possible negative implications as highlighted by Meindl et al. (1985).

VIGNETTE 6.1

Extract from Case Study 3 illustrating the 'dark' side of the romance of leadership – the 'villainization' of a leader

By the end of July, Mike was exasperated. He was working harder and harder to show the way, and everywhere he was meeting passive resistance. The Ops Directors had not bitten on any of the big ideas he had floated with them, choosing only to complain about Procurement's poor level of service and support for basic administration

(Continued)

(Continued)

reported by their people. Much of this Mike felt was unwarranted, and would have been better aimed at Finance, but he let it pass. He had been given a clear mandate to up the game, and nobody – within the department, nor in the company more generally, not even his boss – was interested. How to demonstrate the opportunities for creating more value that were so self-evident to him? Maybe he could commission consultants who specialised in Strategic Procurement to carry out a bench-marking study. That would show them how bad they really were, how far they had to go.

1. Mike was appointed as leader of the procurement department in the organiza-tion of Case Study 3 but failed to win the support of his team. He was trying to implement changes that seemed positive to him but instead was treated as a villain who was trying to destroy what others had created. Drawing on the argu-ments in Meindl et al.'s 'Romance of leadership', what advice would you give Mike in order to become more successful in this organization?

So, while we may not have moved away from the hero or villain image of the leader (Collinson, 2005) and organizational belief in the individual's impact on suc-cess, leadership studies have in recognition of Meindl et al.'s contribution explored the area of follower-centric views of leadership and followership further. Collinson (2006) and Uhl-Bien and Pillai (2007), for example, have challenged the passive nature of followership and explored followers as active agents and co-producers of leadership. Hosking (2007) has taken this a step further in suggesting a focus on the relations in leadership rather than individuals involved. We will explore these critical and rela-tional approaches in the final sections of this chapter.

Approaches to Followers in Leadership Studies

Shamir (2007) has provided an insightful summary of the development of different approaches to followers and their role in relation to the leader and within leadership as a process. He identified six approaches, which we will briefly summarize here in Table 6.1 and in detail below to provide an overview of the existing field of follower-centric approaches to leadership.

Followers as recipients of leadership   The majority of traditional leadership theories outlined in Chapters 2–4 – including traits, styles, and transformational and charismatic leadership theories – focus entirely on the leader and his/her qualities and/or behaviours. The follower is treated as passive and at the receiving end within the leadership process. Leaders act and do things and followers react. Leaders are

Table 6.1   **Approaches to Followers in Leadership Studies**

Category	Contributions	Focus
Followers as recipients of leadership	Traits, styles, transformation and charismatic leadership theories	The follower is treated as passive and at the receiving end within the leadership process
Followers as moderators of leadership	Early contingency theories	Specific aspects of followers' knowledge, attributes and task will influence or moderate effective leadership
Followers as substitutes of leadership	Substitutes of leadership theory	Follower characteristics that can either neutralize or negate the need for leadership
Followers as constructors of leadership	Romance of leadership, psychoanalytic approach, implicit leadership theories, social identity theory	What we see as leadership and what is effective is constructed by those who follow
Followers as leaders	Distributed or shared leadership	Leadership is done by and for everybody and becomes the essence of being and acting in an organization
Followers as co-producers of leadership	Uhl-Bien and Pallai (2007), relational approaches to leadership	The leader–follower relationship is examined further and seen as socially co-constructed by leader and follower

therefore seen to be fully in control of their own destiny and the followers, whereas followers are dependent on the more powerful leader and seemingly locked into this asymmetrical power relationship with the leader. These leadership theories inevitably engage in the process of romanticizing the importance of the leader as discussed by Meindl and colleagues.

Followers as moderators of leadership   The early contingency theories introduced in Chapter 3 – for example, situational leadership, path-goal theory, Fiedler's contingency theory – acknowledged that followers have a somewhat more active role in relation to effective leadership. These theories assume that specific aspects of the followers' knowledge, attributes and task will influence or moderate the particular leadership style or behaviour that will be most effective within a given context. The follower is hence treated as an important contextual variable affecting a leader's effectiveness. These theories further suggest that leaders can learn to 'read' the context they are in, including developing a greater understanding of the needs and specific attributes of their individual followers. While these theories are paying more attention to the role of followers than other traditional approaches to leadership, they are still focusing predominantly on the leader and considering followers in a rather simplistic fashion. They do not explore what happens when a follower does not act or react to a leader's style in the way anticipated by the given model. These theories hence continue to treat the leader and follower as distinct individuals and stable identities with clear boundaries around their relationship and the wider context they are in.

Followers as substitutes for leadership   Shamir (2007) makes here particular reference to Kerr and Jermier's (1978) substitutes for leadership theory that considers follower characteristics that can either neutralize or negate the need for leadership. The followers' skills and knowledge can hence provide the guidance and support normally sought from a formal leader. We have seen this theory in action in many organizations that have moved towards or experimented with the use of self-directed or autonomous work groups over the last century. This has been in an effort to move away from extensive tiers of management and formal leadership. Jackson and Parry (2011) comment, that this focus on leadership could also encapsulate fundamentally critical views on leadership that challenge the importance, existence or necessity of organizational leadership altogether.

Followers as constructors of leadership   Contributions within this particular category take a follower-centric view of leadership and hence suggest that what we see as leadership and what is effective is constructed by those who follow. Within this category falls Meindl et al.'s (1985) work on romancing leadership, psychoanalytic approaches to leadership and social identity theory of leadership. As discussed above, Meindl et al.'s (1985) contribution was crucial for the shift in focus away from the leader and towards the follower. It highlighted the naivety and lack of empirical evidence for the taken-for-granted link between a leader's actions and group or organizational performance. This body of work not only reminded us that without followers there is no leadership but also stressed that followers have as much if not more influence on group and organizational success than the individual leaders in the organization. It argued that it is indeed the exaggerated follower beliefs in the leader's impact on organizational success that construct 'effective' leadership. It also problematized the continuing romanticizing of the leader by both followers and the organization and highlighted the potentially negative implications of this romance.

Another key contribution of our understanding of followers has been through psychoanalytic approaches to leadership that have explored both how a leader's style is significantly influenced by early childhood experiences and particularly the parenting he/she experienced. Similarly, what we experience as a child and how we are raised will also impact on how we choose to follow. Stech (2004) suggests that how a follower will interact with a leader depends on whether he/she reacts to the leader in an independent, dependent or counter-dependent way. This again is influenced by childhood experiences that drive subconscious processes of relating to leaders and situations and are reflected in the emotions and behaviours that followers display. Of key importance to our understanding of followers as constructors of leadership are the psychoanalytical processes of projection and transference. Especially in times of crisis, followers will project their own desire and needs onto the leader or transfer, that is, see the leader as a significant person from their childhood such as a father or mother. Hence what they see as appropriate or effective leadership is then influenced by these subconscious processes and constructs of leadership. These psychoanalytic approaches to leadership will be discussed further in the next section of this chapter.

Shamir (2007) also makes reference to the social identity theory as outlined in Chapter 5. Here it is the shared social identity that will drive followers' interaction with and acceptance of a leader. To be successful, leaders need to be prototypical of the shared identity, and hence behave in accordance with what is deemed appropriate and effective through the lens of the shared values and identity of the group of followers (Hogg, 2008). Shamir (2007) further proposes that these different follower-centric views can be combined to explain different follower elements and why and how he/she comes to construct and engage with leadership. Jackson and Parry (2011) point out that this process of construction is a social, fluid one and ongoing.

Followers as leaders   This category is predominantly concerned with notions of shared or distributed leadership where leadership as a process is distributed throughout the organization. In a sense, leadership is done by and for everybody and becomes the essence of being and acting in an organization. It becomes an activity that is detached from role or function. The boundaries between leader and follower become blurred and in the case of an organization-wide distribution of leadership there would be neither followers nor leaders. Further detailed information on this area of leadership studies can be found in Chapter 9.

Followers as co-producers of leadership   Shamir (2007) concludes his review of existing approaches to followers taken in the leadership literature by proposing a move towards a balanced model – one where followers are seen as co-producers of leadership. Here the leader–follower relationship is examined further and seen as socially co-constructed by leader and follower. The leadership process is hence about the engagement in a mutually beneficial relationship between individuals in a social context. Leader and followers engage in this relationship equally and influence each other and the relationship through ongoing interaction. Uhl-Bien and Pillai's (2007) chapter in the same edited volume as Shamir's (2007) review continues with this idea and explores the nature and context of such social constructions of followers and leaders. They particularly focus on the social construction of followership and look at some of the dominant constructs of followership. We will explore this aspect of social co-construction or co-production in relation to current contributions by Hosking (2011) and Cunliffe and Eriksen (2011) to the notion of relational leadership in the last section of this chapter.

The Study of Followership

More recently and in reaction to the continued focus on the leader and leadership within follower-centric approaches, we have seen conceptualizations of followership and explorations of different types of followers and approaches to followership. Carsten et al. (2010) argue that we should differentiate between follower perspectives of leadership (follower-centric approaches) and follower perspectives on followership (followership approaches). In relation to the latter, Carsten et al. (2010) further explore the many different meanings that followership, that is, how followers view their own engagement and behaviours within leadership, may take and the possible mental models of followership that may be driving this multiplicity. Sy (2010) has taken this research into our understanding of individuals' assumptions on followership further through his empirical exploration of the context, structure and consequences of implicit followership theories. This work has particularly looked at individuals' assumptions on the traits, characteristics and behaviours of followers that form their cognitive schema of followership.

Kelley (1988, 1992), in contrast, has advanced our understanding of different followership behaviours, proposing five styles of followership linked to the dimensions of low-high independent/critical thought and passive-active. Those five styles are:

- the sheep = somebody who is passive and shows little critical/independent thought;
- the yes people = somebody who is active and lively but again shows little critical/independent thought;
- the alienated = somebody who is independent and thinks critically but is relatively passive and hence would not openly challenge a leader;
- the pragmatic = somebody in the middle with regard to both dimensions. This person is sometime active and at other times passive. Equally this follower shows sometimes but not always independent/critical thought;
- the star = this is an effective follower who shows both independent/critical thought and actively engages with the leader and the leadership process.

Kellerman (2008) has more recently offered another list of followership styles that are similar to the above model but where the main focus is on follower engagement with the leader and the organization. The five followership styles developed by Kellerman are the isolates, bystanders, participants, activists and diehards. These styles represent a continuum of positive or negative engagement with a leader depending on their commitment to the leader and/or the organization. These styles have also been linked to notions of bad leadership, such as an exploration of different categories of followers in the Nazi regime and their relative part in the atrocities of the regime. Howell and Mendez (2008) have also explored the different roles that followership can take in organizations and identified followership as an interactive role, as an independent role and as a shifting role. They stress that followership as an independent and shifting role has not received enough attention so far and is an important area for future research.

> **Reflective Question 6.1**
>
> Owing to its popularity, the YouTube clip 'Dancing Guy' is now often identified as 'the classic example' of a demonstration of followership in action. To see this clip, type into the YouTube search engine 'Dancing Guy' and select one of the videos showing a young man dancing at a festival. While commentaries of this clip usually reflect on the need for followers as such, we would like you to reflect in greater detail on the different views on followership outlined above and how these may be used to analyse followership and leadership in this video.What implications can you draw from this analysis for your own understanding and practice of leadership?

Future Trends in Follower-centric Approaches to Leadership and the Study of Followership

Riggio et al.'s (2008) edited book on *The Art of Followership* and Shamir et al.'s (2007) edited book on *Follower-centred Perspectives on Leadership* both represent significant contributions to our understanding of followers, followership and the leader–follower relationship. These volumes not only summarize and review what has emerged in the wider leadership literature on these topics but also provide critical developments and suggestions for future avenues. Kelley (2008), for example, discusses the importance of seven topics for the future study of followership: world events, culture, leader(ship), follower qualities, role of the follower, language of followership and courageous conscience. He uses the example of the suicide bomber as a particular world event and to demonstrate our lack of knowledge on the true power of followers and culture-specific nature of followership. Kelley (2008) also poses questions such as how much do we know about follower qualities and the different roles followers are expected to take on. He recognizes the debates around the language used in connection with followership and the contested words of leader and follower. Future research into the role and meaning of these words in different cultures and languages is needed. Finally, Kelley (2008) addresses the need for further explorations of constructive dissent or 'courageous conscience' of followers especially in light of toxic leadership. How do followers come to dissent and what support mechanisms are needed?

Critical Perspectives

The two edited volumes also feature more critical or radical views on followership and for future research. Stech (2008), for example, challenges the dominant paradigms around leadership and followership and particularly the power relations in the leader–follower relationship and proposes a new paradigm focusing on places or states. In this new paradigm, a person does not have to be either a leader or follower but what is of importance is that whether an individual engaged in leadership or followership is dependent on the state (place) or condition they are in and an individual may hence change between these roles and processes over time. A greater focus on the role of expertise, self-motivation and self-direction enables a move away from the asymmetrical power relations traditionally assigned to leaders and followers. Rost (2008) further challenges the very notion of followership in the era of a post-industrial understanding of leadership where, he argues, leaders and followers are understood to be equally engaged in the process of leadership. He suggests therefore a move towards focusing on what he terms collaborative leadership or 'an influence relationship among people who intend' (Rost, 2008: 57). This specific concept has taken leaders out of leadership and is entirely focused on how individuals relate to each other in organizations in light of their specific goals and intentions and how they consequently influence each other in line with these goals and intentions.

Reflective Question 6.2

Most leaders are also followers within organizations and outside organizations. To what extent can we separate the two and how does an individual switch between them? Reflect on your own work experience to explore this question.

Further, Collinson's (2006, 2008) post-structuralist contributions to the followership debate have been particularly illuminating in relation to the deeply embedded nature of power asymmetry between leader and follower in an organizational hierarchy and modern society. He has highlighted the overly passive view of followers in the leader–follower relationship and particularly in relation to a leader influencing and manipulating follower identities. He suggests that 'post-structuralist perspectives treat followers as frequently more knowledgeable and oppositional than is typically acknowledged in studies of leadership and followership' (2008: 311). From a post-structuralist perspective, identities are not treated as singular, unitary and coherent but are instead seen to be 'multiple, fluid, shifting, fragmented, contradictory and nonrational' (Collinson, 2008: 312). Hence, there are multiple, coexisting follower identities that overlap, mutually reinforce or contradict and hence remain fluid and shifting. We must therefore recognize different and shifting possible follower selves rather than falling into the false illusion of being able to categorize followers into single, stable selves.

Collinson (2008) suggests that some of the recurring follower selves observed in organizations are the conformist, resistant and disguised selves. He discusses the varied forms that these three types of selves can take and the influence the existing leadership literature and dominant leadership discourses have on followers' perceptions of who they should be as followers. It is particularly the conformist selves that have received most coverage in the existing leadership literature. Only a few have written about resistant followers although Chaleff (2008) and others have highlighted the potential constructive nature of resistance. Collinson (2008) further draws readers' attention to the frequent existence of disguised selves where value-based or technology-based surveillance systems are particularly pervasive and followers engage in conscious or subconscious impression management. Collinson (2008) concludes that through a post-structuralist perspective on follower selves we see leader and follower identities as mutually influencing and shifting. Followers are also not always conformist but often resistant, oppositional and knowledgeable as they engage in impression management in the form of disguised selves.

Further Research and Possible Future Trends

In light of the existing literature on followers and followership, Bligh (2011) suggests four main areas of future research and possible trends. First, she proposes that one such area is focused on defining leadership and followership processes. This area of research is particularly linked to existing social constructivist notions of the leader-follower relationship and leadership and followership as such (see Collinson, 2008; Uhl-Bien and Pillai, 2007). Second, another main area should explore contextual and cultural influences on leadership and followership further. While we have seen recent contributions on change and followership (for example, Chen et al., 2007; Pillai et al., 2007), Bligh (2011) argues we are still lacking research into different types of context, the influence of culture on followership and leader–follower relations and particularly the exploration of crisis and follower-centred approaches to leadership. Third, Bligh (2011) suggests a further exploration of the continuing romancing of leaders and subordinating of followers and particularly the roles that leader and follower take in the construction of heroic or villainous images and charismatic leaders (Jackson and Guthey, 2007). Finally, she invites research into the ethical implications of leader–follower processes. This should build on existing explorations of resistance, whistle-blowing, dialogue and the power relationship in leadership (Alford, 2008; Blumen, 2008; Carsten and Bligh, 2007; Collinson, 2006, 2008; Kellerman, 2008).

Psychoanalytic Approaches to Leadership

> The distinguishing feature of psychoanalytic approaches is the assumption of an unconscious dimension to social and individual life. The unconscious is the mental territory where dangerous and painful ideas and desires are consigned through repression and other defensive mechanisms, and also the source of resistances to specific ideas and emotions which present threats to mental functioning. As the territory from which fantasies spring, the unconscious may also be a source of imagination and creativity … (Gabriel, 2011: 393)

The above quote from Gabriel's (2011) recent review of psychoanalytic contributions to the field of leadership studies highlights the different focus that these contributions take. In contrast to most other approaches to leadership, psychoanalytic approaches look into the role the unconscious plays in both the leadership behaviour we see as well as follower preferences for and acceptance of different types of leadership and leaders. As outlined earlier in this chapter, a focus on the unconscious helps us further understand how followers come to accept and follow certain types of leaders and how this is linked to unconscious emotions and desires related to early childhood experiences. Gabriel (2011) particularly stresses the role that fantasies play as another manifestation of the subconscious. It is these fantasies – for example, the ideal leader or follower – that represent our unconscious desires linked to significant experiences that we have had in the past and that influence our behaviour within organizations and the leader–follower relationship. In this section we introduce the reader to key psychoanalytic contributions to leadership studies and particularly with a view to understanding the leader–follower relationship.

The Leader–Follower Relationship

Gabriel (2011) helpfully summarizes several insights into the leader–follower relationship gained through original contributions by psychoanalytic writers. Drawing on Freud's (1921/1985) writings on the primal father, Gabriel notes that the leader–follower relationship is 'inevitably ambivalent as followers may both love the leader, craving protection and support, but they also resent and envy the leader' (2011: 394). Freud (1921/1985) has suggested that following a leader enables a group to form and sustain based on the shared emotional experience of identifying and idealizing that particular leader. Hence, the very formation of follower groups around leaders and seeking engagement in a leader–follower relationship are an inevitable dynamic in societies.

Grint (2010) has similarly suggested that leaderless notions are inevitably going to fail as followers crave leadership, particularly when facing uncertainty as they seek leaders who will hold and silence their anxieties. From a Freudian group perspective, the emotional attachment of a group to a leader can be seen to create fantasies in which followers believe the leader to be omnipotent and in full power and control. Gabriel (2011: 395) also makes reference to Bion's (1961) work on group dynamics and especially his focus on how intense emotional ties can evoke a 'psychological regression to a child-like dependence'. When entering this state of dependency, followers live the fantasy that the leader has extraordinary abilities and is able to save them from whatever uncertainties or complexities they are facing without the followers having to do anything. This delusion of the heroic leader is one that is inevitably failing as a single leader cannot possibly live up to these extreme expectations (Ford, 2010). This then leads to disappointment and disenchantment with the leader.

VIGNETTE 6.2

Extract from Case Study 3 highlighting issues of disappointment when the heroic leader fantasy is not fulfilled

One week towards the end of June, the facilities management contract came up at the Contract Review Meeting. Mike wasn't happy about the way the first lot had been managed, but that was before his time. Feeling that this would be one of the landmark contracts of his tenure, he had made his feelings known to Ken whose buying group were handling the brief. Mike had called for a detailed update on the current status, and Ken had mumbled something about how difficult it was working with Estates, but had not formally responded to the request. So Mike was surprised, and not a little annoyed, to see the next lot appear so suddenly.

At the meeting he had his line of interrogation tightly marshalled. What is happening in the wider FM industry? What are the key trends? What are other companies doing? Why are we going against that trend? The buying group were clearly taken aback. With over 1,000 sites to service, and a legacy of locally owned and operated management contracts, they had been nursing Estates through a painstaking process of aggregation. Mike's questions seemed somewhat academic given the situation on the ground, and they said so. Mike was incensed. And when Ken added 'Besides we're effectively out of contract from Monday, we need a decision now', the red mist came down. 'This is crap. I don't have to put up with this. I asked for a proper report two weeks ago, and you give me a fait accompli! You guys are lost in the dark ages. There is a ton of value to be had in this contract and all you care about is what Estates think. This meeting is over. Ken stay behind.'Ken was evidently unimpressed. They hadn't got a sign-off and something needed to happen before next week. Mike was on to him. 'Now what?' Ken looked blank.' I don't know...' he started. 'Now what will you do?' Ken wanted to say 'report you to Frank for failing to make decisions', but he bit his lip.

1. Ford (2010) argues that the heroic leader fantasy is unachievable and always leads to disappointment in the follower. Explore Ken's disappointment with Mike's behaviour described in this vignette in light of this statement.

We can again see here parallels to Meindl et al.'s (1985) work on the romancing of leaders. Bion (1961) identified two other significant modes to which followers and leaders can regress in time of heightened emotional intensity, for example, stress and anxiety through change and uncertainty. These are the fight or flight mode where groups imagine the dangers they face to be greater than they are and confront these by either attacking the danger or running away from it; and the pairing mode where the group believes that two members of the group will pair up to find a solution that will help them overcome the difficulties they face. In this latter mode the group experiences emotions of exaggerated hopefulness. Gabriel (2011) highlights that Bion's contribution for leadership was to suggest that leaders need to engage in the management of the emotions of themselves and their followers – an idea that was subsequently further explored by Goleman and others' work on emotional intelligence (Goleman, 2001).

Bion (1961) and others (French, 1997; Grint, 2010; Menzies Lyth, 1988) particularly focused on the importance to contain and manage anxieties as a key leadership role or function in organizations. In his seminal work on the difference between leaders and managers, Zaleznik (1977, 1989) suggests that it is sensitivity to the subconscious side of the leader–follower relationship and the ability of leaders for true empathy and to engage with followers at an emotional level that set them apart from managers. Burns (1978) later linked this assertion to the moral engagement of leaders with their followers and suggested that it is an essential role of leaders to recognize and 'make the followers' unconscious desires conscious' (Gabriel, 2011: 396). Through this, followers' desires can be recognized, valued and turned proactively into shared motives guiding the group's actions. Gabriel (2011) notes that while management of emotion is of the highest importance for leadership, it is also a very complex task in itself as followers will inevitably observe and emotionally react to a leader's every word and action.

Reflective Question 6.3

Think about non-hierarchical organizations or those with a minimum amount of hierarchy and hence assigned leadership (for example, small charities or partnerships). To what extent is the desire for and grouping around an individual leader inevitable even in these organizations where everybody is equal in status and importance?

Psychoanalytic Perspectives of Followership

Psychoanalytic studies of leadership have also helped to shed further light on followership as outlined in the previous section and on bad, toxic, dysfunctional or narcissistic leaders. Through the psychoanalytic lens we can explore further how followers' fantasies and unconscious desires drive their relationship and preferences for certain types of leaders and leadership. These fantasies are a product of early childhood experience with the mother and father as the earliest forms of authority. In the leader–follower relationship, these fantasies then influence whether followers enter a relationship of dependency, counter-dependency or interdependence (Stech, 2004) affecting the way they interact with any given leader. This may then further explain the lure and acceptance of those leaders who turn toxic and consciously or unconsciously harm their followers. The fantasy of a leader's omnipotence and heroic attributes (Ford, 2010; Freud, 1921; Gabriel, 1997) is one that offers the illusion or delusion of security and stability and is hence naturally sought by many followers.

Critical Thinking Box 6.2

A parallel has been drawn by Grint (2005a) between leading for the first time and becoming a parent for the first time. He argues that it is the junior person (subordinate or child) that teaches the leader/parent how to lead. Jackson and Parry (2011) reflect further on this parent–child metaphor in relation to psychoanalytic approaches to leadership. They argue that this metaphor highlights the need for joint responsibility for constructive dissent, that is, open and honest communication between leader and follower. Yet, the metaphor also highlights how difficult it may be to keep up constructive dissent and how relatively easy it is for the parent/ leader to tell the child/subordinate what to do and for the latter to rely fully on guidance from the superior.

An increasing body of leadership research now exists that explores how this relationship and fantasy can lead to toxic leadership when the leader either consciously or subconsciously abuses the power, trust and loyalty they are given by their followers (Lipman-Blumen, 2005). Others have explored the dangers of this fantasy leading to narcissism in leaders who come to believe that they are the omnipotent, infallible being of those fantasies (Gabriel, 1999; Maccoby, 2000) and subsequently become preoccupied 'with glamour, image and display' (Gabriel, 2011: 400). In these cases it is their ability to play to those fantasies and work with imagination to inspire their followers that led them to initial success but may turn into their greatest weakness when the protection of that image and vision becomes the only focus and the leader loses touch with reality. The damage that narcissistic leaders can cause to an organization is potentially drastic and hence the need for constructive criticism from followers that is crucial for the survival and success of any organization. We will explore this dark side of leadership in greater detail in Chapter 13 and turn to a deeper exploration of the leader–follower relationship in the next section of this chapter.

Relational Approaches to Leadership

Having introduced the relationship between leader and follower through the lens of LMX theories of leadership in Chapter 3, we introduce here an approach to leader–follower relations that has focused less on the separate role of leader and follower and more on the co-produced relational process itself. Its focus on the 'in-between' leader and follower space is a fundamental shift for leadership studies away of the focus on the individual leader or follower. This emergent field of leadership studies has been called 'relational approach to leadership' and has seen key contributions particularly by Hosking and Morley (1988, 1991), Hosking (1988, 2007), Uhl-Bien (2004, 2006) and more recently Cunliffe and Eriksen (2011).

The Relational Process

Similar to the critical views of Collinson (2008) on follower and leader identities, Hosking (2011) criticizes contingency theories for solely focusing on individual characteristics and behaviours. She argues that this has led to the false assumption of clear and stable boundaries between the individual leader, follower and the wider context, where the individual is in control of the self and individual knowledge. In light of this critique, Hosking and colleagues have developed a different focus on leadership and conceptualized it as a relational process. This relational process is argued to be simultaneously social, cognitive and political (Hosking, 2011: 456) where the social encapsulates processes by which leader and followers construct who they are in relation to the context they are in and ultimately co-constructing the context itself. The cognitive then refers to the element of active sense-making embedded in these social processes, whereas the reference to political illustrates the dominance or support of some constructions over others.

Seeing leadership as such a relational process then blurs the boundaries between the individual selves and the context as all are involved in a co-construction of each other and the leadership process. Cunliffe and Eriksen (2011) have further explored and developed this idea of relational leadership in response to empirical data on US federal security directors. They argue that this is not only a way of 'theorizing leadership' but also potentially of 'being a leader' who is engaged in a true dialogue and is morally and relationally responsive and responsible. This involves understanding and appreciating that who we are as a leader or follower and how we behave is a social construct of our interactions with those around us and the situation we are in. It is an ongoing verbal and non-verbal dialogue and interaction between leader and follower that shapes who they are and what kind of relationship they engage in. As these interactions are ongoing, the notion of who individuals are and their relationship is fluid and co-constructed. It also means recognizing the complexity of the context we are in and how dominant views and discourses influence our expectations towards each other and our self.

The relational approach to leadership hence recognizes that individuals not only influence each other but are also influenced by and influence this wider, complex context. The self can therefore be viewed 'as fundamentally relational and ongoing' (Hosking, 2011: 457) rather than stable and clearly separated from others and context. Equally, leadership as a process is fundamentally relational, ongoing and co-constructed. Further, as Collinson (2008) highlighted, the self is multiple and similarly there are multiple possible versions of the leader–follower relations that exist within and between the individual and context involved. These observations fundamentally challenge the assumption of mainstream leadership theories (as discussed in Chapters 2–4) that there is a universally best or most effective way of leading in a specific context. Instead, they highlight that the very meaning of leadership and effective behaviours of leader and follower within this as well as the specific context is continuously co-constructed 'in-between' the individual actors. Finally, like Collinson, Hosking (2011) argues that a relational approach to leadership implies seeing power as relational and hence shifting and co-constructed between leader, follower and context. Power is then not a fixed attribute that either the leader of follower holds but an influence on and outcome of how these individuals relate to each other and draw on meaning about their own roles and relationship through the context they are in and co-produce.

In line with Cunliffe and Eriksen (2011), Hosking (2011) suggests that relational leadership as a way of being involves working with the fluid, multiple, co-constructed nature of leader–follower relations by encouraging a multiple dialogue, working with different, fluid notions of the self and inviting different views and actions rather than imposing consensus. As part of such relational leadership practice, Hosking (2011) suggests keeping structures, rules and procedures within the group minimal to encourage an open dialogue, enquiry and improvisation. This then also involves what Hosking (2011) calls heart-felt listening and appreciation between leader and followers. In light of Jaworski's (1996) empirical tale of falling into and out of the habit of relating through an over-dependence on staying consistent with the approach adopted and through tensions of being accountable and responsible, Hosking (2011) warns that to be relational means to engage in an ongoing process of deep reflection by the individual and group.

VIGNETTE 6.3

Extract from Case Study 4 in relation to dialogue within a turbulent organizational context

In taking staff through a difficult transition period, the leadership have adopted a strategy of transparency and 'telling it as it is'. This has been painful and challenging. The leadership started with the unions, agreeing a shared vision for the future

(Continued)

(Continued)

and shared principles and values as the framework for on-going dialogue. An understanding that the recession is a market fact that could not be ignored formed the background to these discussions: 'We started with a reality check, and cards on the table. We said if we do nothing, then this is what will happen, we'll go out of business. We opened up a discussion and said we need your help to go forward. We were very careful with our language, conscious of not being them and us.'

1. To what extent can this approach taken by the Brandon Trust senior management team be seen as an attempt to engage in relational leadership? Was it truly an open dialogue between management and employees?
2. In light of the full information offered in this case study, was this attempt to create dialogue rather than impose consensus sustainable?

Summary

This chapter has introduced readers foremost to the field of followership and follower-centric approaches to leadership. We have recognized Meindl et al.'s (1985) historical contribution to a greater focus on the importance of followers in the construction of leadership and reviewed key developments in this area through Shamir's (2007) typology of different follower-centric views of leadership. We have also highlighted work by Kellerman (2008), Kelley (1988, 1992), Carsten et al. (2010) and Sy (2010) that has advanced our understanding of the role of followers and the notion of followership as such. We concluded our review of the field of followership and follower-centric approaches to leadership through a discussion of current and future trends. These suggest that future research needs to concentrate further on a conceptual and empirical exploration of followers and followership as well as understand further cultural and contextual influences on and differences in notions of followership and roles of followers in organizations. More critical scholars have also called for a revisiting of the leader–follower dichotomy and the asymmetrical power relationship embedded within western societies as well as further exploration of resistance and ethics in followership. The second part of this chapter then focused on two more areas related to followership and the leader–follower relationship: psychoanalytic approaches to leadership and relational approaches to leadership. Both areas of leadership studies have most recently moved forward our understanding of leadership as a co-constructed process and relationship between leaders and followers. Psychoanalytic approaches to leadership particularly highlight the deep-rooted fantasy of the strong leader in western groups and organizations and explain the persistence of a child-like dependence on individual leaders in social groups. With a view to the leader–follower relationships, psychoanalytic approaches further help to explain followers' desire for specific good and toxic leaders as they explore the roots of such desire in those followers' subconscious. Relational leadership approaches, conversely, focus in depth on how leadership can be seen to be a relational process that is co-constructed through and between leader and followers. Contributions by Hosking (2011) and Cunliffe and Eriksen (2011) further explore the notion of the relational leader as somebody who engages in and encourages a multiple and open dialogue that strives for enquiry and improvisation rather than enforced consensus.

Additional Reflection Questions

1. What do you see as the main focus of a (a) leader-centric view and (b) follower-centric view? What are the limitations of each approach?
2. Why has Meindl's work on the romancing of leadership been so influential and what are its limitations?
3. What is the difference between viewing followers as constructors of leadership and followers as co-producers of leadership?
4. Reflect on notions of leadership and followership in leaderless or leaderful contexts such as terrorist organizations.
5. What roles do fantasies play in psychoanalytic approaches to leadership?
6. Grint (2010) suggests that societies will always seek individual leaders. Evaluate this statement in light of the psychoanalytic perspective on leadership.
7. Explain how relational leadership differs in its approach to the leader-follower relationship from LMX theories.

Case Study Questions

1. In Case Study 3, Ken is given the leading role in redesigning the structure of the procurement department in the absence of a formal head of department. Critically reflect on his experience with colleagues and his boss during this time, drawing particularly on the idea of followers as leaders and the social identity theory. What are the potential issues and opportunities of being a follower and leader at the same time?
2. Mike Hayesman, the Director of the South Gloucestershire Local Authority is, in Case Study 6, described to be dealing with significant organizational change. While the case study provides a leader-centric account of these events, you are tasked with providing a follower-centric reflection on this change project. Please reflect critically on the likely challenges and possibility of success by drawing on a range of follower-centric approaches to leadership as introduced in this chapter.

3. In Case Study 2, there is reported low morale among engineers who are said to be working alone and lacking contact with managers and the regional offices. Critically analyse the issues that the company in Case Study 2 is experiencing with engineers in light of this lack of access to managers and leader. Draw particularly on the ideas of Bion connected to the psychoanalytic approach to leadership to inform this analysis.

4. Critically analyse Mike's approach in Case Study 3 to and interaction with his team. Drawing on the arguments in the relational approach to leadership, what advice would you give him on how to improve his relationship with his team?

Further Reading

Bligh, M.C. (2011) Followership and follower-centred approaches. In A. Bryman, D. Collinson, K. Grint, B. Jackson and M. Uhl-Bien (eds) *The SAGE Handbook of Leadership*. London: Sage, 425–436.

Cunliffe, A.L. and Eriksen, M. (2011) Relational leadership. *Human Relations*, 64(11): 1425–1449.

Gabriel, Y. (1997) Meeting God: when organizational members come face to face with the supreme leader. *Human Relations*, 50(4): 315–342.

Gabriel, Y. (2011) Psychoanalytic approaches to leadership. In A. Bryman, D. Collinson, K. Grint, B. Jackson and M. Uhl-Bien (eds) *The SAGE Handbook of Leadership*. London: Sage, 393–404.

Grint, K. (2010) The sacred in Leadership: separation, sacrifice and silence. *Organization Studies*, 31: 89–107.

Meindl, J.R., Erlich, S.B. and Dukerich, J.M. (1985) The romance of leadership. *Administrative Science Quarterly*, 30(1): 78–108.

7

Leadership and Power

We have introduced the notion of power in Chapter 4 in relation to management and leadership. In this chapter, we expand our exploration of power further and look at various approaches to power and politics and their relevance for leadership. To this end, we introduce readers to different approaches to power and leadership, different sources of power and their relevance for leaders and leadership as well as different manifestations of power in leadership. As part of this wider exploration of power, we also make reference to more recent contributions by critical leadership scholars and explore the issue of power asymmetry in the leader–follower relationship. Political behaviours and the role of influencing in the process of leadership will be addressed throughout this chapter.

Chapter Aims

- Explore the role of power in leadership and the leader–follower relationship
- Highlight and critically discuss the lack of focus on power within leadership studies
- Introduce individual, social and critical approaches to power and explore their relevance for our understanding of leadership
- Explore the critical view of an existing power asymmetry in our current focus on the leader–follower relationship

Critical Thinking Box 7.1

Some organizational scholars would argue that organizations and relationships are fundamentally about power. Should therefore a focus on and understanding of power be our main drive in leadership studies? Or should we forget about leaders and leadership and only focus on the nature and implications of power for relationships and processes of influencing among individuals and groups in organizations?

Why power?

It can be said that power is fundamentally inherent in the leadership process and that leaders will usually have to engage with political behaviour within organizations. According to Dahl (1957), the active use of power can – at its most basic level – be defined as somebody influencing another to get that other person to do something they would otherwise not do. Most definitions of leadership in turn make reference to the influencing of followers, where some source of power is arguably needed to be able to influence others and where the process of influencing can be seen to be a display of power. Some may go as far as saying that without power there is no leadership. Yukl (2010) discusses a variety of proactive influencing tactics that leaders can draw on such as rational persuasion, inspirational appeals, collaboration, coalition building, personal appeals, ingratiation and so on. These influence tactics can be seen as a manifestation of the leader's building of and use of power within an organization to protect and advance the group or project he/she is leading. Yukl (2010) differentiates between such proactive influencing tactics and political tactics where the latter are linked to influencing decision-making processes within the organization. We will discuss such political behaviours in relation to Lukes' agenda-setting dimension of power later in this chapter. For clarification, we also differentiate in Table 7.1 between the concepts of influencing, persuasion and authority as associated with power.

The topic of power especially has recently received attention within leadership studies from a leader-centric, follower-centric and critical point of view. Yet, power and particularly political behaviour in organizations have not always featured strongly in leadership studies and leadership textbooks due to their negative connotations of abusive and bad leadership. Indeed, Gordon argues that a 'normative apolitical approach to power pervades the mainstream literature' where power is either ignored or treated as something natural to the process of leadership and unproblematic (2011: 195). Critical leadership scholars, such as Gordon (2011) and Collinson (2011), have problematized

Table 7.1   Influence, Persuasion and Authority

	What is it?	Link to leadership and power
Influence	Process of producing an effect on somebody's behaviour, attitude, values, etc.	Can be seen as essential activity of a leader and active use of power to get a group to achieve a set goal
Persuasion	Convincing, urging somebody to do something or believe something	Particular way a leader can influence others; can be seen as a form of political behaviour or tactic
Authority	The right (legal or positional) to determine, control, assign tasks and responsibilities, solve conflict, set rules and procedures, reward and punish	Comes with formal positions of leadership and management within an organizational hierarchy; a particular source of power to influence and effect change in others

this absence of in-depth considerations of power and power asymmetries in leadership studies and practice and argue that this has led to the false assumption of leadership as inherently good and positive. In this chapter, we intend to guide readers through these different foci of leadership studies and power, highlighting the different influences of leader-centric, follower-centric and critical approaches.

> ## Reflective Question 7.1
>
> Before we introduce different types of power, think about your previous and current experiences of organizational power. What kind of power have you encountered, who had it and where did it come from? How important has this been for you or others to get the 'job done'? What were the consequences for the organization and relationships between colleagues?

Power – A Focus on Individuals

Power is often described as the ability or capacity of one individual/group to influence another individual/group. This can be linked to different mechanisms of influencing, such as coercive, remunerative and normative, that are likely to produce different reactions from those who are influenced, such as commitment, compliance or resistance (Etzioni, 1964). Many leader-centred writings on power, as well as textbooks, will take this view and seek to give leaders advice on what types and sources of power they have and how they can use these in light of the different reactions they may evoke. Yukl's (2010) elaborations of influence tactics are an example of this focus on providing proactive advice for practising leaders.

This view of power can also be described as a behavioural view as it focuses on individuals' use of power and interaction with others. It is hence concerned with observable, behavioural actions and reactions and the active use of an individual's power in organizations is often seen in relation to resolving a conflict and/or making decisions. It is therefore particularly concerned with 'management's authority as being relatively automatic, its legitimacy sanctioned through the hierarchy and rules within an organization and exemplified by their leadership roles' (Jackson and Parry, 2011: 96). In other words, the position and role of a manager in an organization give that manager power over his/her subordinates in line with their supervisory role and the organization's rules of conduct. This managerial authority is generally seen as legitimate and defined through the organizational hierarchy. How this legitimate power is used by managers is then linked to the different influencing styles discussed by Etzioni and Yukl above.

VIGNETTE 7.1

Extract from Case Study 3 illustrating managerial authority

One day in May, there was a flurry of excitement as Frank, on one of his rare visits to the department, called everybody together to welcome Michael Langer, the new head of procurement. Mike was a fresh-faced young man who, having started in consumer goods, had moved into heavy industry, and had just spent 3 years as head of out-sourcing in a steel company owned by a private equity firm. He made a brief presentation to the department, detailing his background and his delight at being asked to head up such a prestigious unit as Lowe Power's procurement department. He was polite and well-mannered and made a good first impression. Frank's brief to Mike had been simple and direct: 'Shake 'em up, Mike. A lot of them have been here a long time, and have got very used to the comfortable life.'

1. Mike had been given managerial authority to head up the procurement department. Discuss the influencing style suggested to him by his boss Frank.
2. Reflect on the possible reactions of his new team to this influencing style. What other sources of power may he need to be effective?

Power Sources of the Individual

Legitimate power through the organizational hierarchy is not the only type of power and authority nor the only source of power for individuals. A key concept used within this approach to power and recognized with regard to its relevance for leadership is

Table 7.2   **French and Raven's (1959) Taxonomy of Power**

Type of Power	Description
Reward power	Person A complies with Person B so as to gain a reward that is controlled by Person B. Within organizations such a reward could, for example, be in the form of a bonus, career prospect or esteem related. It needs to be desired by or important to Person B.
Coercive power	Person A complies with Person B so as to avoid punishments controlled by Person B. Within organizations punishments could, for example, be linked to formal performance management procedures or relate to more subtle implications, such as curtailed career prospects, or being excluded from desired tasks/projects.
Legitimate power	Person A complies with Person B because he/she believes Person B to have the right to request and Person A to comply. This type of power is associated with formal positions of authority in organizations and society such as managerial roles or an inherited status (for example, royalty, ownership).
Expert power	Person A complies because he/she believes that Person B has specific knowledge that Person A needs to complete a given task. Such expertise may be formally recognized in the organization or linked more specifically to the very task that Person A is trying to complete and nobody else has that specific knowledge apart from Person B.
Referent power	Person A complies because he/she admires Person B and seek his/her approval. This type of power is most closely related to charisma and involves a strong, positive, emotional engagement between Person A and B.
Information power	Person A complies because Person B has information that Person A needs to complete a given task. This information can be sought through formal and information conversation and network within and outside the organization.
Ecological power	Person A complies because Person B has control over the physical environment and technology that Person A needs to complete a given task. This type of power can be linked to the particular work space, access to other work spaces and technologies.

French and Raven's (1959) taxonomy of power sources/archetypes. We will only briefly introduce each power type here (see Table 7.2) and would advise readers to consult Yukl (2010) for a more detailed reading.

The top three types or sources of power as well as ecological power, on the one hand, have often been associated with organizational structure and are hence closest to notions of authority and the behavioural view on power as introduced by Jackson and Parry (2011). The last three power sources/types are, on the other hand, usually seen as personal attributes or characteristics and therefore not necessarily attached to or dependent on organizational structure. Also, links have been drawn between the first three sources of power and notions of management whereas the last three notions of power have been more readily associated with leadership. While these types of power are treated as personal attributes, they are by no means fixed and an individual can over time lose or acquire different types of power in relation to subordinates, colleagues and superiors. Indeed, owing to organizational changes as well as through influencing and political tactics, individuals can gain or lose different types of power over time.

Reflective Question 7.2

Think about your current or previous position in an organization. Which if any of French and Raven's types of power do/did you hold? How important are these and why?

Being aware of the power distribution within an organization and of the different types of power existing within an organization is highly useful for any individual and particularly those with leadership responsibility. Looking at an organization through this power lens helps us see a whole new structure based on the acquisition of power that allows leaders to make more informed decisions, to be aware of political activities in organizations and to build their own networks and expand their power bases that then help to protect and lead their specific groups of followers. Taking this view on leadership and power does, however, also warrant an exploration of negative consequences, such as a personal abuse of power by those in leadership positions to the detriment of other employees and/or the organization. How a leader engages with and/or attempts to change existing power structures and why a leader may strive to expand his/her power and influence within the organization are therefore significantly linked to organizational ethics and ethical considerations within leadership. We will discuss these issues in relation to ethics and toxic leadership further in Chapter 13.

Power – A Focus on Politics and Relations

While the previous approach to power is located within individuals and can be seen as an attribute or property of individuals, we now consider political and relational views of power (Jackson and Parry, 2011) through the lens of Lukes' (2005) three dimensions of power. Lukes (2005) explores how power works at different levels and how it is linked to political behaviour in organizations. The *first* and basic *dimension* resonates with the behavioural view on power as outlined above, as it is one where power is linked to authority and overt, observable conflict, where Person A influences Person B to do something they would not otherwise have done. It is an act of observable persuasion between individuals and affects decision making and conflict resolution.

Agenda Setting

Lukes' (2005) *second dimension*, however, examines the more hidden aspects of decision making and use of power: agenda setting. Here, the use of power is not manifested in conflict but instead happens prior to the formal decision-making process. It gives the leader of a meeting or decision-making process the power to decide in advance the issues to be discussed and which other issues are to be ignored. The power to set the agenda therefore means that those issues that the person setting the agenda wishes to avoid never make it onto the agenda and are never part of the subsequent decision-making process. At this level, power can bring a bias into what is often seen as a rational decision-making process and give a stronger voice to some organizational members and interests to the detriment of others. Bolden et al.'s review of Lukes' dimensions suggests that since certain issues are never on the agenda and never discussed 'there appears to be universal agreement on the matter as it currently exists, and differences of opinion remain unobservable' (2011: 76). It therefore gives a false sense of unity of individual and organizational interests that covers up or distracts from the real diversity of views and interests as those 'other' interests are silenced in order to avoid any conflict arising.

Within this second dimension of power we see its political aspect working at the individual level and the importance of coalition building, and the impact these social arrangements and individual interests have on agenda setting. Viewing power on this dimension bears several implications for leadership. It highlights the potential for leaders to influence decision-making processes in the organization through their power to set agendas and select members carefully to form decision-making groups. It further highlights again the inevitable bias leaders' actions bring and how their interests may significantly influence decision-making processes. This stresses the potential for a conscious or unconscious abuse of power by leaders for the benefit of their own interests and careers. In Chapter 13 we will explore such bad, toxic or narcissistic notions of leadership further.

Leadership as 'Sense-making'

In addition, Smircich and Morgan (1982) adopt a social constructionist approach to leadership (see Chapter 5 for definition) and focus on the symbolic element of leadership and the significant influence that leaders can have on their followers in relation to the sense-making of organizational reality. Seen through this lens, leaders not only have agenda-setting and rule-setting power but followers will also look to their leader for active sense-making of the situation for their group and organization. They will therefore pay attention to and interpret their leader's actions and language. Hence what meetings the leader attends, what priorities he/she sets and what he/she says or does not say are constantly interpreted by his/her followers in an attempt to make sense of their organizational reality. Smircich and Morgan (1982) highlight particularly the potential for abuse of this type of agenda-setting and symbolic power by leaders.

Reflective Question 7.3

Think about a meeting you have been invited to in your current or previous organizational role. Reflect on the agenda-setting and sense-making processes that happened prior to, during and after this meeting. Who had power, when and why, and how did this change over time?

Linked to Smircich and Morgan's (1982) notion of symbolic power is Lukes' (2005) *third* – institutional – *dimension* that moves on from the individual to the social, collective level and considers the power of the norms and values of professional and social groups and cultures over an individual's behaviours at work. Seen from this dimension, it is the ingrained and taken-for-granted values shared by members of a group/culture that shape how these members see social reality and what they see as right, ethical and a priority in life and in organizations. Agendas are therefore not actually set and decisions not made by specific individuals. The agendas we set, the decisions we make and why, how and when we influence people are instead shaped by shared values and norms invisible to but ingrained within individuals. Power therefore is not situated within individuals but within the shared norms and values that influence and control individuals' behaviours. The lesson here for leadership is that leaders' actions and behaviours are shaped by the norms and values they share – with their group, organization, profession and so on – and these are often enforced through institutionalized mechanisms such as organizational competency frameworks and dominant ideals of effective leadership.

VIGNETTE 7.2

Extract from Case Study 3 in relation to hidden agendas

At their next weekly meeting, Mike gave Frank a watered down account of the events at the contract review meeting. Frank was keen to hear more about Mike's thinking on the way forward for facilities management: 'We discussed this in my interview, Frank. We talked about the major developments in FM.' 'But that was just an interview, Mike. This is the real world. The first lot was a ground-breaker for us. You're still earning the right with Estates. Don't rock the boat.' Mike was flummoxed. How did

(Continued)

(Continued)

don't rock the boat square with shake 'em up? And it was sobering to be reminded how closely involved Frank had been with Lot 1. This was frustrating and perplexing.

1. This quote illustrates a change in underlying agendas for Mike's boss Frank. Mike was asked by Frank to 'rock the boat' and change current practices. Yet, in doing so, he clashed with existing value systems – including Frank's own values. Once this happened, Frank changed his agenda and turned on Mike. How can you explain this turn of events through the second and third dimensions?

Disciplinary Power

Bolden et al. (2011) stress that Lukes' work has received some criticism from other power scholars concerning his underlying assumption that there are people in power and that those in power possess this power and are able to control it. Knights and Willmott (1999) in particular have explored this critical view and argued that power is not something anybody can posses but something that exists in discourse, that is, ways of thinking that help us make sense of our everyday lives and affect our being and doing. Therefore, power through discourse acts as a disciplinary mechanism (Foucault, 1977) and produces what we see as right or wrong, ethical or unethical. But the truth we see is not an objective one. It is a truth that is created through knowledge and knowledge itself is not objective but a product of individuals' and societies' interests and dominant discourses. For example, what we know about leadership is based on theories developed by individual researchers or research groups driven by their own interests, existing knowledge and career aspirations, that in turn are influenced by certain values and discourses existent in organizations and societies. What these researchers then come to study and the theories they subsequently develop are fundamentally influenced by this institutional dimension of power and represent not an objective view on leadership but one that is biased through power asymmetry and political behaviours.

Overall, what we know about leadership so far then needs to be seen in light of the dominance of US/UK-based research embedded in western values and thinking that has formed a dominant discourse (Collinson, 2009) acting as a disciplinary mechanism in the sense that it controls the way we talk about, conceptualize, study and practicse leadership as conforming with this dominant discourse. This has effected our knowledge of leadership to reflect this dominant discourse and with it the western values embedded in it, silencing other equally important values and views of leadership. This has also implications for the practice of leadership, as it reflects the extent to which the dominant literature and popular models and theories on leadership promote a certain dominant leader image that creates expectations in the workplace around what a leader looks like and how they should behave. Those in official leadership positions can then be seen to try and meet these expectations by conforming to the dominant leader images promoted and accepted in organizations and wider society. We will explore this aspect of power further below and in Chapter 14 where we talk about identity and language, making particular references to how the dominant discourse shapes what we see as ideal images of leadership and how these shape leaders' identities.

A Critical Analysis of Mainstream Leadership Studies in Relation to Power

The critical views on Lukes' approach to power and the impact of dominant discourse and institutional power on leadership research have been further explored by critical leadership scholars and will be summarized in this section in relation to Gordon's (2011) recent critical analysis of power in leadership studies and Collinson's (2011) framing of critical leadership studies.

Gordon's (2011: 196) critical review of the leadership literature is focused on the 'dominant trends in the literature which, as Collinson (2009) noted, is US-based and psychologically informed'. To this end, Gordon (2011) divides this dominant leadership literature into theories that are 'traditional' in their approach to leadership and non-traditional. Gordon (2011) identifies trait, styles, contingency and transformational leadership theories with taking a traditional approach and dispersed forms of leadership with a non-traditional approach to studying leadership.

In his review of traditional approaches, Gordon (2011) highlights that all theories falling within this approach share an acceptance of and focus on hierarchical structures in organizations that see the leader–follower relationship as dualistic in the sense that leaders hold a privileged position and are superior to followers (Collinson, 2006, 2008). Gordon stresses that an underlying assumption of these theories seems to be that 'if leaders were not superior, people would not follow them' (2011: 196). This underlying assumption then legitimizes the dualism between leaders and followers and sees the power asymmetry as unproblematic. Gordon (2002) argues that even some follower-centred theories have accepted the leader as superior, giving them further voice while continuing to silence followers. Over time this apolitical stance of mainstream leadership studies has normalized this power asymmetry and it has become accepted as normal and natural. Critical leadership scholars like Gordon argue that this needs to be recognized and problematized as the power asymmetry is not natural or 'right' but has been socially constructed by the dominant approach taken by those studying leadership.

VIGNETTE 7.3

Extract from Case Study 5 on power asymmetry

June's values are lived and breathed through everything she does. They define her as a leader beyond title, and beyond organization, as someone who tries to make a difference in the world through all that she does. June questioned the world she found from a young age, especially '... the kind of social structures that made people inferior or superior which didn't make sense at all ... when I left theatre and worked as team development manager and management consultancy ... I was working with a manager who kept talking about subordinates and I was horrified ... the three words I would eliminate from the dictionary are "should", "ought" and "subordinate" ... it means "less than" ... and hierarchical structure doesn't work for me ... it's not a word you come across much now.'

For June, leadership and the development of any business or organizational practice should be about egalitarianism ...'truly living a sense of equality that is about respect ... if they are doing their job to the best of their ability! If they are not doing their job properly, whoever they are, then they need to be taken to task! I don't think anyone should be given respect purely for their position.'

1. This quote summarizes the beliefs of June Burroughs – founder of a social enterprise – on the power asymmetry embedded in work practices and labels such as subordinate. Critically reflect on the 'need' for power asymmetry between leader and follower across different types of work.

Power and Distributed Leadership

Gordon (2011) further recognizes that dispersed forms of leadership have – in recognition of new organizational forms – shifted our focus away from this duality and instead situated power as equally distributed between leaders and followers. While this shift in focus is an important one that may encourage future research to reconsider the appropriateness of the power asymmetry so often accepted as natural to the leader–follower relationship, the dispersed leadership movement itself has so far fallen short in explicitly exploring power issues. Questions around possible tensions between intended empowerment and institutionalized notions of hierarchy and the leader–follower relationship remain unanswered and under-explored. Grint's (2010) contribution on the sacred in leadership supports Gordon's (2011) concern that the underlying assumption of the superior leader and therefore the dualistic nature of the leader–follower relationship is so deeply ingrained and rooted within western societies that it would require a complete rethink of such underlying power structures to enable dispersed notions of leadership to gain dominance over traditional heroic models of leadership.

Drawing on empirical examples such as offered by Barker (1993), Gordon (2011) argues similarly to Grint (2010) that without such a shift in our social systems, non-traditional forms of leadership will continue to face problems in organizational practice where organizational members seek security and stability through their relationship with superior senior leaders. Especially in times of uncertainty, this institutionalized preference for traditional forms of leadership will take over and non-traditional leaders will be replaced by traditional leaders. Gordon (2011) concludes his critical review that it is not the continuing existence of the leader–follower relationship that is the problem but the normalized power asymmetry within this and its potential for abuse. In Chapter 13 we will take up this discussion of power abuse in the forms of bad, narcissistic and toxic leadership. We will explore further the consequences of western society's acceptance of and conformity with this power asymmetry and particularly how this legitimizes and protects leaders from being exposed for their unethical methods and abuse of the trust, loyalty and commitment invested in them by followers and the organization.

Power Relations between Leader and Follower

Collinson adds to Gordon's (2011) critical review that the power relations between leader and follower are 'likely to be interdependent, as well as asymmetrical, typically ambiguous, frequently shifting, potentially contradictory and often contested' (2011: 185). He argues that 'power relations are always two-way, contingent and to some degree interdependent … Since power relations are always two-way, leaders remain dependent to some extent on the led, while followers retain a degree of autonomy and discretion' (Collinson, 2011: 184). This recognizes that despite the asymmetrical power relationship, followers are not entirely powerless and power relations are not fixed. Rather, the asymmetrical power relationship between leader and follower is shifting over time and followers are recognized to be 'knowledgeable agents' alongside leaders. This view of the leader–follower relationship as interdependent and shifting as well as asymmetrical in power stresses the relational nature of power where it is not the property of one person but instead exists in the relation between two or more individuals and is affected by the changes in this relation over time.

Summary

In this chapter we have introduced readers to a range of views on power and drawn links to political behaviour and leadership. We first defined power, highlighted its relevance for leadership and differentiated it from other concepts, such as authority and influence. We then discussed approaches to power that view it as the property of an individual or group and subsequently explored different sources and types of power in relation to leadership and management. Drawing on Lukes' three dimensions of power enabled us to move our discussion of power onto seeing it as something that is fundamentally relational and shifting. Linked to Lukes' second dimension of power, we discussed it as something we can observe in conflict and decision making but also as something that is related to agenda setting. We further highlighted Lukes' third dimension of power that views power as something that is situated in shared values and socially driven role expectations. We concluded our discussion of different views of power by introducing critical views on power in leadership studies and particularly discussed and problematized the power asymmetry in the leader–follower relationship.

Additional Reflection Questions

1. Without power there is no leadership. Is this statement always true?
2. What is the key difference between a behavioural and a relational view on power?
3. Think of an example from your organizational experience of each of Lukes' three dimensions in action.
4. For each of Lukes' three dimensions, what is the key learning for leaders and leadership?
5. Leaders need to act politically to be successful. Debate this statement drawing on your organizational experience.
6. What is Gordon's key critical reflection on the traditional leader-follower relationship?
7. Reflect on the use of power in distributed leadership. Is equality in power distribution possible in practice?

Case Study Questions

1. Please read carefully through Case Study 1 and analyse the different key players/ groups in this organization and their various sources of power. Does the power distribution change over the course of the case study? What advice would you give each group with regard to increasing and/or maintaining their power sources?
2. Case Study 2 describes the creation and outcomes of an international leadership development programme. Critically analyse the existence and use of power in the creation, running and review of the programme from a second (agenda setting) and third (value systems) dimension of power.
3. Case Study 4 reviews the strong value-based approach at the Brandon Trust to leadership and with a view to the nature and purpose of the organization. The following quote illustrates its particular focus on change as a core value: 'Change

is the norm and a key component of our thinking and our expectations.' Drawing on Foucault's work on power through discourse, explore how this statement – and the dominant discourse at the Brandon Trust that it represents – can be seen as a disciplinary mechanism. What is it like to work at the Brandon Trust and how does this discourse affect the image of an effective leader in this organization?

4. Collinson (2011) and Gordon (2011) discuss the extent to which leaders are assumed to have and need to use power over their subordinates to get things done. They highlight that this puts subordinates in an inferior situation. With reference to Case Study 3, critically evaluate whether a power imbalance is visible between the managers and subordinates in this case study. What are the positive and negative implications of such an imbalance?

Further Reading

Collinson, D. (2011) Critical leadership studies. In A. Bryman, D. Collinson, K. Grint, B. Jackson and M. Uhl-Bien (eds) *The SAGE Handbook of Leadership*. London: Sage, 181–194.

Gordon, R. (2002) Conceptualizing leadership with respect to its historical-contextual antecedents to power. *The Leadership Quarterly*, 13(2): 151–167.

Gordon, R. (2011) Leadership and power. In A. Bryman, D. Collinson, K. Grint, B. Jackson and M. Uhl-Bien (eds) *The SAGE Handbook of Leadership*. London: Sage, 195–202.

Smircich, L. and Morgan, G. (1982) Leadership: the management of meaning. *Journal of Applied Behavioural Science*, 18: 257–273.

Strategic Leadership and Leading Change

In this chapter we combine two prominent issues within the leadership literature. One is how to lead strategically in organizations or the development of the theme of strategic leadership, and the second is the seemingly inherent link leadership has with change and the issue of leading change in organizations. We believe it is important to reflect on issues of strategic leadership and change as they are becoming popular discussions in organizations. As we have already explored in Chapter 1, there appears to be a strong link between concepts of leadership and concepts of change. In this chapter we delve a little further into these connections and also introduce the idea of strategic leadership. We start the chapter by looking at the issue around the term 'strategic leadership' and owing to the nature of what we discover about strategic leadership, this tends to focus our attention towards issues of change in organizations.

Chapter Aims

- Introduce and critically discuss the link between leadership and strategy, hence strategic leadership
- Explore the differing views of what strategic leadership represents in organizations
- Critically discuss the link between leadership and change
- Introduce a debate around the enactment of strategic leadership for change in organizations

---

Reflective Question 8.1

What experiences of strategic leadership have you had? Based on these experiences, what does strategic leadership mean and how important is it in organizations?

Strategic Leadership

The literature on strategic leadership is fairly scarce, which leaves the area relatively poorly understood (Bolden et al., 2011), however, it is a term very often heard in organizations. The literature appears to suggest three differing aspects to leadership:

1. leading the strategy of an organization (Bolden et al., 2011; DuBrin, 2010; Hambrick, 1989; Leavy and McKiernan, 2009; Rowe, 2001);
2. developing and initiating leadership strategically in organizations (Rowe, 2001; Yukl, 2010);
3. or shorthand for describing the leadership at the top of an organization (Cannella and Monroe, 1997; Denis et al., 2011; Hambrick, 1989; Yukl, 2010).

These themes appear to be melded together in theory, for example, Denis et al. (2011) highlight Hambrick's (1989) ideas around distinguishing strategic leadership from other forms of leadership lower down the organization. Hambrick (1989: 5–15) suggests four factors:

1. Strategic leadership involves a focus on internal and external factors in organizations and is concerned with positioning the organization within its context.
2. Strategic leadership involves greater degrees of complexity and ambiguity than leadership at other levels.
3. Strategic leadership is multifunctional and integrative in comparison to other, more specialized roles in organizations.
4. Strategic leadership means leading through others.

This view appears typical of the idea that strategic leadership is at the top of the organization and that it is significantly different from other forms of leadership elsewhere in the organization. Yukl (2010), for example, explicitly relates strategic leadership to executive in one of his chapters in the textbook *Leadership in Organisations*. He goes on to highlight the controversial issue of whether executives in organizations are important for organizational performance, highlighting the two sides of the debate – those that believe executives have a high impact on organizational performance (Finkelstein and Hambrick, 1996; Hambrick, 2007; Katz and Kahn, 1978) and those that suggest they have little influence

(Hannan and Freeman, 1984; Meindl et al., 1985; Pfeffer, 1977). Under this label of strategic leadership Yukl goes on to describe and discuss executive teams, the constraints on executives, issues of political power, CEO research and CEO succession. While he does recognize the idea of strategic leadership as strategically developing leadership across the organization, there is a tendency towards using strategic leadership as shorthand for researching and thinking about leadership at the top of an organization.

Critical Thinking Box 8.1

These ideas expressed by Hambrick (1989) could be challenged in the modern contemporary organization, which can be defined in a more networked and technology driven way. For example, in the modern organization landscape one might challenge the idea that strategic leadership (being used as shorthand for leadership at the top of an organization) is involved in more ambiguity and complexity (or 'wicked problems' as discussed in Chapter 1) or that they are more externally focused than other members of an organization. This suggests a need to develop ideas on strategic leadership that are more dispersed (see Chapter 9) or systemic (discussed later in this chapter).

A similar framework to that of Hambrick picks up on this idea of leadership at differing levels of an organization and tries to differentiate strategic leadership again from other forms of leadership in organizations. Rowe's (2001) distinction of strategic leadership, visionary leadership and managerial leadership suggests that:

- *strategic leadership* is the ability to influence others to voluntarily make decisions that enhance the long-term viability of the organization, while at the same time maintaining its short-term financial viability;
- *visionary leadership* is future-oriented, concerned with risk-taking; control is maintained through socialization and shared norms, values and beliefs;
- *managerial leadership* involves stability and order and focuses on day-to-day activities and is short-term oriented.

Reflective Question 8.2

In relation to Rowe's categories, what instances or experiences of strategic, visionary and managerial leadership have you seen?

There appears to be some empirical evidence for Rowe's model from research conducted using the theory of transformational and transactional leadership by Edwards and Gill (2012). They investigated the perceived effectiveness of transformational and transactional leadership across hierarchical levels in 38 UK manufacturing organizations. They found that while transformational leadership was effective at all levels in these organizations, transactional leadership was shown to be effective only at senior, middle and lower levels. They suggested a diamond shape to describe the variance in the three effectiveness criteria (leadership perceived effectiveness, perceived satisfaction with the leadership and the level to which a person would put in extra effort in response to the manager's leadership behaviour). The model of effectiveness of these behaviours can be seen in Figure 8.1.

As can be seen from Figure 8.1 there are distinct differences at various levels in the organization. For example, at senior, middle and lower levels, there is the need for a mix or transformational and transactional leadership, which may reflect Rowe's 'managerial leadership', whereas at the top and director levels of the organization there is the need only for transformational leadership, which of course has visionary elements and hence could be linked to Rowe's 'visionary leadership'. In addition it appears that Rowe's 'strategic leadership' is best described somewhere between the senior and director

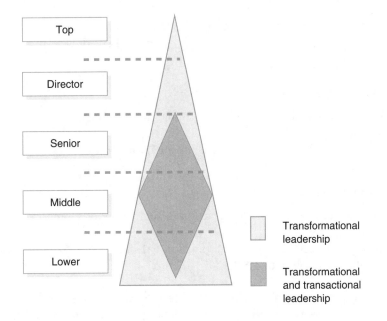

Figure 8.1   Leadership Across Hierarchical Levels

Source: Edwards, G.P. and Gill, R. (2012) Transformational leadership across hierarchical levels in UK manufacturing organizations. *Leadership and Organisation Development Journal*, 33(1): 25–50.

levels in organizations. This would suggest that the idea of strategic leadership being the very top of the organization is questionable, but reflects that interaction and tensions between senior and director levels in organizations are the nature of strategic leadership. This model, however, also leans too much towards a hierarchical explanation of strategic leadership and in reality it is probably more dispersed across an organization and could be similar to ideas around systemic leadership.

In addition, Bolden et al. (2011) seem to take a 'setting the direction' perspective on strategic leadership. Similarly to Rowe (2001) they draw on the work of Achua and Lussier (2010) and suggest that the purpose of strategic leadership is to turn the vision of the organization from the idealistic to the specific via a process of strategy formulation, implementation and evaluation. Leavy and McKiernan (2009) also take a similar view and highlight the following aspects as important in strategic leadership:

- Context – defining the opportunity
- Conviction – fuelling the performance
- Credibility – keeping the stakeholders on board
- Enhancing differentiation – the difference is culture
- Strengthening Corporate Identity – competing for a share of hearts and minds
- Generating a trust premium – promoting inclusive capitalism

Lastly, and most recently, Denis et al. (2011) map out the strategic leadership literature through two frames of reference, each broken down into two further sub-themes.

1. Who strategic leaders are:

    a. strategic leadership as collective cognition (Hambrick, 2007; Hambrick and Mason, 1984);
    b. strategic leadership as individual inspiration (Zaleznik and Kets de Vries, 1975).

2. What strategic leaders do:

    a. strategic leadership as political action (Eisenhardt and Bourgeois, 1988; Pfeffer, 1992a, 1992b);
    b. strategic leadership as social practice (Alvesson and Sveningsson, 2003b; Knights and Willmott, 1992).

This dichotomy is useful in mapping the terrain within the subject of strategic leaders, yet it still sits within the paradigm of strategic leadership and the strategic leader being at the top of organizations. A slightly different view is provided by those who investigate ideas such as systemic leadership (addressed later in this chapter).

> **Reflective Question 8.3**
>
> Reflect on your own organizational experiences: what model(s) of behaviours across organizational levels have you seen?

Criticism of Strategic Leadership Approaches

As we have already seen in this chapter the strategic leadership approach can be criticized for being 'shorthand' for researching and thinking about leadership at the top of organizations and therefore could be described as not contributing much as a topic in itself. There are other criticisms that have been cited in the literature. For example, Bolden et al. (2011) mention the focus on the individual at the expense of more distributed or process ideas of leadership (see Chapter 9). They suggest that strategic leadership is not just the product of the leader but also requires a process of cooperation and a sense of shared values. Bolden and colleagues (2011) also refer to the work of Levy et al. (2003) who suggest a political, power and identity laden process of strategic management in organizations, which is not represented in the leadership literature. There is further work therefore to be done to define strategic leadership as a topic in and of itself as opposed to what seems to be a labelling process of leaders at the top of organizations. To do this some investigation along the lines of Levy et al. (2003) into the identity and political issues incumbent in the strategic leadership process would seem merited.

Systemic Leadership

Beerel (2009) provides a differing and more dispersed perspective (see Chapter 9 for further information regarding distributed and dispersed notions of leadership) on what we might call strategic leadership, that of systemic leadership. Here the leader role is to keep organizations relevant in contemporary climates by being alert to 'new reality' signals from external sources. Beerel goes on to describe systemic leaders as those who ensure that organizations are always an open system by remaining attentive to networks, relationships and patterns in the organizational system. These forms of leaders are also attentive to levels of distress in the system and work with organizational members to diffuse this distress. This view seems to show a more networked version of what we might call strategic leadership and fits with views around leadership as a network (Balkundi and Kilduff, 2006). Although the idea of systemic leadership is intuitively appealing from the sense of a distributed perspective, it is difficult to see how this differs from other notions of leadership (for example, transformational leadership). It still concentrates on identifying *the* leader and the model does not seem to acknowledge organizational issues of power and politics (discussed in Chapter 7). From here the chapter now looks at issues of change in organizations in more detail.

Reflective Question 8.4

Reflect on an organizational change experience and apply this experience to the following models and discussion on leading change: what observations can you make along the way?

VIGNETTE 8.1

Extract from Case Study 4 highlighting strategic leadership and values

For Lucy, values form the bedrock of both leadership and strategy: 'In Winterbourne View, adults with learning disabilities were locked up in large groups and despite charging high fees, the company took the money and failed to deliver personalised support. As the recession began to bite, we had a discussion with our Board in relation to our values given the financial squeeze from government and commissioners. We upheld the fact that we are wholly against the institutional large scale warehousing of vulnerable people, no matter how financially attractive this may be. We are clear that this is against our values. But there is a tension between the amount of money available and the quality of care we want to provide. Despite this our solution cannot be to pile 'em high! Instead we have gone down the line of focusing on developing a service journey that provides highly creative models of individual support, adopting assistive technology where possible and taking on-going action to increase efficiencies and reduce overheads. Our strategy is quite broad based but it has clear principles. We also know that the bottom line for our survival depends on growth and increasing our market share.'

Holding onto core values in a tough market requires taking a firm stand and on the right occasions it also means balancing this with the tension of the reality of the marketplace. In these difficult times being a successful Chief Executive can be hard; in standing up for the people you serve and your employees who directly support them there is always a dialogue going on with stakeholders. And the arguments and the answers are no longer easy. Whether it be paymasters or politicians,

(Continued)

(Continued)

or indeed families and the people with learning disabilities themselves, everyone is seeking quality services but the financial purse strings are always very tight. As Steve put it: 'Values are at the heart of what we do. We are values driven, but we are also a product of the market itself. We won't be standing to present these values if we are inconsistent with the market.'

1. Use this extract to critically reflect on the strategic leadership literature discussed above. To what extend do values underpin the theory of strategic leadership? You may also want to reflect on the theory highlighted in Chapter 13.

Leading Change

Change and leadership have been closely linked by leadership scholars for some time. As we saw in Chapter 1, John Kotter (1990) has described the difference between management and leadership as:

- management produces orderly results which keep things working efficiently;
- leadership creates useful change.

He goes on to suggest that both are needed in organizations, avoiding the issue of denigrating management, also highlighted in Chapter 1. Previous to this work Kotter and Schlesinger (1979) suggested the following techniques for change management, which can also be linked to leadership:

- Education and commitment – Educating people above the change and hence gaining commitment to the change.
- Participation and involvement – Involving people in the change.
- Facilitation and support – Enabling people through change.
- Negotiation and agreement – Negotiating with resistors to change.
- Manipulation and cooptation – Using power and politics to control those involved in the change process.
- Implicit and explicit coercion – Using threats and punishments to control change processes.

Kotter and Schlesinger (1979) do not advocate all these techniques, instead they are observations of processes that occur within organizations. From his later work Kotter (2002) recommends eight steps to successful change in organizations:

1. create a sense of urgency, get people ready to move;
2. develop a guiding team that has trust and emotional commitment;
3. the guiding team then creates uplifting visions and sets of strategies;
4. communication of those visions and strategies;
5. empower people to remove obstacles to people engaging with the vision – give power;
6. create short term wins;
7. keep momentum;
8. make change stick by nurturing a new culture.

While these steps are helpful in tracking change, there are elements that are too simplistic, such as empowering and nurturing a new culture. As is highlighted in Chapter 1 culture is more complex an issue than is given credit by Kotter (2002) in this list.

Using Models of Change to Lead

Lewin (1951) proposed the, now famous, module of change in organizations, that of *unfreezing, changing and refreezing*. This is a simple model but useful to managers and leaders in organizations in (1) tracking where change efforts are in the process and (2) reminding managers and leaders that there are inherent cultural issues in unfreezing and refreezing processes (an issue discussed in more detail in Chapter 10).

Figure 8.2   **The Change Process**

   In addition to Lewin's model there is also the 'coping cycle' (Kübler-Ross, 1969), which helps managers and leaders track the potential emotional impact of change on the people involved. Originally developed to describe the process of bereavement the model tracks a typical emotional journey for those coping with loss. This model is now being used quite extensively in management and leadership development to explain the morale of a person as they shift through a change process. These emotions include denial, anger, bargaining, depression, and acceptance (see Figure 8.3).

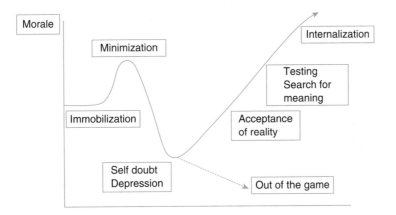

Figure 8.3 **The Coping Cycle**

> **Reflective Question 8.5**
>
> In the models described above what is the role of the leader or leadership? What other theories of change might be useful in developing ideas of leading change?

Change Agents

The idea of change agents came out of the work of Kanter (1984). Kanter developed an idea, similar to systemic leadership (noted above), that managers and leadership of change in organizations do not require formal positions in organizations, and moreover will have certain behaviours or attitudes to change. She suggested the following:

- an ability to work independently, without management power, sanction and support;
- an effective collaborator, able to compete in ways that enhance cooperation;
- the ability to develop high-trust relationships based on high ethical standards;
- self-confidence tempered with humility;
- respect for the process of change as well as the content;
- able to work across business functions and units: 'multi-faceted and ambidextrous';
- a willingness to stake any reward on results and gain satisfaction from success.

Resistance to Change and Failure to Change

An opposite side to looking at leading change is developed by investigating why people resist change efforts and why change efforts fail. For example, Connor (1995) describes the main reasons to the resistance to change as:

1. lack of trust;
2. belief that change is unnecessary;
3. belief that change is not feasible;
4. economic threats;
5. relative high costs;
6. fear of personal failure;
7. loss of status and power;
8. threat to values and ideals;
9. resentment of interference.

This list enables managers to identify certain behavioural and emotional factors in why people resist change, enabling them to respond in an appropriate manner. The model falls short, however, in providing information on how managers and leaders can react to this resistance. Further discussion regarding resistance and framing as a leadership process itself is found in the next section. In addition to this work on the resistance to change Kotter (2007) also highlights the main reasons for a failure in change efforts:

1. not establishing a great enough sense of urgency;
2. not creating a powerful enough guiding coalition;
3. lacking a vision;
4. under-communicating the vision by a factor of 10;
5. not removing obstacles to the new vision;
6. not systematically planning for, and creating, short-term wins;
7. declaring victory too soon;
8. not anchoring changes in the corporation's culture.

Again this is helpful to managers and leaders in organizations as it enables them to focus on what to avoid and what to concentrate on in the leading change process. However, it is difficult to see from this work what is meant by 'failure' – what does it mean to 'fail'? This would need further exploration through case study work.

Critical Thinking Box 8.2

Many of the change models represented in the literature are too linear. This is to enable some form of sense making in regard to issues of change in organizations. However, this linearity also covers over the inherent complexity in change processes in organizations.

Leadership as Resistance to Change

A recent development along the lines of leadership and change appears to be developing that challenges the mainstream view of just connecting leadership with the drive for change. Levay (2010) and Zoller and Fairhurst (2007) both developed ideas around investigating the 'flip side' and looked at leadership in the resistance to change. Levay (2010), for example, investigates through two case studies the role of charismatic leadership in resisting change. They conclude that the idea of the 'charismatic leader' is as much evident in the resistance to change in organizations as it is in the drive for change (which is the prevailing discourse in leadership studies). Zoller and Fairhurst (2007) take a more critical perspective and again challenge leadership being the driving force of change, but also challenge the notion of 'agency' and individualism that is inherently linked to the idea of leading change in organizations. They do not discuss 'leading change' or the 'leadership of resistance', instead they describe resistance as leadership and suggest an approach whereby resistance leadership emerges from dynamic and evolving relationships between resisters, as well as between resistors and their targets. This all happens, they suggest, in particular social and historical contexts. They then go on to suggest relationships or tensions (concepts are mutually dependent and flow into each other) between:

- resistance and reproduction;
- covert and overt resistance;
- individual and collective;
- leader and follower;
- reason and emotion;
- worker and manager;
- discourse and discourse;
- fixed and fluid meaning.

Ultimately, in taking this view, Zoller and Fairhurst (2007) describe the mobilization of collectives and how this is achieved in organizations, which is reminiscent of a distributed leadership approach discussed in Chapter 9.

VIGNETTE 8.2

Extract from Case Study 1 highlighting the use of change models

Adding to this, in March 2012 Space Engineering Services went through an organization-wide restructure, making a 20% reduction in overheads. At the same time the company

(Continued)

(Continued)

had a large (150 engineers) transfer of undertaking (protection of employees) (TUPE) out of the company. The engineering industry is renowned for continuously winning/ losing contracts. With this comes TUPE, where employees who work on that contract are transferred across with the contract to the new supplier. For leaders, this means fresh talent, and it can also mean a diverse mix of capabilities, cultures and work standards. There have been instances where companies have used TUPE to transfer across employees who are not as capable, to ensure they keep a good talent pool in their organization. With all this change and movement, employees were now working in different job roles and for different managers. The completions of performance reviews were stagnant, and mid-year reviews were put on hold.

There was an underlying rumour from employees that morale was extremely low. Despite the amount of change, this didn't seem to be the cause of this change in mood. Instead the reason for the unrest was the lack of communication from management and senior leaders. Employees were on consultation for redundancy, and yet were not being consulted. They were not receiving updates on timeframes, or on changes in the organization such as new job positions. When looking into this problem further, it seems that department leaders were not being told by senior managers about the changes, and so could not update the process or send out communications.

1. Use the change models described in this chapter to analyse and explain the situation here.

Managerial and Organic Views of Leading Change: The Issue of Organizational Becoming

In the leading change literature there are two forms of understanding that appear to be dominant. The first is a 'managerialist' view, which suggests that we can control an organization in a top-down manner. This is reminiscent of the work of Kotter (1990, 2007). A second viewpoint is what we might call a distributed or organic view of leading change in organizations which appears to be advocated by writers and researchers such as Kanter (1984) and Zoller and Fairhurst (2007) and signifies a bottom-up or a collective approach. Neither is necessarily advocated, but both viewpoints should be noted. The issue in either case, however, is how can people can cope with the constantly evolving in organizations, as Tsoukas and Chia highlight:

> … change is inherent in human action, and organizations are sites of continuously evolving human action. (2002: 567)

They go on to suggest that we should treat change as a normal condition of organizational life. This is reminiscent of the old adage – 'change is the only constant'. Nonetheless however, this adage is to extraordinize change, whereas Tsoukas and Chia wish to make it part of our ordinary management, leadership and organizational lives. As they suggest, change is inherent in human action and organizations are sites of continuously evolving human action. Change is part of our everyday lives and organizations are 'in a state of perpetual becoming ...' (Tsoukas and Chia, 2002: 576).

The issue of 'becoming' we will pick up again in Chapter 11, when we discuss the idea of 'leader becoming' (Kempster and Stewart, 2010).

Reflective Question 8.6

Reflect back on the organization change experience we asked you to think about at the beginning of this section. Relate the resistance (Zoller and Fairhurst (2007) and organizational becoming (Tsoukas and Chia, 2002) views to your experiences. Does this notion help make sense of change in organizations? If so why? If not why?

VIGNETTE 8.3

Extract from Case Study 4 looking at change and leadership

In the leadership team they have a phrase in common usage: 'Change is the norm and a key component of our thinking and our expectations.' We see change as a norm, because none of us live in a static world, we live with ambiguity: 'As leaders we expect to be continuously moving forward. It can be exhausting, but it's game on – part of being in the real world. It's much more than just changing the corporate colours, mere appearance. It's about behaviours. We are introducing coaching for all our managers. We believe that everyone is a leader and an innovator, so what does this mean for how we behave? It's how you do your job that is key.'

1. Read this short paragraph and provide a critical perspective on the messages regarding change and leadership.

VIGNETTE 8.4

Extract from Case Study 1 highlighting the importance of an understanding of strategic leadership and change

'When starting the knowledge transfer partnership project, I asked to see the business plan to ensure the HR and project objectives were aligned with the overall strategic direction. However, this was more difficult than originally thought, for the following reasons;

- Long-term strategic direction is challenging to determine.

As the nature of the industry is extremely reactive, long-term planning can be difficult. The strategic direction can change in terms of priorities at a given time.

- Directors were rarely 'seen' by the wider workforce

Although the directors are visible in head office, the directors are not seen in the regional offices or out in the field. There have been comments about asking if the directors care, and even asking what their names are. There is a gap and a disconnection between senior management and front line employees.'

1. Based on the chapter you have just read, what recommendations would you make to top management concerning the issues highlighted above?
2. How might change be affecting workers in this instance and how might leadership help?

Summary

This chapter has investigated the linked notions of strategic leadership and leading change in organizations. First, it highlighted the lack of empirical and theoretical consideration regarding the notion of strategic leadership and suggested three ways in which it appears to be shown in the literature. This is either as leading strategy in an organization, strategically initiating and modelling leadership in organizations, or as a shorthand way of describing research into top management in organizations. The chapter goes on to define leadership in relation to ideas about managerial and visionary leadership, courtesy of Rowe (2001). The chapter also highlighted some empirical evidence to support this definition and distinction. However, it also developed a more critical discussion regarding notions of strategic leadership in which it criticizes these for not considering the impact of power and politics in the leadership process in organizations (see Chapter 7). The chapter offered a discussion on an alternative way of viewing strategic leadership through the notion of systemic leadership, which appears to be a more distributed notion (see also Chapter 9). Finally, it looked at leading change through the work of John Kotter alongside some generic models of change in organizations. The chapter concludes with some critical perspective around leading change through perspectives of the resistance to change and leadership and ideas of organizational and leadership becoming.

Additional Reflection Questions

1. What do you see when you hear strategic leadership?
2. What do you see when you hear strategic leader?
3. How does change manifest itself in organizations?
4. How might we lead or manage change in organizations?
5. What are resistance and resistance leadership?
6. How might we conceptualize 'organizational becoming'?

Case Study Questions

1. Read carefully through Case Studies 1 and 5 where there are discussions on an engineering company and a self-development organization. To what extent is strategic leadership evident? How is it similar or different between these case examples? Which is more effective and why?
2. From Case Study 2, a leadership development programme in Iraq, highlight what level of strategic leadership is being developed. To what extent is this in relation to leading change and what models would be useful in the development programmes and why?
3. Read carefully through Case Study 3 where there is a discussion around management practice. What advice would you give the company on their approach to leading change? What recommendations would you make based on the information within this chapter?
4. Using the change models discussed in this chapter reflect on Case Studies 4 and 6 and identify critical instances and incidents that impact on how change is being led in these organizations. How might ideas on leading resistance and organization becoming be represented in these case examples?

Further Reading

Beerel, A. (2009) *Leadership and Change Management*. London: Sage.

Denis, J., Kisfalvi, V., Langley, A. and Rouleau, L. (2011) Perspectives on strategic leadership. In A. Bryman, D. Collinson, K. Grint, B. Jackson and M. Uhl Bien (eds) *The SAGE Handbook of Leadership*. London: Sage, 71–85.

Hambrick, D.C. (2007) Upper echelons theory: an update. *Academy of Management Review*, 32(3): 334–343.

Leavy, B. and McKiernan, P. (2009) *Strategic Leadership: Governance and Renewal*. London: Palgrave.

Levay, C. (2010) Charismatic leadership in resistance to change. *Leadership Quarterly,* 21: 127–143.

Rowe, W.G. (2001) Creating wealth in organizations: the role of strategic leadership. *Academy of Management Executive*, 15(1): 81–94.

Tsoukas, H. and Chia, R. (2002) On organizational becoming: rethinking organizational change. *Organization Science*, 13: 567–582.

Zoller, H.M. and Fairhurst, G.T. (2007) Resistance leadership: the overlooked potential in critical organization and leadership studies. *Human Relations*, 60(9): 1331–1360.

Distributed Leadership

9

In this chapter we explore the writing and research in the area commonly known as distributed leadership. As we shall see there are a number of differing ways to describe distributed leadership, but holistically this body of work marks a shift from an individualistic focus on the 'leader' towards more widespread notions of leadership and processes of leadership. Within the chapter we will explore how and why distributed leadership has become a popular subject over the last 10 years, we will make a link to community and culture, and, finally, we will explore a methodology for exploring leadership that holds promise for uncovering notions of distributed leadership – the Leaderful Moment – where a snapshot of leadership is taken within definitive contexts.

Chapter Aims

- Introduce and critically discuss concepts of distributed leadership
- Explore the differing views of what distributed leadership represents in organizations
- Critically discuss the link between distributed leadership and concepts of community and culture
- Introduce a methodology for researching and identifying instances of distributed leadership in organizations

What Is Distributed Leadership?

The literature surrounding distributed leadership is not new. As Gronn (2008) suggests, and Leithwood et al. (2009) reiterate, reference to the term distributed leadership was made back in 1954 by C.A. Gibb in the *Handbook of Social Psychology* and further back by Benne and Sheats (1948) who made a reference to the diffusion of leadership functions. Indeed, notions around emergent leadership (as this chapter highlights, sometimes confused as distributed leadership) have also been around for decades (Whyte, 1943). Even the popular notion of transformational leadership (Bass, 1985a, 1998) could be described as being based on notions of emergent leadership as it has no connotations to power based on organizational position. In 2002, however, Peter Gronn suggested that a problem with the majority of leadership theory up until the early 21st century was an assumption regarding a twofold division of labour – leaders and followers – and, therefore, suggested viewing leadership in a much more dispersed sense. He went on (Gronn, 2009b) to describe the idea of distributed leadership as a rallying point for those commentators searching for 'post heroic' leadership alternatives. Ideas around distributed leadership generally suggest that leadership is a widely dispersed activity throughout teams and organizations and that leadership capabilities and the development of these capabilities are needed at all levels within organizations (Bolt, 1999; Charan et al., 2001; Conger and Benjamin, 1999; Khaleelee and Woolf, 1996; Nicholls, 1994; Tichy, 1997). There are a number of ways that the literature portrays distributed (Bolden, 2011; Currie et al., 2009; Edwards, 2011; Gronn, 2002; Oborn et al., 2013; Thorpe et al., 2011) or dispersed leadership (Gordon, 2010), institutional leadership (Askling et al., 2004; Currie et al., 2009; Pasternack et al., 2001; Tikhomirov and Spangler, 2010; Washington et al., 2008), co-leadership (Heenan and Bennis, 2000; Vine et al., 2008), collective leadership (Contractor et al., 2012), shared leadership (Pearce and Conger, 2003; Pearce and Manz 2005; Pearce and Sims, 2000, 2002; Pearce et al., 2008a, 2008b, 2009), multi-directional leadership (Edwards et al., 2002) and rotated leadership (Erez et al., 2002). Although this is indicative of the confusion that surrounds the topic it could also be described as highlighting differing levels of dispersedness. For example, where there is duopoly (co-leadership), wider group involvement (shared leadership) and even an organizational sense of distributed leadership (institutional leadership). Table 9.1 provides further information regarding each differing view of distributed leadership.

With the varied labels to account for distributed leadership comes the issue of definition (Fitzsimons et al., 2011). Bolden et al. have provided a definition, where they suggest that distributed leadership:

> … argues for a less formalized model of leadership where leadership responsibility is dissociated from the organizational hierarchy. It is proposed that individuals at all levels in the organisation and in all roles can exert leadership influence over their colleagues and thus influence the overall direction of the organisation. (2008: 11)

Table 9.1   Perspectives on Distributed Leadership

Label	Description
Distributed	Gronn (2002) describes distributed leadership as a 'unit of analysis' by which one could understand leadership in a more holistic or gestalt sense, moving away from an individual or dualistic (leader/follower) sense.
Dispersed	According to Gordon (2010), dispersed leadership appears to be described as an espoused sharing of power between leadership and followers and represents the distribution of leadership skills and responsibilities throughout an organization.
Institutional	Institutional leadership seems to refer to two aspects. The first is a unifying voice in an organization (e.g. Pasternack et al., 2001; Tikhomirov and Spangler, 2010), or as Pasternack and colleagues call it '... a chorus of diverse voices singing in unison'. The second interpretation appears to derive from the educational and public sector paradigm and describe a particular organization or sector taking the lead (e.g. Askling et al., 2004; Wasserstein et al., 2007).
Co-leadership	According to Vine et al. (2008), co-leadership is described as '... the process by which two leaders in vertically contiguous positions share the responsibilities of leadership'.
Collective	Used by Contractor et al. (2012) in a similar way to distributed or dispersed leadership as way of describing a variety of concepts that take a more holistic approach to the study of leadership. Contractor et al. go on to provide a topology that includes the forms, roles and dynamics of collective leadership.
Shared	Shared leadership is described by Conger et al. (2009) as the sharing of duties, so that the person in charge at any moment in time is the one with the key knowledge, skills and ability for the aspect of the job at hand.
Multi-directional	Described by Edwards et al. (2002) as deriving from the notion of leadership based on personal power (our character, charisma, expertise, etc.), where positional authority has little impact. This form of leadership therefore enables one to have influence in a number of directions in an organization, with our team, peers, customer, clients and our boss. The use of 360-degree questionnaires enables us to glimpse these differing influences at any one time.
Rotated	Rotated leadership refers to the idea of self-managed teams and relies on members of a group stepping forward to carry out leadership functions (Erez et al., 2002). Furthermore, like a jazz band this is a fluid process over the life span of a group or team where different members take turns in performing the leadership role.

This definition, however, appears to negate important considerations of power and politics in organizations (as discussed in Chapter 7). As Leithwood et al. (2009) summarize the definition of distributed leadership is varied, ranging from the normative to the descriptive (Harris, 2004), and the literature remains diverse and broad based (Bennett et al., 2003). Indeed, although the evidence is encouraging with regard to the applicability of distributed leadership in organizations (Harris, 2009b), there is an appreciation that that evidence is mixed (Leithwood et al., 2009) and is largely from one contextual domain – the education sector. Leithwood et al. (2009) are rightly unsurprised about this broad range of understanding especially given the highly contested nature of leadership (in that it is difficult to agree on a single definition or conceptualization of leadership) in general (Grint, 2000).

Extract from Case Study 5 highlighting an example of distributed leadership

June considers the idea of leadership as shared, something everyone has responsibility for: '... this role of leader ... I am questioning whether this word works at all ... leading into a world where people lead themselves and everyone is a leader ... and being a manager means everyone has their own bit of leadership ... in some ways the Pierian Centre did put that level of responsibility out there ... for example when I was away I said to people "you have my absolute backing to make a decision if needed, because it's not fair to encourage and then say you can't make decisions ... you know you have my unadulterated support ... it may be that they make mistakes and we have a debrief and learn from it ... if people are given that level of responsibility and treated as if it's their own business then they are much more likely to make a good decision" ... I can't think of a single occasion where people made a horrendous decision ... sometimes they made innocent decisions, where they didn't have sufficient information ... I never had to really call someone on major decisions unless they really didn't get the fundamental philosophy underlying what we did ... there were one or two people who really didn't get it and I had to sit them down ... I think that happened twice ...'

1. To what extent is this distributed or dispersed leadership? To what extent does this example relate to the different perspectives highlighted in Table 9.1?
2. How is decision making related to leadership in this example? To what extent is this developed in theories and frameworks of distributed leadership?

Theories and Frameworks of Distributed Leadership

Despite these concerns there appear to be a number of categorical or typological approaches to gaining a better understanding of distributed leadership in organizations. One is that put forward by Gronn in 2002, where he suggested two forms of thinking about leadership in a distributed or dispersed sense:

- aggregated pattern of distributed leadership (for example, a pool of leaders);
- holistic pattern of distributed leadership (for example, the whole has a unique structural entity that acts back on the parts).

In parallel, Pearce and colleagues (Pearce and Conger, 2003; Pearce and Manz, 2005; Pearce and Sims, 2000, 2002; Pearce et al., 2008a, 2008b, 2009) highlight the idea of *shared leadership.* Shared leadership suggests a more positional perspective than distributed leadership where leaders are seen in a number of differing leadership positions in groups (Fitzsimons et al., 2011). Other categorical accounts have been given by Gosling et al. (2009) as *Descriptive, Corrective, Empowering and Rhetorical.* Also cited are Gronn's (2009a, 2011) idea of *leadership configurations,* Leithwood et al.'s (2009) idea of *patterns of distributed leadership* and Spillane's (2006) ideas of distributed leadership by *Design, Default and Crisis.* In a recent special issue (Thorpe et al., 2011) on the subject, these notions were reviewed and developed. For example, there are further links to community (Edwards, 2011) (discussed further below alongside issues of culture and to distributed leadership), to the small business context (Cope et al., 2011) and to the health sector (Currie and Lockett, 2011). These explorations in differing contexts are important given that most studies and theoretical considerations of distributed leadership have been in the education sector (Currie et al., 2009; Gosling et al., 2009; Harris, 2008, 2009a, 2009b; Leithwood et al., 2009; Spillane, 2006; Thurston and Clift, 1996). Despite these developments, one might argue that distributed leadership is not a new concept.

VIGNETTE 9.2

Extract from Case Study 1 highlighting an example of distributed leadership

Space Engineering Services engineers are primarily remote, working either solely or in pairs. They see their line manager perhaps once a month as the core communication is on the telephone. Engineers also do not have access to E-mail, and so any company-wide communication is sent via post. After initial focus groups and interviews, it was found that the engineers' morale was generally low. They believed that senior management did not care, and they were always the last to find out core company decisions that would directly affect them.

1. How might this be conceptualized as distributed leadership?
2. What advantages and disadvantages are created by working and leading remotely?

Reflective Question 9.1

Think of an organization, either one from your own experience or one in the press. How might concepts of distributed leadership work in this organization?

Distributed Leadership, Culture and Community

Edwards (2011) has highlighted the idea of community as a framework for developing ideas around distributed leadership, suggesting a more context rich and cultural approach to understanding leadership. Edwards draws attention to various perspectives on community, such as symbolism (Cohen, 1985), a sense of belonging (Delanty, 2003), a sense of community (Hyde and Chavis 2007; McMillan and Chavis, 1986), individualism (Delanty, 2003; Lichterman, 1996), community as communicative (Delanty, 2003), language (Habermas, 1984, 1987), friendship (Delanty, 2003; Phal, 2001) and liminality (Turner, 1969; Van Gennep, 1960). Edwards (2011) goes on to hold a discussion around ideas of the postmodern community (Agamben, 1993; Blanchot, 1988; Corlett, 1989; Maffesoli, 1996; Nancy, 1991) that suggests we need to think about leadership from a multiple identity and multiple belonging perspective. Finally, Edwards highlights the need to consider distributed leadership in relation to notions of space and place (Low and Lawrence-Zúñiga, 2003) and 'virtual' communities that are technologically mediated (Bateman Driskell and Lyon, 2002; Castells, 2001; Jones, 1995; Rheingold, 1993; Shields, 1996; Smith and Kollock, 1999). The links to concepts of distributed leadership and the research implications are summarized in Table 9.2. There are criticisms of the notion of community, which must be recognized. For example, Touraine (1995, 1997) suggests that notions of community are closely aligned with nationalism and that the notion of community may have been debased by nationalism (Delanty, 2003). In addition, Bauman (2001) suggests that notions of community tend towards the nostalgic or utopian. While community may be able to give one a broader notion of leadership and hence distributed leadership one must not forget the boundary effects of community; while some are included in a community others are excluded. This raises a question regarding the true nature of inclusivity in the idea of distributed leadership in itself, a concept which appears, on the surface, to suggest a more inclusive notion of leadership.

Reflective Question 9.2

How might leadership be described in these more community-oriented ways? For example, think about leadership in groups of friends or virtual groups, and note what leadership might be for these circumstances.

Critical Thinking Box 9.1

Distributed leadership is too idealistic. It will never truly work in organizations owing to the fascination with heroic individual leaders. Critically explore these statements.

Table 9.2   Concepts of Community, Distributed Leadership and Research Implications

Concept of community	Link to distributed leadership	Research implications
Symbolism	Relates through the aesthetic; sees distributed leadership as represented by the symbolic construction of boundaries.	Calls for an aesthetic form of methodology. For example, using the 'leaderful moment' method highlighted by Wood and Ladkin (2008).
Sense of belonging	Suggests a co-constructed mutual sense of belonging based on cultural connections.	Could be investigated through methodologies that develop an understanding of a connective sense of belonging. Calls for a methodology that develops a group-based inquiry over time; could also involve observation-based data.
Sense of community	Would be based on a mutual sense of a supportive network of relationships (relates to a sense of belonging).	Could use frameworks such as membership, influence, integration and fulfilment of needs and shared emotional connection (McMillan and Charvis, 1986). Because related to a sense of belonging, could usefully explore parallels and differences between the two.
Individualism	Brings out the tension between a shared sense of identity and individual self-identity.	Could use co-produced auto-ethnographic forms of research (similar to Kempster and Stewart's (2010) research on leadership development). Could explore how these tensions materialize in the construction of self in relation to context.
Community as communicative	Involves understanding distributed leadership from the perspective of common values, ethics and morals.	Co-produced auto-ethnographic forms of research would highlight tensions between individually held beliefs and how these inter-relate with contextual group norms (there is an overlap here with ethical leadership research).
Language	Notion of distributed leadership as bounded by language, discourse and dialect.	Understanding how leadership is conceptualized within and through differing languages and for different contexts to uncover latent constructs. Qualitative investigation based on word usage, meaning and enactment.
Liminality	Suggests that notions of distributed leadership may be virtual, contextually bound, fluid and shifting based on ideas of space and place.	Ethnographic to enable an understanding of leadership situated in context and time. Could be centred on specific tasks or projects in organizations to gain a sense of the shifting and rotating basis of leadership. Artistic or aesthetic forms of data collection could help to represent the fluidity of distributed leadership by giving research participants a broader scope to explore interpretations of leadership.
Friendship	Suggests an informal notion of distributed leadership linked to social networks.	An ethnographic approach might make it possible to uncover social networks within organizations and the impact on how decisions are made or not made. Demands an ability to 'go behind the scenes' of the formal organizational structure to uncover underlying social and friendship networks. Need to collect data within and outside the organization in more social settings (e.g. Sturdy et al., 2006).
The Postmodern Community	Highlights distributed leadership as inter-connected and multi-distributed; individuals are members of a number of differing forms of distributed leadership based on emotional connections.	Implications from all other concepts could be relevant here, as the issues of community, in the context of postmodernity, apply throughout.

Source: Edwards, G.P. (2011) Concepts of community: a framework for contextualising distributed leadership. *International Journal of Management Reviews*, 13(3): 308.

VIGNETTE 9.3

Extract from Case Study 5 highlighting an example of distributed leadership and community

The Centre was based in a five-storey Georgian building in Grade I listed Portland Square which June lovingly transformed from a state of neglect to dignified splendour. Number 27 was lucky to have retained many of its original features – and delegates and visitors were greeted by a working environment filled with the aesthetic and spiritual ethos of the Enlightenment. From the 20 ft well in the basement to the conical lantern that crowns the spiralling staircase, the building radiates a deep and productive calm. But the Pierian Centre was never a museum, it was a 21st-century working building used for practical purposes by people from every walk of life. During Bristol's Doors Open Day when unusual private buildings are open to the public, the Centre received between 300 and 600 visitors every year!

The Centre attracted a wide range of people, from blue-chip management teams to community groups, musicians, healers and voice coaches. From June's first involvement with the Zimbabwean community and Refugee Week in 2005, the Centre steadily expanded the role it played in the wider life of Bristol. Bells Unbound in 2007 was a global event (Antarctica to Zimbabwe), marking the 200th anniversary of the Abolition of the Slave Trade. The next year the Centre hung 17 four-metre high banners of Tom Stoddart's photo-journalism on Platform 5 at Temple Meads station – and the 2009 Anne Frank [+ you} exhibition at Bristol Cathedral was a breakthrough in terms of partnerships and collaboration.

The Centre became a Community Interest Company (CIC) in 2008, and the first CIC to be awarded the Social Enterprise Mark. It was appointed lead project partner for Bristol's response to EY2010: the European Year for Combating Poverty and Social Exclusion. Events included the community art installation Portents, filling College Green with 49 tents each printed with artwork by groups and individuals from across Bristol. June considers the Centre's crowning achievement to be the launch of Bristol as a City of Sanctuary – the culmination of 4 years' work that saw 750 people fill the Council House, College Green and Bristol Cathedral with passion, laughter and dancing blue brollies, with care expressed for those without a country or home.

1. Reflect back on the section on distributed leadership and community. How might this extract be linked to the perspectives developed by Edwards (2011)?

The Leaderful Moment

As first introduced in Chapter 5 and linked to Raelin's idea of 'leaderful practice' (Raelin, 2004), the Leaderful Moment (Wood and Ladkin, 2008) concept suggests a methodology for studying leadership that has resonance with ideas around distributed leadership. As with distributed leadership the idea of leaderful moment moves away from the individual leader or even the dyadic relationship and concentrates more on frames of leadership as an unfolding emergent process. The argument is that this gives a richer appreciation of the role played by context, culture, history and geography. The idea is to frame leadership as an event and use photographs and film to explore parallel existing frames of leadership in context. There is an exercise below that will help students to create this notion and therefore discuss frames of leadership that are from a distributed perspective.

VIGNETTE 9.4

Extract from Case Study 4 highlighting an example of distributed leadership

In the Chief Executive's view communication is central: clarity, and an honest and constant dialogue. Brandon Trust uses social media effectively. For example, people who are supported by Brandon's service contribute to the Brandon weekly blog, as do front line staff right through to the top team. This is bottom-up communication rather than top-down. Brandon holds large forum events for the people who use their services, but this is not consultation. These forums are used to drive strategy – 'these 100 voices shape strategy'. The Brandon Trust is constantly innovating because its starting point is its 'customers'. As Lucy Hurst-Brown states with real passion: 'The only point of being here is to serve the people we support.'

1. Reflect back on the chapter and use the various theories and frameworks to critically examine this extract from a distributed leadership perspective. How might this be conceptualized as distributed leadership? What advantages and limitations do you observe?

Summary

This chapter has explored a number of differing perspectives on what we might call distributed leadership, such as dispersed, instutional, collectice, shared, multi-directional, rotated and co-leadership. It has also looked at the historical context of the notion and how it has been revived over the past 10 years to become a prominent area for theory, research and reflection. The chapter has also taken a community perspective on distributed leadership and suggested differing frames with which to explore the notion – symbolism, sense of belonging, sense of community, individualism, language, liminality and friendship. The chapter also reflected on notions of the virtual community and on leadership in the increasingly virtual-driven world of remote working. Lastly, the chapter highlighted the idea of developing distributed leadership in a more contextual, cultural and community sense and promoted the use of 'Leaderful Moment' methodology to discover notions of distributed leadership.

Additional Reflection Questions

1. What is distributed leadership? Think of examples from your managerial and/or organizational experience.
2. Why has distributed leadership gained ground in the literature over the last 10 years?
3. How might differing notions of distributed leadership (for example, shared, multi-directional, institutional, dispersed, rotated and so on) compare and contrast to each other?
4. How might culture be linked to ideas of distributed leadership?
5. How might leadership be influenced by remote working and the virtual community?
6. Use 'the leaderful moment' exercise to reflect on the question of where is leadership?

Case Study Questions

1. Read carefully through Case Study 1 where there is a discussion about an engineering company. To what extent can you identify differing forms of distributed leadership in practice (co-leadership, shared leadership, multi-directional leadership and rotated leadership)?
2. From Case Study 2, a leadership development programme in Iraq, highlight what skills are being developed for leadership. To what extent is distributed leadership a factor in the development process?
3. Read carefully through Case Study 3 where there is a discussion around management practice. Relate the discussion in the papers by Bolden (2011) and Gordon (2010) to this case study. To what extent do they relate to the experiences of the managers involved?
4. Read carefully through Case Studies 4, 5 and 6. To what extent can we see these examples as 'leaderful moments'? If so, why? If not, why not? Critically reflect on your learning from considering these case examples as leaderful moments.

Further Reading

Bolden, R. (2011) Distributed leadership in organisations: a review of theory and research. *International Journal of Management Reviews*, 13(3): 251–269.

Contractor, N.S., DeChurch, L.A., Carson, J., Carter, D.R. and Keegan, B. (2012) The topology of collective leadership. *Leadership Quarterly*, 23: 994–1011.

Edwards, G.P. (2011) Concepts of community: a framework for contextualising distributed leadership. *International Journal of Management Reviews*, 13(3): 301–312.

Gordon, R.D. (2010) Dispersed leadership: exploring the impact of antecedent forms of power using a communicative framework. *Management Communication Quarterly*, 24: 260–287.

Gronn, P. (2011) Hybrid configurations of leadership. In A. Bryman, D. Collinson, K. Grint, B. Jackson and M. Uhl-Bien (eds) *The SAGE Handbook of Leadership*. London: Sage, 437–454.

Harris, A. (ed.) (2009) *Distributed Leadership: Different Perspectives*. London: Routledge.

Leithwood, K., Mascall, B. and Strauss, T. (2009) *Distributed Leadership According to the Evidence*. New York: Routledge.

Thorpe, R., Gold, J. and Lawler, J. (2011) Locating distributed leadership. *International Journal of Management Reviews*, 13(3): 239–250.

Wood, M. and Ladkin, D. (2008) The event's the thing: brief encounters with the leaderful moment. In K. Turnbull-James and J. Collins (eds) *Leadership Perspectives*. Basingstoke: Palgrave, 15–28.

Leadership and Culture

10

In this chapter we look at leadership as a cultural activity and therefore explore what culture is, how leadership is linked to culture and what different types of culture may be relevant for the study of leadership. We first discuss the link between organizational culture and leadership in recognition of Schein's contributions in this area as well as Alvesson's more critical views. We then go on to review the benefits of two fundamentally different approaches to studying leadership across regional cultures – the etic and emic – and their representation in and relevance for the wider leadership literature. Against this background, we then discuss the GLOBE project as the most successful example of etic cross-cultural research and counter-balance this section with recent critical reviews of the GLOBE project and the wordliness perspective as an example of research taking an emic approach to studying leadership in different regional cultures.

Chapter Aims

- Introduce and critically discuss the link between organizational culture and leadership
- Explore the difference between emic and etic approaches to studying leadership in different regional cultures

- Critically discuss the link between societal culture and leadership drawing on etic and emic studies
- Introduce worldly leadership as an emic approach to cultural leadership studies

What is Culture and Why is it Relevant for Leadership?

At the most basic level, culture has been identified as 'the glue' that binds together a group of people (Martin and Meyerson, 1988). Other definitions are more explicit about a culture's nature and development: a shared set of values, beliefs, attitudes and basic assumptions on reality and the group itself that has developed through interaction and exposure to specific problems and challenges as well as successes (Schein, 2004). These basic assumptions, values and beliefs are further manifest in the group's artefacts such as traditions, rituals, myths, jokes and stories. Membership of a culture is achieved through adaptation and integration of the group's set of values and beliefs into the self and can arguably be traced through focusing on shared meaning embedded in conversations. Becoming a member takes time and it is difficult to ascertain when this moment is reached as a culture is never fixed but constantly evolving. Schein (2004) argues that culture pervades everything in the group and is set deep in the individual's subconscious. When truly ingrained, the norms and values of a culture are defining the shared sense of belonging within a group and then have a stabilizing effect on the group as they are acting as a deep-set enforcement mechanism of behaviours aligned with the culture. This shared sense of belonging further provides meaning of the group, the self in the group and the group's outlook on reality as such. It is not static but has evolved through the group's history and is continuously evolving through current and future new experiences and reinterpretations of the shared set of assumptions within a given group (Schein, 2004). New members as well as existing members will through interaction with each other and the environment contribute to these subtle or radical changes in the existing culture.

The Link Between Culture and Leadership

Culture and leadership are hence both processes that take place and evolve within a group setting. There is an abundance of both culture and leadership definitions and various different approaches to studying the two phenomena separately as well as their link. Depending on which type of culture we are looking at there will be different links identified in the literature between the two concepts. National culture and leadership have, for example, often been linked through the lens of implicit leadership theories whereas occupational and organizational cultures may be more closely identified with Schein's model of culture. This chapter will explore in detail the different approaches to culture and leadership as well as their link in different contexts.

VIGNETTE 10.1

Extract from Case Study 2 highlighting the importance of understanding culture in creating an appropriate leadership development programme

The role of a group leader in Iraqi culture is quite different from the western model. It is essential to understand and acknowledge this, consulting the group leader for all important decisions and briefing them ahead of modules and key activities. Sometimes the dialogue is solely with the group leader – with others listening in or occasionally contributing. There is much more collaboration and less competition in an Iraqi (Deans') group compared to an English (Principals') group. Deans search for 'the wisdom' in tasks, lectures and even ice-breaker exercises. And this is seen as a function of the group rather than the individual take-away it would be in the UK. Feedback flows differently in an Iraqi group. It firstly depends on the level of trust present (as in the UK) but even in high trust groups it defaults to a discussion of the positives and avoids anything which might be seen as negative. This protects the 'face' of the hearers or facilitators. Reframing developmental feedback to 'it would be even better if …' could sometimes help. The quality of feedback was also in inverse proportion to group size – small groups worked better than large ones, pairs better still, and one-to-one feedback from the tutor gave the greatest scope for a discussion of 'negatively perceived' issues, subject always to obtaining the permission of the hearer and watching closely for non-verbal reactions which might indicate psychological distress from feedback.

1. Reflect on how this role of group leader differs from or is similar to your own experiences with group leadership.

Alvesson's (1993) book on 'cultural perspectives on organizations' provides a detailed and insightful overview of a number of different approaches to studying and conceptualizing culture in organizations as such. For the purpose of this chapter, it is worthwhile picking up on a specific part of these wider approaches that represent a fundamental divide in the perceived importance and role of leadership in relation to culture: seeing culture as a variable or as a root metaphor (Smircich, 1983). Seeing culture as a variable within organizations further leads us to the basic assumption that this variable is manageable and ought to be managed in order to align employees' behaviours and attitudes with the dominant corporate culture. In connection with this approach to culture, leaders throughout the organization have been given the key role of cultural change agents and cultural enforcers, creating, maintaining and changing organizational cultures to improve their overall performance (Schein, 2004). We will critically explore this view of leadership and organizational culture further below with reference to Schein's work.

In contrast, seeing culture as a root metaphor draws on anthropological views of culture (Geertz, 1973) and subsequently approaches organizations as naturally evolving and unmanageable cultures in their own right and as systems of 'common symbols and meanings' (Alvesson, 2011: 153). Focusing on organizations through this latter cultural lens means to explore the symbolic in organizations and organizational life as a 'subjective experience' (Smircich, 1983) that does not 'exist in people's heads but somewhere between the heads' and through interactions within a group (Alvesson, 2011: 153). Leadership is equally seen as a symbolic activity, engaging in sense and meaning making (Smircich and Morgan, 1982). In the rest of this chapter, we elaborate on these different approaches to studying culture further and the differences this brings in how we think about culture in relation to leadership.

Different Types of Culture

As a group phenomenon and in its essence as a shared sense of belonging, a culture may exist in all kinds of format at different levels of society. An individual is hence linked with a diverse mix of cultures as he/she will naturally be part of various different groups and share their specific sense of belonging. These different group memberships may vary in their importance for the individual's own value set and will change over time (Jepson, 2009b). Types of culture that have received the most attention through research into leadership are organizational cultures and national or societal cultures.

Yet, we also need to recognize that there are many cultures beyond these two types and that there may further be variation within each dominant culture, also known as counter- or sub-cultures. Some of the less explored yet potentially important types of cultures for leadership are, for example, occupational ones that may span across different organizations and potentially across societies (Jepson, 2009a). These occupational cultures may lead to sub- or counter-cultures of the main organizational one and are usually reinforced through professional bodies and member-specific events, hence becoming more or less important for the individual's set of values depending on the context and situation the individual finds him/herself in at a specific moment in time. Within societies, not enough attention has been paid to regional diversity and the overlap of the national or societal culture with other dominant cultures.

Relatively under-explored in relation to leadership is also the nature of individual value-sets of a leader and of a group of followers. To what extent can we assume unity in value sets among all followers within a group interacting with a leader? Some approaches seem to expect complete unity in leader–follower expectations while others recognize that there may be more variation and fluidity for both individual leaders and followers at all levels of a given culture. Below, we will explore further the two most prominent fields of leadership research into culture: the organizational and the national/ societal. We will further explore with reference to the national/societal level notions of unity or variation within cultures and interaction with other possible dominant cultures.

Reflective Question 10.1

What different cultures do you belong to (for example, regional, professional, organizational, religious)? Which of these is/are the most important culture(s) for you and who you are? Is your answer the same now as it was 5 years ago?

Organizational Culture and Leadership

The existing literature on the role of leadership in organizational culture has been especially influenced by Schein's seminal book *Organizational Culture and Leadership* and can further be connected to the multitude of existing autobiographies and biographies of chief executive officers (CEOs), such as that of Lee Iacocca as CEO of Chrysler in the 1980s, who have become known as major culture change agents in the past (Trice and Beyer, 1993). Alvesson (2011) has further contributed to a more critical review of the link between leadership and organizational culture in *The SAGE Handbook of Leadership*, which we will turn to after a discussion of Schein's work.

A Model of Organizational Culture

In his model of organizational culture, Schein (2004) explores the different levels of a culture and the extent to which each culture is unique, complex and rooted in taken-for-granted assumptions shared by members of that culture. Schein's model (illustrated opposite) explicitly recognizes the unconscious elements of a culture and its constantly evolving nature as the membership of cultures change and sub-cultures may be formed. Yet, Schein also acknowledges the more concrete behavioural, attitudinal consequences of the abstract, unconscious concept of culture. He focuses his work on leadership on how leaders may – through their consistent engagement with artefacts at the most superficial level of a culture – change behaviours and attitudes over time. This may then over an even longer period of time change the culture at the deepest, most unconscious level as the changed behaviours, attitudes and values become taken-for-granted and form a revised set of basic assumptions on reality and relationships within the culture. Schein's work on organizational culture and leadership hence treats culture as something that is to some extent manageable (although slowly) and consequently attributes a key role to leaders at the top and role models throughout the organization. His model of cultural levels may also help in

Table 10.1   Schein on Key Leadership Roles

Culture creation through founder: the individual's view of the world drives the beliefs, values and assumptions of the organization through the initial vision, member selection and processes. If it leads to success, members adopt this view through ongoing learning experiences. Eventually it develops into a culture on its own.

Cultural embedding at all leadership levels (taken from Schein, 2004: 246):

Primary embedding mechanisms

- What leaders pay attention to, measure, and control on a regular basis
- How leaders react to critical incidents and organizational crises
- How leaders allocate resources
- Deliberate role modelling, teaching and coaching
- How leaders allocate rewards and status
- How leaders recruit, select, promote and excommunicate

Secondary embedding mechanisms

- Organizational design and structure
- Organizational systems and procedures
- Rites and rituals of the organization
- Design of physical space, façades and buildings
- Stories about important events and people
- Formal statements of organizational philosophy, creeds and charters

understanding further the cultural roots of organizational conflict and disagreement, where observable, seemingly 'irrational' behaviour or resistance and misinterpretations of leaders' actions and communication may be seen as manifestations of different or clashing values sets and basic assumptions. Through such exploration, Schein's work may enable leaders to be able to work proactively with understanding and possibly changing such cultural distances.

Leadership and Culture Management

More specifically, Schein sees leadership and culture as essentially entwined concepts where 'On the one hand, cultural norms define how a given nation or organization will define leadership … On the other hand, it can be argued that the only thing of real importance that leaders do is to create and manage culture; that the unique talent of leaders is their ability to understand and work with culture; and that it is the ultimate act of leadership to destroy culture when it is viewed as dysfunctional' (2004: 11). It is therefore leaders who design and identify new organizational cultures and align the organization's processes to promote and enforce this new organizational culture, while it is the role of management and administration to work within existing cultures. The type of leaders you need for this ranges from the charismatic founders,

CEOs or managing directors, who act both as engineers and role models of a specific organizational culture, down to the line managers who again role model and measure their subordinates against the set values of the organizational culture. A summary of the various roles of leaders in creating, embedding, transmitting and changing organizational cultures can be found in Table 10.1. Schein (2004: 11) critically acknowledges that the impact of leaders may not be absolute as culture is 'the result of a complex learning process' and hence only partially influenced by a leader's actions and behaviour. This also recognizes the likelihood that sub-cultures develop over time, where a group of people within the organization develop a different set of values from that of the corporate culture. These sub-cultures may be enhancing the corporate culture (that is, extreme adherence to corporate culture), exist in addition to but not in conflict with the corporate culture or indeed form a counter-culture that resists the corporate culture (Martin and Siehl, 1983). These limitations of cultural management and the role of leaders will be further explored in the next section.

VIGNETTE 10.2

Extract from Case Study 4 highlighting the complexities of and challenges for culture management

For Lucy, values form the bedrock of both leadership and strategy: 'In Winterbourne View, adults with learning disabilities were locked up in large groups and despite charging high fees, the company took the money and failed to deliver personalised support. As the recession began to bite, we had a discussion with our Board in relation to our values given the financial squeeze from government and commissioners. We upheld the fact that we are wholly against the institutional large scale warehousing of vulnerable people, no matter how financially attractive this may be. We are clear that this is against our values. But there is a tension between the amount of money available and the quality of care we want to provide. Despite this our solution cannot be to pile 'em high! Instead we have gone down the line of focusing on developing a service journey that provides highly creative models of individual support, adopting assistive technology where possible and taking on-going action to increase efficiencies and reduce overheads. Our strategy is quite broad based but it has clear principles. We also know that the bottom line for our survival depends on growth and increasing our market share.' Holding onto core values in a tough market requires taking a firm stand and on the right occasions it also means balancing this with the tension of the reality of the marketplace. In these difficult times

(Continued)

(Continued)

being a successful Chief Executive can be hard; standing up for the people you serve and your employees who directly support them, there is always a dialogue going on with stakeholders. And the arguments and the answers are no longer easy ... everyone is seeking quality services but the financial purse strings are always very tight. As Steve put it: 'Values are at the heart of what we do. We are values driven, but we are also a product of the market itself. We won't be standing to present these values if we are inconsistent with the market. We have both our soft and hard hats on! Taking a tough stand can also mean deciding with the Board of Trustees where to draw the line. Lucy responded to a suggestion that Brandon compromise its stance by saying "She would rather stack shelves"'

1. What are the key challenges for Lucy – the CEO – of the Brandon Trust in her attempt to maintain a specific culture within the company?

A Critical View on Leadership and Cultural Management

The idea of culture management dates back to the 1980s and has further been embedded in values-based leadership theories, such as transformational leadership. Yet opinions have since been divided between scholars exploring and fine-tuning the task of culture management and the role of the leader and those who view culture as something quite uncontrollable. The latter group of scholars can be associated with Alvesson's (2011) recent critical review of culture and leadership studies as well as Ladkin's (2010) and Smircich and Morgan's (1982) exploration of the complex task of meaning making that leaders engage with on an ongoing basis. Alvesson (2011) voices concerns with the leader-centric approach taken by Schein and related publications and suggests that the cultural context within which a leader is working is far more complex, shifting and outside that leader's control. He stresses that followers' views, values and behaviours 'are hardly only or mainly formed by their boss but by societal, industrial, occupational, generational cultures, by the material work situation, by group interactions etc.' (Alvesson, 2011: 154).

In line with a Geertzian approach to culture, Alvesson (2011) further stresses the symbolic nature of leadership and the relational influence of a leader within and on a group's sense-making process of reality and their culture. Followers look instinctively to their leader for active sense-making of the here and now as well as the future and the past (Smircich and Morgan, 1982). This is subconsciously done by looking at the leader's every move, action, conversation and so on as a symbolic manifestation of the underlying basic assumptions and values of the leader and

Table 10.2   **The Role of Leaders**

Schein: Leaders as cultural change agents	Smircich and Morgan: Leaders as meaning-makers
• Leaders as engineers of strong organizational cultures	• Leaders as co-creators of organizational cultures through symbolic activities
• Leaders embed and reinforce through practices and procedures of the existing culture	• Leaders are influenced by an existing culture and influence the culture through social interactions with followers
• Leaders challenge and change the culture through vision, practices and procedures	

subsequently of the wider organization. With regard to a leader's role, this could then also be associated with conscious efforts to shape followers' values, ideals and attitudes. Such 'cultural orientation' could then be seen as the essence of leadership and leadership as such as essentially cultural (Alvesson, 2011). Any changes in the organization and wider environment need to be communicated and made sense of at such a local level and through the leader's conscious meaning making this effort may lead to subtle or stark differences in interpretation of an organizational culture. It is crucial, however, to recognize the limits of such conscious efforts and the far more complex nature of individual followers' value sets and their socially constructed and evolving nature as alluded to above by Alvesson (2011). Other sociological approaches to studying the link between leadership and organizational culture are, for example, the study of leadership as local cultural understandings, that is, variations in leadership may be seen as reflecting wider local cultural patterns of values and belief sets, as well as the influence organizational cultures may have on the form, nature and meaning of leadership itself, that is, leadership as a cultural outcome (Alvesson, 2011: 158).

Reflective Question 10.2

Think about your own organizational experiences and managers you have known. How does your experience relate to the different views on the role of leaders in culture management expressed in Table 10.2? What role have leaders taken?

Social Identity Theory, Culture and Leadership

There is some overlap between the latter view on the influence of organizational cultures on leadership itself and the notions of social categorization (Turner, 1987, 1991) and social identity (Haslam, 2004) as introduced in Chapter 5. To briefly recap, at an individual and group level, leaders as well as followers are always members of different social groups and categories. Group membership is associated with a common characteristic, value/belief or identity that all members of the group share. Boundaries of groups may hence be drawn explicitly – such as departments or project groups in organizations – or implicitly through mutual recognition of members as a group. A leader and all the followers will naturally belong to a multitude of groups, yet the specific context they are in and task they face may trigger a stronger affiliation to one group rather than another and this will change over time.

Haslam (2004: 45) has argued that 'leadership is intimately bound up with the shared concerns of followers' and 'issues relating to the social identity that they share' where the leader's central concern is not only one of embracing the shared social identity but also one of shaping and defining said social identity. A leader who is prototypical of the group's shared social identity is more likely to be accepted and his/her decisions supported. A new leader will need to adjust to and find out what a group's value set is in order to be accepted by the group as a legitimate and trustworthy leader and may only over time be able to work on changing said value set. As the group's shared social identity may not always align with the organization's, it could further be seen to be the leader's role is to nurture a group's shared value set that does align with the organization. Yet, Alvesson (2011: 160) stresses that this social identity view is too focused on the personal, individual level and does not – unlike culture – take into consideration the 'broader and richer understanding of socially shared meaning, beliefs and values of followers' at a group level.

Approaches to Studying National/Societal Culture and Leadership

The dominant focus of leadership textbooks and indeed research projects has been on the national/societal level. This has been further enhanced through two distinctly different yet closely connected recent phenomena: the GLOBE project and the worldliness perspective. These two developments in the literature represent two ends of the methodological spectrum and conceptual thinking on leadership and national/societal culture: the etic and the emic.

Etic Research on Societal Culture and Leadership

Etic research has been dominant throughout the 20th century and can be indentified with the dominant approach of cross-cultural leadership. It is characterized by psychologically-based, large-scale, cross-country/societal questionnaire research that has been largely informed by the use of leadership styles as pre-determined categories of effective leadership behaviour. It has been driven by international teams of researchers working with leadership models originally developed and tested in the USA, seeking to compare the applicability of these models and styles across different countries and cultures (Guthey and Jackson, 2011).

Etic research: studying certain characteristics or phenomena across various cultures, for example, finding universal leadership behaviours or comparing the effectiveness of specific leadership styles across cultures.

This type of research has approached national/societal culture in line with Hofstede's (1980) original cross-cultural work (see Table 10.3) and looked at the existence of measurable culture dimensions that distinguish one country's/society's culture from another. It therefore also shares Hofstede's assumptions on culture as 'the collective programming of the mind which distinguishes the members of one group or category from another' (1991: 5) and that national culture is the earliest and most determinable cultural identity affecting individuals' behaviours. Through the use of questionnaires, this type of research has then been able to link culture and leadership by showing what type of culture prefers what type of leadership style. This approach to studying leadership across cultures has been very successful and has provided us with insights into the possible links between the two phenomena as well as reliable data on different leadership preferences in different countries that can be used for culture sensitivity training in organizations. The next section of this chapter will review the GLOBE project in its role as the largest and most successful cross-cultural leadership research project to date.

Critical Thinking Box 10.1

The Hofstedian approach to cultural research assumes stable membership of a specific culture. Yet, individuals nowadays often do not stay in the country and culture they have grown up in but move on to study, work and live in other cultures throughout their lives. This challenges the assumption that an individual belongs to a single culture. Instead, we need to see cultural membership as multiple and changing over time. An individual can hence belong to different cultural groups at any point in time and any of these cultural groups may be more or less important over time.

Emic Research on Societal Culture and Leadership

Emic research: studying a phenomenon within its local context and through the lens of natives of the local culture, e.g. in-depth studies of relevance, form and meaning of leadership in a local culture.

Alongside but also recently in reaction to limitations of this etic approach, we have seen the existence and development of an emic approach to studying leadership across cultures. This emic approach is drawing on anthropological methods of ethnographies, observations and in-depth interviews to engage with people's understanding and interpretations of culture and is hence more closely aligned with the root metaphor approach to culture as it treats culture as complex, naturally evolving and uncontrollable. This type of research is concerned with the symbolic in language – what is said and what is taken for granted – as well as behaviours and attitudes as these will carry meaning that has been and is socially constructed within

Table 10.3   **Hofstede's Cultural Dimensions**

Hofstede's cultural dimensions (taken from www.geert-hofstede.com):

Power distance = extent to which the less powerful members of organizations and institutions (like the family) accept and expect that power is distributed unequally. This represents inequality (more versus less), but defined from below, not from above. It suggests that a society's level of inequality is endorsed by the followers as much as by the leaders. Power and inequality, of course, are extremely fundamental facts of any society and anybody with some international experience will be aware that 'all societies are unequal, but some are more unequal than others'.

Individualism = on the one side versus its opposite, collectivism, that is the degree to which individuals are integrated into groups. On the individualist side we find societies in which the ties between individuals are loose: everyone is expected to look after him/herself and his/her immediate family. On the collectivist side, we find societies in which people from birth onwards are integrated into strong, cohesive in-groups, often extended families (with uncles, aunts and grandparents) which continue protecting them in exchange for unquestioning loyalty. The word 'collectivism' in this sense has no political meaning: it refers to the group, not to the state. Again, the issue addressed by this dimension is an extremely fundamental one, regarding all societies in the world.

Masculinity = versus its opposite, femininity, refers to the distribution of roles between the genders which is another fundamental issue for any society to which a range of solutions are found. The IBM studies revealed that (a) women's values differ less among societies than men's values; (b) men's values from one country to another contain a dimension from very assertive and competitive and maximally different from women's values on the one side, to modest and caring and similar to women's values on the other. The assertive pole has been called 'masculine' and the modest, caring pole 'feminine'. The women in feminine countries have the same modest, caring values as the men; in the masculine countries they are somewhat assertive and competitive, but not as much as the men, so that these countries show a gap between men's values and women's values.

Uncertainty avoidance = deals with a society's tolerance for uncertainty and ambiguity; it ultimately refers to man's search for Truth. It indicates to what extent a culture programs its members to feel either uncomfortable or comfortable in unstructured situations. Unstructured situations are novel, unknown, surprising, different from usual. Uncertainty avoiding cultures try to minimize the possibility of such situations by strict laws and rules, safety and security measures, and on the philosophical and religious level by a belief in absolute Truth; 'there can only be one Truth and we have it'. People in uncertainty avoiding countries are also more emotional, and motivated by inner nervous energy. The opposite type, uncertainty accepting cultures, are more tolerant of opinions that are different from what they are used to; they try to have as few rules as possible, and on the philosophical and religious level they are relativist and allow many currents to flow side by side. People within these cultures are more phlegmatic and contemplative, and not expected by their environment to express emotions.

Long-term orientation = versus short-term orientation: this fifth dimension was found in a study among students in 23 countries around the world, using a questionnaire designed by Chinese scholars It can be said to deal with Virtue regardless of Truth. Values associated with Long Term Orientation are thrift and perseverance; values associated with Short Term Orientation are respect for tradition, fulfilling social obligations, and protecting one's 'face'. Both the positively and the negatively rated values of this dimension are found in the teachings of Confucius, the most influential Chinese philosopher who lived around 500 BC; however, the dimension also applies to countries without a Confucian heritage.

the specific culture and will shape, make sense of and reinterpret the existing culture on an ongoing basis. Notions of effective leadership are seen from this perspective as subjective, changing and socially constructed. Studying leadership as a phenomenon within a given culture and from within the culture, that is, giving voice to the culture-specific language, behaviour and attitudes in depth will be a key focus of this approach.

Understanding leadership across cultures is hence less about comparisons of similarities and differences and more about a greater focus on the culture-specific and allowing for possible bridges and links between cultures. Membership of a culture and the importance of a culture are seen as less stable and individual leaders and followers may therefore change in their view on and enactment of leadership over time as well. The outcomes of this type of research are arguably of great importance and can possibly be seen as providing essential complementary insights into effective leadership within and across culture on top of the cross-cultural leadership outputs. More critical views may suggest that where etic approaches can be seen to be perpetuating stereotypes, emic approaches are working against stereotypes and giving voice to minorities and diversity within cultures.

Reflective Question 10.3

Think about a culture you belong to. How could you use an etic or an emic approach to analyse this culture? How would either approach help you to understand this culture, explain it to somebody else and compare it with another culture?

The GLOBE Project

Aim of GLOBE: To determine the extent to which the practices and values of business leadership are universal (that is, are similar globally), and the extent to which they are specific to just a few societies).

The GLOBE (Global Leadership and Organizational Behaviour Effectiveness) project constitutes a major contribution to the field of cross-cultural leadership studies. It is to date the largest research project of its kind and has not only triggered a new wave of interest in the subject but due to its size and rigorous methodological approach has also been the most successful project in providing supporting evidence for the very link between leadership and culture. The published results of the GLOBE project show a clear indication of culture-specific preferences for effective leadership and existing culture-specific differences in leadership practices. They further show evidence that certain leadership attributes and behaviours are universally desired or alternatively seen as undesirable. The GLOBE findings have therefore supported other existing studies in the field (see Dorfman, 2004, for review) as well as enhanced our understanding of cross-cultural differences in leadership practices and preferences on a global scale. A detailed description of the study itself, its methodology, scale and all detailed findings, can be found in *Leadership, Culture and Organizations: The GLOBE Study of 62 Societies* by House et al. (2004) as well as in country-specific journal publications. We will therefore only discuss the key facts and figures and illustrate some of the findings as a taster for the overall project and its approach to studying leadership across countries.

The Empirical Research

The GLOBE project and its worldwide team of 170 scholars have been led by Robert House in the USA since 1993. It represents the largest etic study to date and deployed a standardized questionnaire approach (House et al., 2004) that was later supplemented by a smaller scale qualitative research project (see Chhokar, 2007). The actual sample size of the original questionnaire-based data set covered 62 societies and 17,000 middle managers from 951 organizations in three industries: financial services, food processing and telecommunications services. The 62 societies were roughly in line with official country borders apart from three countries where two regions within the countries were treated as separate societies (for example, South Africa, Germany and Switzerland). The questionnaire itself was influenced partly by Hofstede's work on cultures yet the culture dimensions (see Table 10.4) used in the GLOBE project have been significantly improved as a construct and research method on Hofstede's original design, including separate measures for current societal practice (as is) and societal value (as should be). A detailed discussion of the limitations of Hofstede's work and the GLOBE project is provided on pages 199–202 in this chapter.

The link between leadership and societal culture was based on the assumptions of the implicit leadership theory and value-belief theory, seeking to find the essential

Table 10.4 GLOBE's Cultural Dimensions

Culture dimension	Definition
Uncertainty avoidance	Extent to which members of an organization or society strive to avoid uncertainty by relying on established social norms, rituals and bureaucratic practices.
Power distance	Degree to which members of an organization or society expect and agree that power should be stratified and concentrated at higher levels of an organization or government.
Institutional collectivism	Degree to which organization and societal institutional practices encourage and reward the collective distribution of resources and collective actions.
In-group collectivism	Degree to which individuals express pride, loyalty and cohesiveness in their organizations or families.
Gender egalitarianism	Degree to which an organization or society minimizes gender role differences while promoting gender equality.
Assertiveness	Degree to which individuals in organizations or societies are assertive, confrontational and aggressive in social relationships.
Future orientation	Degree to which individuals in organizations or societies engage in future-oriented behaviours such as planning, investing in the future and delaying individual or collective gratification.
Performance orientation	Degree to which an organization or society encourages and rewards group members for performance improvement and excellence.
Humane orientation	Degree to which individuals in organizations or society encourage and reward individuals for being fair, altruistic, friendly, generous, caring and kind to others.

leadership characteristics and attributes that are seen as prototypical for effective leadership within a specific culture (Guthey and Jackson, 2011). In line with Hofstede's approach to culture, the GLOBE project hence treated culture also to be the determining factor of what is seen as prototypical of effective leadership and if a leader in a culture does not share these prototypical characteristics, then he/she is unlikely to be accepted or followed. Similar to other cross-cultural leadership studies, the GLOBE team developed six global leadership behaviours (listed in Table 10.5). These global leadership behaviours were used alongside the cultural dimensions in a questionnaire to (1) support the link between culture and leadership as suggested by implicit leadership theories and to (2) be able to identify what is seen as effective leadership behaviour in different societies/cultures. Written first in English, the questionnaire was then carefully translated and back-translated by specialists in each country to ensure its validity and reliability. The findings were again back-translated and largely communicated in English through the above-mentioned academic outlets.

Table 10.5   **GLOBE's Leadership Prototypes**

Prototype	Definition
Charismatic/value based	Visionary, inspirational, self-sacrificial, integrity, decisive, performance oriented
Team oriented	Team collaborative, team integrator, diplomatic, malevolent (reversed), administrative
Self-protective	Self-centred, status consciousness, conflict inducer, face saver, procedural
Participative	Autocratic (reversed), participative, egalitarian, delegator
Humane orientation	Humane orientation, modesty
Autonomous	Individualistic, independent, autonomous, unique

Key Findings

The findings showed, similar to Hofstede's work, country-specific differences in the culture dimensions included in the study. They further showed that quite a few countries could be grouped together according to their culture dimensions and the GLOBE data subsequently revealed 10 different culture clusters with 3–10 countries within each cluster (see Table 10.6). Leadership style preferences were found to be linked to these culture clusters and we can therefore see cluster-specific as well as country-specific trends and results in this vast data set.

To exemplify the GLOBE findings with regard to cultural practices and leadership preferences, Tables 10.7 and 10.8, respectively, compare three clusters – Anglo, Middle East and Latin America – according to their culture and leadership style GLOBE ratings. Focusing here on the Anglo cluster as an example, we can see from Table 10.7 how the Anglo cluster is characterized by medium results for uncertainty avoidance, power distance, gender egalitarinism, assertiveness, future orientation and human orientations. Of notable difference is the Anglo cluster's low scores for in-group collectivism and its high score for performance orientation. These value scores for the Anglo cluster can then be linked to the leadership preferences as summarized in Table 10.8. The relatively high ratings for charismatic, autonomous and participative leadership styles can arguably be associated with the relatively high values score on performance orientation, whereas a medium score for team orientation may reflect the low values score for in-group collectivism. The GLOBE project questionnaire also contained 112 leadership items/attributes and the findings revealed 22 universally desirable and 8 undesirable leadership attributes summarized in Table 10.9.

There have been a multitude of follow-up publications focusing on single cluster results or comparisons of different cluster results that have contextualized these general findings further with regard to cultural practices and leadership preferences within specific clusters.

Table 10.6 GLOBE's Culture Clusters

Confucian Asia	Southern Asia	Middle East	Nordic Europe
Singapore	Philippines	Turkey	Denmark
Hong Kong	Indonesia	Kuwait	Finland
Taiwan	Malaysia	Egypt	Sweden
China	India	Morocco	
South Korea	Thailand	Quatar	
Japan	Iran		
Anglo	**Germanic Europe**	**Latin Europe**	**Sub-Saharan Africa**
USA	Austria	Israel	Zimbabwe
Australia	The Netherlands	Italy	Namibia
Ireland	Switzerland	Switzerland	Zambia
England	Germany-East	Spain	Nigeria
South Africa	Germany-West	Portugal	South Africa
New Zealand		France	
Eastern Europe	**Latin America**		
Greece	Ecuador		
Hungary	El Salvador		
Albania	Colombia		
Slovenia	Bolivia		
Poland	Brazil		
Russia	Guatemala		
Georgia	Argentinia		
Kazakhstan	Costa Rica		
	Venezuela		
	Mexico		

Table 10.7   **An Example**

Value dimensions	Cluster ratings		
	High	Mid	Low
Uncertainty avoidance		Anglo	Middle East, Latin America
Power distance		Anglo, Middle East, Latin America	
Institutional collectivism		Anglo, Middle East	Latin America
In-group collectivism	Middle East	Latin America	Anglo
Gender egalitarianism		Anglo, Latin America	Middle East
Assertiveness		Anglo, Middle East, Latin America	
Future orientation		Anglo	Middle East, Latin America
Performance orientation	Anglo	Middle East	Latin America
Humane orientation		Anglo, Middle East, Latin America	

Table 10.8   **An Example**

Leadership styles	Cluster ratings		
	High	Mid	Low
Charismatic/value based	Anglo, Latin America		Middle East
Team oriented	Latin America	Anglo	Middle East
Self-protective	Middle East	Latin America	Anglo
Participative	Anglo	Latin America	Middle East
Humane orientation	Anglo	Latin America, Middle East	
Autonomous	Anglo, Middle East, Latin America		

Table 10.9   **Universal leadership attributes**

Universally desired leadership attributes:	Universally undesirable leadership attributes:
Trustworthy, Just, Foresight, Positive, Plans ahead, Dynamic, Confidence Builder, Motivational, Intelligent, Decisive, Win-win problem-solver, Communicative, Administrative skilled, Coordinator, Excellence oriented, Honest, Encouraging, Motive arouser, Dependable, Effective bargainer, Informed, Team builder	Loner, Irritable, Ruthless, Asocial, Nonexplicit, Dictatorial, Noncoooperative, Egocentric

Reflective Question 10.4

Using the GLOBE project findings, what can you learn about your own values and preferences for leadership styles based on your cultural background?

Critical Evaluation of the GLOBE Project

Alongside the continuing contributions of the cross-cultural leadership field, we have also seen similar criticism emerging regarding the GLOBE project (Graen, 2006; Guthey and Jackson, 2011; Jepson, 2009b) as has been voiced on Hofstede's dimension approach to culture (Ailon, 2008; McSweeney, 2002; Tayeb, 2001). Both streams of critique centre on:

- the limitations of the simplistic conceptualizations of culture that Hofstede and the GLOBE project have adopted;
- the resulting misrepresentations of specific cultures through this etic, cross-cultural approach and its negative implications on the perpetuation of stereotypes (Clausen, 2010);
- the lack of truly representative sampling and the oversampling of middle manager;
- the questionnaire as an inferior methodological tool for cultural studies and generally explorative studies and its ignorance of the symbolic, cultural meaning carried by language.

Guthey and Jackson (2011) highlight the deterministic approach to leadership that these dominant cross-cultural studies take as they explore how national culture shapes leadership behaviours – hence treating leadership as passive and ignoring the dynamics of leadership and the two-way nature of the influence relationship between leadership and culture.

It is important at this point to pause and direct readers to the robust responses that Hofstede (2002, 2009) has provided to the critiques introduced above as well as the GLOBE project's wider publications that equally challenge the criticisms highlighted here. Recognizing these responses we will now focus more explicitly on the critiques as these are often marginalized in standard texts on leadership and culture.

Pitfalls of Simplistic Conceptualizations and Measures of Culture

The first set of criticisms introduced above challenges the predominant focus of cross-cultural research studies, such as the GLOBE project, on the use of culture dimensions/categories, rather than a holistic, anthropological study of culture. Jepson (2009a) argues that this has led to a fundamentally simplistic conceptualization and measure of culture as it takes a static approach to culture, ignoring its evolving and ever changing nature. Through its assumption that culture dimensions/categories are core, systemically causal, territorial unique and shared (Graen, 2006; McSweeney, 2002) studies like the GLOBE project assume that the culture-specific characteristics found will apply to a whole society. Tayeb (2001) and others have highlighted that this ignores the variation within cultures (for example, regions, religions and so on) and the importance of other contexts on an individual's value set and behaviours. Jepson (2009b) has further argued that these studies also seem to conflate the individual with the societal level of analysis, making deterministic claims about the importance of national culture that ignore the potentially more important influence of other cultural contexts. Finally, the minimalist approach of culture dimensions (Tayeb, 2001) embraced by studies like the GLOBE project has been criticized for not providing information about national/societal cultures from a historical, institutional and linguistic perspective, hence limiting the outsider's understanding of how a culture has evolved, what it is today and how it is further changing (Jepson, 2009b). Clausen (2010) warns that this approach therefore leads to a perpetuation of national stereotypes and differences between countries. Instead Clausen (2010) suggests, we should be concerned with breaking down these stereotypes of cultures and recognize similarities in leadership practices and challenges across the globe that may be rooted in alternative but equally important contexts from the national one.

Limitations of the Methodological Approach

A further set of criticism targets the methodological approach of etic studies. Jepson (2009b) posts that, despite some of the GLOBE project's exploratory aims, it has failed to truly investigate how and to what extent national culture influences leadership preferences and leadership behaviours. Through its predominant use of quantitative questionnaire tools, the GLOBE project has hence only been able to successfully achieve its explanatory aims of discovering universally desired and culture-specific leadership behaviours. Bryman's (2011) recent review of research methods in leadership studies and Conger's (1998) critique of the use of standardized questionnaires in leadership research can be used to address further key limitations of quantitative cross-cultural research. Based on abstract models of reality and simplistic behavioural and values-based categories, the standardized questionnaire tool fails to capture the contextual complexity and evolving nature of cultures and leadership behaviour within these. It can only focus on the individual level and therefore ignores the interactional nature of leadership as well as the interactions and influences of varying contexts on leadership and on each other (Jepson, 2009b). Jepson (2009b) argues that cross-cultural research such as the GLOBE project that is unable to explore dynamic, evolving interactions between societal culture, other contexts and leadership may hence be wrongly attributing leadership behaviours and leadership preferences of individuals to the national context, that is, confusing different levels of analysis.

Implications of Treating Language as a Neutral Tool

A third key major concern voiced especially by Jepson (2009b) as well as Graen (2006) is linked with the above two strands of criticism and focuses on the use of language within cross-cultural research studies and its problematic implications. The GLOBE project, like other quantitative survey-based studies, has despite careful translations and back-translations of the questionnaire tool fundamentally ignored the possible language-specific meanings of cultural values and leadership styles across different languages as it has analysed the results at face value. They have hence treated language as a neutral device for studying leadership differences and preferences across countries. Yet, Tayeb (2001) and Tietze et al. (2003) stress the important role of language as a cultural voice and other scholars (Alvesson and Skoldberg, 2000; Van Maanen, 1979; Wittgenstein, 1953) have further argued that language as a transmitter of meaning is a product of historical, social interaction that is hence unique and specific to individuals and social groups. Questionnaires that are focused on robust, reliable, standardized measurements of links between predefined leadership styles and cultural dimensions are fundamentally incapable of taking into account such varied meanings and are hence through their design likely to under- or misrepresent the nationally specific meaning assigned to specific leadership behaviours. The GLOBE questionnaire, for example, was originally written in the English language and hence took the existence of leadership and management within an organizational context as taken-for-granted. Yet, in other languages such as German, Italian or Spanish, the equivalent word for 'leader' is unavailable owing to its specific historical connotations, for example, the German word *Führer* is closely linked to Hitler and the Nazi atrocities in the Second World War. Any attempts to provide equivalent translations will inevitably change the associated meaning with the term leader in an organizational context. If translated back into English, this local meaning is lost. We will further explore these language-specific differences in meaning and the existence of equivalent words to manager and leader in Chapter 14.

Ailon (2008) in his critique of Hofstede's original questionnaire-driven design of cultural dimensions adds that the use of standardized questionnaires not only neutralizes language but also silences other language and meanings than the one the results are published in. He adds that due to the cultural meaning imbued in the language the questionnaire is originally written in, it is from the start value-laden rather than scientifically neutral. With regard to the GLOBE project, we therefore need to also take into consideration the importance of the English language and its role as a cultural voice as it is this language that the GLOBE questionnaire tool was designed in and in which subsequent findings have been published. The leadership and cultural measures are hence biased towards western values embedded within the English language and potentially silencing rather than empowering other values embedded in other languages. As the results have been back translated and evaluated within the English language, they certainly do not take into consideration possible alternative culturally embedded meanings of individual participants, which means that the results as they are currently published may be misrepresenting the participants' own view on culture and leadership. Jepson (2010) supports this possible limitation of the GLOBE findings through her research into the importance of national language as a cultural voice and its influence on an individual's ability to talk about, think about and enact leadership. She stresses that different languages may have quite different culturally and historically embedded words and indeed not all languages have an equivalent word for manager or leader.

There may hence be more accurate words and culturally important meanings in other languages in relation to leadership that the GLOBE project was never able to tap into due to its questionnaire design. We will look into the importance of language in greater detail in Chapter 14 and discuss some of these issues further. Finally, Guthey and Jackson (2011) further call into question the extent to which the 22 positive universal attributes and the eight negative universal attributes identified by the GLOBE findings can really have a universally shared meaning and suggest that attributes such as integrity or ruthlessness are indeed likely to carry very specific cultural as well as local, individual meanings that may change over time and depending on the context an individual is facing.

Reflective Question 10.5

The previous reflective question asked you to explore your own culture(s) using the GLOBE research results. How satisfying did you find this experience? If you experienced any difficulty with your initial cultural analysis, did any of the critical reflections in this section help you to understand these limitations in your cultural analysis?

An Alternative Approach to Studying Societal Culture and Leadership

In light of these limitations of the dominant approach taken in cross-cultural leadership studies, there have been some suggestions towards alternative approaches to studying leadership within and across different cultures. Guthey and Jackson (2011) point towards studies such as Henry and Pene (2001), Jones (2005), Prince (2006) and Warner and Grint (2006) that have taken an emic approach and studied specific cultures from within and explored the notion of leadership within this analysis. The last section of this chapter will discuss the worldliness perspective as a recent move aiming to give further voice to such alternative approaches. Here we would like to introduce the approach taking by Jepson (2009b) in her work on leadership as an initial example of an alternative framing of research into different cultures. The 'dynamic approach' she proposes takes a social constructionist approach to leadership and looks at it as an outcome of social interaction between individuals and contexts. Taking this approach is argued to overcome the above problems of minimalism, overly objectivist assumptions and a static nature as it embraces 'greater sensitivity to contextual factors and flexibility to explore unexpected phenomena or symbolic dimensions of leadership in different countries' (Jepson, 2009b: 68). This dynamic, interactional approach was inspired by Ailon-Souday and Kunda's (2003) work on national identity, which stressed that individuals are free to define what national belonging means and that their national identity is a fluid and changing social construct.

Extract from Case Study 2 illustrating the multiple important cultural influences and their interactions

Every opportunity was taken to honour the heritage of Iraq by making links to its culture and history. The oldest known writing in the world is a Sumerian clay tablet found near Babylon, which contains a leadership parable making this the oldest recorded leadership wisdom. Erbil – where we were delivering – has the oldest continuously inhabited settlement in the world. We were working with people from the land of great biblical figures such as Noah, Abraham and Daniel.

We had intriguing discussions about the Qur'an and the role of faith in leadership. Spirituality is an inseparable part of Iraqi life and leadership. The five calls to prayer reminded us of this daily. Iraq's isolation under sanctions had decayed the research skills of participants and independent study was made harder due to the loss of so much of the country's infrastructure. Information resources, libraries and internet access were patchy and unreliable. Power cuts were a daily occurrence. Verbal story telling was a natural teaching medium for our Iraqi friends. This was very useful whenever our modern technology decided not to work!

The Deans had grown up in a leadership culture which was command and control, underpinned by patriarchy with tribal affiliations. Most had learned to keep their opinions to themselves to avoid trouble or personal disaster. Those with prior western contact demonstrated more subtle leadership styles. Our pilot group were mainly engineers and scientists typically educated to PhD level. Their academic curiosity allowed them to make new connections out of seemingly disparate leadership models.

1. What different cultures seem to influence the participants in this leadership development programme?
2. Reflect on the strengths and challenges of emic and etic approaches to researching into the cultural roots of these participants.

Jepson (2009b) stresses that similarly national cultures are social constructs that are fluid and changing over time and are indeed interacting with other contexts such as the immediate social and wider institutional or occupational ones. Individuals' changing value sets and preferred or displayed leadership behaviours can hence be seen to be an outcome of interacting contexts over time, with the national context not always being the most important or determining one. Jepson's (2009b) dynamic approach to studying leadership across different countries therefore stresses the active, dynamic element in culture and leadership and stresses that individual leaders and followers actively draw on different value sets in different contexts over time. That they are not only being influenced by the cultures they are part of but also influence the extent to which any such culture and its associated value set is important for the leader's sense-making and behaviour at any point in time. Subsequently, it becomes important to recognize the multicultural nature of leadership and followership and to avoid over-emphasizing the importance of any one specific culture (for example, national, organization) over the lifetime of an individual.

The Worldliness Perspective

The Worldly Mindset

In this final section of the chapter, we would like to introduce readers to a more recent stream of leadership research that has been associated with the term 'worldliness' and has been more widely connected to Gosling and Mintzberg's (2003) publication on the 'five mind sets of a manager'. The original contribution by Gosling and Mintzberg (2003) discussed more widely how a manager today must draw on different mindsets and intelligences to be successful in a complex world filled with conflicting and confusing demands, facing more often wicked, complex problems rather than simple, rational ones. The worldly mindset was identified to be one of these needed mindsets and focused particularly on a manager's ability to manage the context through being aware of his/her own value set, ethical code, religious beliefs and those of others around him/her.

The worldly mindset went beyond stereotypes and was clearly concerned with the individual and understanding in depth the individual's background, presence and future in order to understand their behaviours and actions in context. Managers were held to 'become worldly when their feet are planted firmly on the ground of eclectic experience' (Gosling and Mintzberg, 2003: 59). This also clearly distinguishes the worldly view from 'global views of leadership' as the latter is more concerned with generalizations of management practices and the blurring of differences rather than paying attention to specific conditions, behaviours and consequences and celebrating a plurality of views. Links can be drawn and will be explored further between this work and that around authenticity, ethics and sustainability in leadership covered in Chapter 13.

VIGNETTE 10.4

Two extracts from Case Study 5 illustrating the active use of a worldly mindset

'If you look at the Pierian centre ... the whole place was based on the belief that everyone in the world is remarkable ... the whole place was there to support people in discovering how remarkable they are ... we delivered inspiration or support and that people knew they were cared about ... this is distinctly lacking in the world ... I try and do it wherever I am ... relate to whoever is there ... we live in a disjointed and an unrelated world and we need to connect with people.

You have to earn it in my world, by living and being the best that we can be. For some people that may be minimal because its restricted, by the world you are born into. For example if you are born into a refugee camp and there is no food and no teachers and little water and you are living on the verge of death, you are just trying to survive the circumstances into which you have been put, but that doesn't mean they are not still trying their best to be their best ... The mothers are still raising their children and when they can't milk them any longer it's not because they are bad mothers. There's a real sense for me that that deserves as much respect as someone working really hard in a 9-5 job and looking after their team and producing good quality work We don't seem to have that real sense of equality (in this world)'.

1. Reflect on how and to what extent the two quotes above by June Burrough can be seen as illustrating a worldly mindset.
2. How is cultural context and its importance for organizations and leadership expressed?

Research into Worldly Leadership

Gosling and Mintzberg (2003: 59) encouraged managers to develop their worldly mindset through 'immersion in the strange context'. The last five years have seen immersion in other contexts through an influx of connected contributions to the field of leadership studies that are in one way or another associated with the worldliness perspective and tend to embrace an emic approach to studying culture and leadership. This new wave of research can also be linked to (1) the increasingly dominant critical voices on cross-cultural approaches to leadership outlined above and (2) leadership as such, stressing the extent to which dominant leadership discourses have been predominantly western, masculine and individually oriented (see for example, Ford et al., 2008; Jepson, 2010;

Western, 2008) and hence have silenced other cultural voices and views on the relevance and nature of leadership. This recent wave may also be a reaction to recent problems of ethical and sustainable leadership in western countries and organizations, a topic explored further in Chapter 13. A quest for answers to western leadership problem and dilemmas in other cultures is hence part of this new wave of research as are the breaking down of clear, distinct national borders and the increasingly popular idea of the global leader and global mindset (Beechler and Javidan, 2007) that is required in a world where leaders and followers may be at home in many countries and not easily allocated to just one culture. The worldliness perspective has found several outlets, such as research streams at conferences, books and more practitioner-oriented conferences and pro-grammes. Turnbull et al. (2011)'s book on worldly leadership is an example of such publications as it not only includes chapters considering the different lenses on worldli-ness in general but also gives voice to a number of locally situated, emic studies of leadership in various different cultures such as those of Russia, Turkey, UAE and Ghana.

Critical Views of the Worldly Perspectives on Leadership

While such outlets are serving a significant purpose of encouraging other voices to be heard, other languages to be empowered and some of the longstanding western con-cepts of leadership to be challenged, there remains a risk that we embark on another holy grail mission to find alternative definitive wisdoms on leadership. In light of the critical reflections throughout this chapter on culture and leadership and the dangers of taking western concepts and imposing them on other cultures, we must equally be careful not to take alternative wisdoms at face value and try to transfer them into western contexts. Instead the future of cultural leadership studies needs to celebrate a more emic, anthropological approach to culture – exploring it as a thick description of the complex meaningful web of values and morals that relate the members of a specific culture (Geertz, 1973) – as well as help us to understand leadership in greater depth across the globe. There may be transferable lessons to be learned but those should be second to the goal of reducing false stereotypes through rigorous research.

Summary

This chapter has explored the link between leadership and organization and societal culture in depth and breadth. It has also highlighted the importance of recognizing the diversity of different cultures that a leader is part of and linked into apart from the organizational and national/societal one. We have discussed Schein (2004) and Alvesson's (2011) work on organizational culture and the role of leadership in cultural management, including the opportunities as well as the limitations that a leader faces. In the global, interconnected environment that leaders work in today, it is also important to recognize the influence of societal/national culture on leadership. Research into this type of culture has largely taken one of two different approaches: an etic approach as demonstrated by the GLOBE project or an emic approach as represented by the wordliness perspective (Turnbull et al., 2011). We have explored the difference between these two approaches and illustrated their achievements through details on the GLOBE project, worldliness perspective and their respective strengths and limitations. In summary, etic studies such as the GLOBE project have provided valuable data that support the assumption that national culture does influence individuals' leadership behaviours and preferences. However, these studies can be criticized for treating culture as too simplistic and leadership as too passive. Their findings may hence suffer from an overgeneralization and if used as a sole insight into a specific culture may lead to a perpetuation of culture stereotypes as well as possible misinterpretations of a culture. Emic studies and the wordliness perspective have through their anthropological approach to studying culture and leadership tried to overcome these limitations as they avoid generalizations and focus on the specific, in-depth, local cultural insights. They hence attempt to give voice to local cultures and languages to uncover meaning and work against stereotypes and misinterpretations. Nonetheless, these emic studies may be seen of lesser value for leadership development programmes due to their inability and opposition to generalize beyond the small data sets studied. With a view to these different approaches to culture and leadership as highlighted in this chapter, it can be concluded that leadership is indeed a cultural activity (Jackson and Parry, 2008) at multiple levels, for example, group, organizational, occupational, societal and so on, and it continues to be an important task for leaders in practice, as well as leadership scholars, to explore to what extent leaders are affected by and do influence cultural beliefs and values at these multiple levels.

Additional Reflection Questions

1. What is culture? What is the link between culture and leadership?
2. To what extent can leaders influence the culture of a group or organization they are leading? How would they do this?
3. What type of culture is the most important one for leaders to take into consideration and why? Under what circumstances?
4. What is the difference between emic and etic approaches to studying cultures? What lessons can we learn from this for leaders leading multicultural teams?
5. Think about your own cultural values and beliefs. What are they? Where do they come from and how do they affect what you see as effective leadership?
6. Think about your national origin and compare yourself to the culture dimensions and leadership style that the GLOBE project identified as determining for the cluster you belong to according to national origin. Do you agree? Does this align with your answer to question 5?
7. To what extent are leadership characteristics truly universal? Can you name a leader who would be equally effective and popular all around the globe? What does that mean for leadership development within globally operating organizations?

8. What is the difference between global leadership and worldly leadership? What is the significance of either of these for leaders in organizations?

Case Study Questions

1. Case Study 1 focuses on engineers as a specific employee group within the organization. Use the information provided in Case Study 1 to analyse the extent to which engineers form a sub-culture within the organization and its implications for leadership.
2. Case Study 6 outlines a strategic organizational change. Drawing on Schein's model or organizational culture and Alvesson's critique, critically evaluate the importance and role of cultural management within this change project. What advice would you give the CEO leading this change project in relation to organizational culture?
3. Explore different cultural influences on the leadership development programme described in Case Study 2, for example, professional, industry, societal, religious and so on. Discuss their importance in relation to the articles by Ailon (2008) and Jepson (2009b) in the further reading list.
4. The worldliness perspective encourages in-depth research that helps to understand the importance and nature of leadership in other cultures. Analyse and provide a detailed picture of the Iraqi culture and leadership within this culture, drawing on Case Study 2 and any other information that you can find.

Further Reading

Ailon, G. (2008) Mirror, mirror on the wall: *Culture's consequences* in a value-test of its own design. *Academy of Management Review*, 33(4): 885–904.

Alvesson, M. (2011) Leadership and organizational culture. In A. Bryman, D. Collinson, K. Grint, B. Jackson and M. Uhl-Bien (eds) *The SAGE Handbook of Leadership*. London: Sage, 151–164.

Gosling, J. and Mintzberg, H. (2003) The five minds of a manager. *Harvard Business Review*, 81(11): 54–63.

Guthey, E. and Jackson, B. (2011) Cross-cultural leadership revisited. In A. Bryman, D. Collinson, K. Grint, B. Jackson and M. Uhl-Bien (eds) *The SAGE Handbook of Leadership*. London: Sage, 165–178.

House, R.J., Hanges, P.J., Javidan, M., Dorfman, P.W. and Gupta, V. (eds) (2004) *Leadership, Culture and Organizations: The GLOBE Study of 62 Societies*. London: Sage.

Jepson, D. (2009) Studying leadership at cross-country level: a critical analysis. *Leadership*, 5(1): 61–80.

Schein, E.H. (2004) *Organizational Culture and Leadership*, third edition. San Francisco, CA: John Wiley & Sons.

11

Leadership Learning and Development

In this chapter we will explore the issues of leadership development and learning. We will highlight sources of leadership learning, leadership development best practice and ideas around leader becoming and leader identity in relation to leadership development. We start this chapter by exploring the most common form of leadership learning, which is linked to self-development, where we, as leaders, are expected to work on creating high levels of self-awareness to enable us to carry out the role of leader most effectively. We will look at some ways in which leaders can create self-awareness and hence develop self through differing experiences. This leads nicely into the growing area of critical and alternative views of leadership learning and development, leader becoming and leader identity, where, as leaders, we use these experiences or triggers to become a leader or they shape our identities as leaders. Finally, we will look at some contemporary and critical comments on leadership development and learning that help us question the purpose of leadership development and learning in our organizations.

Chapter Aims

- Introduce and critically discuss the link between leadership, learning and development
- Explore the differences and similarities between differing forms of leadership development

- Critically discuss the link between leadership development, learning, identity and becoming
- Introduce a debate around the enactment of leadership development in organizations

The Development of Leadership Learning

Over the last 20 years there has been evidence of an increased interest in leadership development courses and programmes (Adair, 2005; Charan et al., 2001; Collins and Holton, 2004; Conger, 1992; Conger and Benjamin, 1999; Day, 2000; Gill, 2011). Some researchers see leadership development programmes as a source of competitive advantage (McCall, 1998; Vicere and Fulmer, 1998) in organizations that have significant financial impact (Collins and Holton, 2004) and have been seen for a while as increasingly popular (Cacioppe, 1998) and expensive (Fulmer, 1997). In a publication in 2001 Kim Turnbull James and John Burgoyne set out some principles for leadership development best practice for organizations. They suggested that leadership development should have three strategic principles, and these were as follows:

- Leadership development must be driven from the top: if the CEO is not intimately involved and committed to it, it is not worth starting.
- Leadership development supports and drives the business: if it is not central to an organization's strategy, it will not happen.
- A leadership model must be culturally attuned: it must reflect the culture of the organization.

These principles were set out when leadership development was largely based on principles of self-development (see for example, Edwards et al., 2002) that were developed outside the organizational context. The focus of this best practice, therefore, was on integration into the organization through top level management, strategy and culture.

Reflective Question 11.1

Think about your experiences. What have been the triggers to your leadership development and learning?

Leadership Development as Self-development

The traditional view of leadership development reflects the notion of self-development. This view of leadership development is epitomized by the following quote:

Leaders know themselves; they know their strengths and nurture them. (Bennis, 1984: 17)

These ideas are played out in a number of leadership development programmes that are of a self-improvement and experiential nature (Edwards et al., 2002). The idea being that one can develop in a Maslowvian (Maslow, 1954, 1968) sense towards ideals of self-awareness, self-control and self-realization or actualization in conjunction with methodologies of an experiential nature (Baker et al., 2005; Edwards et al., 2002; Kolb, 1984; Mainemelis et al., 2002) and grounded in learning styles theory (Honey and Mumford, 1989; Mainemelis et al., 2002). This appears to have been the norm outside business schools until the 1990s where the transformational leadership concept (Bass, 1985a) started to ingrain itself in the academic as well as the practitioner worlds. With this we see the development of the FRLP (Avolio, 1999; Avolio and Bass, 1993) that promoted the development of transformational leadership skills over transactional behaviours, sometimes to the detriment of other perspectives and certainly in favour of transactional leadership skills (Edwards and Gill, 2012), owing to the promotion and allure of transformational behaviours (see Chapters 4 and 13 for further discussion). Edwards and Gill (2012), however, have provided empirical evidence to suggest that transactional behaviours are also important for leadership at certain levels of an organization, hence suggesting an understanding of contextual issues is also important for leadership development.

In addition to these forms of programme the psychometric analysis of leadership behaviour has also become the norm in organizations with tools such as the MLQ (Bass and Avolio, 1995) and the transformational leadership questionnaire (Alban-Metcalfe and Alimo-Metcalfe, 2000; Alimo-Metcalfe and Alban-Metcalfe, 2001). Questionnaires such as these are still used in leadership development programmes and are seen as a useful tool in understanding one's own behaviours and those perceived by others in relation to leadership. Again, however, the problem is how to gain some understanding of context with questionnaire tools that take us out of context (see Chapter 10 for a critical review of questionnaire tools). Finally, and most recently, there has been a focus on authentic leadership development (Cooper et al., 2005), which suggests a process of ethical awareness alongside leadership development. Issues of ethicality, morality and authenticity within leadership are discussed further in Chapter 13. In the next section we highlight some common tools that are used on leadership development programmes.

Reflective Question 11.2

What have been your experiences of using questionnaires to develop self? How have they helped? How have they not helped?

VIGNETTE 11.1

Extract from Case Study 2 highlighting tools for self-development

Dr Mahmood wanted a programme which was robust and externally accredited. I initially used assessors from the UK programme to validate the written assignment from each participant. I established a partnership with the Chartered Management Institute so that successful graduates of DQP would be assessed to become Chartered Managers. This was the first time this external accreditation had happened in Iraq.

The content of the 16-month programme included taught elements on high performance working, change leadership, engaging with external stakeholders, innovation culture, motivation and coaching skills. It also included an experiential learning workshop to stimulate peer feedback and self-awareness. Participants were required to undertake a 360-degree feedback process. They had to prepare a personal leadership development plan and also manage a change project in the workplace.

Almost all of this approach was new to the Iraqi culture in terms of content. In order to be a source of useful learning for Deans every aspect of the programme needed to be contextualized for a Middle East, Arab group. This contextualization took place beforehand when possible but in the pilot often occurred as 'work in progress' in the classroom. Deans had been raised on didactic teaching methods. An informal style of learner-centred delivery was ground breaking for them.

1. Reflect on each element of the programme described and critically discuss the extent to which this will help or hinder self-development for leadership.

Triggers of Leadership Development and Learning

A survey in the UK of senior managers and directors in the manufacturing sector suggested 10 triggers to their leadership development and learning (Bentley and Turnbull, 2005). These were:

- a significant leadership challenge at an early age (for example, captain of a sports team);
- observing positive role models;
- mentoring, coaching and consultant relationships;
- experiential leadership development training courses;

- impact of negative role models;
- MBAs and professional qualifications;
- international and multicultural experiences;
- voluntary and community work;
- team sports;
- being thrown in the deep end.

Bentley and Turnbull picked up particularly on the 'being thrown into the deep end' discussion that most executives had with interviewers. This aspect was described as their becoming accountable and responsible for a part of the organization for the first time. For example, some participants in the research described the first time their line manager was away from the manufacturing plant and they were left in charge or their boss was taken ill and they had to take responsibility. These moments of 'being thrown into the deep end' appear to be lucid in the minds of managers when thinking about their leadership development. These aspects are discussed further by Gill (2011), who also highlights the work of McCall (2009), who suggests that experience, similar to how it is discussed above, is key to developing leadership. He highlights the following experiences as important:

- early work experiences;
- short-term assignments;
- major line assignments;
- other people (very good and very bad bosses);
- hardships of various kinds;
- miscellaneous events, such as training courses.

Gill goes on to highlight others who have pointed out various experiences, such as Rajan (2000), who highlights the following leadership development methods in rank order:

- coaching by the CEO;
- learning from peers;
- experience;
- skills training.

Finally, Gill (2011) points to the consensus reflected in academia and practitioners initially highlighted by Furnham (2010) regarding what develops leaders. Furnham suggests the following are the main factors in developing leaders:

- early work experience which reveals likes and dislikes, interests, abilities and talents;
- the influence of other people, usually immediate bosses, who are positive or negative role models;

- short-term assignments, such as projects, which provide opportunities for new experiences and learning;
- the first big assignment, the first promotion or a foreign posting;
- hardships, which provide learning, coping in a crisis;
- formal management and leadership development, such as 360-degree feedback and coaching.

What seems interesting from this list is not just the programming of leadership development activities for managers in organizations, but also the making use of experiences for leadership learning. These experiences are often more powerful when they connect with the manager at a high level of emotional impact. Bennis and Thomas (2002) point to this as 'crucibles of leadership', which are described by Gill as:

> ... experiences, often unexpected and traumatic, always intense, that will cause leaders to stop in their tracks and question who they are and what really matters. (2011: 347)

It is these moments that epitomize the idea of leader becoming, which we will now discuss.

Reflective Question 11.3

What have been your 'crucibles of leadership'? How did you feel and what did you learn?

Leadership Development Evaluation

A question that remains elusive in the leadership studies world is whether leadership development initiatives are effective in delivering effective leadership capacity in organizations. To respond to this question, alongside the growth in leadership development literature, there has also been a growth in the research and literature on the subject of evaluating leadership development. This has been highlighted by two special issues in academic journals being devoted to the subject (Edwards and Turnbull, 2013a; Hannum and Craig, 2010).

The first of these special issues (Hannum and Craig, 2010) addresses the paucity of scholarly literature on leadership development – at the time of publication – and challenges the notion that this may indicate that leadership development evaluation is either not important or not possible. In the introduction to the special issue, the authors (Hannum and Craig, 2010) highlight that leadership development evaluation is important, and possible. If, for example, certain leadership development programmes or initiatives use certain models as the basis of the development intervention, then this enables a level of evaluation to take place. However, they also highlight the inherent challenge that this represents owing to the contextualized nature of leadership (see Chapters 5 and 10) and hence the inherent contextualized nature of leadership development and learning. Hannum and Craig (2010) go on to describe problems that occur in this contextualized environment that include difficulties in gaining comparison groups, environmental instability and the contamination of performance criteria over time. They therefore introduce papers that offer a range of techniques that advance and promote leadership development evaluation. For example, there are discussions regarding a framework for evaluating leadership coaching (Ely et al., 2010), the use of Social Network Analysis (SNA) to provide a classification of different types of leaderships networks (Hoppe and Reinelt, 2010), a data collection tool for evaluating collective leadership (Militello and Benham, 2010), a model for evaluating changes over time in a leadership development context (Gentry and Martineau, 2010), a mixed-method approach for the evaluation of leader self-development (Orvis and Langkamer Ratwani, 2010) and a mixed-method approach for the evaluation of a case example leadership development programme looking at leadership skills assessment and leadership mentoring (Solansky, 2010). In addition to these papers, Avolio et al. (2010) hold a discussion regarding another thorny issue in leadership development – return on investment (ROI). In this paper Avolio and colleagues promote the use of return-on-investment models in relation to leadership training. They review the experiences of leadership development by interviewing 10 leaders from across 10 different organizations. They used different guiding assumptions, scenarios, length of intervention and level of management to estimate a range of return on development interest (RODI) of between a low negative percentage up to a 200%. This paper, while based on a low sample size, suggests a way or working with models of ROI in evaluating leadership development programmes.

A second special issue on the subject of leadership development evaluation (Edwards and Turnbull, 2013a) takes a different perspective and challenges conventional survey-related techniques of evaluating leadership development programmes, instead highlighting new paradigms in the evaluation of leadership development programmes. For example, they recognize the issues of evaluation in a contextualized environment, highlighted by Hannum and Craig (2010) above, however, they suggest ways of working that are ingrained and work with context and culture. The special issue includes case study examples from New Zealand, Canada, the UK and Australia that exemplify ways of evaluating leadership learning and development based on mindsets (Kennedy et al., 2013), complexity theory (Jarvis et al., 2013), culture (Edwards and Turnbull, 2013b), a social capital perspective (Grandy and Holton, 2013), distributed leadership (McCauley-Smith et al., 2013) and a whole system approach to evaluation (Hanson, 2013). These new paradigms in leadership development evaluation represent a move towards more contemporary and critical notions of leadership being distributed, relational, cultural and complex (as also explored in previous chapters) that then inform the perspective with which an evaluator might explore the impact of leadership development and learning.

Leader Becoming and Leader Identity

Becoming

More recent studies of leadership development and learning appear to resonate with the experiential nature of leadership learning (Lowe and Gardner, 2000; Stead and Elliott, 2009; Waldman et al., 2006) and the development of leadership practice from a relational, social and situated perspective through a process of 'becoming' (Cunliffe, 2009; Kempster and Stewart, 2010; Parker, 2004). This research has also encouraged leadership development practices to be more contextually situated and therefore has built on Burgoyne and Stewart's (1977) work on naturalistic leadership learning and wider notions of situated leadership learning (Bennis and Thomas, 2002; Janson, 2008; Kempster, 2006, 2009a; Luthans and Avolio, 2003; McCall, 2004). From the literature around the process of 'becoming' in particular, there appears a need for leadership development and learning literature to appreciate the aspects of emotion, in particular anxiety and desire, in the process of 'becoming' a leader and in 'being' a leader (Schedlitzki et al., 2011). In addition, it appears that leadership learning and development should reconnect with context (Fairhurst, 2009; Fry and Kriger; 2009; Jepson, 2009a; Liden and Antonakis, 2009; Osborn et al., 2002; Osborn and Marion, 2009; Porter and McLaughlin, 2006) and community (Edwards, 2011). Kempster and Stewart's (2010) contribution, for example, is part of a new trend to enhance our insight into leadership development in a more rigorous way. They suggest an autoethnographic (e.g. Chang, 2008) approach to understanding how mangers progress in becoming a leader. They highlight leadership development through situated learning of leadership practice in organizations. In this sense situated means within a historical and social context and through interaction with notable others. By adopting a leadership role, we engage in behaviours that we have learned from experience in this context, then act and reflect on our actions to inform these behaviours. This also links to ideas about identity development around concepts of leadership learning.

Identity

Ford et al. (2008) highlight the performative role of leadership literature in relation to ideas of leadership development and learning. For example, they suggest that reading the literature has a lasting impact on who we think leaders are and how they should be. They go on to suggest that leaders are largely portrayed as transcendental, perfect beings and also as masculine, competitive, aggressive, controlling and self-reliant individuals (see Chapter 14). Within leadership development programmes and processes within organizations managers are increasingly asked to do not just a role but to become leaders, that is, adopt the identity prescribed by literature. In reality, Ford et al. (2008) suggest that nobody can live up to the expectations set by the literature and in organizations. They go on to propose a multiple identity perspective in which we have multiple competing identities, not just one fixed one, and that leaders often have to ignore their preferred identity in favour of those expressed in their organizations, literature or leadership development programmes. So what does this mean for leadership development?

Some suggestions from the work of Kempster and Stewart (2010) and Ford et al. (2008), would promote the following aspects within leadership development and learning.

- Avoid presenting leadership as a fixed role or identity that we can adopt and develop.
- Encourage awareness of different possible selves as leaders, followers and both.
- Deal with emotions and anxieties during the process of becoming and being a leader.
- Strengthen the voices of alternative leadership models rather than the masculine, competitive, aggressive, self-reliant, individualist one.
- Reconnect with context and community (see Chapter 9) and become inclusive and welcoming of the critical and creative views of others.

Finally, we will now review some further critical and alternative approaches to leadership development and learning.

Critical Thinking Box 11.1

Leadership development and learning are too focused on the individual. They do not consider more dispersed notions of leadership (Chapter 9), nor do they consider differing identities and concentrates on the masculine, competitive and individualistic perspective.

VIGNETTE 11.2

Extract from Case Study 1 highlighting issues of identity

A second challenge for managers that emerged was the lack of training managers had received. There was a tendency to give a higher emphasis and dependence to engineering skills rather than people. As there were such stringent service-level agreements in place, senior management had a tendency to promote and reward engineering skills – as they got the work done. For instance,

(Continued)

(Continued)

productive engineers were made into managers, rather than looking at who would make a good leader. Therefore managers had not received any training for things such as people management, or support during the period of taking on new responsibilities. Some managers had found HR issues difficult in the past, such as how to hold disciplinaries, or more broad issues, such as the consequences of speaking to an employee in a particular way. With no formal training on how to interview someone, engineers were recruited by a quick chat in the café. Therefore it may not be the best possible candidate that comes on board. With no formal training, managers were not necessarily equipped to perform their duties to the best of their ability.

1. To what extent is identity or identities evident in this passage? How might you cope with this as an issue on a leadership development programme?
2. What issues may arise from the leadership development intervention and how might the organization respond?

Critical and Alternative Approaches to Leadership Learning and Development

Another recent special issue in the journal *Management Learning* was deveoted to leadership development and learning. This special issue explored more critical perspectives and alternative approaches to leadership development and learning to lead (Edwards et al., 2013). This developed further already existing critical views on leardership learning and development.

There has been criticism of the traditional approaches (including activities such as 360-degree feedback, coaching, mentoring, networking, job assignments and action learning) to leadership development and learning, highlighted above, of being too individually focused and that there is a need for more socially orientated forms of leadership development (see Day, 2000, for further elaboration). There is some evidence that organizations are taking a more systemic approach to leadership development (Collins, 2001; Collins and Holton, 2004), similar to the recommendations made by Turnbull James and Burgoyne (2001). However, there is also some work that has started this trend towards critical leadership studies (Cunliffe and Linstead, 2009; Ford and Harding, 2007; Sinclair, 2007b, 2009) and there are some fledgling areas being developed that might be termed alternative or aesthetic approaches to leadership learning and development (Baruch, 2006; Gayá Wicks and Rippin, 2010; Hansen and Bathurst, 2011; Hansen et al., 2007; Ropo et al., 2002; Taylor et al., 2002). An aesthetic approach appears important in leadership learning and development, as tools based on traditional logic and rationality assume that the world is stable, knowable and predictable, which does impact on the emotionality of leadership processes, as highlighted above (Schedlitzki et al., 2011). Non-logical activities enable people to solve problems and enact their potentials: accessing intuitions, feelings, stories, improvization, experience, imagination, active listening, awareness in the moment, novel words and empathy. The contribution of arts-based methods to the development of managers and leaders was highlighted by Taylor and Ladkin (2009):

- *skills transfer* – learning artistic skills that can be applied to an organization setting;
- *projective technique* – accessing inner thoughts and feelings;
- *illustration of essence* – apprehend the essence of a concept, situation, tacit knowledge;
- *making* – deeper experience of personal presence and connection to counteract feelings of disconnection and fragmentation among leaders.

The notions of aesthetics and art-based approaches to leadership are discussed further in Chapter 15.

The special issue *Management Learning* highlighted earlier develops these themes with papers based on aesthetic methods for leadership development (Schyns et al., 2013; Sutherland, 2013), gender (Kelan, 2013; Stead, 2013) and a critical exploration of leadership development in the UK public service (Tomlinson et al., 2013)

VIGNETTE 11.3

Extract from Case Study 1 highlighting a need for leadership development

Between the years 2008 and 2011, Space Engineering Services grew rapidly due to several contractual wins. More resources were needed to cope with the demand. As a result of this, more managers needed to be recruited, and thus engineers who were very good at their job became managing engineers or managers. However, with this new-found responsibility came no formal training on how to manage people. HR issues were not being handled by the managers but by the HR department – distancing the front-line managers even further away from people management duties.

1. Based on what you have read in this chapter what would you recommend as an approach to leadership development for these managers?
2. What issues may arise from the leadership development intervention and how might the organization respond?

Summary

The chapter began by looking at the historical development of thinking on leadership learning and development. The chapter then reviewed traditional approaches to leadership development and learning, based on the pursuit of self-awareness and self-actualization. These ideas appear to be the mainstay of leadership development practice. The chapter then changed focus slightly by looking at various triggers to leadership development and learning that have informed notions of becoming and identity in leadership learning. The chapter also looked at the practical need to evaluate leadership development programmes: this includes the need to assess the return on investment of a programme and issues of the relevance of what is increasingly becoming an expensive part of an organization's budget. The chapter also highlighted recent research that looks at alternative paradigms of leadership development evaluation that include taking a culturally, complexity, and critically appreciated view of leadership development and learning. It then briefly explored wider discussions regarding issues of becoming and identity and related these to leadership development. Finally, it highlighted the growing literature on critical and alternative approaches to leadership development and learning, which emphasize issues of power, gender and aesthetics in the process of leadership learning and development.

Additional Reflection Questions

1. What is leadership development and what is leadership learning? How might the two concepts differ?
2. What methods of leadership development and learning have you experienced?
3. How have you developed or 'become' a leader?
4. What identity do your assume in taking leader roles?
5. What creative methods would you employ in a leadership development programme?
6. How might we develop leadership as well as leaders?
7. What is meant by taking a critical approach to leadership development?

Case Study Questions

1. Read carefully through Case Study 1, which presents a discussion about an engineering company, and Case Study 5, from a self-development organization. What triggers to leadership development are evident in the discussion?
2. Read carefully through Case Study 2, regarding a development programme in Iraq. Relate the discussion to the chapter above. Develop a critical discussion on how you might evaluate such a programme. What factors would be important to your evaluation and why?

3. Read carefully through Case Study 3 which includes a discussion about management practice. Relate the discussion in the papers by Bolden (2005 and 2006) and Day (2000) to this case study. To what extent do they relate to the experiences of the managers involved?

4. Relate the discussion held in Case Studies 4 and 6. To what extent can you relate these examples to the critical issues developed in this chapter? What advice would you give the characters in each case example based on your knowledge of alternative ways of developing and learning leadership?

Further Reading

Avolio, B.J., Avey, J.B. and Quisenberry, D. (2010) Estimating the return on leadership development investment. *Leadership Quarterly*, 21: 633–644.

Bolden, R. (ed.) (2005) *What Is Leadership Development?* Exeter: Leadership South West and the University of Exeter.

Bolden, R. (ed.) (2006) *Leadership Development in Context*. Exeter: Leadership South West and the University of Exeter.

Day, D.V. (2000) Leadership development: a review in context. *Leadership Quarterly*, 11(4): 581–613.

Edwards, G.P., Elliott, C., Iszatt-White, M. and Schedlitzki, D. (2013) Critical and alternative approaches to leadership learning and development. *Management Learning*, 44(1): 3–10.

Edwards, G.P. and Turnbull, S. (2013) Special issue on new paradigms in evaluating leadership development. *Advances in Developing Human Resources*, 15(1): 3–9.

Gill, R. (2011) *Theory and Practice of Leadership,* second edition. London: Sage.

Kempster, S. (2009) *How Managers Have Learnt to Lead: Exploring the Development of Leadership Practice*. Basingstoke: Palgrave.

Kets De Vries, M.F.R. and Korotov, K. (eds) (2011) *Leadership Development*. Cheltenham: Edward Elgar.

Turnbull James, K. and Burgoyne, J. (2001) *Leadership Development: Best Practice Guide for Organizations*. London: Council for Excellence in Management and Leadership.

Part III
Critical Issues in Leadership

12

Leadership, Gender and Diversity

Gender and diversity have been a focus in the field of leadership studies for quite some time now and considerations of gender and diversity have predominantly focused on differences and similarities between female and male leaders and pondered the relevance of diversity within groups as something that a leader or manager has to enhance and cope with. The focus on gender, in particular, has recently taken a more critical turn in which stereotypical views of male/female and masculinity/femininity have been questioned and gendered representations in leadership theory and discourse have been problematized. In this chapter, we will outline and discuss a wide range of approaches to gender and diversity in relation to leadership. We will explore generally whether and why gender may matter for leadership and critically evaluate views on a feminine advantage in leadership. We will further discuss persisting challenges for women as leaders and outline other forms of diversity and their relevance for leadership.

Chapter Aims

- Introduce the links between gender, diversity and leadership
- Critically evaluate the differences between male/female and masculine/feminine leaders
- Explore the arguments for and against a feminine advantage
- Discuss critically informed views on the study of gender and leadership
- Outline other forms of diversity and their link to leadership

> ## Critical Thinking Box 12.1
>
> Critical leadership scholars have increasingly highlighted the masculine nature of many 20th-century leadership theories and the extent to which this silences other, more feminine forms of leadership. This dominance of masculinity associated with leadership is deeply embedded within western societies and organizations.

Why Gender Matters

One of the most popular questions, according to Jackson and Parry (2011), in relation to leadership is that of whether and what the difference is between a male leader and a female leader. At the beginning of the field of organizational leadership studies there was the great man theory and with it the prime focus on what we can learn from great male leaders in history. Subsequently, many of the early leadership theories outlined in Chapters 2–4 were developed from research conducted in male dominated contexts and have long been criticized for therefore being too masculine in nature and focus. Since then, and particularly in the 1990s, we have seen a certain feminization of leadership studies through which feminine characteristics of care and support have been viewed as a strategic advantage for organizational effectiveness and well-being (Jackson and Parry, 2011). Transformational leadership has also been acclaimed to fit into this wave of seeing feminine traits and behaviours as a leadership advantage.

Glass ceiling: an invisible barrier that hinders women and other minority groups from reaching elite leadership positions despite their qualifications

Yet, there have also been more critical views on the possible perpetuation of gender stereotypes that these considerations may bring (Billing and Alvesson, 2000). What is relatively certain is the continuing glass ceiling that many female leaders face in their career; often related to their child-bearing and -rearing duties as well as dominant societal and cultural structures across many organizations and countries. Yet, what deserves further consideration is whether our concerns for gender differences should be focused on the body (that is, male/female) or certain personal characteristics (that is, feminine/masculine) or indeed an interaction of both. If the question is one of equality, then there is certainly still a lot to be done to unpack gender stereotypes in relation to modern society, organizations and leadership, as well as to ascertain whether gender is indeed of such importance to leadership.

Male Leaders or Female Leaders?
What is the Difference?

The question or difference in relation to gender and leadership has particularly focused on leader effectiveness. We will review in this section some of the most well-known studies that have investigated this particular question.

The difference between male and female leaders has been manifold in research studies, particularly since the 1970s (Bass, 1985b; Book, 2000; Eagly and Carli, 2003; Eagly et al., 1995; Helgesen, 1990), yet with rather mixed results. No 'hard' evidence exists to suggest that female leaders are more or less effective than male leaders and are indeed consistently different in traits and behaviours compared to male leaders (Dobbins and Platz, 1986; Engen et al., 2001; Powell, 1990).

Key Findings of Gender Differences

Among these research studies on the gender difference, there are some notable meta-analyses of existing research studies in the literature that we will address here. Meta-analyses by Eagly and Johnson (1990) and van Engen (2001), for example, showed that female leaders do not necessarily fall into the stereotypical assumptions of feminine versus masculine leadership behaviours. They were therefore not found to be more interpersonally and less task-oriented than male leaders. These studies as well as other studies on transformational leadership did, however, provide some evidence that female leaders are more participative and democratic in their preferred leadership style compared to male leaders. Eagly et al.'s (2003) recent study showed indeed that female leaders tended to be more transformational and engage more in contingent reward behaviour than male leaders. Although this difference was small, Eagly et al. (2003) concluded that the findings were robust and represented a feminine advantage as these leader behaviours are linked to higher leader effectiveness. We will explore this argument further later on in this chapter.

Hoyt (2007: 267) highlights other interesting findings such as a meta-analysis by Eagly et al. (1992) that discussed research findings that showed how female managers were 'devalued compared to men when they led in a masculine manner', worked in masculine roles and masculine industries and when they were evaluated by men. These findings stress the prejudice that female leaders have for a long time encountered and continue to face in many countries and industries. Other studies such as Eagly et al. (1995) add to this insight by demonstrating that female and male leaders tend to be more effective in gender congruent roles, that is, female leaders were found to be less effective than men in military positions but more effective in, for example, education. This was linked to different uses of interpersonal skills in these different gendered contexts.

> **Reflective Question 12.1**
>
> Think of female and male managers you have known. To what extent did they differ in their leadership style? If there were differences did this matter? How and why?

Outstanding Questions

What we can conclude at this point is that research so far has not provided robust insights that would confirm a clear difference between leadership styles and leader effectiveness in relation to the gender of the leader. But, as Jackson and Parry (2011) suggest, maybe we are not asking the right questions? Indeed, these studies have not unpacked what exactly we mean by gender. They have studied the differences between men and women without questioning in detail whether it is indeed the biological difference, that is, male/female that needs attention or whether it is personal characteristics of feminine and masculine often associated with one sex more than the other that we should consider (Ely and Padavic, 2007). Some studies have indeed conflated the two rather than explored where these interact.

Yukl (2010) summarizes key limitations of the dominant comparative studies on gender and leadership and suggests that other contextual variables affecting the comparability of male and female leadership behaviours have seriously contaminated the results of these studies. We recommend the exchange of articles between Vecchio (2002, 2003) and Eagly and Carli (2003) in *The Leadership Quarterly* for an in-depth reading of the methodological and conceptual issues around these meta-analyses of gender related differences in leadership. In this chapter, we help readers unpack gender further by introducing some of the main problems that women in leadership positions have faced in recent history and critically considering feminine leadership as an alternative approach. Here we will also address the interaction of body and character in the genderizing of leadership and organizations.

Female Leaders and Feminine Leadership – Opportunities and Persistent Challenges

In light of the positive changes over the last few decades in terms of percentage of female graduates, employees and female managers, the greater part of research into challenges for female leaders is focused on their access to top managerial positions. The statistics for leaders in top political and organizational positions continue to show a relatively low proportion of women in these positions. Despite the rise in numbers of women in managerial positions overall and some top hierarchical positions over the last few decades many scholars suggest that inequalities and persistent challenges continue to exist (Carli and Eagly, 2011; Hoyt, 2007). We will first highlight several theories and ideas as well as research findings that try to explain these challenges. We will then also review some of the literature on what has been termed a 'feminine advantage' as a counter-movement or possibly remedy to the seeming inequalities for female managers. Through this contribution, we will also highlight the differences between female and feminine and their relevance for more critical current and future gender and leadership studies.

Challenges for Female Leaders

Hoyt (2007) has looked in particular at the so-called 'glass ceiling' that is preventing women from being promoted into top hierarchical positions and therefore perpetuating the unequal distribution of female and male leaders across an organization's hierarchy. She identified three main reasons for the persistence of this invisible barrier: human capital differences, gender differences and prejudice. Hoyt draws on a wider range of research (Eagly and Carli, 2004; Haslam and Ryan, 2008; Powell and Graves, 2003) to explore the different forms and impact of human capital differences, that is, the relatively lower level of education, training and work experience of women compared to men. One of the key issues discussed here is the culturally, socially and legally ingrained notion of child-bearing and -rearing responsibilities where women seem to naturally take more time out of work, seek less full-time employment, drop out of employment more often and find re-entry into employment more difficult than men in many countries. Yet, with rising numbers of female graduates, the increasing number of women chosing not to have children and the more active involvement of men in child-rearing responsibilities (Carli and Eagly, 2011), this cannot be seen as the only explanation for low numbers of female leaders throughout all hierarchical levels.

Hoyt (2007) also addresses other interesting research such as Powell and Graves' (2003) work into women's weaker access to key informal mentoring relationships and general development opportunities than their male counterparts. Bowles and McGinn (2005) have further argued that women tend to be more strongly represented in organizational roles and departments that do not naturally lead to top leadership positions, for example, HR. Haslam and Ryan (2008) have further explored this latter aspect of career transition and found a 'glass cliff' rather than a glass ceiling. This means that female leaders are more likely to be promoted into top positions in times of crisis or poor organizational performance. These appointments into higher positions are seen as highly risky and female leaders inevitably end up being associated with the current failures in organizations, which are out of their control yet lead to a problematic continuation of their career in top managerial positions.

Linked to this first explanatory area of the glass ceiling is the issue of natural and nurtured gender difference, that is biological as well as socially constructed gender notions. This area is linked to some extent to the research introduced in the previous

Glass cliff: female leaders get promoted to elite positions in time of crisis and are subsequently associated with pre-exisiting organizational failures, which are out of their control, that then affect their careers negatively

section on differences in leader style and effectiveness in relation to gender. As noted previously, the evidence to justify the outright support of a clear difference in female and male leaders is rather mixed and weak. Another gender difference highlighted by Bowles and McGinn (2005) is the relative hesitance by many women to identify themselves and promote themselves as leaders. This may be also linked to the historically masculine definitions of what is deemed to be appropriate and effective leadership (Ford, 2010) and has to be seen in light of research findings into the gender bias in perceptions of the appropriate ways of behaving as women and female leaders. Other research by Small et al. (2007) further suggests that women are less inclined to negotiate than men – a skill that they posit is crucial for leadership. This ultimate nature–nurture debate of whether these gender differences are biologically imposed or socially constructed (developed in line with social norms and expectations) is ongoing and there has arguably not yet been enough exploration of dominate, transitional and resistant notions of the body, gender attributes and sexuality in different societies.

A third area of concern is that of prejudice, that is, stereotypical assumptions and judgements in relation to gender. Eagly and Carli (2003) make reference to 'sex-typed' theories of leadership that suggest men and women behave consistently differently and hence impose stereotypical judgements on those they observe. Bolden et al. (2011) draw a link here to leadership in the sense that leadership has been stereotyped over time as masculine and hence associated with competition, control and change and as therefore standing in clear contrast with feminine stereotypes of care, support and stability. As biological gender difference is often conflated with the personal characteristics associated with feminine/masculine, we can see how this leads to female leaders being expected to be feminine and hence are perceived as inapt to perform the masculine leadership roles that society provides. Eagly's (1987) social role theory further argues that in order to avoid being outcasts and to receive praise leaders want to behave in accordance with society's gender expectations. This leads to continuing gender stereotyping into the caring and task-focused camps of female and male leaders.

Reflective Question 12.2

Reflect critically on an organization you know. How masculine/agentic (that is, competitive, controlling, focused on change) is the organization? Alternatively how feminine/communal (that is, caring, supporting, focused on stability) is it? What implications does this have for 'real' equal opportunities?

Carli and Eagly also talk about a double bind situation in which 'highly communal female leaders are criticized for not being agentic enough, but highly agentic female leaders may be criticized for lacking communion' (2011:108). Communal is here defined as warm, supportive, kind and helpful and associated with female leaders whereas agentic is seen as assertive, dominant, competent and authoritative and as stereotypical for male leaders (Carli and Eagly, 2011). It is this double bind situation that has proven particularly limiting in female leaders' ability to work against the organizational and culturally ingrained assumptions around success of management and leadership as an outcome of agentic behaviours.

Addressing the Challenges

Attention has, of course, also been paid in the literature to ways in which we can work towards reducing this invisible barrier, the glass ceiling or glass cliff. Hoyt (2007) usefully summarizes some of the existing suggestions and highlights the need for a wider role renegotiation of women at home and at work – both at an immediate social and wider societal level. She draws on Powell and Graves (2003) who suggest that women have the choice to circumvent the glass ceiling through seeking organizations that are dominated by women entrepreneurs. A compelling alternative opportunity that has also become more widely known as the feminine advantage is the popularity of an allegedly feminine leadership style: that of transformational leadership.

Feminine Advantage

We highlighted earlier in this chapter research by Eagly et al. (2003) that has shown women to be more natural at engaging with transformational and contingency-reward type leadership behaviour which has been – over the last few decades – seen as particularly successful and popular in organizations. This finding is not entirely surprising as transformational leadership is associated with more traditionally feminine characteristics such as caring, supporting and considering followers than necessarily masculine attributes. Based on their research findings Eagly et al. (2003) suggest that women should play this feminine advantage and embrace their natural tendency for transformational leadership behaviours as future organizations will only continue to promote and value this type of leadership style. Vecchio's (2003) critical response to meta-analyses carried out on the subject of the feminine advantage warns that the research findings supporting the assumption that a feminine advantage does exist are rather weak and inflate the real existence of such an advantage. He calls for a more cautious evaluation of such research, especially also in light of the limitations and danger of over-relying on the wonders of transformational leadership (see Chapter 4). Finally, Carli and Eagly (2011) also draw on research by Twenge (1997, 2001) to argue that women have changed and have become more assertive, dominant and masculine and hence better able to combine the communal and agentic aspects of leadership that have previously created tensions and a double bind situation for female leaders.

Critical Views on Gender and Leadership Studies

Whether or not a feminine advantage exists in the way it has been formulated in the literature, we contend that we have not unpacked enough of what we mean by feminine and masculine and how this interacts with the more biologically focused notion of gender. Jackson and Parry (2011) also suggest that future research needs to focus more on issues of power, context, style, identity and social construction in relation to gender and leadership. Indeed, more recent critically focused leadership research into gender has addressed these interconnections of the feminine/masculine and the female/male body and explored the socially co-constructed and power infused nature of the meaning of these. Billing and Alvesson, for example, have critically reviewed the suggestions of a feminine advantage or feminine leadership and argue that 'constructing leadership as feminine may be of some value as a contrast to conventional ideas on leadership and management but may also create a misleading impression of women's orientation to leadership as well as reproducing stereotypes and traditional gender division of labour' (2000: 144). They argue that both biological notions of gender and notions of femininity and masculinity have been overly focused on opposites and assumed to be clearly different and separate from each other. Billing and Alvesson (2000) suggest that this is a rather simplistic view of gender and that we need to recognize the constantly changing and culturally constructed nature of what is feminine and masculine and how this is linked to biological notions of gender. This calls for research that sheds further light on different constructions of gender across cultures and over time and also on how feminine and masculine interact on their own and with the biological notions of gender in a particular context.

Other research has further explored the performative impact that the dominant, masculine discourse has had on women managers (Ford, 2010; Stead and Elliott, 2009). It has particularly highlighted the extent to which women in leadership positions feel pressured to conform to the dominant image of a successful – masculine – leader in speech and behaviour in order to be accepted by and have influence on others. This has also been found to create tensions for those female managers with regard to who they would like to be and how they would like to interact with others and the style they feel they have to adopt to conform and be successful. Carli and Eagly (2011), in contrast, argue that notions of leadership are changing and becoming more communally focused and consequently less masculine. Collinson (2011) recognizes the latter changes in leadership studies but argues that it continues to be highly gendered and polarizes the similarities and differences between women and men as well as between women and between men. He argues we are therefore no step further from the categorizations of biological and personal notions of gender. Drawing on critical feminist contributions (Bowring, 2004; Bligh and Kohles, 2008), Collinson (2011) also highlights the possibly interlinked nature of gender and power in society and leadership where women – similar to followers – are seen as the Other (rather than the leader). Similar to Billing and Alvesson (2000) he calls for a more nuanced view of gender in different contexts and particularly as interlinked with ethnicity and class.

Related to the above, Hoyt (2007) stresses that the key weakness of current gender and leadership research is its heavy emphasis on research conducted in western societies. It is hence in itself biased by its culturally limited view of gender roles and the meaning of masculinity and femininity. More research in different cultures needs to be conducted to broaden our view on this. Hoyt (2007) further argues that gender could be subsumed under the broader heading of diversity. We would argue the other way round, that gender currently receives more attention in leadership textbooks and leadership studies than diversity as a broader phenomenon. It is hence diversity that we address in the final section of this chapter.

VIGNETTE 12.1

Extract from Case Study 5 highlighting the complexity of what is gender

When asked whether as a woman June brought something different to the table, she found this was difficult to answer. Perhaps her response would be this: June feels for humanity and acts in all she does to make the world a better place.

1. June Burrough is the successful founder of a social enterprise and has quite strong views on many aspects of leadership. Yet when asked about gender, she is lost for words. What is your interpretation of her belief in humanity and striving to make the world a better place. Is this a feminine approach?
2. Is our definition of feminine as communal and caring applicable here? Could there be other culturally informed views of gender and femininity?

Diversity and Leadership

The broad term of diversity has served as an umbrella for many specific foci such as ethnicity, age, gender, education, class and sexual orientation (Yukl, 2010). Diversity as a catchphrase has then within the wider field of business and management received a lot of attention over the last couple of decades owing to the increasing importance it has for global organizations where employees from a large range of diverse backgrounds come to work together. Rickards (2012) stresses particularly the literature's focus on diversity in teams at all hierarchical levels and the complexities of expatriate leaders' work. Within leadership studies, diversity has not achieved as much attention on its own but has rather in the past been subsumed within three different areas: gender as a form of diversity; cross-cultural studies of leadership (and expatriate leaders); and in leadership textbooks as an element of groups and group leadership in organizations.

Reflective Question 12.3

Critically reflect on an organization you know. How diverse is this organization? Does it matter? What are the implications for employee opportunities within the organization?

Queer theory: ciritcally explores texts and phenomena focusing on gender as part of the essential self and the socially constructed nature of sexual acts and identities

So, with regard to the first area mentioned above, we can see strong parallels between what we have said throughout the chapter about the challenges for women as leaders and feminine leadership and the challenges that minorities face within organizations. Critical leadership scholars are highlighting similar issues of exclusion and prejudice that the dominant white, male, middle-class image of leaders has for leaders from other ethnicities and classes (Collinson, 2011). Rickards argues that this has encouraged minorities to circumvent this 'diversity dilemma' by 'becoming entrepreneurial founders of business of various kinds' (2012: 178). It is then the overcoming of the glass ceiling that women and minorities face that creates their shared social identity and drives their entrepreneurial aspirations. More recently we have also seen work using queer theory (Harding et al., 2011) to unpack sexuality and leadership in organizations further and particularly with a view to homosexual and heterosexual aspects of dominant leader images and a queer reading of dominant leadership texts.

Expatriate Leadership

The second area of leadership in different cultures, leading followers from different cultures and expatriate leaders, has to a large extent been addressed in Chapter 10 in this book. It is the latter complexity of expatriate leadership that has not received as much attention within leadership studies per se. It has been explored, particularly in relation to the technical training and competence of expatriate leaders in the cross-cultural and comparative management literature (Black and Mendenhall, 1990; Toh and Denisi, 2003) but remains under-explored with reference to the exploration of the expatriate leader–local follower relationship. Hailey (1996) has stressed the culture shock that many expatriates experience owing to inadequate cultural training and awareness. Western expatriates often find it difficult to adjust to local culture and their behaviours and attitude are then often perceived as a 'colonial mentality' by local employees (Hailey, 1996: 263). The expatriate leader–follower relationship is bounded by the complexity of this culture clash and indeed the short-term, fixed nature of the expatriate's placement in the local culture. The perception of the expatriate as stranger (Richards, 1996) by the locals and equally the perception of the local context as a strange environment for the expatriate leader create an immediate tension that is very difficult to subsequently overcome. More research is needed to unpack and understand the added complexity that these time and culture issues bring to the leader–follower relationship.

Diversity Management

Finally, Yukl (2010) draws our attention to the work that has been done on the management of diversity in groups and the potential benefits and challenges that this poses for leadership and the organization (Kochan et al., 2003; Triandis et al., 1994). The main advantages of having a diverse workforce are the likely increase in creativity and innovation as well as a greater potential talent pool and more balanced decision-making process that an influx of different views and values of a diverse workforce brings. Yukl (2010) warns though that with greater diversity in the workforce may also come more opportunities for distrust and conflict due to less shared commitment and identity in the group. With a view to the management of diverse groups, this research has also focused on ways in which an appreciation of and tolerance for diversity can be enhanced and equal opportunities created. Insights from critical and feminist studies on gender and diversity as highlighted above do, however, call into question the extent to which any such diversity training measures are able to make a difference and to what extent they may instead lead to a perpetuation of stereotypes and an emphasis on the difference between different forms of diversity.

VIGNETTE 12.2

Extract from Case Study 1 highlighting diversity in action

The engineering industry is renowned for continuously winning/losing contracts. With this comes a transfer of undertaking (protection of employees) (TUPE), where employees who work on that contract are transferred across with the contract to the new supplier. For leaders this means fresh talent, and it can also mean a diverse

(Continued)

(Continued)

mix of capabilities, cultures and work standards. There have been instances where companies have used TUPE to transfer across employees who are not as capable, to ensure they keep a good talent pool in their organization.

1. Reflect on how this example of 'diversity management in action' relates to Yukl's (2010) views on the opportunities and challenges of diversity.
2. What may be the challenges of frequent changes in staffing for leadership?

Critical Thinking Box 12.2

A significant problem with equal opportunities policies and diversity management programmes is their inevitable perpetuation of gender and other diversity related stereotypes. This is because they have to define diversity categories and locate individuals within these in order to ensure that each individual falling into a minority category is given equal opportunities within the organization. Unfortunately, this deepens rather than removes stereotypes in organizations and society. What can organizations do to ensure equal opportunities without naming and perpetuating stereotypes?

Summary

In this chapter, we have introduced the reader to several key fields of leadership studies in relation to gender. We have particularly focused on the research and meta-analysis conducted over the last three decades on the existence of differences between female and male leaders and their effectiveness in organizations. Through this review we have also highlighted some of the persistent challenges that female leaders face in light of the well known notions of the glass ceiling and glass cliff in organizations. We have also highlighted claims in the wider literature for a feminine advantage in leadership and sought to unpack further how this holds up to critical and feminist views on a deeply ingrained structural and cultural bias towards the male and masculine. In light of these more critical views of gender and leadership we have also highlighted the danger of viewing biological notions of gender as well as personal gender characteristics as separate, distinct entities and as clearly different and opposite. This therefore recognizes research that explores feminine and masculine as fluid, shifting and socially constructed notions of gender and looks at how these interact with each other and with biological forms of gender in the context of organizations. A final section then drew the link to the broader term of diversity that includes not only gender but also ethnicity, class, sexual orientation and education. We highlighted similarities in opportunities and challenges for these other forms of diversity in light of the dominant white, male, middle-class image of the successful leader in western countries. We also stressed that the wider notion of diversity has often been subsumed under other topics such as gender, culture and team leadership and briefly reviewed each of these areas. We concluded on the note that more in-depth research is needed on different forms of diversity and their influence on dominant leader identities as well as the leader–follower relationship.

Additional Reflection Questions

1. What is the difference between research into female leaders and feminine leadership? What can we learn from either about leadership?
2. There is a clear difference in styles between female and male leader. Critically discuss and relate to your own organizational experience.
3. Is there a feminine advantage?
4. What are the dangers of promoting a feminine advantage?
5. Critical leadership scholars argue that women are seen as the 'Other'. What does this mean?
6. Critically reflect on the opportunities and limitations of gender studies into leadership and their potential to work against or reinforce stereotypes.
7. What can be described as a diversity dilemma and what solutions can we find to it?
8. How does diversity affect the leader-follower relationship? Critically reflect on organizational examples.

Case Study Questions

1. Read carefully through Case Study 3 and note down specific behaviours and attributes that Ken, Mike and Frank display. To what extent are these behaviours and attributes masculine or feminine (as defined in this chapter)? How masculine or feminine are the organization and culture they are working in? What influence may this have on their effectiveness as a leader and follower?
2. Case Studies 4 and 5 describe the particular views of two female leaders on their approach to running organizations. Compare and contrast the relative agentic

and/or communal nature of their views and set these in the context of the particular organizations their work in. Link your analysis back to mainstream and critical ideas on gender as discussed in this chapter.

3. Diversity is often associated with either gender or ethnicity. What other forms of diversity are visible in the three case studies? What does diversity mean in the context of each case study?

4. This chapter has highlighted the problematic nature of diversity management. June Burrough reflects in Case Study 5 on equality and the importance of showing everybody equal respect. How can she embed this belief in an active practice of equal opportunities in her organization and avoid the pitfalls of traditional diversity management?

Further Reading

Billing, Y. and Alvesson, M. (2000) Questioning the notion of feminine leadership: a critical perspective on the gender labelling of leadership. *Gender, Work and Organization*, 7(3): 144–157.

Carly, L.L. and Eagly, A.H. (2011) Gender and leadership. In A. Bryman, D. Collinson, K. Grint, B. Jackson and M. Uhl-Bien (eds) *The SAGE Handbook of Leadership*. London: Sage, 103–117.

Collinson, D. (2011) Critical leadership studies. In A. Bryman, D. Collinson, K. Grint, B. Jackson and M. Uhl-Bien (ed.) *The SAGE Handbook of Leadership*. London: Sage, 181–194.

Haslam, S.A. and Ryan, M. (2008) The road to the glass cliff: differences in the perceived suitability of men and women for leadership positions in succeeding and failing organizations. *The Leadership Quarterly*, 19: 530–546.

Hoy, C. (2007) Women and leadership. In P.G. Northouse (ed.) *Leadership: Theory and Practice*. Thousand Oaks, CA: Sage, 265–299.

13

Leadership: Issues of Ethics, Sustainability, Authenticity and Toxicity

So far in this textbook we have looked at questions like what is leadership (Chapter 1), who is the leader (Chapter 2), and even where is leadership (Chapter 9)? We have not asked, however, what is leadership for or what is its purpose? The focus of this chapter, therefore, is to explore the reasons behind leadership. We will thus explore issues of sustainability, ethical leadership, links to altruism and authentic leadership. Then we explore the 'flip side', writing and theory concerning narcissism and leadership and recent theory concerning toxic or bad leadership. Finally, we will explore some more critical comments in this area of research and ponder the future.

Chapter Aims

- Introduce and critically discuss the link between leadership and ethics, sustainability, altruism and authenticity
- Explore the differences and similarities between these concepts
- Critically discuss the link between leadership and toxicity
- Introduce a debate around the enactment of leadership and ethics in a community context

> **Reflective Question 13.1**
>
> What is success and effectiveness in organizations? How do we measure success and effectiveness? Can we, and if so should we, measure success and effectiveness?

What Is Leadership For?

Hemphill (1958) has provided three stages to the leadership process:

- *attempted leadership* – is an act by which an individual intends to influence a group for the purpose of solving a mutual problem;
- *successful leadership* – is an attempted leadership act that has been followed; that is, an individual has influenced the group toward solving a mutual problem;
- *effective leadership* – has not only influenced the direction of the group but also contributed to the group's solution to the problem.

The challenge is that this appears to be the extent to which leadership has been studied up to and including the 'new leadership approaches' described in Chapter 4. Our challenge in this chapter is that there are elements outside the basic (and sometimes ill-defined or undefined) idea of effectiveness that one needs to consider. Longer-term issues such as ethics also appear to be fundamental to the idea of leadership (Ciulla, 2004) and could provide ideas as to the purpose of leadership in and across organizations, cultures, communities and countries. First, however, we briefly discuss a similar issue, that of sustainability.

> **Reflective Question 13.2**
>
> What is sustainability in and outside of organizations? How do we measure sustainability? Can we, and if so should we, measure sustainability?

Leadership for Sustainability

Bolden et al. (2011) raise the issue of leading responsibly and link this to issues in saving our planet. They suggest an agenda for leadership that is sustainable, that takes the ethics of leadership further by suggesting a responsibility of leaders for engendering sensitivity to the environment. This view is challenging traditional business models of profit orientation and wealth creation towards more sustainable and environmental agendas. This has been incorporated into a recent initiative at the University of Exeter – the One World MBA (http://business-school.exeter.ac.uk/mba/). This new form of business education works with the World Wildlife Fund (WWF) and businesses to look at developing a plant-minded business education. This form of business education epitomizes the contemporary view that links leadership responsibility to ethical considerations, which is explored below.

Ethical Leadership

Ciulla (2004) equates the central issues of ethics with those of leadership, hence providing a strong link between the two. She goes on to suggest that the issue of morals or morality is magnified by issues around leadership (Ciulla, 2012). However, Mendonca and Kanungo (2007) suggest that it is an increasing societal concern that it is unacceptable for leaders in organizations to be unaware of moral responsibility and unethical behaviour which drives an interest in ethics and leadership or ethical leadership. Mendonca and Kanungo go on to suggest that effective leadership occurs when the leader's behaviour and leadership influence is consistent with ethical and moral values. In her work, however, Ciulla (2004) concentrates on understanding ethical leadership as linked to the challenges of being ethical, which she connects to challenges of authenticity, self-interest and self-discipline as well as moral obligations that are related to notions of justice, duty, competence and the greatest good. Ciulla (2005) suggests there are three categories of ethical leadership:

1. *intentions* – the ethics of leaders themselves – the intentions of leaders; their personal ethics;
2. *relational* – the ethics of how a leader leads or the ethics of the process of leadership; the means by which a leader gets things done and/or the relationship between the leader and other stakeholders;
3. *the ends* – the ethics of what a leader does – the ethics of the outcomes of the leader's actions.

Furthermore, Ciulla (2012) has also developed a discussion of ethics and effectiveness and proposes that the distinction between the two is not necessarily a clear one. She suggests that sometimes being ethical is effective and sometimes being effective is ethical. She therefore also suggests that ethics is effectiveness in certain circumstances. Here she uses the example of the Secretary General to the United Nations as an example and posits that because the power and resources of this position of UN Secretary General are low, it is difficult to uphold this position without acting ethically.

The literature also discusses other issues linked to ethics and leadership, such as morality, altruism and authenticity. We will explore each of these in turn.

Moral Luck

Ciulla (2012) brings into the ethical leadership discussion the term 'moral luck'. She uses Bernard Williams' (1982) description of moral luck, which suggests there is an aspect of how well one thinks through a decision and the extent to which this thought process turns out to be 'right', but also accepts extrinsic factors, that leaders have little or no control over, such as bad weather, accidents and so on. Ciulla (2012) suggests that moral luck is important for leadership studies as it helps us reconcile issues of decision making, risk assessment and moral accountability. Ultimately, she goes on to point out, some leaders are ethical but unlucky, while others are not as ethical and very lucky. It is because of the issues surrounding moral luck that Ciulla (2012) advocates more study in the area of decision-making processes of leaders and the ethicality of such decision processes.

The Moral Manager

From the literature on ethical leadership that has been discussed so far there appears to be a descriptive focus: how leaders ought to behave – what do leaders need to do to be ethical? In response to this focus some scholars have offered a view on ethical leadership from a social learning perspective (Brown and Treviño, 2006; Brown et al., 2005). From a social learning theory (Bandura, 1977) perspective the proposition is that for leaders to be seen as ethical by their followers, they need to be credible role models. Further to this, ideas regarding the *moral manager* (Treviño et al., 2000, 2003) suggest that ethical leadership is represented by a leader's proactive efforts to influence followers' ethical behaviour. Here, therefore, there is a prominent link to leaders developing followers along an ethical or moral path. One aspect that appears to be an enduring question within the ethics and leadership literature is that of the tension between self-interest and collective good (Ciulla and Forsyth, 2011). It is this tension that the chapter now discusses by exploring altruism, authentic leadership, narcissism and toxic or bad leadership.

Altruism

Kanungo and Mendonca (1996) make an explicit link between ethical leadership and altruism in their three-dimensional framework. In a later version of their book Mendonca and Kanungo (2007) suggest that ethical leadership comes about when a leader fulfils obligations because of their moral principles as opposed to considerations of media impact, and the leader fulfils these moral obligations because of virtue. They see it as essential for leaders to be altruistic. This resonates with earlier ideals of servant leadership (Greenleaf, 1977), which suggest that a leader's responsibility is to serve those who follow. Similar to servant leadership, Mendonca and Kanungo go on to explain that if a leader is subsumed with self-interest they are prevented from being sensitive to the concerns of others. Effective leaders, therefore, are those who can consider followers' needs and aspirations and have a concern for the welfare of the organization.

Avolio and Locke (2002) initiated an interesting discussion regarding altruism and debated the level to which leaders are actually motivated by altruistic terms as opposed to egotism. Edwin Locke, for example, asked how realistic is it to find leaders who have ultimately a selfless pursuit of goals. This links to Manfred Kets de Vries' (2003) work around the narcissistic leader, which we discuss in more detail below, but before we do, a discussion of authentic leadership would be useful.

VIGNETTE 13.1

Extract from Case Study 5 highlighting the importance of understanding leadership and altruism

June started the Pierian Centre in a quiet and evolutionary kind of way, without a big vision or big plan. As June describes it 'I don't think I started with a vision! I started with principles and values and the sort of idea that it would be nice to set up a place that ran along different principles and philosophies from what I had experienced elsewhere. If that was the vision well then ... I wanted to set up something where the growth of the individual was the focus, that something could be part of the community and that was there to open the door ... that framework ... I guess the way we got people to see what the place was all about was one of the challenges: it was to live it and be it as the leader ... and it was challenging ... so there were never any doubt for me that if you stand up and say these are the principles, that you must live and breathe them. There is no choice and I think that what goes wrong in the world is that leaders pontificate but then don't live it. That's fundamentally where things in this world go wrong. To live and be what we say is a very deeply challenging process. And it means almost every day something happens where I think what shall I say ... if every time we have a decision to make we think about how our decision will have the best impact on the most marginalized in our society we cannot go wrong. That's about making an altruistic as opposed to a selfish decision ... it will always be a better decision.

June's approach to leadership clearly starts from the premise of her own deeply held personal values which include authenticity, social justice, service and creativity. June feels these are manifested in the belief that everyone is remarkable; the principle that every organization is part of the community in which it exists; and an ethos of welcoming and taking care of everyone who comes through the door.

1. To what extent is June being altruistic?
2. What impact does this have on her leadership? How is she able to lead?

Authentic Leadership

Developed from the transformational leadership paradigm (Bass and Steidlmeier, 1999; Price, 2003), an alternative response to the question of ethics and leadership highlights the need for authenticity as a leader (Avolio et al., 2004; George, 2003; Luthans and Avolio, 2003). The theory and research around authentic leadership and authentic leadership development have proved popular and often been linked to contemporary organizational issues regarding how leaders conducted themselves (Caza and Jackson, 2011; Gardner et al., 2011). The theory around authentic leaders has been dichotomized into three types or levels and has assumed an important role in contemporary discussions regarding leadership (Caza and Jackson, 2011). Caza and Jackson (2011) go on to highlight the three levels of authentic leadership described in the literature (Gardner et al., 2005; Shamir and Eilam, 2005; Yammarino et al., 2008):

1. individual personal authenticity – the level to which one know one's self and acts in accordance with that notion of self (see Harter [2002] and Kernis [2003] for wider discussions regarding definitions of authenticity);
2. a leader's authenticity as a leader;
3. authentic leadership as a phenomenon in itself.

There is a suggestion (Gardner et al., 2005) that these levels are hierarchically ordered, in the sense that authentic leadership is not possible without an authentic leader and it is not possible to be an authentic leader without first being an authentic person (Caza and Jackson, 2011). From a behavioural perspective and drawing on the work of Kernis (2003), Caza and Jackson highlight how the literature (Gardner et al., 2005; Walumbwa et al., 2008) defines authentic leaders through their exhibiting certain behavioural tendencies:

* self-awareness – an accurate knowledge of one's self – strengths, weaknesses and qualities;
* relational transparency – a genuine representations of self to others;
* balanced processing – the collection and use of relevant and objective information, which in some circumstances challenges pre-existing beliefs;
* internalized moral perspective – self-regulation and self-determination.

In their chapter, Caza and Jackson (2011) go on to describe the theoretical claims (antecedents, consequences and mechanisms of authentic leadership) and research findings from the area. We would therefore recommend this as further reading. Finally, Caza and Jackson point out some potential disadvantages with the authenticity perspective, one of which is the almost pervading viewpoint that authenticity is wholly desirable and that it always has positive outcomes (Caza and Jackson, 2011). This is contended by some writers and researchers (Harter, 2002; Kernis, 2003). Caza and Jackson go on to suggest that this is a possible area for future research. The authentic leadership literature and the link it has with self-awareness are connected to ideas around leadership development (Avolio and Gardner, 2005) and self-development. We will discuss this link in more detail in Chapter 11. There is, however, also a link to the literature on narcissism and leadership, which could be described as the flip side of leader authenticity and is addressed below.

VIGNETTE 13.2

Extract from Case Study 3 highlighting the importance of understanding ethics and authenticity

One day in May there was a flurry of excitement as Frank, on one of his rare visits to the department, called everybody together to welcome Michael Langer, the new head of procurement. Mike was a fresh-faced young man who, having started in consumer goods, had moved into heavy industry, and had just spent three years as head of out-sourcing in a steel company owned by a private equity firm. He made a brief presentation to the department, detailing his background and his delight at being asked to head up such a prestigious unit as Lowe Power's procurement department. He was polite and well-mannered and made a good first impression.

Frank's brief to Mike had been simple and direct: 'Shake 'em up, Mike. A lot of them have been here a long time, and have got very used to the comfortable life'.

1. What could Mike do to 'shake 'em up'?
2. What ethical issues may Mike need to consider and how might he overcome these issues?
3. Can Mike remain authentic – and if so how?

Toxic and Bad Leadership

In this section of the chapter we will look at the opposite of ethical leadership and explore toxic and bad leaders.

Leadership and Narcissism

The concept of narcissism comes from the Greek myth of Narcissus who fell in love with his own reflection. This has been linked to leadership through the work of Manfred Kets De Vries (2003). He recognizes the narcissistic leader as exhibiting an uninhibited behaviour filled with self-righteousness and arrogance. He goes on to explain that leaders considered to be narcissistic have a selfish and individualistic outlook on life to the extent that they display an inattention to organizational processes and structures they are supposed to be leading to heighten their own self-gain. What Kets De Vries found interesting was that these types of leaders were found frequently at the top of organizations. Research by Boddy et al. (2010) supports Kets de Vries' initial observations. They discuss the 'corporate psychopath', described as 'ruthless employees' who enter organizations and get promoted to positions within senior management. Boddy and colleagues' research suggests that these individuals are again found frequently at the top of organizations. This self-serving behaviour appears to be a powerful force in climbing the career ladder. If so many top leaders can be described as self-serving, narcissistic and psychopaths then this, in turn, brings into question the purpose and image of leadership in and for organizations. This has been explored in a growing literature on toxic or bad leadership.

Toxic and Bad Leadership

In the last 10 years or so the leadership literature has been fascinated not just with 'heroic' or charismatic leaders but also with the dark side of leadership; those leaders that could be termed as toxic (Lipman-Blumen, 2005) or bad (Kellerman, 2004). Below we highlight the literature that discusses these topics.

Toxic Leadership   Toxic leadership was a phrase coined by Jean Lipman-Blumen (2005) in *Allure of Toxic Leaders*. In this book she highlights the role some leaders play in attracting and then ultimately destroying followers, defining these leaders as toxic. She also highlights the psychological need for leadership and suggests that in some cases followers tolerate toxic leaders and even aid and abet their toxic endeavours. This book has developed a critical discussion regarding the moral and ethical guidelines for leadership. This issue has also been described as the Hitler problem by Joanne Ciulla (2004), where she identifies an issue when asking students whether Adolf Hitler was a good leader. Indeed, in classes students tend to have a heated discussion regarding this question and it relates to the word 'good' having two connotations – 'good' as competence or effectiveness as a leader and 'good' as morally ethical. These reflections regarding toxic and bad leaders usually lead to a further discussion with regard to psychological drivers and the follower part in the process of bad, toxic or unethical leadership. In addition a similar piece of literature discusses bad leadership and highlights the dual role of leaders and followers in bringing about this form of leadership.

Bad Leadership   Bad leadership is a similar concept to toxic leadership and was developed around the same time in a book by Barbara Kellerman (2004). Kellerman suggests that bad leaders exhibit a number of characteristics or orientations. These include:

- *incompetence* – the leader and at least some followers lack the will or skill (or both) to sustain effective action (with regard to at least one important leadership challenge, they do not create positive change);
- *rigidity* – the leaders and at least some followers are stiff and unyielding – although they may be competent, they are unable or unwilling to adapt to new ideas, new information or changing times;
- *intemperance* – the leader lacks self-control and is aided and abetted by followers who are unwilling or unable to intervene effectively;
- *callousness* – the leader and at least some followers are uncaring or unkind – ignored or discounted are the needs, wants and wishes of most members of the group or organization, especially subordinates;
- *corruptness* – the leader and at least some followers lie, cheat or steal – to a degree that exceeds the norm, they put self-interest ahead of the public interest;
- *insularity* – the leader and at least some followers minimize or disregard the health and welfare of 'the other'; that is, those outside the group or organization for which they are directly responsible;
- *evilness* – the leader and at least some followers commit atrocities. They use pain as an instrument of power. The harm done to men, women, and children is severe rather than slight. The harm can be physical, psychological, or both.

In addition, Kellerman highlights the importance of taking a relational perspective on this theory in the sense that the leaders are not the only ones to blame, as the followers also have a responsibility in moderating the behaviour of leaders. This is similar to concepts discussed in Chapter 6 where Shamir et al. (2007) discuss the relational perspective on leadership and followership. Although toxic and bad leadership theories have provided a particular critical comment on the leadership literature, there are some writers who go further and we explore these writers below.

Reflective Question 13.3

Think about a toxic or bad leader you have known. What did they do? How did they act?

Critical Perspectives

The Problem of Individualism   Knights and O'Leary (2006) critique ethical leadership, and in turn, the leadership literature more generally, for being too focused on an individualistic perspective. They suggest that an obsession with the self seems to be pervading the leadership literature and this has an impact particularly on models and theories of ethical leadership as discussed above. Knights and O'Leary go on to suggest that if one is too concerned with one's self image – a criticism lined at MBA students and programmes particularly – then the danger is that it is likely to be problematic for ethical leadership ideas, as there is a potential lack of acknowledgement of the ethical responsibilities of leadership. We highlight this topic in more detail in the section on community and ethics below.

Fuzzy Toxicity   Edwards et al. (2010) use film to highlight the fuzzy nature of toxicity. They ultimately challenge the notion of toxic leadership being a static entity that one can prescribe without understanding the power and political aspects linked to organizations, cultures and communities. This paper discusses the relational basis of toxic or bad and moral and ethical standpoints and uses the film *Batman: The Dark Knight* as a basis for exploring the fuzzy nature of toxicity and highlights three issues to be considered:

- *Good or evil?* – This reflection discusses the level to which we categorize leadership as ultimately 'good' or 'heroic' and that the toxic leadership literature responds by providing the villain to the previous literatures 'heroes'. Edwards and colleagues go on to suggest a blurred representation of the boundaries between good and evil.
- *Tyrannical tradition* – This reflection relates to identifying toxic, bad, good, moral or ethical leadership as socially constructed and that we are subjected to a tyranny of tradition, where we rely on tradition to inform our interpretations of what is good or bad. The labelling effect on 'toxic', 'good', 'bad' or 'ethical' leadership serves to mask the reasoning behind acts. This is elaborated on with examples from the discourse of The Joker, whereby he see his acts as not toxic or bad but ultimately about challenging the established order and power structures – a discourse that appears to be less than toxic.
- *Moronic morality* – Here the paper draws on the work of Durkheim (1951, 1965) to explore the pressure to conform to social norms. The language of leadership, therefore, provides a reason for inclusion and is used in organizations for this benefit. Organizational members then become trapped in discourses and culturally shaped narrative habits as highlighted in previous work by Ford (2010).

The use of film is becoming an increasingly popular and useful way of exploring leadership both in classroom situations and as a research methodology (Comer, 2000; Harrington and Griffin, 1990; Islam, 2009; Komaki, 1998; Warner, 2007). Billsberry and Edwards (2008) have highlighted other films that can be used to explore the notion of toxic leadership in organizations. They suggest films such as *Path to War*, *The Bounty*, *Star Trek II: The Wrath of Khan*, *Swimming with Sharks*, *The Smartest Guy in the Room*, *Erin Brockovich* and *Harry Potter and the Goblet of Fire*.

Reflective Question 13.4

Reflect on the last film you saw. What messages of leadership (good or bad) did it engender?

Ethics, Leadership and Community

From the theories discussed above the issue of individualism in leadership studies and research and especially ethical leadership appears to be problematic. Therefore, to develop more community perspective on ethical leadership is an avenue some researchers are taking. For example, as Knights and O'Leary suggest:

> [E]thics is not only choosing what to do as individuals, but also, and essentially, discovering who we are in relation to others – in short our membership of organizations, communities and societies. (2006: 133, referring to the work of MacIntyre, 1991)

> Local communities [as opposed to political or cultural community] are important vehicles for the recovery and expression of moral recognition and the building of personal identities. (Delanty, 2003: 71)

The link between ethics and community is not necessarily a new avenue for theoretical or empirical consideration (see Chapter 9). Donaldson and Dunfee (1994), for example, developed a framework based on integrative and social contracts theory which attempts to blend community-based perspectives of ethics and universal norms (Cunha et al., 2010). The model suggests that a norm would be: (1) created within a given community; (2) generally accepted by the members of that community; (3) abided by the majority of the members of that community; (4) in line with universal indisputable ethical principles; and (5) subject to prioritization by rules previously agreed upon. Cunha et al. (2010), however, criticize this model for being functionalist in nature and therefore as not adding much more than those models and theories highlighted above. In addition, this would highlight the lack of a theoretical consideration of community and the differing perspectives and fluidity of concepts associated with community (Delanty, 2003). Cunha et al. (2010) go on to suggest that notions of ethics and leadership need to be developed along five motives: (1) avoid 'black and white' views of ethical leadership and appreciate the 'grey areas' (Bruhn, 2008) or 'twilight zones' (Nel et al., 1989) of ethics; (2) adopt a process/relational approach (Bradbury and Lichtenstein, 2000) to ethical leadership; (3) avoid dispositional and situational deterministic explanations; (4) present ethical leadership as a social construction; and (5) incorporate the role of ambiguity in the process of ethical leadership (Cunha et al., 2010: 200).

> ## Reflective Question 13.5
>
> Think about your community. What does leadership look like? To what extent does this differ from organizations you have experienced?

Summary

In this chapter we have responded to the question of what is leadership for? To do this we have reviewed literature and research on core concepts of sustainability, ethical leadership, morality, altruism and authenticity. This literature suggests that leadership needs to include all of the above and these tend to be quite prescriptive regarding what a leader should do to be ethical, authentic and altruistic. In addition, we discussed the opposite to these positions and looked at the contemporary literature around toxic and bad leadership, which highlights issues of narcissism, incompetence in the role as a leader, rigidity, intemperance, callousness, corruptness, insularity and evilness. Again this body of literature also appears prescriptive, saying that leaders should not do all of the above. In response to these essentialist views we have suggested a presupposition with the self, the individual that appears to pervade the literature in this area, and suggested a need to take a more social, relational and community look at these ideas and concepts in further research. This highlights the relational and contextual nature of ethical and toxic leadership: what is seen as 'good' or 'bad' leadership is dependent on the relations between leaders, followers and the context.

Additional Reflection Questions

1. How might one reconcile the idea that self-confidence and self-assertion are important for career progression to the top of organizations and the leadership of others?
2. Who might we categorize as a toxic leaders? And why?
3. What examples of fuzzy toxicity can we identify in organizations and society?
4. Who are authentic leaders? And what might we recognize about them?
5. When is one exhibiting ethical leadership? And what does this look like?
6. How might we make leadership more sustainable for organizations and society?

Case Study Questions

1. From Case Study 2, a leadership development programme in Iraq, highlight how this development programme might be a factor in avoiding toxic and bad forms of leadership. What specific factors will help?

2. Read carefully through Case Studies 3 and 4. To what extent can you identify differing forms of toxic (Lipman-Blumen, 2005) or bad leadership (Kellerman, 2004)? And how do these forms of leadership manifest?

3. Read carefully through Case Study 5, which looks at a self-development organization. Critically reflect on the literature above regarding ethical, authentic and morally based leadership: to what extent does this case study embody these forms of leadership? How might these be effective? How might these be ineffective?

4. Reflect on Case Studies 1 and 6. To what extent is leadership behaviour being driven by sustainable and ethical issues? What evidence is there for a moral basis for leadership behaviour in these case examples and why?

Further Reading

Caza, A. and Jackson, B. (2011) Authentic leadership. In A. Bryman, D. Collinson, K. Grint, B. Jackson and M. Uhl Bien (eds) *The SAGE Handbook of Leadership*. London: Sage, 353–364.

Ciulla, J.B. (2012) Ethics and effectiveness: the nature of good leadership. In D.V. Day and J. Antonakis (eds) *The Nature of Leadership*, second edition. Los Angeles, CA: Sage.

Ciulla, J.B. and Forsyth, D.R. (2011) Leadership ethics. In A. Bryman, D. Collinson, K. Grint, B. Jackson and M. Uhl-Bien (eds) *The SAGE Handbook of Leadership*. London: Sage, 229–241.

Gardner, W.L., Cogliser, C.C., Davis, K.M. and Dickens, M.P. (2011) Authentic leadership: a review of the literature and research agenda. *Leadership Quarterly*, 22: 1120–1145.

Kellerman, B. (2004) *Bad Leadership: What It Is, How It Happens, Why It Matters*. Boston, MA: Harvard Business School Press.

Knights, D. and O'Leary, M. (2006) Leadership, ethics and responsibility to the other. *Journal of Business Ethics*, 67: 125–137.

Lipman-Blumen, J. (2005) *The Allure of Toxic Leaders*. Oxford: Oxford University Press.

14

Leadership, Language and Identity

The concepts of language and identity have to date not been discussed in standard leadership textbooks (except for *The SAGE Handbook of Leadership*) and represent a smaller sub-area of the wider field of leadership research in comparison to the other topics we have discussed so far in this book. Nevertheless, recent developments on the link between both concepts and leadership deem it important to be included as a main chapter in a comprehensive textbook on the study of leadership. While we will discuss the links between language and leadership and identity and leadership separately, we would like to encourage readers to remain open to considerations of links between all three concepts. The section on identity and leadership will certainly make reference to the role and importance of language where appropriate.

Chapter Aims

- Introduce and explore different aspects of language and their relevance for leadership
- Introduce and critically evaluate the relevance of discourse for leadership
- Critically discuss the importance of national language for our understanding of leadership
- Outline the ways in which communication is an important aspect of leadership
- Introduce the identity perspective on leadership
- Draw links between leadership, language and identity

Language – Why Is it Relevant?

There are as many reasons why language is relevant for leadership as there are different approaches to and forms of language currently studied. While language is often touched upon in other topics on leadership, such as culture, leadership development, context and so on, it deserves separate attention as a phenomenon and in its relation to leadership. Within the field of leadership studies, language has been predominantly addressed as a rhetorical device that leaders use and communication more widely as a key aspect of leader–follower interaction and hence as a factor influencing the success of leadership.

Alternatively, language can also be explored as 'constituting reality' (Wittgenstein, 1953), meaning that a phenomenon only becomes 'real' through our naming of it and the meaning we attach to that phenomenon – how we think about it and describe it – will impact our behaviours in relation to it. Although this latter interest in language has been vastly ignored by many streams of leadership research, it has been given greater voice more recently by critical leadership scholars. In this chapter we will address both approaches to language and its relationship with leadership. We have selected three main areas of language research that empower the role of language in our conceptualization and thinking of leadership as well as our practice of leadership. These three areas are those of discourse of leadership, national language as a cultural voice, and a leader's strategic use of language through the art of storytelling and the study of rhetoric. We will now discuss each in turn and make reference to the implications for leadership theory, practice and leadership development.

Leadership and Discourse

The study of discourse has received vast attention within the wider field of organization studies and will not be reviewed in detail here. For a good introduction to this field of research we would suggest Hardy (2001) for further reading. In relation to leadership and for the purpose of inclusion in this chapter, we will predominantly explore the study of discourse through its link to the social constructionist approach to leadership (introduced in Chapter 5) and the topics of culture, power and social categorization.

Hardy defines discourse as 'a system of texts that brings objects into being' and as constructing social reality (2001: 26). Texts can stem from or be shared by a variety of discourses yet are interpreted/translated differently through the lens of different discourses. Discourses themselves are contextual and historically as well as socially constructed and fluid in their nature and being. Alvesson and Karreman (2000) have differentiated between 'discourse' and 'Discourse' to reflect the two different foci that discourse studies can take and have taken with regard to leadership studies. Discourse, on the one hand, with a small 'd', looks at the local meanings within social interactions and is hence concerned with local issues and negotiated meanings of leadership at the individual and group level. Discourse with a big 'D' is, on the other hand, concerned with the Foucauldian study of the existence and power of dominant socio-historical conversations in organizations, societies and more generally, the social groups we belong to, and how these dominant conversations and themes affect the way we think, theorize on and practise leadership.

Discourse: exploring local meanings within social interactions
Discourse: study of dominant socio-historical discourse in organizations and societies

Reflective Question 14.1

One of the dominant discourses of the last century has been 'the need for constant change to advance'. Its influence on ideal leadership behaviours is particularly reflected in the popularity of transformational leadership and its emphasis on significant change as a leader's role. Has this discourse affected the priorities and practice of leadership in organizations you have worked in? If yes how, and what were the consequences?

Discursive Leadership Studies

Fairhurst (2011a: 495) has recently reviewed existing 'discursive approaches to leadership studies' and draws attention to the focus on local meanings and local situatedness of leadership within these approaches. This is quite contrary to the dominant focus of 20th-century leadership research on generalizable models of leadership. Instead discursive studies pay attention to how language and communication construct leadership 'in situ' (local context) and are hence linked to processes of social interaction. Fairhurst introduces two research examples (Fairhurst and Cooren, 2004; Sheep, 2006) of the still under-explored area of small 'd' discourse studies in leadership, and illustrates through these examples how such discourse studies are concerned with exploring the 'mundane, immediate, instrumental, and material aspects of organizational life where leadership action is concerned with making and managing meaning' in everyday life (2011a: 497).

VIGNETTE 14.1

Extract from Case Study 4 on small 'd' discourses at Brandon Trust

In the leadership team they have a phrase in common usage: "Change is the norm and a key component of our thinking and our expectations". We see change as a norm, because none of us live in a static world, we live with ambiguity. As leaders we expect to be continuously moving forward. It can be exhausting, but it's game on – part of being in the real world. It's much more than just changing the corporate colours, mere appearance. It's about behaviours. We are introducing coaching

(Continued)

(Continued)

for all our managers. We believe that everyone is a leader and an innovator, so what does this mean for how we behave? It's how you do your job that is key'.

Both Chris and Philippa echo Lucy's sentiments. As a leader 'You have to be able to stand back and not be conceited. To take advice by someone who is further down the line. A lot of people are too fond of themselves ... It's like King Arthur, his table was round so that everyone was equal. There was no head of the table. I think you can run Brandon like this. Everyone to treat everyone with respect. And if they don't, there's the door! I would say Brandon is run like that.'

1. Read carefully through this extract and make sense of any dominant organizational discourses at the Brandon Trust.
2. What are the implications for leadership and followership in this organization?

'D' Discourse Studies of Leadership

Fairhurst (2011a) also makes references to wider leadership and management large 'D' discourses that have led to socio-historically embedded systems of thought and that influence how organizations as well as individuals talk about leadership and differentiate it from management. For example, Meindl et al. (1985) and Bligh and Schyns (2007) have reflected on the romanticizing of leadership that we have witnessed in the leadership literature since the 1970s (see also Chapter 6). This has not only denigrated management but more importantly has also attributed organizational success and failure to leadership, turning leaders into heroes or villains. Ford et al. (2008) and Ford (2010) add to this through their discussion of how leaders are often depicted as transcendental beings in the wider leadership literature and organizational talk. In reflection on this dominant leadership discourse, mainstream leadership studies seems to be part of the search for the holy grail of organizational success as it produces linear, generalizable models of leadership that predict effective leadership.

One aspect of the most dominant discourse has been that of change embedded in academic, consulting and organizational talk through popular theories such as the transformational leadership theories. Alvesson and Spicer's (2010) book on 'metaphors we lead by' illustrates the extreme leader ideals that have been formed through these dominant Discourses embedded in and promoted through such popular theories as well as their limitations within leadership practice.

Gendered Leadership Discourse

Several of the above scholars involved in large 'D' discourse studies of leadership have drawn on Foucault's post-structuralist views on the role of power and gender in this. In

Chapters 7 and 12, we introduced this field of leadership studies by reference to the work of Collinson (2011), Ford (2010), Ford et al. (2008) and Elliot and Stead (2008). As highlighted in Chapter 12, Ford et al. (2008) have explored the performativity of the leadership literature and how through its existence and the engagement of individual actors with it, it has influenced organizational discourse, talk and subsequently behaviour as well. Ford (2010), Elliott and Stead (2008) and Kempster (2009b) have further explored the influence that the largely male image of the 'right leader' promoted through mainstream leadership literature has had on the nature of leadership development and the self identity of female leaders in organizations. This research has explored how the dominant discourse embraced in the leadership psychologist literature (Fairhurst, 2011a) of the heroic, male leader has been embedded in organizational competency and the appraisal framework. It is through these organizational structures that male and female leaders in organizations are then disciplined to conform to this ideal, heroic, male leader image.

> ## Reflective Question 14.2
>
> In the organization(s) you have worked in, has the heroic, masculine leader been an important identity? To what extent was this promoted by the organization through recruitment, appraisal and promotion processes?

Several discursive research studies have illustrated some of the consequences of this dominant discourse in organizational life. Ford (2010) with her research in a UK local authority has, for example, shown female senior managers who conform with the dominant discourse and subsequent identity of the heroic, masculine leader and have as a result experienced stress and anxiety as this dominant leader identity was not their own preferred identity. Zoller and Fairhurst (2007), in contrast, have explored the notion of resistance leadership as a response to this dominant discourse in organizations.

Interaction of Different Discourses

Fairclough (2003) has further explored how individuals are linked into and influenced by not just one discourse but multiple levels of small 'd' as well as large 'D' discourse that span across different social groups (at a local and societal level). As mentioned above and introduced in Chapter 5, these discourses are fundamentally contextual as they are historically and socially constructed and continually reconstructed within social groups. A specific discourse can hence also be seen as reflective of a group's social identity and acts as a mechanism for defining and reinforcing membership of the group as well as the shared sense-making of reality. This further highlights the power of discourses where organizations and society are subject to the continuing power struggles of competing discourses trying to dominate the shaping of social reality in a way that serves the affiliated group's own interests. An individual's identity as discussed further in the last section of this chapter can then be seen as a fluid, ever changing and evolving construct affected by this competition of discourses and associated social identities.

Koivunen's (2007) study of the local culture of symphony orchestras in two different countries illustrates the existence and interrelatedness of four specific leadership discourses within this setting. These discourses were described as 'constantly on the move' (Koivunen, 2007: 297) and potentially contradictory and in competition with each other 'for the status of offering the best and most truthful interpretation of social knowledge' (Koivunen, 2007: 298). The historical and social context of these interrelated discourses was further found to be translocal and fluid, affecting individuals' understanding of leadership and being leaders across distinct social groups.

This discursive view of leadership bears a significant importance for leadership theory and development as it suggests that the way we talk about leadership is influenced by the dominant discourses we are linked to. As discourses change over time in nature and importance, this will then also change and affect the individual's view and understanding of leadership. If we assume that our thinking and the way we speak about leadership affects our actions, we can see a direct link between dominant discourses and real leadership behaviours, actions and, as discussed in the last section of this chapter, leadership identities. Discourses of leadership can hence be seen to have power over individuals' thinking on leadership and leadership practice. The next section of this chapter will look at the national language as a cultural voice and as a potentially important level of discourse that affects individuals' ability to talk about, think and practise leadership.

Critical Thinking Box 14.1

The words leader/leadership and manager/management have been embedded in the English language and organizational talk within English-speaking countries for quite some time. Within leadership research we have taken for granted that the concepts of leader and manager exist and are somehow different. Yet other languages, such as French, Swedish and German, do not have a generic word for manager/management. This is connected to a different historical context of the profession of management and the existence of leadership in these countries. Future leadership studies need to explore the importance of national language for our greater understanding of the existence and relevance of what we call leadership and management in non-English speaking countries.

National Language

This section will explore the role that national language may play in an individual's sense-making process of leadership and is linked to our discussion of the limitations of cross-cultural leadership research in Chapter 10. We will highlight how important it is to recognize the fundamental differences in linguistic resources across different national languages and the significant impact this has on the meaning, existence and relevance of concepts such as leadership and management in different languages. Through this discussion we challenge the universal nature and importance of leadership and its relation to management and instead stress the need for explorations of these concepts in languages other than English. Recognizing the importance of such future linguistic research, we also review Jepson's (2010) research into the national language as a discourse competing with other discourses to explore the relative importance of national language for an individual's understanding and practice of leadership.

The field of leadership studies has only recently paid direct attention to national languages and differences in the representation of leadership in such (Jepson, 2010; Prince, 2006). This lack of focus on the national language may to some extent be attributed to the historically quantitative, standardized questionnaire driven focus of cross-cultural leadership studies and the subsequent treatment of language as a neutral device. Prince's (2006) research into Taoism and ancient Chinese has illustrated the problems with such an approach as he found leadership representations in this non-western language to be significantly different from western conceptualizations of leadership in its focus on context and action. Jepson's (2009b) critique of the use of standardized questionnaires for cross-cultural leadership research supports these concerns and highlights the dangers of misrepresenting how leadership is thought about, talked about and subsequently enacted in different language contexts. Social psychology has long stressed the 'inseparability of language and meaning' (Jepson, 2010: 427) and indeed pays specific attention to the ways in which individuals attach meaning to words that then shape thought and action in relation to a phenomenon like leadership. The meanings attached to words are contextually linked to an individual's current and prior experiences and are continuously changing through an individual's interaction with the wider social context and gathering of new experiences. Consequently, language is neither static nor neutral, but instead fluid and contextually bound.

Languaculture

Tietze et al.'s (2003) review of the relationship between language and culture draws on Agar's (1994) concept of 'Languaculture' to suggest that language and meaning are inseparable from culture. Slobin (2000) indeed argues that a national language is the cultural voice of a nation. These arguments are linked to the linguistic relativity hypothesis that suggests – and has been empirically supported – a national language to influence patterns of thinking and subsequently action from an early age onwards. It does so through its grammatical structure as well as the shared cultural meaning imbued in the language. Agar explains that a national language lays down 'habitual patterns of seeing and thinking and talking when you learn its grammar and vocabulary' (1994: 18). He recognizes as well, however, that languages and their habitual patterns of seeing and thinking change over time and are hence not 'a prison' (Agar, 1994: 18) of thought but can rather be seen as boundaries and ground rules guiding conversations between those who share this language.

Tietze et al. (2003) further draw our attention to the different impact that mother-tongue and second languages may have on an individual's thoughts on a phenomenon like leadership. The mother-tongue 'remains the comfortable room' and even when speaking in a second language, individuals will always remain in that 'comfort zone of their own meaning system' (Tietze et al., 2003: 94–95). This would then suggest that we cannot assume a shared sense of meaning attached to the phenomenon leadership. Conversations we hold in English – our business lingua franca – on leadership are hence affected by potential misunderstandings and misrepresentations if those having this conversation have mother-tongues other than English. These linguistic arguments on the inseparability of language, meaning and culture would hence suggest that it is vital to fully understand and embrace 'the lasting impact of the cultural codes and meaning systems of national languages on effective inter-cultural communication' (Jepson, 2010: 428) and to empower other languages by exploring their language-specific representations of leadership. As leadership studies has so far been dominated by publications and theories of leadership in the English language, future research needs to fundamentally challenge the taken-for-granted assumptions that this has brought in relation to the existence and importance of leadership and management in organizations and give voice to linguistically specific meanings of ways of leading and organizing.

Reflective Question 14.3

Reflect on interactions you have had with individuals who have not shared your mother tongue. Have you had any of the above described experiences of miscommunication? What implications if any may these have had in a leadership context?

National Language and Other Discourses

Yet, in light of above arguments for the importance of discourse, it is also interesting to explore the extent to which national language matters for an individual's understanding and enactment of leadership and is more or less important than other discourses on leadership. Jepson's (2010) research into representations of leadership in the English and German languages in a small-scale qualitative study in the chemical industry has shed some light on this question. Her data showed evidence of coexisting as well as competing national, organizational and transnational discourses on leadership affecting individuals' action theories of leadership. While she found evidence for the importance of the national language as a cultural voice and examples of the historically and socially situated meanings of leadership in the German language in the majority of individual accounts in her data, her analysis also revealed tension and competition between the national and organizational as well as translocal discourse of leadership. Jepson (2010) suggests that this shows the national language is not always the dominating discourse and that it may indeed be other organizational or occupational discourses that are affecting an individual's action theory of leadership more at a specific point in time.

Jepson (2010) stresses further that the dominating discourse, be it the national one or not, is likely to change as an individual's context and circumstances constantly change, hence leading to an unstable and fluid individual action theory of leadership. She concludes that the national language is of importance as it 'sets the parameters within which conversations on leadership can and do take place' (Jepson, 2010: 441) but we can certainly not say that it is the only discourse that matters and affects individuals' thinking on and practice of leadership.

Understanding and Working with Language

A longstanding interest for several leadership scholars such as Grint (1997, 2000) has been a focus on how language is being used and can be used by leaders to help encourage their followers towards achieving a set goal. This section will review some of these rhetorical devices but will also turn more widely towards language as a tool for meaning making and link this idea to aesthetic work such as storytelling and Habermas's notion of communicative rationality.

Grint's (1997) book on classical, contemporary and critical approaches to leadership provided an important contribution to the strand of leadership studies that is concerned with exploring language and communication as a practical means to understanding leadership and developing leadership. In his book, Grint (1997) dedicates a whole section to carefully chosen extracts from classical writings by Plato, Sun Tzu, Machiavelli and Pareto to engender a discussion from these classical texts to very current leadership issues around power, organizing and the importance of leaders and leadership. This is further embedding the study of leadership more widely in the field of art, poetry and politics through a focus on communication on leadership and communication by leaders throughout history. Grint's (2010) recent article on the sacred in leadership further talks about the non-verbal aspects of communication in the process of leadership and explores the importance of seeing leadership also as a space within which the distance between leaders and followers is important as well as the role of leader as silencers of followers' anxieties.

Communication Models

Unlike most other existing textbooks, Bratton et al. (2005) devote an entire chapter to looking at the importance of communication in the interaction between leaders and followers. Drawing on earlier work by Stech (1983), Hughes et al. (1999), Smither (1988) and Hartley and Bruckmann (2002), they discuss various models of communication, leadership communication styles and barriers to communication. Bratton et al. (2005) draw attention to the importance of good communication skills and an exchange model of communication instead of a transmission model. Effective communication within leadership means that the leader is not only able to transmit information effectively but also communicate ideas, tell stories and be an active listener.

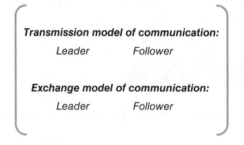

Figure 14.1 **Communication model**

Hatch et al. (2005) expand on the usefulness of storytelling as a means for leaders to communicate important ideas more effectively to their followers. They argue that this is a key skill for leaders in the face of today's complex and messy problems and change intensive work environments. Drawing on Smircich and Morgan's (1982) concept of meaning making, leaders should not aim to primarily transmit facts but are inevitably looked at for meaning making by their followers. It could hence be seen as a key leadership skill to be able to see effective communication with followers as an interactive meaning making process and to be able to make proactively meaning of information and reality in the organization for and with followers.

Barriers to Effective Communication

Yet, effective communication does not necessarily come easy for leaders and Bratton et al. (2005) draw on Smither's (1988) work to describe six barriers to effective communication: serial communication (that is, too many links in the communication chain creating too much noise around the original message), status differences (that is, hierarchical relationships, political behaviours), social conformity (that is, strict conformity or groupthink within a group allowing only one opinion), spatial distance (that is, physical locality), defensiveness (that is, self-protective behaviour on behalf of the leader or follower) and cultural differences (see previous section). Most of these barriers seem inevitable within medium and large companies as detailed managerial hierarchies create long communication chains between those at the top and the bottom of the organization, and enforce status differences based on hierarchical positions and political behaviours across the hierarchy and physical distance between different groups and hierarchical levels. This physical distance and cultural differences may also be present when working with a group that is geographically dispersed and/or culturally diverse. Finally, and coupled with political behaviours is the possible tendency for either leader or follower to be defensive of their own opinion and/or knowledge base in order to not be excluded or disadvantaged. This can be particularly true in small- to medium-sized organizations where the pressure is strong to conform to and with the decisions and opinions of senior management, especially when those at the top have very strong views about the identity and direction of the company and where criticism is felt to be directly linked to a lack of loyalty to the company.

VIGNETTE 14.2

Extract from Case Study 1 highlighting the importance of proactive communication

Between the years 2008 and 2011, Space Engineering Services grew rapidly due to several contractual wins. More resources were needed to cope with the demand. As a result of this more managers needed to be recruited, and thus engineers who were very good at their job became managing engineers or managers ...

Space Engineering Services engineers are primarily remote, working either solely or in pairs. They see their line manager perhaps once a month as the core communication is by telephone. Engineers also do not have access to E-mail, and so any company-wide communication is sent via post. After initial focus groups and interviews, it was found that engineers' morale was generally low. They believed that senior management did not care, and they were always the last to find out core company decisions that would directly affect them.

Over the past three years, the engineers had been subject to several amounts of change. This made employees extremely nervous about their positions. This uncertainty was not helped again by the lack of communication from senior management.

(Continued)

(Continued)

Within the organization and the engineering industry, there is a precarious nature of annual (no longer) service contracts to key customers. The customer typically draws contracts for between 1 and 2 years, decreasing the risk on service delivery. The effects for the supplier tend to create an ethos of uncertainty which is echoed throughout the company. It was seen throughout Space Engineering Services that it also created a culture of gossiping and 'story telling', where a lack of communication from senior leaders allowed for gossip to prevail across all employees.

1. Evaluate Smircich and Morgan's (1982) concept of meaning making in relation to this vignette. How could meaning making be done in this context?
2. Reflect on the barriers to affective communication. What issues does senior management need to address to improve communication in this organization?

Reflective Question 14.4

In light of the above barriers to effective communication, what can leaders do to counteract these difficulties?

These barriers to effective communication illustrate the value-ladenness of language and the political aspects and role of power within communication processes affecting how a message is sent, received and interpreted. This further highlights the interactive, fluid and negotiated nature of communication between leaders and followers. Skilful communication can, according to Bratton et al. (2005), be seen as not only a reflector of reality but more importantly as also a constructor of reality. They draw on the example of Martin Luther King's 'I have a dream' speech and how this through its rhetorical devices skilfully targeted meaning, and through its delivery managed to excite and move its audience. The message itself is not exciting but the use of metaphors, irony, emotion, repetitions and so on demonstrated the speaker's ability to relate to the audience and construct a new reality through the words and non-verbal cues together with the audience. Seeing storytelling as a key communicative skill for leaders further enhances this element of co-construction of reality through the story and the message. Not only can the past and present be re-storied to meet the current needs of the idea or message to be shared but the leader as storyteller can also demonstrate new, alternative endings to a story and hence co-create with the audience visions for the future. Taylor and Ladkin (2009) stress in their review of aesthetic and art-based forms of leadership development, how important such skills of improvisation and alternative ways of engaging with the essence of a phenomenon or idea are for leaders in dealing with messy, complex problems and changing realities.

Communicative Action

Finally, a link is made by Bratton et al. (2005) to Habermas's work on communicative action, rationality and leadership. Communicative action means that every dialogue should end with mutual understanding and agreement. He recognized that communicative statements are inevitably shaped and influenced by existing ideologies and social conventions within society and organizations, and subsequently argued that for communication to be successful a conversation needs to be undistorted and uninterrupted and that there needs to be communicative rationality: 'a way of responding to the validity claims of various statements. A high level of communicative rationality thus signifies that perceptions are being based upon statements which are intelligible, that the statements reflect honesty and sincerity, that the statements are true or correct and that they accord with the prevailing norms' (Alvesson and Skoldberg, 2000: 119). Habermas (1984) argued that in an ideal situation where communicative rationality prevails, every member of the situation has an equal right and chance to speak as only the argument, and not the position, power or ideology, matters.

From a leadership perspective, this seems to describe an ideal scenario for effective communication and arguably effective leadership. Yet, Bratton et al. (2005) stress that such an ideal situation is, unfortunately, hardly ever achieved in an organizational setting where leadership and followership are often embedded in a hierarchical relationship, status differences and a different real or perceived access to power and information. Consequently, communication should maybe be seen as always distorted by the power, values, politics and status in organizations – something a leader needs not only to be aware of but also to understand and deal with on a daily basis.

Leadership as an Identity

Identity and identity constructions are well established research areas within the field of organization studies but have to date received relatively little attention from leadership scholars. They have been considered in the past as part of leadership development and scholars have written about the identity development of leaders. More recently though, publications in the UK by Ford et al. (2008), Kempster and Stewart (2010) and Kempster (2009b) have provided further bridges between the study of leadership and that of identity and identity construction from a critical and social constructionist perspective. We will hence consider all these contributions in turn, make linkages back where appropriate to language, and finally reflect on notions of anxiety and desire in light of leadership identity.

It is important to be aware of the two strands of leadership studies focusing on identity construction and identity work in leadership. The longer standing one, and arguably more closely tied to popular literature and leadership development practices, approaches identity from a psychology perspective as 'a unitary coherent construction produced by the individual' (Sinclair, 2011: 508). By this we mean that we assume that an individual has one single identity that is developing and can be developed over time. The focus here is hence an introspective one, that is, identity within the individual. This perspective is closely linked to continuous self-development, aiming to foster a coherent and stable self in leaders and in Sinclair's (2011) view has tended to promote the marketing of the self, turning the leader into a brand.

Psychology perspective on identity: a unitary coherent construction produced by the individual

A more recent second, critical strand of leadership studies – influenced by critical accounts from sociologists and cultural theorists – has moved away from such essentialist approaches to leader identities (Ford et al., 2008) and focused instead on how identities are produced, controlled and resisted (Alvesson and Sveningsson, 2003a; Collinson, 2003; Ford et al., 2008; Sveningsson and Larsson, 2006). This strand recognizes and explores the increasing organizational and societal pressure on managers to conform to the dominant leadership discourse and become the ideal leader depicted in this discourse. It also develops the view of identity as multiple, temporary, changing and socially constructed rather than single, consistent and introspective. This includes an exploration of the multiple possible selves of an individual and possible tensions in the individual's process of becoming an identity (Ford, 2010; Kempster 2009b; Kempster and Stewart, 2010).

Sociology perspective on identity: self identities are temporary, fluid and co-constructed within the social context

---

Reflective Question 14.5

Consider your views, behaviour, attitude and values in different contexts at work, such as when chatting with colleagues in the office, attending your appraisal and in an official meeting with your managing director. Do you change your behaviours and attitudes in these situations? If you do so why do you think they are different?

Dominant Leader Identities

Linked to discursive studies on leadership, these identity studies of leadership also draw on Foucauldian notions of power and explore identities as discursive, social constructs. This new strand of leadership and identity studies problematizes the notion that managers have to 'become' leaders (Ford and Harding, 2007) and dominant identities promoted through wider leadership discourse of the heroic (Grint, 2010), the transcendental (Ford, 2010) and the saint (Alvesson, 2010). Ford's (2010) psychosocial study of female senior managers in a UK local authority illustrates the organizational compliance and self-regulatory mechanisms in place where these senior managers repress preferred identities in order to conform to what is perceived to be the 'ideal' leader identity in the workplace.

As mentioned above in the discourse section of this chapter, this ideal identity is often a masculine, competitive and heroic one. The suppression of other preferred selves was illustrated to lead to anxieties and stress in these leaders (Ford, 2010). This gender issue within these dominant leader constructions and the subsequent pressure to conform to this identity is further reflected in research by Elliott and Stead (2008) and Kempster (2009). Ford et al. (2008) argue in their book *Leadership as Identity* that it is the dominant leadership literature and wider media – for example, the leader persona of Lord Alan Sugar in *The Apprentice* (a popular BBC television programme about a competition for a lucrative apprenticeship with Lord Sugar) – that have created a dominant discourse that enforces this dominant leader identity. Sinclair (2011) makes reference to the social identity theory of leadership (Hogg et al., 2003) and authentic leadership literature (see Guthey and Jackson, 2005, for critique) as examples of leadership studies that actively ask managers and leaders to shape and adapt themselves to the social identity of the group or to become 'the authentic leader'. The use of psychometric testing, competency frameworks and 360-frameworks has further embedded this pressure to become and be a specific leader within organizations.

VIGNETTE 14.2

Extract from Case Study 3 demonstrating an influential leader and his potential impact on the ideal leader image in this organization

Despite the amount of preparation that Ken had put into Frank's presentation, Frank had simply prefaced the event with a 10 minute chat on what was needed and why, leaving it to Ken to present the detailed proposal. It didn't help that Frank later left the meeting, only returning to close what had obviously been a bad-tempered session. The main objections had been (a) disagreement on the problems and opportunities faced by the department, (b) that the new structure would not address them, and (c) a petty process point, 'why consult us now if you have already made up your mind what you are going to do?' Frank's 'You're not taking them with you, Ken' seemed a poor return for all the hard work he had put in.

1. Based on this vignette, what is the dominant leader identity portrayed through Frank's behaviour in this presentation? How may this affect the behaviour of other leaders?
2. What impact may this have on followers' image of ideal leadership?

Leader Becoming

Linked to this second strand of leadership and identity studies – and first introduced in Chapter 11 – is also work by Kempster and Stewart (2010) and Kempster (2006, 2009b) on leadership construction and the process of becoming a leader. Kempster and Stewart (2010), for example, analysed an autoethnographic account of the process of becoming a leader that a specific senior manager went through. The analysis shows this process to be a socially constructed and locally situated one, where the leader is drawing actively and subconsciously on previous and current on-the-job experiences with existing leaders in the organization. Kempster and Stewart (2010) argue that this illustrates how one's own practice and experience of other's leadership are mutually constructing processes. The leader identity one becomes is hence one that is locally situated and constructed in relation to important others – both positive and negative.

It is through the experiences of what we perceive as good or bad leadership in a specific context that we come to identify with the ideal leader identity we wish to become. The self and the social context are here interlinked through the experiences that the individual has in a given community with what leading looks like and means within the context of that very community (Wenger, 1998). These experiences will shape their self identity of leadership as well as influence the community's shared sense of what leadership is through their own leadership practice. There is further an aspirational element to a leader identity, which lies in the temporal, continuously changing nature of identity, that leads to an individual forever striving to become a leader but never actually 'being' that ideal leader as the very notion of what is 'ideal' is subject to continuous change. An individual will carry a multitude of 'provisional selves' (Markus and Wurf, 1987) that resemble the internal process of identity prototyping based on a comparison between the self and important others in specific contexts. As important others, self and specific contexts are changing, and so are these multiple provisional selves and their relative importance in the process of becoming the individual's leader identity.

Parallels have also been drawn by Kempster (2006) between the process of learning to become a leader and an apprenticeship that is equally aspirational and truly locally situated in its nature. The notion of a multitude of provisional selves also means that theoretically there is a multiplicity of possible leader identities for an individual at any given point in time and the most important leader identity that the individual draws on or strives for is dependent on the context. It is further temporary as the individual continues to interact with important others in practice, gains experiences through own practice and deploys other possible leader identities in the course of this development. This research then supports the argument against essentialist approaches to leader identity and the falsity of the assumption that an individual could ever have a stable and coherent identity. Instead, Kempster and Stewart's (2010) autoethnographic study illustrates the socially constructed, locally situated and never-ending, continuous process of becoming instead of being a leader.

> ## Reflective Question 14.6
>
> Who are the 'important others' for you in relation to leadership? Are these positive or negative associations? Reflect on whether this is reflected in your views on leadership.

Critical Views on Identity Construction

Finally, it is important to note the role of anxiety and desire in these processes of leadership identity and construction – an area that has not been addressed by psychological approaches to leader identity and leadership development but has most recently been brought into the wider discussion within the sociological, critical stream of leadership studies (Ford, 2010; Grint, 2010; Schedlitzki et al., 2011). As noted above, Ford's (2010) psychosocial study with senior female managers has highlighted the anxieties carried by these managers stemming from preferred leader identities that are being suppressed in order to conform to the dominant leader identity embedded in organizational discourse and the wider leadership literature. It has further been argued (Ford et al., 2008; Sinclair, 2011; Schedlitzki et al., 2011) that the wider leadership literature still tends to portray successful leaders as heroes and provides lists of ideal leadership behaviours and attributes that are unattainable in real life by one individual. The wider literature further fails to acknowledge fully that individuals work in organizational contexts that are political, emotional and cultural in their nature which limits the degree to which individuals have control over their own and others' actions. The experience of not being able to live up to the expectations of ideal leaders promoted in popular discourse may hence lead to and reinforce anxieties within managers, as illustrated by Ford (2010).

While Ford et al. (2008), Ford (2010) and Ford and Harding (2007) call for non-essentialist leadership development that is reflective on multiple competing possible leader identities and the falsity of the assumption that an individual can develop a stable, coherent self that matches the heroic ideal stipulated in the leadership literature, Grint (2010) further highlights that such a move away from the focus on the heroic individual in leadership may be quite difficult. Grint (2010) argues that leaders 'emerge out of the consequence of the existentialist angst created within individuals resulting from a permanently unstable world associated with uncertainty and ever present equivocation over purpose' (Schedlitzki et al., 2011: 16). He notes that it is easier to look for leaders to carry or alleviate this burden of anxiety than to live with it.

Implications for Leadership Development and Practice

There is hence a 'natural', 'social' drive to identify individual leaders – heroes – who offer 'certainty, identity and absolution from guilt and anxiety' (Grint, 2010: 100).

Following Grint's (2010) argument, it therefore would seem that leadership construction is fundamentally linked to follower anxiety and equally creates distance between the individual, heroic leader and follower that is necessary to quieten that follower's anxieties. This separation may in turn lead to loneliness and anxieties on the part of the leader who is himself an individual filled with existential angst. The focus on the individual 'saviour' who brings certainty and identity for followers certainly feeds into the popular heroic leader identity that Ford's (2010) study showed to be so problematic for managers in practice. As it is a fictitious, unrealistic identity, managers will continue to strive to become this leader but inevitably fail in doing so – leading to further deep-set anxieties concerning their own expectations and perception of others' expectations on who they should be as a leader and how they should behave. These reflections on the role of anxiety in leadership construction or leader becoming and identity have then key implications for the leadership development and leadership in practice. It most importantly calls for an embracing rather than silencing of multiple possible leadership selves as well as a careful exploration and acknowledging of anxieties as a natural aspect of leadership and indeed followership. This may then enable individuals aspiring to be leaders, in formal or informal organizational positions, to come to terms with the existing tensions in popular and preferred leadership identities as well as exploring and understanding the anxieties embedded in this ongoing process of becoming.

Summary

This chapter has introduced the relevance of language and identity for our understanding and practice of leadership. With regard to language, we highlighted the insights of discursive leadership studies that are also important for leadership development programmes in order to help leaders become more aware of the impact of dominant discourses on their own actions and expectations on them within their group and wider organization. We discussed the importance of national language as one such important discourse. Drawing on the notions of languaculture and linguistic relativity, we have highlighted the influence that an individual's mother tongue has on their ability to talk about and think about leadership. Unless language-specific representations of leadership are hence explored and communicated, leaders of multicultural teams may find themselves unaware of these different understandings of leadership within their group. Miscommunication happens not only across multi-language settings but can quite easily occur in any leadership context owing to the value-leadenness of language and the political nature and role of power within communication processes. It is therefore important for leaders to be aware of and develop their communication and rhetorical skills. Finally, we explored psychological and sociological approaches to identity and their relevance for leadership and leadership development. This review focused on the different notions of identity offered by either approach and explored in depth the power of dominant leader identities in western leadership literature and societies and their influence on leader becoming, leadership practice and development.

Additional Reflection Questions

1. What is a discourse? Can you think of a societal discourse and/or of an organizational discourse that has affected your view of leadership and management?
2. How does a discourse affect a leader's effectiveness?
3. What is the linguistic relativity hypothesis? How does it affect a leader's effectiveness?
4. Reflect on previous conversations you have had with individuals whose mother tongue was different from yours. Did you experience any miscommunications as highlighted by Tietze et al. (2003)?
5. Think of a leader with good communication skills. What are these skills? What does the leader do?
6. Reflect on miscommunication you have experienced in the past. What went wrong? How can a leader avoid this from happening?
7. Reflect on arguments for and against the existence of stable leader identities. What are the implications for leadership development?
8. What role does anxiety play in leadership?

Case Study Questions

1. Case Study 2 describes an international leadership development programme. Critically evaluate Jepson's (2009b) arguments on the importance of national language for our understanding of leadership in relation to this programme. What challenges may those running this programme encounter in relation to language? Can you illustrate the meaning of 'language as a cultural voice' through this case study?
2. Case Study 6 provides a brief overview of a strategic change project. Drawing on the different views on communication (for example, Smithers, Haberman, Smircich and Morgan) discussed in this chapter, explore the potential challenges and barriers to communication that the CEO running this change project may encounter. Reflect on how you would advise him in relation to effective communication.
3. Please read carefully through Case Study 3. What are the key priorities of the organization in relation to leadership? How is this reflected in the Ken, Mike and Frank's talk (discourse)? How does this affect individuals' behaviours?
4. Vignette 14.2 has highlighted the influence of Frank's behaviours on the dominant leader identity in the organization of Case Study 3. Read carefully through Case Study 3 and analyse what kind of leader Mike is trying to be and how this is

similar to or clashes with Frank's behaviour. How may this impact on Mike's success in the organization?

Further Reading

Alvesson, M. and Karreman, D. (2000) Varieties of discourse: on the study of discourse analysis. *Human Relations*, 53(9): 1125–1149.

Fairhurst, G.T. (2011) Discursive approaches to leadership. In A. Bryman, D. Collinson, K. Grint, B. Jackson and M. Uhl-Bien (eds) *The SAGE Handbook of Leadership*. London: Sage, 495–507.

Ford, J. (2010) Studying leadership critically: a psychosocial lens on leadership identities. *Leadership*, 6(1): 47–65.

Ford, J. and Harding, N. (2007) Move over management: we are all leaders now. *Management Learning*, 38(5): 475–493.

Jepson, D. (2010) The importance of national language as a level of discourse within individuals' theorising of leadership – a qualitative study of German and English employees. *Leadership*, 6(4): 425–445.

Kempster, S. and Stewart, J. (2010) Becoming a leader: a co-produced autoethnographic exploration of situated learning of leadership practice. *Management Learning*, 41 (5): 205–219.

Sinclair, A. (2011) Being leaders. In A. Bryman, D. Collinson, K. Grint, B. Jackson and M. Uhl-Bien (eds) *The SAGE Handbook of Leadership*. London: Sage, 508–517.

Sveningsson, S.F. and Larsson, M. (2006) Fantasies of leadership: identity work. *Leadership*, 2(2): 203–224.

Leadership, Arts and Aesthetics

In this chapter we follow current research that challenges the seeming overreliance in leadership studies and leadership development on logical reasoning and rational decision making. This increasing body of research draws on arts and aesthetics in order to emancipate leadership studies and to shift the dominant focus towards an emphasis on embodiment, sense-making and symbolism. This shift is argued to enable organizations to deal with and embrace ambiguity and uncertainty better and enable transformation. In order to give the reader an overview of this emerging field, we introduce notions of aesthetics in the study and practice of leadership as well as insights into perspectives on leadership as art and art as leadership. For further information on the use of arts and aesthetics in leadership development please refer to Chapter 11 in this book.

Chapter Aims

- Introduce the notion of aesthetics and sensory knowledge and explore their relevance for the study and practice of leadership
- Discuss current research on aesthetic approaches to leadership and highlight their argument for an emancipation of leadership studies from the dominance of rational and cognitive-based models
- Introduce and discuss the role of arts for our understanding of the concept and practice of leadership

Critical Thinking Box 15.1

Leadership and leadership development have so far been predominantly approached from a rational, reasoned perspective. Indeed this rational paradigm has driven emotions and awareness of other bodily experiences out of organizations and our dominant view of leadership and management.

Why Arts and Aesthetics in Leadership?

Many leadership and management scholars (Hatch et al., 2005; Wheatley, 1994) have for some time now argued that modern organizations are complex, uncertain and ambiguous environments where managers face wicked, complex problems in a context of frequent external and internal changes. These scholars have further suggested that a reliance on rational, logic decision making is inadequate as it falsely assumes control, knowledge and certainty (Grint, 2005a). Instead we need to engage not only with the mind but also with the body and emotions to deal with ambiguity, the un-knowable and uncertainty. It is with a view to achieving the latter, and understanding what this can mean for our knowledge of leadership and how we can develop relevant skills in leaders, that these scholars have drawn on arts and aesthetics to inform leadership studies. Hansen and Bathurst (2011), for example, highlight that through our engagement with notions of aesthetics we may be able to transform our understanding and praxis of leadership through a stronger focus on sensory experiences and sense-making as a core focus of leadership. This then departs from the rational image of management and leads towards an embodied sense of management and leadership, where a focus on emotions, sense-making and sense-giving is seen to be equally as important as cognitive thinking.

Parallel to the work on leadership aesthetics, we have also seen contributions on art and leadership where poetry, philosophy, visual and oral art are seen as sources of creative understanding of the concept of leadership. There are further lessons that can be drawn from these alternative sources on modern leadership phenomena and for leadership practice (Grint, 2001). However, any form of art can be seen as leadership in itself in terms of influencing others' mindsets, feelings and values. Finally, and as a link to aesthetics, we can see the practice of leadership – particularly as embodied sense-making – as an art. We will now explore these avenues in greater detail in the following two sections of this chapter.

Aesthetics and Leadership

Aesthetics as a concept can be described as 'sensory knowledge and felt meaning in relation to objects and experiences' (Hansen and Bathurst, 2011: 257). This has increased in importance within organization and leadership studies since an original contribution by Strati (1992) who argued that aesthetics – as emphatic knowledge, feeling and intuition – was 'central to management science' (Jackson and Parry, 2011: 124). Subsequent key foci within organizational aesthetic approaches have been the study of emotions and embodiment in organizations. This focus has also informed research into the use of arts and aesthetics as alternative methods and approaches to leadership development where the emphasis is less on cognitive models and more on activities that create a focus on felt meanings and develop sensory knowledge (Taylor and Ladkin, 2009).

Aesthetics and the Importance of Sensory Knowledge

Hansen and Bathurst (2011) provide a very compelling argument for the relevance of aesthetic notions of leadership alongside more traditional technical, competence-based and psychologically driven approaches to leadership. They suggest that a pre-dominant focus on technical competencies and preferable traits or behaviours helps to clarify organizational roles but works inevitably towards a reductionist approach to complexity. The perceived need to bring in control and predict effectiveness is at odds with the daily paradoxes and complex problems and relationships that managers are really facing in organizational contexts (Collinson, 2005). Hansen and Bathurst (2011) hence argue for a more qualitative, sensory approach to thinking about leadership praxis and dealing with complexity and paradoxes.

A move towards focusing less on the individual traits and attributes and more on the social processes involved in leadership is seen as essential as is a greater emphasis on sensory knowledge within these processes. The lived experiences of both leaders and followers in the process of leadership therefore take centre stage and the importance of body and emotions within this is being explored. Hansen and Bathurst (2011) propose that such an aesthetic turn in leadership studies is particularly important for our understanding of leadership in crisis and in relation to creativity where overly complex and logic-based approaches and solutions do not work (Wheatley, 1994).

The Aesthetic Perspective on Leadership

The last two decades have seen several contributions to the aesthetic perspective on leadership. Ladkin (2006), for example, has explored the aesthetic assumptions underlying authentic leadership and how beauty being in the eye of the beholder affects notions of authenticity. The notion of beautiful leadership or leading beautifully has been explored further since (Ladkin, 2008) and linked to classical philosophy. Kotter (1996) has also made reference to the importance of aesthetic awareness in change leadership where leaders need to carefully engage with processes of sense-making and sense-giving. This includes listening to and understanding felt meanings by those involved in the change process. Sutherland (2013) adds to these insights with his empirical exploration of the value of arts-based methodologies in leadership development to leverage aesthetic experiences that engage actively with complexity and ambiguity in leadership and organizations. He develops a three-stage model that explores aesthetic workspaces, aesthetic reflexivity and memories with momentum as a way of de-routinizing and aestheticizing the leadership learning and development environment. The outcomes of such alternative and aestheticized learning and development environments are shown to enable more memorable experiences and scope for changing of frames of reference compared to traditional, cognitive-based learning scenarios. Of relevance here is work by Ropo and Eriksson (1997) and Ropo et al. (2002) on the need for leaders to develop bodily knowledge alongside cognitive knowledge. Their concept of bodily knowledge refers to a 'sixth' sense that is developed through a greater emphasis on sensing and feeling as much as doing.

VIGNETTE 15.1

Extract from Case Study 5 to explore aesthetic notions of leadership

June's approach to leadership clearly starts from the premise of her own deeply held personal values which include authenticity, social justice, service and creativity. June feels these are manifested in the belief that everyone is remarkable; the principle that every organization is part of the community in which it exists; and an ethos of welcoming and taking care of everyone who comes through the door. As June puts it, '... the whole place was there to support people in discovering how remarkable they are ... this is distinctly lacking in the world ... I try and do it wherever I am ... relate to whoever is there ... we live in a disjointed and an unrelated world and we need to connect with people.'

1. Based on the above extract and wider information on June Burrough's particular leadership style provided in Case Study 5, please reflect on the extent to which June is engaging in sensory and bodily knowledge. What are the implications of this for her leadership of a social enterprise?

It is important to note that aesthetic leadership scholars do not argue for a greater importance of sensory knowledge over intellectual knowledge but treat the two as interrelated and influencing each other. Artful leadership can then be seen as a careful interaction of the mind and the body (Bathurst, 2008). What is, however, seen as essential is that managers and leaders are encouraged to engage in deeper, more holistic sense-making and therefore engage all senses of the mind and body. Artful leadership can then also be seen as an outcome of greater self-awareness of how the mind and body interact (Singer, 2003; Witz et al., 2003). This is linked to leadership development that enhances managers' sensitivity to and openness for a wider range of sense-making processes.

Emancipation of Leadership Studies

Hansen and Bathurst (2011) argue that the aesthetic turn in leadership studies may enable emancipation from the dominant traditional views of managers and leaders as rational, powerful and in control. They see this turn therefore as a crucial contribution to a more critical understanding and practice of leadership where critical self-reflection and self-transformation are a core part of the emancipatory process. It is in this sense further linked to seeing realities as multiple and socially constructed and where aesthetic processes of drawing on sensory knowledge and aesthetic philosophy may help to unpack and engage with our understanding of such social constructions and reconstructions of leadership (Grint, 2005a; Meindl et al., 1985). In Chapter 11, we touched on the usefulness of the aesthetic perspective for leadership development and highlighted how an engagement with artful tools and activities can enable the development of heightened sensitivity to other senses, that is, strengthening sensory knowledge and deep self-reflection in managers (see also Taylor and Ladkin, 2009).

Hansen and Bathurst conclude their argument for an aesthetic turn in leadership studies with reference to the 'revelatory elements of aesthetics: that by being alert to our sense perceptions we are better placed to discern the ways in which structures control and inhibit a full range of human expression at work' (2011: 262) – and thereby are emancipating both leadership as well as organizational work to open up to such wider sensory perceptions that embrace the irrational as much as the rational and the ambiguous, un-knowable, unspeakable as much as the controllable, logic elements of working life. O'Sullivan (2006) stresses, though, that such aesthetic action is difficult as it sets out to rupture deep set routines and habitual ways of living through critical introspection and intra-spection. Yet again through rupture, he posits, may emerge creativity and renewal in leadership and organizations as we let go of our false sense of complete control and start to explore holistically and with all our senses. Leadership can then be seen as a relational process of ongoing sense-making of self and others.

Reflective Question 15.1

How and why can a leader's senses help him/her to deal with change and other complex situations? Can you think of an organizational experience that would illustrate this?

Art and Leadership

The Art of Sense-making

Sense-making (Pye, 2005) and meaning-making (Smircich and Morgan, 1982) have been argued to be the essence of leadership. One could say that the ultimate aim in leadership is to master the art of deep, active and ongoing sense-making and meaning-making. By this we mean, the ability of a leader to distil and translate what is going on inside and outside the organization to the group they are leading in a way that is meaningful to that group. It is an art that calls for aesthetic processes of sensory knowledge and self-reflection and highlights the great responsibility the leader has not to abuse their ability to influence the group. It is therefore linked to our understanding of ethical practices of leadership. Jackson and Parry (2011) argue that art has been seen as a particularly useful and creative source to enable these processes of sense-making and meaning-making. They make particular reference to Grint (1997, 2001) and his contributions to our understanding of how leaders can draw on different kinds of arts – poetry, philosophy, music, painting and so on – to enhance their communication and sense-making skills. Hatch et al. (2005) have similar to Grint (2001) explored ways in which metaphor, mythology and storytelling can be used as rhetorical and meaning-making devices by CEOs. They skilfully highlight the element of drama in leadership and the usefulness of different plotlines in a story that conveys the essence and moral of a situation more convincingly than any report or presentation could. Humour as another form of sense-making has also been explored and research by Hughes and Avey (2009) that particularly links humour to successful transformational leadership where humour enables greater trust building with and commitment from followers. Other arts such as dance, visual arts and poetry have further been investigated (Cammock, 2002; Griffey and Jackson, 2010) as sources of sense-making for leadership. Schyns et al. (2013), for example, have employed a research approach centred around a drawing activity that has enabled them to gain unique insights into students' implicit models of leadership, highlighting issues of power, gender and race stereotypes. In Chapter 11 we also reflect on how these arts can be used in leadership development to develop skills of and for sense-making as well as provide transferable skills that are relevant for leadership practice.

VIGNETTE 15.2

Extract from Case Study 2 on the use of religious artefacts in leadership development

The oldest known writing in the world is a Sumerian clay tablet found near Babylon which contains a leadership parable, making this the oldest recorded leadership wisdom. Erbil – where we were delivering – has the oldest continuously inhabited settlement in the world. We were working with people from the land of great biblical figures such as Noah, Abraham and Daniel.

We had intriguing discussions about the Qur'an and the role of faith in leadership. Spirituality is an inseparable part of Iraqi life and leadership. The five calls to prayer reminded us of this daily. Iraq's isolation under sanctions had decayed the research skills of participants and independent study was made harder due to the loss of so much of the country's infrastructure. Information resources, libraries and internet access were patchy and unreliable. Power cuts were a daily occurrence. Verbal story telling was a natural teaching medium for our Iraqi friends. This was very useful whenever our modern technology decided not to work!

1. The clay tablet described in this vignette has cultural and religious value and meaning specific to the cultural context of the leadership development programme described in this case study. How may these be used in the programme?
2. What benefits would this bring to participants?

Art as Leadership

Another way of looking at the link between leadership and art is to see art and its symbolism as leadership. This perspective recognizes the power of art to influence an audience through its embedded meanings and shared truths. Schama (2006) has, for example, demonstrated how paintings have been able to influence and drive a shared identity through their shared sense- and meaning-making of a specific historical and social movement. The paintings can hence be seen to have influenced and contributed to social transformation. Similar impacts of aesthetic representations can be seen in theatre and drama where social movements are played out and driven further, enabling audiences to 'see the light' (Lancaster, 1997: 76). When we unpack this perspective on leadership further, we have to consider though the role of the author and creator of any form of art. This can be seen either as providing leadership themself through the creation of vision and symbolic meaning – through framing (Fairhurst,

2011b) the movement – or alternatively as a medium between societal movements, ideologies and meanings and the wider audience. The art product itself can then also be seen as a medium between the artist and the audience where both interact through the creation and active interpretation of the art product. More research is clearly needed into this perspective on leadership.

Reflective Question 15.2

Choose one or more images/pictures/diagrams to represent leadership. What are the images? What do they mean in relation to leadership? How is this linked to your personal experience of leadership? What emotions does this image evoke in you? Now write down a definition of leadership. How is your experience of the written word similar to or different from that of the image? Link your reflection to Taylor and Ladkin's (2009) article referenced in this chapter to further your analysis.

Summary

In this chapter, we have introduced the emergent field of aesthetics in leadership studies and highlighted the various ways in which art can be used for sense-making in leadership. We have also argued that art itself can be leadership through its symbolic power and influence on an audience. We have introduced the reader to work by scholars within this emergent field of leadership studies that stresses the limitations of a purely rational, cognitive and competence-based approach to leadership practice. They argue that technical competence and intellectual knowledge need to be balanced and supplemented with sensory knowledge. This enables leaders to interconnect mind and body, emotions and rationale with a view to more active and ongoing sense-making. Such connecting of mind and body further allows leaders to deal better with complexity and uncertainty as it recognizes the limits of our control over situations and others and starts to embrace the irrational and ambiguous in leadership and organizational practice.

Additional Reflection Questions

1. What is the difference between sensory knowledge and intellectual knowledge?
2. Reflect on examples where either a rationally-based or an aesthetic approach to leadership is more useful?
3. Why do we need a balance between sensory knowledge and logical reasoning in leadership?

4. Reflect on the use of dance for the leader–follower relationship. What are the transferable skills? What knowledge can be gained about leadership?
5. Sense-making is the essence of leadership. Why and how is this true?
6. Can art create leadership?

Case Study Questions

1. In reflection on the leadership development programme described in Case Study 2, how could the programme develop sensory knowledge further in the participants? What would be the benefits?
2. Mike, the procurement manager in Case Study 3, demonstrates a strictly cognitive focus on his role and the tasks of his team. How could the development of his sensory awareness and knowledge improve his ability to lead successfully?
3. Kotter (1996) suggests that aesthetic awareness in change leadership is crucial, particularly with a view to listening to and understanding felt meanings by those involved in the change process. Explore how and to what extent this may aid or has already been employed in the change project outlined in Case Study 6.
4. Case Study 5 describes the Georgian building that was carefully restored by June Burrough to be the home of and physical inspiration for the social enterprise she founded. Reflect on what the physical and symbolic influence of this building may have been on the organization. Has the building provided a form of leadership?

Further Reading

Griffey, E. and Jackson, B. (2010) The portrait as leader: commissioned portraits and the power of tradition. *Leadership*, 6(2): 1–25.

Hansen, H. and Bathurst, R. (2011) Aesthetics and leadership. In A. Bryman, D. Collinson, K. Grint, B. Jackson and M. Uhl-Bien (eds) *The SAGE Handbook of Leadership*. London: Sage, 255–266.

Ladkin, D. (2006) The enchantment of the charismatic leader: charisma reconsidered as aesthetic encounter. *Leadership*, 2(2): 165–179.

Ladkin, D. (2008) Leading beautifully: how mastery, congruence and purpose create the aesthetic of embodied leadership practice. *The Leadership Quarterly*, 19(1): 31–41.

Pye, A. (2005) Leadership and organizing: sense-making in action. *Leadership*, 1(1): 31–50.

Witz, A., Warhurst, C. and Nickson, D. (2003) The labour of aesthetics and the aesthetics of organization. *Organization*, 10(1): 33–54.

Epilogue: The Future of Leadership Studies

Within this textbook we have taken readers through traditional, current and critical frames of leadership research, theory and practice. Within each chapter we have drawn their attention to historical developments and divergent epistemological and ontological debates in leadership studies. Through such an integrative approach, we have been able to bridge the gap between sociological and psychological as well as mainstream and critical approaches to leadership. We hope that this has given a holistic overview of leadership studies. In this concluding chapter we draw on the discussions in this book to reflect on, debate and extrapolate the possible future foci of leadership research. We have found the experience of writing this book extremely satisfying, not least in the collation of information about a subject we hold dear to our hearts, but also the reflection and reminiscence this exercise creates for leadership scholars such as ourselves. It is from this standpoint that we reflect on the future.

We start our reflection here through the lens of our fellow leadership scholars who have featured most in this textbook and whom we have asked to provide personal statements and opinions on the future of leadership studies.

> I think leadership studies has to date managed to resist, to some extent, the pressure to focus entirely on how to increase performance, and in so doing to carve out a space for a critical sociological perspective on matters of authority, obedience, cooperation and shared belief (among others). In doing so, we have pursued an ideal of 'the good' characterised by intellectual rigour, ethical integrity, academic independence. However, I think there is a good chance that the effects of climate change will be very, very challenging to existing social structures, including academia; and that leadership studies will be drawn to focus more on contributing (albeit critically) to social and economic continuity amidst sometimes catastrophic change. In other words, we will want to help. In my view, we should start now to focus on contributing to the major transformations implied by a 'green economy'. Our analyses and conclusions should be just as rigorously researched, but their focus should be more towards action. We should take a lead ourselves, in our business and management schools. (Jonathan Gosling, Professor of Leadership Studies, University of Exeter, UK, 10 October 2012)

Leadership research appears to have settled on a general acceptance that it is a relational phenomenon. As such the historic obsession with the leader, and the leader alone, is increasingly seen as very partial. The relational orientation will enable a rich opportunity to explore leadership as a dynamic. A processual dynamic that draws on a social history of past relational experiences that inform on expectations of leadership; a dynamic that is contextualised; a dynamic that focuses on the practices of leading and following. The notion of 'leadership-as-practice' (Carroll et al., 2008) will become a fruitful area of leadership exploration. Practice has been overlooked and for far too long. Practice seen as both activity of leading and following and meanings associated with such activity can enable leadership studies to make a significant contribution to enhancing leadership development. This is because it addresses directly the link between how we learn to lead and follow drawn imperceptibly from lived experience and the ongoing application of what we have learnt. A corollary will be greater attention to follower learning. Finally I would draw attention to the associated notion of ongoing leader and follower becoming. This last point on becoming captures the essence of the relational perspective of leadership studies. Unlike the notion of becoming a leader (a leader centric perspective) leader and follower becoming is ongoing, never ending. It is shaped by past learning, is enacted by current practice and has a sense of future expectations and aspirations. Becoming is associated with meaning and associated with identity: an identity that is provisional, under constant flux and change, full of hope, excitement, aspiration, desire, disappointment and anxiety. Follower becoming is constantly entangled with leader becoming – the two feed off each other and are mutually constitutive in a malleable relationship.

This orientation to the contextualized relational perspective will by necessity stimulate the development of novel methodological approaches to reveal deep insight into the nature of the dynamics of leader-follower relationships. Arguably we are at a most exciting time in leadership research, almost a revolution. We are beginning to examine the fundamental aspects of leadership that have been overlooked in search of the great, sacred and heroic leader. In a sense exploration the everyday ordinariness of relational leadership practice will provide an extraordinary insight to the complexity of the phenomenon. (Steve Kempster, Director of Leadership Development, University of Lancaster, UK, 12 October 2012)

We will see much more evidence of people studying leadership as opposed to studying leaders. For too long, the study of the heroic leader has been a stain on the good name of 'leadership'.

We will see less focus on the leadership processes by which people have made money and created business empires; and more focus of how they have used that success to achieve more noble goals for their communities. For example, we might not look at how Bill Gates made his fortune, but how Bill Gates has used his fortune to make the world a better place. The successes of Mutuals and Co-Operatives is another example of how leadership within the organization has given way to the study of leadership within a community, as a criterion of success.

We will see more people studying business leadership by studying leadership outside the business domain. Leadership will be looked at through the lenses of music, drama, aesthetics and of the performing arts much more than in the past. (Ken Parry, Professor of Leadership, Bond University, Australia, 14 October 2012)

I'm quite optimistic about the future of leadership studies. As more scholars from different disciplines and from a wider range of national contexts become engaged, this young field of inquiry will continue to become intellectually enriched and culturally dynamic. My main concern for the future is ensuring that the gap between leadership research and leadership development is properly bridged in a generative and interdependent manner. If this is not attended to, we will be in danger of losing one of the key strengths of leadership studies which is its ethical action orientation. (Brad Jackson, Fletcher Building Education Trust Chair in Leadership, University of Auckland, New Zealand, 15 October 2012).

The last fifty years of leadership research has generated a proliferation of approaches and methods that undermines any assumption about the emergence of a consistent, let alone universal, understanding of the phenomenon. It seems unlikely that this trend will be reversed in the near future and more likely that the opposite will occur – diversity rules – OK! (Keith Grint, Professor of Public Leadership and Management, University of Warwick, UK, 16 October 2012)

The importance of making social scientific progress in understanding leadership cannot be underestimated. The work of the world takes place in groups, organizations, cities, nations, and international organizations. Individuals rise into leadership roles in these social contexts, where some leaders prove to be effective, but unfortunately many do not. If scientific knowledge could influence the selection of leaders, or at least provide useful insights about the potential pitfalls of traditional processes of leaders' emergence and selection, the quality of leadership should improve. In addition, for leaders themselves, research could provide guidance about how to be effective. Principles of leader effectiveness could be imported into training programs with the result that leaders might come to function better for the benefit of the people whose goals they are attempting to facilitate. (Alice Eagly, Professor of Social Psychology, Northwestern University, USA, 18 October 2012)

The future of leadership studies depends on the development and integration of humanities research into the field. The humanities provide the context and various interpretations of leader/follower relationships. The social sciences measure whether these assumptions about leaders and followers are true. Without the insights of history, philosophy, religion, and the arts, the future of leadership studies consists of nothing more than a collection of studies. With them, leadership studies will progress and be able to offer useful and timeless insights on leadership to scholars and practitioners alike. (Joanne Ciulla, Coston Family Chair in Leadership and Ethics Jepson School of Leadership Studies, Richmond, Virginia, USA, 17 October 2012)

In reflecting on the history of leadership studies, I note the shift between the earliest studies which focused almost exclusively on individual 'leaders' to more contemporary theories which recognize the critical role played by followers, and even context, in delivering 'leadership'. With the increasing democratization of society resulting from higher levels of wealth and education, not to mention the impact of technology and social media, I imagine this trend will only continue. The 'Occupy Movement' offers a glimpse of social mobilization which simultaneously appears to be 'leader-less' and ' leader-ful'. If it is to remain in any way a vital and enlightening source of insight into this phenomenon, leadership studies needs increasingly to recognize leadership not as a person, but as a social force, a crucial way of being together – sometimes as leaders, sometimes as followers – as we navigate the waters of our uncertain times. (Donna Ladkin, Professor of Leadership and Ethics, Cranfield University, UK, 18 October 2012)

I see a possible future of leadership studies as one in which we know more and more about less and less: that the study of leadership will become even more esoteric and fragmented than it is now, so that we produce more and more pieces of the jigsaw puzzle that characterizes leadership but still no clear unitary picture. I see the desirable future of leadership studies as one that integrates both quantitative and qualitative research methodologies in a blended way, agrees on a single definition of leadership – such as 'leadership is about showing the way…', and presents to the world of leadership practitioners and scholars a universally accepted paradigm for leadership. (Roger Gill, Visiting Professor of Leadership Studies, Durham University, UK, 19 October 2012)

Contemporary leadership studies is both flourishing and in intellectual crisis. We live in times of fascination with and great hopes invested in leadership, at the same time as this 'it' is extremely vague. Given the expansion of perspectives, ideas and exploitation efforts, we see an increasing ambiguity in the field of leadership studies. Leadership fuels into managers' identity projects and most people's wishes to attribute responsibility for outcomes as well as leadership developers' interest in selling people improvement projects. It is certainly a challenge to retain an intellectually meaningful and sharp understanding of 'leadership' and use it as a framework for managers and others in the influencing business. Two ingredients seem crucial in particular: use the concept in a less all embracing way so that covers less and reveals more and avoid framing it in an ideological (positive) manner. (Mats Alvesson and Stefan Sveningsson, Lund University, Sweden, 24 October 2012)

There has never been a more exciting time to both research and study leadership. Traditional approaches continue to privilege the leader within hierarchical formulations. Emerging theories of leadership recognize the more dispersed, flexible and decentralized forms of organizations that encourage a shared, distributive and relational leadership dynamic. There is mounting interest in more critical leadership studies that focus on plurality rather than homogeneous forms, presenting us with new opportunities of understanding leadership from within much richer, contextual empirical studies.

The future looks encouraging for further critical studies that focus on the relational, situated, reflexive, discursive and embodied dimensions of thinking about leaders, followers and leadership. Micro-revolutions in thinking and influencing practice are made possible through challenging the taken for granted, asymmetrical power bases of leaders and led; through exploring the interactions between people at work and through encouraging putative leaders to be more self-aware and less destructive of both themselves and others. Other recent initiatives include challenging the 'West is best' phenomena and the ongoing privileging of Western, Male, Anglo Saxon-informed models and approaches to studying leadership. Source of future productive research include the potential for learning from broader, interdisciplinary and multicultural perspectives – embracing spirituality, eastern studies and other forms of leadership relationships. (Jackie Ford, Professor of Leadership and Organization, Leeds University Business School, UK, 25 October 2012)

We need to go beyond mainstream functionalist and positivist perspectives with their underlying tendencies towards romanticism, essentialism and dualism to explore the constructed, situational and contested nature of leadership. More critical studies ask important questions about power, inequality and followership, and the shifting contexts in which they are enacted. They highlight the ambiguities, paradoxes and contradictions of global and local leadership dynamics as well as the importance of (fragmented) identities, insecurities and diversities for understanding leader-follower dialectics. After so many recent cases of destructive leadership in various sectors, critical perspectives should have a key role to play in the future study and practice of leadership. (David Collinson, Professor and Head of Department for Management Learning and Leadership, University of Lancaster, UK, 30 October 2012)

This series of statements is evidence to the breadth of current trends in the field of leadership studies across US, UK and European scholarly communities and the many possible avenues that this field may take in the near and distant future. As Keith Grint suggests, further diversity is the future of leadership studies! Among these diverse avenues are, for example, those exploring sustainable and ethical forms of leadership (Jonathan Gosling, Ken Parry, Joanna Ciulla) as well as continued enquiries into effectiveness and leader development (Alice Eagly). The individual statements further give voice to the continuing value of both sociological and psychological perspectives on and approaches to leadership studies. Joanna Ciulla and Brad Jackson indeed invite greater interdisciplinarity in leadership studies and stress the value of connecting with other fields such as history, philosophy and the arts to advance our understanding of leadership.

Major Trends in Leadership Studies

In light of both this series of statements and our own review of the field of leadership studies, it seems clear to us that one of the most significant developments in the history of leadership studies has been – and continuous to be – a shift of focus towards social constructionist, relational and critical frames of reference. This development appears as a response to the negative outcomes and implications that essentialist, standardized and stereotyped ideas of what leadership embodies have created for leadership theory and practice. For example, the field of leadership studies has seen a move towards feminized interpretations of leadership in response to predominantly masculinized notions on the subject (Chapter 12); distributed ideas in response to predominant individualized notions (Chapter 9); and ideas of worldliness and cultural interpretations of leadership in response to the predominant western ideals in the leadership literature (Chapter 10). Embedded in these changes is an attempt to move away from the tradition of normative leadership theories focused on organizational effectiveness. Instead, and partly in response to the numerous cases of unethical or toxic leaders and leadership incidences, leadership studies has moved on to explore the messy, complex, shifting and grey sides of leadership as a process and relation. Looking into the future, Mats Alvesson and Stefan Svenningsson warn scholars with their statement to avoid all-embracing and ideological (positive) frames of leadership. David Collinson further suggests going beyond romantic, essentialist and dualist notions of leadership and instead to continue to explore leadership as constructed, situational and contested. Jackie Ford agrees and sees the future of leadership studies as a space for critical studies on relational, reflexive, discursive and embodied notions of leadership that challenge taken-for-granted assumptions on power in leader–follower relationships.

Associated with this move we see a second major development: artistic and aesthetic approaches to leadership that can be linked to developing theory and experiences in practice (Chapters 11 and 15). This development has been particularly dedicated to bringing back emotion, felt meaning and sensory knowledge to our understanding and practice of leadership – an area that has long been silenced in our wake for professionalism in organizations and particularly management. In their statements on the future of leadership studies, Donna Ladkin, Ken Parry and Steve Kempster strongly agree with the importance of the aesthetic perspective on leadership and a greater focus on social dynamics between leaders and followers. Finally, we have through the critical and aesthetic turn in leadership studies seen a growing concern for other, so far silenced, discourses in leadership studies and ways of being and subsequently witnessed attempts to give these a stronger voice. Among these are issues of gender and other notions of diversity such as sexuality. We need to recognize that there are dominant voices in the field that may override others and that we should push to amplify the quieter voices.

Personal Reflections on the Future of Leadership Studies

In reflection on these three major changes in the field of leadership studies and the future statements of other scholars in the field, we see a continued focus on leadership as constructed, situational and contested as a key priority for the future of leadership studies. This includes diverse, robust empirical and conceptual explorations of leadership that strengthen the currently quieter voices of aesthetic, critical, relational and follower focused perspectives on leadership.

To realize this future priority of leadership studies, we would argue that we need to learn from both traditional, mainstream and critical, aesthetic perspectives on leadership and to take a more symmetrical or balanced approach to studying leadership. *Symmetry provides proportion to parts of the body and any whole to each other.* We see the goal of symmetry here not as one of unifying agendas but one that recognizes and values the importance of strengthening areas and discourses that have so far been neglected and in bringing these into balance with mainstream or traditional approaches to leadership studies and leadership development. We hence believe that symmetry is important for a number of aspects of leadership studies and will dedicate the rest of this chapter to explore three such issues here: leadership as process, leadership and context, and epistemology of leadership studies.

First, arguably the most fundamental shift in leadership studies of the previous century has been the change in our level of analysis from the person towards the process. We see the future of leadership studies developing ideas of leadership as process further and particularly through the lens of relationality (see Chapter 6). By seeing the leadership process as ultimately relational we are able to connect and recognize and explore the importance of all elements and components involved in this process. This may include individuals engaging in a relationship focused on leadership and exploring how these come to relate to each other in space and time. It will certainly entail exploring the roles we take up in this relationship as leader and follower and challenging the taken-for-granted asymmetry of the relationship we build through these roles. The study of leadership as a relational process must further and more deeply explore the elements of time and space as well as identity and power within it. Future research, we therefore suggest, needs to investigate the component contributors to this relational process, hence developing an understanding of symmetry inherent in the relational process of leadership.

Second, and connected, we see a need to develop our understanding of context in leadership studies. There have been for some time calls to explore context more deeply within the study of leadership (Chapter 5). However, we believe there is further work that needs to be done in this area. We believe that issues of time, space and place are still unnoticed in the theory, practice and research of leadership. Most leadership research is devoid of discussing space and place – physical and symbolic – in relation to leadership in practice. In addition, issues of time are also commonly left out of leadership discussions. Various questions arise, such as, is leadership a phenomenon of the moment or does it build up over time and if so, how? How, where and when do we take up roles that relate to the leadership process? Is it the space we share that binds us together as leader and follower or is it the time we invest in this relationship? These are all questions that might be responded to through more historical, longitudinal, ethnographic and reflective approaches to the study of leadership – which brings us to our final concluding point.

We believe that symmetry also has relevance for epistemological approaches to the study of leadership. We challenge that the question should be one of qualitative over quantitative research but more importantly that we need to ask what we can learn from the substantial body of knowledge and criticism of leadership studies that already exists and how we can contribute to this and move forward. We argue that such as way forward needs to embrace an epistemological approach that is about providing equal recognition for the different aspects of leadership we study and the elements that contribute to the process of leadership. This entails strengthening the voice of those elements that have been quietened in the study of leadership so far. Yet when we give voice we need to ensure that we do not repeat history and silence those that were previously dominating. Instead we need to provide balance through paying equal attention to all aspects of leadership. We would therefore call for parity and harmony in the approaches used to study leadership.

Doris Schedlitzki and Gareth Edwards, Bristol, UK, April 2013.

Appendix: Case Studies

Within this appendix, you will find six case studies that have been written by colleagues in reflection on their work with and experiences in organizations. We advise that you read all case studies in advance of your specific study of each chapter. You can then engage with these case studies in the following ways.

- Read each case study in full and reflect on the links you can find and make to chapters and specific ideas and models within this book, that is, make sense of what is going on in this case study through the lens of academic leadership models and ideas.
- Use the 'Case Study Questions' in each chapter to analyse in depth specific aspects of each case study in relation to specific ideas and models from the respective chapters. Again, we would advise that you read the cases studies in full prior to attempting these specific questions.
- Read the vignettes – taken from the case studies – in each chapter as an illustration of key ideas and models within the respective chapters. As the vignettes only show small parts of the full case study, it may help to also draw on the rest of the case study to engage more deeply with the reflective questions associated with each vignette.

Each of the six case studies looks at a different aspect of leadership and organizational life and is based on real organizations and real experiences of leadership and leadership development. Case Study 1 was written by a graduate working on a Knowledge Exchange Partnership with a refrigeration engineering company. It reviews her experience with this company over the course of 18 months and the organizational challenges she was trying to address as part of the project she was working on with the organization. Issues of change, leadership context and communication are pertinent in this first case study. Case Study 2 is more narrowly focused on the description and evaluation of a leadership development programme in an international context. It therefore addresses specifically issues of leadership development, culture, diversity and context. Case Study 3 introduces an interesting and complex series of events within the procurement department of a large utility company. It particularly highlights real issues of change, power, strategic leadership, authenticity and toxicity as well as illustrating different leadership styles. Case Studies 4–6 were written by one of our colleagues either in collaboration with a client company or as reflection on specific work with an organization from the public or third sector. Case Study 4 is the success story of the Brandon Trust, a charitable organization working with adults with learning difficulties, which has had to go through significant changes when faced with a turbulent external climate. It offers interesting observations on strategic leaders and leadership and delves into issues of context, change, gender, authenticity, culture and ethics. Case Study 5 provides a detailed picture of the female founder and director of a social enterprise. As such, it explores issues of leadership development, context, charisma, leadership, authenticity, gender, identity and culture. Finally, Case Study 6 is a short summary of the transformation of a local authority and as such provides particularly relevant observations on leadership and change, context, strategic leadership and power and politics.

Case Study 1: Space Engineering Services

Space Engineering Services has been established for 22 years as a refrigeration engineering company. By 2012, they had 700 employees (450 of which were engineers), were now nationwide and developing into different specialisms such as heating and air conditioning, and mechanical and electrical engineering. The organization is now established internationally, with offices in Hungary and Poland. Their main customers are supermarket chains; however they have started to branch into non-food retail and supplying/maintaining heating, ventilation and air conditioning.

Between 2008 and 2011, Space Engineering Services grew rapidly owing to several contractual wins. More resources were needed to cope with the demand. As a result of this more managers were needed, and engineers who were very good at their job became managing engineers or managers. However, with this new found responsibility came no formal training on how to manage people. HR issues were not being handled by the managers, but being dealt with by the HR department – distancing the front line managers even further away from people management duties.

Space Engineering Services engineers are primarily remote, working either solely or in pairs. They see their line manager perhaps once a month as the core communication is by telephone. Engineers also do not have access to e-mail, and so any company-wide communication is sent via the post. After initial focus groups and interviews, it was found that the engineers' morale was generally low. They believed that senior management did not care, and they were always the last to find out about core company decisions that would directly affect them.

Over the past thee years, the engineers had been subject to several amounts of change. This made employees extremely nervous about their positions. This uncertainty was not helped again by the lack of communication from senior management.

Within the organization and the engineering industry, there is a precarious nature of annual (no longer) service contracts to key customers. The customer typically draws up contracts for between one and two years, decreasing the risk on service delivery. The effects for the supplier tend to create an ethos of uncertainty which is echoed throughout the company. It was seen throughout Space Engineering Services that it also created a culture of gossiping and 'storytelling', where a lack of communication from senior leaders allowed for gossip to prevail across all employees.

Strategic direction

When starting the knowledge transfer partnership project, I asked to see the business plan to ensure HR and project objectives were aligned with the overall strategic direction. However, this was more difficult than originally thought, for the following reasons:

- Long-term strategic direction is challenging to determine.

As the nature of the industry is extremely reactive, long-term planning can be difficult. The strategic direction can change in terms of priorities at a given time.

- Directors rarely 'seen' by wider workforce.

Although the directors are visible in head office, the directors are not seen in the regional offices or out in the field. There have been comments about asking if the directors care, and even asking what their names are. There is a gap and a disconnection between senior management and front line employees.

September 2010

I joined Space Engineering Services as part of a knowledge transfer partnership scheme in order to join academia and industry. My position here was to design and implement a performance management process, looking at measuring and monitoring performance through an appraisal.

Also during this period I developed a SWOT analysis for the project, and a stakeholder analysis to think about who could be involved in the project team. These stakeholders identified were contacted to explain the project and where their involvement may lie if they wished to be involved.

To supplement this, I conducted consultation focus groups and interviews with employees to understand opinions from all stakeholders. I also designed an employee opinion survey to give a baseline indication of where employees' engagement stood. This included measures such as job security, opinions on managers, training and development, and performance management. The results from this employee opinion survey showed that employees in the service and compliance department (primarily engineers) were dissatisfied with the level of leadership and communication from management. They didn't necessarily receive any feedback on performance, or understand how their performance was measured. The other two departments (projects, and central services) scored better in these areas, however the overall score showed employees were 'dissatisfied'. Communication of the survey results spurred information on the performance review system, indicating that the low scores from the survey would be addressed through performance appraisals. The focus groups and interviews highlighted the low morale among the engineers. The engineers are mainly lone workers, and do not regularly see managers or regional offices. They stated that they felt that they were not important enough to receive information.

This highlighted the first challenge for managers. Employees, and in particular engineers, were disengaged with the company, and with managers. The focus groups illustrated that engineers lacked faith in the capabilities of their managers, mainly because they rarely communicated information to them. There is a tendency for engineers to talk among themselves, and so gossip is high in the organization. As soon as one engineer starts talking about something negative, it gets around the workforce quickly.

January 2011

The second quartile at Space Engineering Services focused on designing the new system. This included the performance review form, guidelines for use for both management and employees, the core competencies which all employees were to be measured on, and the policy and procedures behind the appraisals. Once the design was completed, I had started to focus on the pilot. With this in mind, I created a training package for the managers to understand performance management, as well as use the performance reviews. I trained 16 managers in performance management, interviewing skills, and how to conduct appraisals.

A second challenge for managers that emerged was the lack of training managers had received. There is a tendency to give higher emphasis and dependence to engineering skills rather than people. As there are such stringent service level agreements in place, senior management has a tendency to promote and reward engineering skills – as they get the work done. For instance, productive engineers are made into managers, rather than looking at who would make a good leader. Therefore managers have not received any training for things such as people management, or support during the period of taking on new responsibilities. Some managers had found HR issues difficult in the past, such as how to hold disciplinaries, or more broad issues, such as the consequences of speaking to an employee in a particular way. With no formal training on how to interview someone, engineers are recruited by a quick chat in the café. Therefore it may not be the best possible candidate that comes on board. With no formal training, managers are not necessarily equipped to perform their duties to the best of their abilities.

May 2011

The third quartile of the project was managing the pilot. This involved monitoring the performance reviews that were coming in, and advising managers with issues as and when they come through.

In August 2011, the pilot was completed. This gave me an opportunity to evaluate the effectiveness and performance of the pilot system. With this I conducted one on one interviews with the managers who participated in the performance interviews, and focus groups to gain group feedback. I collated the information and used the qualitative data to feed into the full implementation, and the e-system. The main points in the feedback were:

- Employees were dubious as to the reasons behind the performance reviews – they though they may be linked to giving them more work, or demoting them.
- Employees did not understand the relation to development, as all training throughout the organization was frozen.
- Managers wanted extra support through the process as they had not used these before.

These points were all taken into consideration. A communication piece was written to address employees and these concerns before the full roll-out across the organization.

One challenge for managers that emerged was their resistance to conduct performance management activities. Some had seen similar schemes that had failed, and some were dubious about the amount of additional time this would take, eating into operational duties. A few had an attitude where they felt they could get away with not doing it if they were bringing in money. This is a challenge for senior managers with regard to how to handle these managers.

November 2011

The performance reviews start coming though. Again I needed to monitor the completion rate, the quality of the performance reviews, and the levels of performance. There was a definite lack of people management shown in the reviews, as some were extremely basic. Some managers had still not bought into the process and did not start the performance reviews until they were individually spoken to by their senior managers.

After the performance reviews had taken place, I gained feedback from the managers that some employees were still hesitant about why they were happening, and thought it was a micro-management exercise. When asked how they explained the performance reviews, they replied 'I don't really know.'

January 2012

At the beginning of 2012, I was still monitoring the completion rates of the performance reviews, as well as finishing up any management training that was missed. This was coaching more than facilitation.

There were difficulties with getting managers to submit the reviews. There seemed to be a lack of commitment and leadership from the directors, which may have affected the buy-in from managers. With this in mind the overall completion rate was slightly lower than expected (76%).

After another round of employee opinion surveys in February 2012, the results reflected a drop in morale. There were some results that were below the baseline level of morale taken in December 2010, especially relating to items on management and training. These items were mainly in the service and compliance department. The items showed employees in this area were dissatisfied by the level of communication, support, and leadership displayed by their managers. They were also dissatisfied with the amount of training opportunities available to employees. A key management challenge in an organization without a clear communications strategy is this – how do you maintain regular communication with your employees?

Adding to this, in March 2012 Space Engineering Services went through an organization-wide restructure, making a 20% reduction in overheads. At the same time the company had a large (150 engineers) TUPE transfer out of the company. The engineering industry is renowned for continuously winning/losing contracts. With this comes a Transfer of Undertaking (protection of employees) (TUPE), where employees who work on that contract are transferred across with the contract to the new supplier. For leaders this means fresh talent, but it can also mean a diverse mix of capabilities, cultures and work standards. There have been instances where companies have used TUPE to transfer across employees who are not as capable, to ensure they keep a good talent pool in their organization. With all this change and movement, employees were now working under different job roles and for different managers. The completions of performance reviews were stagnant, and mid-year reviews were put on hold.

There was an underlying rumour from employees that morale was extremely low. Despite the amount of change, this didn't seem to be the cause of this change in mood. Instead the reason for the unrest was the lack of communication from management and senior leaders. Employees were on consultation for redundancy, and yet were not being consulted. They were not receiving updates on timeframes, or on changes in the organization such as new job positions. When looking further into this problem, it seems that department leaders were not being told by senior managers about the changes, and so could not update the process or send out communications.

May 2012

I completed an evaluation task, conducting focus groups with managers who took part in the performance reviews to gain feedback on the successes and the development areas. The outcomes of these focus groups included a standardization of technical skills for job posts, more options on performance measurement, and clear options on statutory training.

The next couple of months were reliant on me creating a version 2 of the performance reviews on HR.net.

Another management challenge has developed through the new structure within the organization. It means that employees now work under one single contract, rather than for multiple contracts. However, the management structure under this new regime would mean that potentially managers and employees may not be under the same geographical remit – making people management even harder, and creating a severe lack of visible leadership.

Case Study 2: Arabian Knights by Tony Nelson

Summary

The Iraqi Foundation for Technical Education (FTE) wanted a world-class development programme for its college deans. It drew from the UK's acclaimed leadership development programme which was adapted to become the Dean's Qualifying Programme (DQP).

FTE wanted to move from top down, centralized control to more flexible management in order to better meet the training needs of local employers and areas. This was against a background of national security problems, political change, economic challenges and a patriarchal culture.

A pilot programme was successfully run over 18 months to develop a cadre of Iraqi coaches and assessors able to support a wider roll-out. Cohorts two and three commenced in 2011 and 2012 for a further 36 senior leaders in Iraqi colleges and schools.

Context

FTE is based in Baghdad and is the government agency responsible for technical colleges and Institutes throughout Iraq, excluding the Kurdistan region. It has over 72,000 students and 14,000 staff in 40 colleges and institutes. Since 2003 many of their buildings had to be reconstructed and all had to be re-equipped after looting. Some have been repeatedly targeted for attack by insurgents. Deans have faced attempts on their life.

The existing system of technical education is highly centralized, working under the auspices of the Ministry of Higher Education. Iraq was pre-eminent in the region for education and training but after 1980 this changed and it now suffers from educational deprivation, high drop-out rates from schools and up to 40% adult illiteracy in rural areas.

Then FTE President Dr Mahmood wanted new models of senior leadership to help them cope with economic reconstruction. He knew these models should be adapted to the Iraqi context and culture. He showed vision in seeking to redefine the work of leadership and wanting to place leadership power locally.

Dr Mahmood said 'We strongly supported DQP from the start. This is an accredited programme which is helping Deans achieve our vision to strengthen the Iraqi economy through local communities. DQP is helping professionalise our senior management.'

Colleges faced the challenge of equipping young people and adults with the vocational skills that are desperately needed to rebuild local economies. Society was divided and infrastructure decimated. Few leaders ever face such challenges in their lifetime.

Rawabit (arabic *partnership*) was set up in 2004 by FTE, a group of UK FE colleges, the Association of Colleges and other UK agencies. It subsequently attracted funds from the UK government (now the Department for Business, Innovation and Skills) and UNESCO. In 2009 I was running the UK's leadership programme for Principals of Further Education Colleges. One of the UK participants was Iraqi-born Ali Hadawi CBE, who was Vice-Chair of Rawabit. Ali shared with Dr Mahmood how his own leadership had changed as a result of the programme he attended. Dr Mahmood brought to England a group of policymakers and I spent two days with them explaining the leadership programme and discussing how it could be contextualized for them.

Key Innovations and Timeline

I talked to anyone I could find with experience of leadership development in the Middle East. There is a paucity of published material on leadership in an Arab let alone an Iraqi context. I attended the Leadership Trust Foundation's first Worldly Leadership Conference on non-western forms of leadership wisdom.

Dr Mahmood wanted a programme that was robust and externally accredited. I initially used assessors from the UK programme to validate the written assignment from each participant. I established a partnership with the Chartered Management Institute so that successful graduates of DQP would be assessed to become chartered managers. This was the first time this external accreditation had happened in Iraq.

The content of the 16-month programme included taught elements on high performance working; change leadership; engaging with external stakeholders; innovation culture; motivation; and coaching skills. It included an experiential learning workshop to stimulate peer feedback and self-awareness. Participants were also required to undertake a 360-degree feedback process. They had to prepare a personal leadership development plan and also manage a change project in the workplace.

Almost all of this approach was new to the Iraqi culture in terms of content. In order to be a source of useful learning for Deans every aspect of the programme needed to be contextualized for a Middle East, Arab group. This contextualization took place beforehand when possible but in the pilot often occurred as a 'work in progress' in the classroom. Deans had been raised on didactic teaching methods. An informal style of learner-centred delivery was ground breaking for them.

Each dean was required to:

- be assessed for Maber/Fellow status by the Chartered Management Institute, to their usual UK standards;
- submit a 5000-word assignment evidencing their applied leadership learning – this was assessed by former assessors of the English principal's programme;
- undergo a rigorous four-hour, face-to-face interview with a CMI assessor looking at managing people and leading change competences for chartered manager (CMgr) status, with triangulated evidence from peers.

Looking back and looking forward

Every opportunity was taken to honour the heritage of Iraq by making links to its culture and history. The oldest known writing in the world is a Sumerian clay tablet found near Babylon which contains a leadership parable, making this the oldest recorded leadership wisdom. Erbil – where we were delivering – has the oldest continuously inhabited settlement in the world. We were working with people from the land of great biblical figures such as Noah, Abraham and Daniel.

We had intriguing discussions about the Qur'an and the role of faith in leadership. Spirituality is an inseparable part of Iraqi life and leadership. The five calls to prayer reminded us of this daily. Iraq's isolation under sanctions had decayed the research skills of participants and independent study was made harder due to the loss of so much of the country's infrastructure. Information resources, libraries and internet access were patchy and unreliable. Power cuts were a daily occurrence. Verbal story telling was a natural teaching medium for our Iraqi friends. This was very useful whenever our modern technology decided not to work!

The deans had grown up in a leadership culture which was command and control, underpinned by patriarchy with tribal affiliations. Most had learned to keep their opinions to themselves to avoid trouble or personal disaster. Those with prior western contact demonstrated more subtle leadership styles. Our pilot group were mainly engineers and scientists typically educated to PhD level. Their academic curiosity allowed them to make new connections out of seemingly disparate leadership models.

Benefits

The programme was designed to support participants in achieving the following personal learning outcomes:

- understand and apply strategic leadership to improve the effectiveness of your institution and its position in the market and community;
- understand the impact you make as a leader on your team and organization;
- apply selected theories, models and concepts from the programme in a project to strengthen your adaptive leadership of change;
- develop reflective leadership practice through feedback, coaching, change leadership and self-awareness;
- help create a community of leadership practice among peers to support continuous leadership improvement.

CMI Assessors found that contemporary leadership and management skills are still in their infancy in Iraq and in their CMgr assessment the deans all showed an advanced understanding of theory. During DQP they have been able to apply these leadership and management theories within their institutes and colleges. Assessors Gaynor Thomas and John Sephton contextualized and triangulated the evidence offered to reflect the unique setting and challenges of Iraq. Deans shared their stories of creating business impact including de-politicizing their learning institutions; stabilizing local communities through vocational education among former insurgents and prisoners; introducing new vocational and academic qualifications to Master's/PhD level; and rebuilding colleges destroyed by terrorist activity.

Gaynor commented 'The most impressive stories were those of rebuilding the human soul.'

Programme Outcomes

The nine deans all achieved the triple accreditation of DQP graduate, Fellow of the Chartered Management Institute (FCMI) and Chartered Manager (CMgr).

The robust nature of assessment assured the quality of the applied learning. The programme also developed leadership standards with FTE. The nine deans were all trained to be able to coach future participants on DQP, thus building organizational capacity to support an Iraqi-led, wider roll-out of the programme. Four deans were selected to undertake the assessment of written assignments. The leadership competences used were to the highest UK standards.

Wider roll-out commenced in November 2011 for cohort two of 26 deans and vice deans (including the first female dean). This cohort embraced delegates from across the whole of Iraq including Kurdistan, now involving all three FTEs in the country. A third cohort commenced in July 2012 of 10 headteachers (three were female). These later cohorts have been funded by the EU through the British Council, contracting with the Association of Colleges.

Lessons

The pilot programme was evaluated to draw out the learning and lessons.

Relationships

- These are the key to learning in an Iraqi group.
- Tutors need to establish credibility with an Iraqi group – but this is more than professional background, qualifications and relevant experience. It covers working with trust, dignity and respect at all times. We learnt to empathize with cultural difference and to research and reflect on cultural imperatives.
- Building relationships takes time and is a layered process in Iraq – for example, we experienced a deepening bond each time we visited Iraq.
- Dave Peel (tutor) reflected 'we held in tension the need to adopt and role model a style of coaching which was supportive and challenging whilst not reinforcing patriarchal dependency. To do this needed us to reflect on and adapt our approach. The deans were great teachers in this endeavour and allowed us to learn through real practice with them, always seeking "the wisdom" in what we were doing and how this could positively affect the hearts and minds of those who they lead.'

Planning

- Planning is good but we learned to increase our personal flexibility – working 'in the moment' rather than to a fixed idea of what had to happen next. This is how Iraqi culture works.
- Delivery took twice the time it would with a group of English principals because of the need to work with in-group translation and also to allow time for the group members to discuss new concepts and theories. This meant a need to adjust the pace, adapt content and avoid colloquialisms which only served to confuse.
- We learnt to assume nothing – we repeatedly discovered aspects of western leadership development which are not present in Iraqi culture.

Groups work differently

- The role of a group leader in Iraqi culture is quite different from that in the western model. It is essential to understand and acknowledge this, consulting the group leader for all important decisions and briefing them ahead of modules and key activities. Sometimes the dialogue is solely with the group leader – with others listening in or occasionally contributing.
- There is much more collaboration and less competition in an Iraqi deans' group compared to an English principals' group.
- Deans search for 'the wisdom' in tasks, lectures and even ice-breaker exercises. And this is seen as a function of the group rather than the individual take-away it would be in the UK.
- Deans make lateral connections *across* leadership models and theories (whereas English principals tend to drill down into one particular model to examine it in depth). Deans could then create a new model out of the inter-connectedness. This was outstanding conceptualization.
- Feedback flows differently in an Iraqi group. It firstly depends on the level of trust present (as in the UK) but even in high trust groups it defaults to a discussion of the positives and avoids anything which might be seen as negative. This protects the 'face' of the hearers or facilitators. Reframing developmental feedback to 'it would be even better if ...' could sometimes help. The quality of feedback was also in inverse proportion to group size – small groups worked better than large ones; pairs better still, and one to one feedback from the tutor gave the greatest scope for a discussion of 'negatively perceived' issues, subject always to obtaining the permission of the hearer and watching closely for non-verbal reactions which might indicate psychological distress from feedback.

Tony Nelson CMgr FCMI FRSA MBA/LS, Director of BrQthru, heads up the Dean's Qualifying Programme. He is passionate about helping leaders create high performance organizations by maximizing the potential of their people.

Email: tony@BrQthru.co.uk. or see www.rawabit.org

Case Study 3: Procurement Transformation at Lowe Power Company

The procurement department of a large utility company, Lowe Power, had evolved pretty successfully from the old rule-bound model of the corporate policeman to a leaner, more commercial model of supply chain management. Even though relationships internally could be difficult and fractious, the department had scored some big wins and was operating with roughly two-thirds of the staff from the previous year. However, Frank Illingworth, the Finance Director, to whom procurement reported, was pretty sure that re-organizing the department into market facing teams would yield a step-change in procurement performance, not just in cost improvement, but also in enhanced service to the operations.

The sudden departure of the head of procurement in September 2008 provided Frank with his opportunity. While pursuing the external recruitment of a new head of procurement, he assumed direct responsibility for the department, giving the task of drawing up new designs to Ken Tweedy, a relatively new member of the procurement management team. Ken was thrilled to be asked. He had some misgivings about the existing structure, and was keen to make an impression. Who knew, this might even position him as the most likely second-in-command to the new head of procurement when he arrived.

Ken set about steadily creating and evaluating alternative organizational models for the department. He found the design work interesting and rewarding, but really didn't like what happened after that. His colleagues seemed to be able to give him endless reasons why a particular proposal would not work, but seemed very short on alternatives. Equally, presenting options to Frank was frustrating. Not only would Frank refuse to hear a proposal out before interrogating it, but he also seemed to have an inexhaustible fund of new criteria for assessing what the new organization should do.

Progress was slow. But by December, Ken had pretty much got a model that, while not wildly popular with the department – 'change for the sake of change' – did at least seem to meet Frank's requirements.

By the end of March 2009 the implementation was complete. There had been some uncomfortable moments along the way. Ken had not enjoyed the presentation to the department early in January to unveil the proposals. Despite the amount of preparation that Ken had put into Frank's presentation, Frank had simply prefaced the event with a 10 minute chat on what was needed and why, leaving it to Ken to present the detailed proposal. It didn't help that Frank later left the meeting, only returning to close what had obviously been a bad-tempered session. The main objections had been (a) disagreement on the problems and opportunities faced by the department, (b) that the new structure would not address them, and (c) a petty process point, 'why consult us now if you have already made up your mind what you are going to do?' Frank's 'You're not taking them with you, Ken' seemed a poor return for all the hard work he had put in.

In February, two of the noisier objectors left the department to join the previous head of procurement at his new company. While publicly bemoaning the loss of talent and experience, Ken was privately relieved. He didn't relish the challenge they provided. And these, together with two other leavers, made it easier to make the portfolio adjustments required to land the new organization. And so come April the department settled into its new structure.

One day in May, there was a flurry of excitement as Frank, on one of his rare visits to the department, called everybody together to welcome Michael Langer, the new head of procurement. Mike was a fresh-faced young man who, having started in consumer goods, had moved into heavy industry, and had just spent three years as head of out-sourcing in a steel company owned by a private equity firm. He made a brief presentation to the department, detailing his background and his delight at being asked to head up such a prestigious unit as Lowe Power's procurement department. He was polite and well-mannered and made a good first impression.

Frank's brief to Mike had been simple and direct.

> 'Shake 'em up, Mike. A lot of them have been here a long time, and have got very used to the comfortable life'.

Mike was energized. In the interviews he had been able to demonstrate some pretty leading edge thinking about modern procurement techniques, and he had liked the way Frank had picked these ideas up. He was keen to put them to work. He had guessed Lowe Power would be a long way behind best practice and the little he had picked up from the head-hunter and other contacts in the know had confirmed this. He could see an opportunity to transform the department, deliver significant gains for the business and make a name for himself in short order. And in two years he could be looking for a bigger role in Lowe, or for a directorship somewhere else.

Mike spent the first week on formalities, meeting the people, and getting an idea of who did what. He booked meetings with the operations directors as well as other divisional heads. What he heard did not surprise him. There were a lot of complaints about the procurement department. 'Too bureaucratic', 'hide-bound by process', 'not sufficiently focused on value' were just some of the criticisms. He also carried out his own assessment. He quickly came to the opinion that, apart from learning the vocabulary of strategic procurement, not so much progress had been made in this direction. He also observed that workload was unevenly distributed across the new department. The stationery contract and corporate travel for example were getting a lot more resource and attention than some business critical engineering requirements.

Inspired by a strong sense of purpose, Mike set a blistering pace. Alarmed that he couldn't find them, he asked for contracting calendars from each of the buying area managers. Unable to make sense of the different monthly reports from the market teams, he set about creating a standard report format with a lot more detail. This was necessarily an iterative exercise, and caused a deal of moaning and groaning, but at the end of May he was able to present the report in full to the monthly executive meeting. Mike noted, with some satisfaction, that his submission passed without remark.

Meanwhile, Mike was dismayed at the apparent lack of enthusiasm from his management team. They were sullen and uncommunicative in the weekly meeting. He'd talk, they'd listen, but it didn't feel right. Next steps would get recorded but were rarely completed on time. A month after the request for contracting calendars, he still hadn't seen one. Once he had got the department on an even keel, he resolved to take time out to figure out what made them tick. In the meantime, there was a lot to do and a pressing need to get on. Determined to get to grips with the fundamentals, he called for detailed market and contract reviews from each buying group.

Other management routines were problematic. A standing contract review meeting, on Wednesdays at 4pm, was used as a forum to sign off newly arranged contracts. Mike struggled with these. Not only was he unused to making these decisions in public, but he also disliked the feeling that it was a mere formality, and all he was being asked to do was to rubber stamp decisions already taken. That didn't sit well with the requirement of his role to ensure probity for the business. In fact, when he started to ask questions about what work had been done, what criteria had been used and what alternatives had been looked at, he got short change from the buying groups. He tried to get the buying groups to submit work a week in advance so he could provide more of a critique, but rarely did they make this. Mostly, he would get the papers on Tuesday night.

Mike shared his feelings with Frank at their weekly catch-up meeting: 'I'm worried about the management team, Frank. There's not a lot of get up and go in the group, and we are short of real professional procurement capability within the department'. 'That's what you are there for, Mike. I told you. Shake 'em up.' He asked if there was any feedback from the Exec. 'No. They don't know what to make of you, but nothing yet.' Mike didn't know what to do with this. Mike also kept his misgivings about the organization structure to himself, knowing that Frank had been instrumental in creating it. He would have to pick and choose his fights …

One week towards the end of June, the facilities management contract came up at the contract review meeting. Mike wasn't happy about the way the first lot had been managed, but that was before his time. Feeling that this would be one of the landmark contracts of his tenure, he had made his feelings known to Ken whose buying group were handling the brief. Mike had called for a detailed update on the current status, and Ken had mumbled something about how difficult it was working with estates, but had not formally responded to the request. So Mike was surprised, and not a little annoyed, to see the next lot appear so suddenly.

At the meeting he had his line of interrogation tightly marshalled. What is happening in the wider FM industry? What are the key trends? What are other companies doing? Why are we going against that trend? The buying group were clearly taken aback. With over 1000 sites to service, and a legacy of locally owned and operated management contracts, they had been nursing estates through a painstaking process of aggregation. Mike's questions seemed somewhat academic given the situation on the ground, and they said so. Mike was incensed. And when Ken added: 'Besides we're effectively out of contract from Monday, we need a decision now', the red mist came down: 'This is crap. I don't have to put up with this. I asked for a proper report two weeks ago, and you give me a fait accompli! You guys are lost in the dark ages. There is a ton of value to be had in this contract and all you care about is what Estates think. This meeting is over. Ken stay behind.'

Ken was evidently unimpressed. They hadn't got a sign-off and something needed to happen before next week. Mike was on to him:

'Now what?'

Ken looked blank. '… I don't know', he started.

'Now what will you do?'

Ken wanted to say 'report you to Frank for failing to make decisions', but he bit his lip:

'Okay. Since you don't know, I'll tell you what you'll do. You'll roll the existing contracts until this unholy mess is sorted out. And another thing. I want to see your contracting calendar on my desk first thing tomorrow morning, or I will be putting you on disciplinary.'

At their next weekly meeting, Mike gave Frank a watered down account of the events at the contract review meeting. Frank was keen to hear more about Mike's thinking on the way forward for facilities management:

'We discussed this in my interview, Frank. We talked about the major developments in FM.'

'But that was just an interview, Mike. This is the real world. The first lot was a groundbreaker for us. You're still earning the right with Estates. Don't rock the boat …'

Mike was flummoxed. How did *don't rock the boat* square with *shake 'em up*? And it was sobering to be reminded how closely involved Frank had been with Lot 1. This was frustrating and perplexing.

The market review meetings were staged for the second week of July. The run-up to them had not been promising. After the FM debacle tensions were running high, and Mike guessed the gossip machine was working overtime. Despite briefing the management team, there had been several petitions to clarify what was needed. In the end Mike had put out a format for the presentation he wanted to see from each team. And in the last instance there had been a flurry of last minute re-arrangements, with 'more important' operations meetings to go to, as well as two people phoning in ill.

In the event, the presentations were reasonably coherent. Each group seemed to have a plan and a supporting rationale. Mike's concern was to check the thinking, and to try and raise the bar. He was struck by how incremental the plans were and struggled to find good things to say even when he was impressed by the underlying thinking.

There were no real breakthrough moments, but he didn't want to let the event pass without impressing upon the buyers the importance of raising their game. *Have you ever thought about?* ... became the by-line of the event. Invariably the answer was *yes, but* ... and some combination of *we/they are not ready for that yet, our systems won't support it*, and *we tried it and it didn't work.*

By the end of July, Mike was exasperated. He was working harder and harder to show the way, and everywhere he was meeting passive resistance. The ops directors had not bitten on any of the big ideas he had floated with them, choosing only to complain about procurement's poor level of service and support for basic administration reported by their people. Much of this Mike felt was unwarranted, and would have been better aimed at finance, but he let it pass. He had been given a clear mandate to up the game, and nobody – within the department, nor in the company more generally, not even his boss – was interested. How to demonstrate the opportunities for creating more value that were so self-evident to him? Maybe he could commission consultants who specialized in strategic procurement to carry out a benchmarking study. That would show them how bad they really were, how far they had to go. He resolved to raise this with Frank at their weekly meeting the following Tuesday.

However, on that Tuesday morning on the way to work, Mike is surprised to get a BB message from Frank asking him to meet him on the top floor as soon as he arrives at the office. Mike doesn't know what to make of this, but dutifully attends. 'What is it, Frank?' Frank comes straight to the point. 'Mike, bad news I'm afraid, there have been rumblings now for several weeks, both from inside and outside your department, but last week I received a formal complaint about you and your conduct from a member of your staff, and I have been obliged to ask HR to carry out a formal review. The complaint is one of bullying ...'

Case Study 4: Leadership Through Values and Integrity – Brandon Trust

The Brandon Trust has hit the news headlines in recent years on numerous occasions, for the very best of reasons: as a sage and respected voice in the world of services for adults with learning disabilities. The Trust has charitable status and provides high quality personalized support services to people with learning disabilities across the South West region of the UK, and now also in London, having recently taken on board a smaller charity with similar values and client group; in 2011 Odyssey Care became a subsidiary of the Brandon Trust. Now they are fully integrated and the London team is known under the Brandon Trust name. There is a shared a common history in that Lucy Hurst-Brown, Brandon Trust's Chief Executive, had had the same role at Odyssey until she moved to Bristol and the Brandon Trust in 2005. Clearly it is a growing and ambitious organization dealing with a very tough fiscal and a constantly changing, complex policy environment.

Through a period of high turbulence, taking on staff from the statutory sector, renegotiating terms downwards to match that of the charitable sector where pay is in some cases up to a third lower, the Brandon Trust has achieved a high trust brand and growing visibility. This has occured in a world rocked by shocking scandals and abuse against adults with learning disabilities, such as the recent closure of Winterbourne View, a private sector residential 'assessment and treatment' centre for adults with learning disabilities and challenging behaviour run by Castlebeck Care Ltd.

A government review[1] was called in response to this scandal. This abuse (physical and mental) only came to light through secret filming for a television documentary. Commentators[2] warn that the care sector risks slipping back into an institutional culture typified by a Victorian asylum system in a financial recession, where the focus is on cutbacks rather than the development of quality services for vulnerable people. The Brandon Trust was one of the first charities to speak out against the institutional 'care' of people with learning disabilities.

So how have the Trust achieved growth, a trustworthy brand and the transformation of services in such a tough climate? In this case study, Chief Executive Lucy Hurst Brown, and Director of Communications Steve Day, share some of their thoughts on the role of leadership in leading change through a highly turbulent environment.

For Lucy, values form the bedrock of both leadership and strategy: 'In Winterbourne View, adults with learning disabilities were locked up in large groups and despite charging high fees, the company took the money and failed to deliver personalized support. As the recession began to bite, we had a discussion with our Board in relation to our values given the financial squeeze from government and

[1] www.dh.gov.uk/health/2012/12/final-winterbourne/.

[2] Such as David Brindle, writing in the *Guardian*, Monday 10 December 2012.

commissioners. We upheld the fact that we are wholly against the institutional large scale warehousing of vulnerable people, no matter how financially attractive this may be. We are clear that this is against our values. But there is a tension between the amount of money available and the quality of care we want to provide. Despite this our solution cannot be to pile'em high! Instead we have gone down the line of focusing on developing a service journey that provides highly creative models of individual support, adopting assistive technology where possible and taking ongoing action to increase efficiencies and reduce overheads. Our strategy is quite broad based but it has clear principles. We also know that the bottom line for our survival depends on growth and increasing our market share.'

Holding onto core values in a tough market requires taking a firm stand and on the right occasions it also means balancing this with the tension of the reality of the marketplace. In these difficult times being a successful chief executive can be tough; in standing up for the people you serve and your employees who directly support them, there is always a dialogue going on with stakeholders. And the arguments and the answers are no longer easy. Whether it be paymasters or politicians, or indeed families and the people with learning disabilities themselves, everyone is seeking quality services but the financial purse strings are always very tight. As Steve put it: 'Values are at the heart of what we do. We are values driven, but we are also a product of the market itself. We won't be standing to present these values if we are inconsistent with the market. We have both our soft and hard hats on! Taking a tough stand can also mean deciding with the Board of Trustees where to draw the line. Lucy responded to a suggestion that Brandon compromise its stance by saying "She would rather stack shelves."'

Brandon's values are lived and acted upon. It encourages the development and advocacy of all the people who use its services. For example, several people who do so were commissioned by the national review as expert witnesses to speak on behalf of vulnerable people with learning disabilities in the enquiry following the Winterbourne View scandal. These expert witnesses played a key leadership role in advocating on behalf of those who were unable to speak for themselves.

As Phillipa Hamilton, one of the expert witnesses put it, 'They (businesses in the care sector) need to learn to care.' Philippa is active in shaping the services she uses. Much more than a customer, she is actively engaged in encouraging voices around her to be heard and in shaping the way Brandon delivers its services. As Philippa puts it 'Since I've been here I feel I've had the confidence to speak out. Before here I was in my flat doing nothing. I've brought my inner self out.' Philippa is an active member of Brandon's consultative forum and sees this as important in helping to shape effective services for her and others.

Chris Schumacher sits on the Board of Trustees and has been using the services that Brandon provides for the last 10 years. Chris describes Brandon Trust as 'a cloak for the disabled. It covers you from anything that's not right. That might get the better of you.' As a young 19-year-old soldier, Chris suffered a terrible accident, and was written off by the medical staff as 'a cabbage'. Chris has some difficulty with mobility and has lost the use of one of his legs. He also suffers from speech impediments. But Chris wouldn't change any aspect of his life and says 'I have learned about how others cope with disabilities. It's brought me down to their level. I don't look down. I look up. Leadership (and life) is about what's inside (the heart). After I came out of intensive care, my Mum was told to put me in a home for cabbages. She said she couldn't do that, he's my son. They told her I would never do anything or be anybody. I am proud that I am able to help others. We are able to help Brandon Trust move forward. Even if I wasn't on the Board, I'd be listened to anyway. I've been involved for 10 years. I've seen a lot of changes.'

In taking staff through a difficult transition period, the leadership have taken a strategy of transparency and 'telling it as it is'. This has been painful and challenging. The leadership started with its unions, agreeing a shared vision for the future and shared principles and values as the framework for ongoing dialogue. An understanding that the recession is a market fact that could not be ignored formed the background to these discussions: 'We started with a reality check, and cards on the table. We said if we do nothing, then this is what will happen, we'll go out of business. We opened up discussion and said we need your help to go forward. We were very careful with our language, conscious of not being them and us.'

However, the top team also model their values through behaviour. They have not had a pay rise in three years. In addition, the leaders advocate on behalf of the staff and the people they serve, as a campaigning organization. As the chief executive put it: 'Social care staff do not get paid enough, so we are fighting on both fronts. Our greatest asset is our staff.' Lucy has also just come back from a sabbatical, using this to focus on mindfulness and to consider the development of strategy for the well-being of staff. In leaving the organization for an extended period she signalled her belief and faith in her staff to hold the reins in her absence, which they ably did. She also modelled the importance of taking care of self as the leader of the organization. She has modelled the values she espouses for well-being, creativity and mindfulness, especially potent in such tough times. As a top team, Lucy feels 'we need to be thinking, planning, creating and NOT doing!' Part of the strategy for growth includes recognition of the need to support staff in this next phase and to foster a better sense of well-being by focusing on what makes for a great organization.

However, it is not plain sailing. Steve voiced the tension he sees between, 'Holding and looking after staff and pushing them forward.' As the Chief Executive, Lucy put it, 'There is a direct link between staff performance and outcomes for the people we support. How well we function as a team is what we sell in the marketplace – the talent of our staff, not just their skills, but also their attitudes and values. The first can be taught, the latter cannot. So we recruit on the basis of values and attitudes first and foremost.'

Director Steve referred to the chief executive's 'angry editorial' in Brandon Trust's own internal staff magazine where she vented her anger at the state of the economy and the subsequent impact on both vulnerable people and the staff who support them. For as Steve said, the short article was a tightrope balancing act since Lucy was articulating the anger she felt on behalf of her staff, standing up for them, while at the same time holding the difficult position of asking the staff to do more for less.

Transparency, honesty and plain speaking are the hallmarks of this leadership team who freely admit that morale is low right now, and yet staff continue to give up their own free time to support the adults with a learning disability that they serve: for example, caring for young adults with a learning disability at a summer camp. The leaders of the Brandon Trust do not shy away from uncomfortable truths, they act to address the difficulties.

In the Chief Executive's view communication is central; clarity, and an honest and constant dialogue. The Trust uses social media effectively. For example, people who are supported by Brandon's service contribute to the weekly blog, as do front line staff right through to the top team. This is bottom-up communication rather than top-down. Brandon holds large forum events for the people who use their services, but this is not consultation. These forums are used to drive strategy – 'these 100 voices shape strategy'. Brandon is constantly innovating because its starting point is its 'customers'. As Lucy Hurst-Brown states with real passion: 'The only point of being here is to serve the people we support.'

These values are translated through to the experience in life of the people who use Brandon's services. As Philippa and Chris put it:

> 'I try and speak up and feel more confident in speaking my views. When I first came here I was very nervy.' And 'It inspires confidence in the people behind you. I have grown in confidence.'

In the leadership team they have a phrase in common usage: 'Change is the norm and a key component of our thinking and our expectations'. We see change as a norm, because none of us live in a static world, we live with ambiguity. 'As leaders we expect to be continuously moving forward. It can be exhausting, but it's game on – part of being in the real world. It's much more than just changing the corporate colours, mere appearance. It's about behaviours. We are introducing coaching for all our managers. We believe that everyone is a leader and an innovator, so what does this mean for how we behave? It's how you do your job that is key.'

Both Chris and Philippa echo Lucy's sentiments. As a leader 'You have to be able to stand back and not be conceited. To take advice from someone who is further down the line. A lot of people are too fond of themselves … It's like King Arthur, his table was round so that everyone was equal. There was no head of the table. I think you can run Brandon like this. Everyone to treat everyone with respect. And if they don't, there's the door! I would say Brandon is run like that.' When asked for advice to business leaders, Chris said 'watch and listen', and Philippa added 'yes, sometimes people think they are listening!'

In concluding our conversation, Lucy reflected that her leadership role is part of a continuous journey and 'part of our job is to make sure that the journey continues whether we are here or not. It's work in progress, a bit like life! It's good to reflect though; finding the moments of contemplation, like in music, the silence between the notes!'

Contributors

Lucy Hurst Brown, Chief Executive

Steve Day, Director of Communications

Philippa Hamilton, Member of the Consultative Forum and service user

Chris Schumacher, Board of Trustees and service user

Anita Gulati, Director, interviewer and author. InPerspective UK Ltd

Case Study 5: Organization as Purpose: Leadership as Relationship and Values Through Social Enterprise

June Burrough, Founder and Director of the Pierian Centre

June Burrough founded the Pierian Centre in 2002 as a centre for training and self-development – expanding it over the years into a unique conference centre and busy focus of community development in the heart of St Pauls, a deprived inner city area of Bristol. The Pierian Centre's strap line was 'Time, space and clarity.'

June started the Centre in a quiet, evolutionary kind of way, without a big vision or big plan. As June describes it, 'I don't think I started with a vision! I started with principles and values and the sort of idea that it would be nice to set up a place that ran along different principles and philosophies than what I had experienced elsewhere. If that was the vision well then … I wanted to set up something where the growth of the individual was the focus, that something could be part of the community and that was there to open the door … that framework … I guess the way we got people to see what the place is all about was one of the challenges: it was to live it and be it as the leader … and it was challenging … so there were never any doubt for me that if you stand up and say these are the principles, that you must live and breathe them. There is no choice and I think this is what goes wrong in the world is that leaders pontificate but then don't live it. That's fundamentally where things in this world go wrong. To live and be what we say is a very deeply challenging process. And it means almost every day something happens where I think what shall I say … if every time we have a decision to make we think about how our decision will have the best impact on the most marginalized in our society we can not go wrong. That's about making an altruistic as opposed to a selfish decision … it will always be a better decision.'

June's approach to leadership clearly starts from the premise of her own deeply held personal values which include authenticity, social justice, service and creativity. June feels these are manifested in the belief that everyone is remarkable; the principle that every organization is part of the community in which it exists; and an ethos of welcoming and taking care of everyone who comes through the door.

As June puts it, 'if you look at the Pierian centre … the whole place was based on the belief that everyone in the world is remarkable … the whole place was there to support people in discovering how remarkable they are … we delivered inspiration or support and that people knew they were cared about … this is distinctly lacking in the world … I try and do it wherever I am … relate to whoever is there … we live in a disjointed and an unrelated world and we need to connect with people.'

June's recent decision to close the Pierian centre after 10 years leading the organization, was as distinctive as her reasons for opening it. The Pierian Centre was never about making money, though finance certainly had to be taken into account. June's views are perhaps unusual in mainstream business, but not in the third sector, social enterprise or community led organizations. June articulated a view that 'I would never make a decision purely on the basis of money. And I didn't. Money comes into it. You have to be sensible. It's a finite resource. But never, never, did I make a decision based purely on finance. The one that came closest to it was to become a community interest company in order to do something to achieve more work … we could do City of Sanctuary … it gave service to the people of Bristol as a result. But for me it was a little too close to the bone … the reason for wanting the money was solid … there was always a question for me around this because it was based on an old paradigm that the only way you can get money is this way … If I had put a message out to the world that we wanted to do these wild and wacky things … who knows … we just don't know! What's true is that I got four legacies from members of my family dying and I would never have been able to keep the Centre going without this … so I look at that and I think, who knows.'

So as the Pierian Centre's website explains, it was fundamentally a social enterprise that was about creating a space that enabled people to explore who they were and how they might be in the world, inspired by the lines from Alexander Pope's 'Essay on Criticism' (1711):

'A little learning is a dangerous thing, Drink deep or taste not the Pierian Spring.'

Pieria is the ancient home of the Muses on Mount Olympus, and the adjective Pierian therefore means of knowledge or inspiration. June reached a point in her life where she felt it was time to move on. Practicalities meant that the Pierian Centre needed to close, but it had provided significant inspiration to many, including June, through the course of its existence.

The Centre was based in a five-storey Georgian building in Grade I listed Portland Square which June lovingly transformed from a state of neglect to dignified splendour. Number 27 was lucky to have retained many of its original features – and delegates and visitors were greeted by a working environment filled with the aesthetic and spiritual ethos of the Enlightenment. From the 20ft well in the basement to the conical lantern that crowns the spiralling staircase, the building radiates a deep and productive calm. But the Pierian Centre was never a museum, it was a 21st-century working building used for practical purposes by people from every walk of life. During Bristol's Doors Open Day when unusual private buildings are open to the public, the Centre received between 300 and 600 visitors every year!

The Centre attracted a wide range of people, from blue-chip management teams to community groups, musicians, healers and voice coaches. From June's first involvement with the Zimbabwean community and Refugee Week in 2005, the Pierian Centre steadily expanded the role it played in the wider life of Bristol. Bells Unbound in 2007 was a global event (Antarctica to Zimbabwe), marking the 200th anniversary of the Abolition of the Slave Trade. The next year the Pierian Centre hung 17 four-metre high banners of Tom Stoddart's photo-journalism on Platform 5 at Temple Meads station – and 2009's Anne Frank [+ you] exhibition at Bristol Cathedral was a breakthrough in terms of partnerships and collaboration.

The Centre became a community interest company (CIC) in 2008, and the first CIC to be awarded the Social Enterprise Mark. The Centre was also appointed lead project partner for Bristol's response to EY2010: the European Year for Combating Poverty and Social Exclusion. Events included the community art installation Portents, filling College Green with 49 tents each printed with artwork by groups and individuals from across Bristol. June considers the Centre's crowning achievement to be the launch of Bristol as a City of Sanctuary – the culmination of 4 years' work that saw 750 people fill the Council House, College Green and Bristol Cathedral with passion, laughter and dancing blue brollies with care expressed for those without a country or a home.

June's values are lived and breathed through everything she does. They define her as a leader beyond title, and beyond organization, as someone who tries to make a difference in the world through all that she does. June questioned the world she found from a young age, especially

> the kind of social structures that made people inferior or superior which didn't make sense at all … when I left theatre and worked as team development manager and management consultancy … I was working with a manager who kept talking about subordinates and I was horrified … the three words I would eliminate from the dictionary are 'should', 'ought' and 'subordinate' … it means 'less than' … and a hierarchical structure doesn't work for me…it's not a word you come across much now.'

For June, leadership and development of any business or organizational practice should be about egalitarianism, '… truly living a sense of equality that is about respect … if they are doing their job to the best of their ability! If they are not doing their job properly, whoever they are, then they need to be taken to task! I don't think anyone should be given respect purely for their position. You have to earn it in my world, by living and being the best that we can be. For some people that may be minimal because its restricted, by the world they are born into. For example, if you are born into a refugee camp and there is no food and no teachers and little water and you are living on the verge of death, you are just trying to survive the circumstances into which you have been put, but that doesn't mean they are not still trying their best to be their best … The mothers are still raising their children and when they can't milk them any longer it's not because they are bad mothers. There's a real sense for me that that deserves as much respect as someone working really hard in a 9–5 job and looking after their team and producing good quality work We don't seem to have that real sense of equality (in this world). It's so much about hierarchy and position and I think why?'

When asked whether as a woman June brought something different to the table, this was difficult for her to answer. Perhaps her answer would be this: June feels for humanity and acts in all she does to make the world a better place.

June considers the idea of leadership as shared, something everyone has responsibility for: '… this role of leader … I am questioning whether this word works at all … leading into a world where people lead themselves and everyone is a leader … and being a manager means everyone has their own bit of leadership … in some ways in the Pierian Centre did put that level of responsibility out there … for example, when I was away I said to people "you have my absolute backing to make a decision if needed, because it's not fair to encourage and then say you can't make decisions … you know you have my unadulterated support" … it may be that they make mistakes and we have a debrief and learn from it … if people are given that level of responsibility and treated as if it's their own business then they are much more likely to make a good decision' … I can't think of a single occasion where people made a horrendous decision … sometimes they made innocent decisions, where they didn't have sufficient information … I never had to really call someone on major decisions unless they really didn't get the fundamental philosophy underlying what we did … there were one or two people who really didn't get it and I had to sit them down … I think that happened twice …'

June sees the development of human relationships and treating people as equally significant and part of a team as fundamental to leadership and living, whether it be the cleaner, the taxi driver, the bank manager or the Queen. June put it this way 'Nobody was just a bank manager. It was a relationship and an integral part of the whole thing working, so he [the bank manager] was part of the team as far as I was concerned. And he gave advice and suggestions and he engaged with things and came to events and I am quite sure that it had an impact on him. I hope it gets passed on to other businesses in some way!'

June saw her bank manager and her suppliers such as cab drivers, florists and caterers as part of the same team: 'I refused to call people our suppliers. I called them our external partners … that hierarchical thing of people coming to the back door and if they are lucky they get a box of chocolates at Christmas because they've been so good! So for me, I didn't often get angry, but there was somebody on duty one day and someone came to order a cab and they rang the cab company and the way they spoke to the woman they were ordering the cab from as though she was a servant. I don't get irate often, but it was 'how dare you talk to the people, who drop people off and help them out with their baggage ... that is the last memory they have of the Pierian Centre, they are so important and they are part of our team, we don't pay them on the books, but my God they are important, they are part of the service we offer!' There's a local cab company, mainly black African guys in unmarked cars, trying to make a living and doing their bit who certainly treated me with a load of respect because they really valued what the Pierian Centre was doing for the local community. They really understood. And who still when I get a cab ... say 'how are you June, what's going on?' They really care and I can say that the way they treated Pierian Centre passengers was quite a lot better than some of the other cab companies. They really understood what the Pierian Centre was about and we took care of them ... anyone who came to us was treated in exactly the same way ... we didn't do red carpets ... the odd visitor from the Minister for example, all got the same (excellent) chocolate biscuits, just like everyone else.'

June admits that sometimes it was very difficult indeed living and breathing her values and putting them into practice. Sometimes members of the team did not see things the same way, sometimes staff behaviour was severely challenging to the fundamental principles of the organization. But each time this occurred, June came back to her values as the underpinning bedrock of leadership and the basis of the Centre.

June recruited staff primarily on the basis of their values. But sometimes staff would try to please her and as she put it, from her perspective, 'It was always about finding the best way to care for people when they came to us. It's not about keeping me happy or quiet. The frustration was when staff didn't quite get that. It's not about doing something because I say so! It's not about ego. Yes, we'd have someone new in and they'd come and proudly tell me they've changed something and I would say, great, have you told everybody else? You need to think about the impact on everyone else ... we would have a team meeting, because the processes and systems need to serve something, they are there to serve the purpose of the Centre ... The test for me was there wasn't much place for ego. You needed a level of self-confidence, to be who they were with something to offer that would add to the Centre. They were prepared to say what they thought ... they weren't frightened to say something is not working ...'

So in this organization, leadership was about encouraging shared responsibility and an attitude of servitude towards the people the Centre served, a fundamental primary focus on the goals and values of the Centre, emanating from its leadership. Sometimes the challenges of translating this into reality felt overwhelming and June doubted her ability to carry on. But she made a conscious choice to dig deep and continue and was supported by her close working relationships that buoyed her up, as well as a refocusing on her core values. June's legacy as a leader has been the many seeds that have been sown for new organizations and individuals seeking and making positive change in Bristol.

Case Study 6: Leadership in Transforming Services in a Local Authority

South Gloucestershire Local Authority was brought into existence in 1996 from the merger of three neighbouring authorities. It serves some 265,000 people, in a key locality on the M4/M5 corridor and in close proximity to Bristol, and is the equivalent in size to a London borough. The revenues and benefits service, which employs in the region of 100 staff, serves a vital role in helping vulnerable and often the poorest citizens (elderly and disabled people for example) access the benefits they are entitled to to help them live. The service also collects council tax from householders and local businesses rates, large and small, amounting to some £200 million a year.

The director of this service, Mike Hayesman, arrived into his role to find that the earlier merger had resulted in an ongoing state of crisis, a short-term view, poor communications both internally and externally, a loss of expertise, major inefficiencies across two distinct geographic patches, demotivated staff and the lack of a coherent approach to the use of technology and ICT – the service had three different suppliers and systems in concurrent use. In short, there was a lack of long-term sustainable vision for the transformation of the service. The benefits service at the time served some 18,000 households, handling £50 million of benefit monies from government coffers.

At this stage, the department was being fined by the Department of Work and Pensions for its inability to comply with statutory regulations in the calculation of benefits and was ranked in the bottom 10 among league tables for performance across the country. The revenues service was faring adequately, but sat in the mid quartile in terms of national indicators and was not fulfilling its potential, and with responsibility for collecting around £200 million per annum, the new director felt that this position was unacceptable.

With the backing of the senior management team and elected members, he sought to turn around the position, negotiating a new contract under a public private initiative (PFI) to strengthen the IT services, while working on skills development, and shifting the department culture to one that was responsive to the needs of its citizens as 'customers'. PFI was introduced by the then Labour government to inject capital and business 'know how' as a route to transforming and modernizing public sector delivery.

The director took stock of the position and focused on the development of appropriate single site accommodation, analysis of data to identify problem 'hot-spots', addressing poor staff performance by investing in training and changes to key personnel, as well as gaining of efficiencies through a reduction of staff by 10%. The new integrated systems contract negotiated for IT commenced in 2003 and ran for seven years with a whole life value of just over £4 million. Over time credibility was rebuilt as performance improved.

All of the above sounds very factual and step by step. The reality as Mike puts it felt very different. In his view it was 'all about the psychology of change, about creating a different physiology even, and an atmosphere of thinking differently'. In his opinion 'you should never be a victim of your own environment' and under his leadership the service was transformed and achieved 30% savings through the life of the PFI, making itself financing and turning around abandoned call rates from frustrated customers as high as 40%. Now, under the current economic environment, the team are being asked to dig deep and work even smarter, and have now achieved a further 25% savings.

The team that heads up the service has a strong gallows sense of humour, and works in a relaxed, mutually supportive but focused way. Mike's openness to new ideas, his view and confidence that his management team and staff are highly capable, his investment in them through management development, and their capacity in finding solutions, his own sense of humour , together with a 'hardnosed' focus on the role of data intelligence and integrated technology to target areas of the business and new ways of working in creating streamlined services, are critical factors in his team's success. Challenging existing systems and ways of working while using ideas and methods not traditionally associated with the UK public sector culture has set them apart as a high performing resilient team able to deliver more with less.

Glossary

action centred leadership a model of leadership that takes into consideration three elements – the task, the team and the individual

aesthetics sensory knowledge and felt meaning in relation to objects and experiences

altruism the regard for others as a principle of action

biological gender male or female body

cognitive resources theory explores how the performance of a group is affected by a complex interaction of leader intelligence and experience, a specific type of leadership behaviour, and two situational variables (that is, interpersonal stress and subordinate knowledge)

communicative action every dialogue should end with mutual understanding and agreement

communicative rationality a way of responding to the validity claims of various statements. A high level of communicative rationality thus signifies that perceptions are being based upon statements which are intelligible, that the statements reflect honesty and sincerity, that the statements are true or correct and that they accord with the prevailing norms

contingency theories of leadership models and theories exploring the role and importance of contextual variables in leadership, that is, how different situations require different types of leadership

discourse a system of texts that brings objects into being and constructs social reality

discourse studies exploring local meanings within social interactions

discourse studies study of dominant socio-historical discourse in organizations and societies

discursive studies of leadership   focus on local meanings and local situatedness of leadership

embodiment   state of being and body shaping the mind

emic   exploring a culture from the inside

empirical   the reliance on observation and/or experimentation rather than theory alone

etic   looking into a culture from the outside

etymology   the study of the origin of words

extraversion   the direction of thoughts and interests to things outside oneself, sociable, unreserved

factor structure   a term used to described how models and frameworks are empirically developed from questionnaire responses

feminine   personal characteristics such as caring, supporting, nurturing, communal

feminine advantage   the assumption that feminine characteristics of leaders are more effective in modern organizations than masculine characteristics

Fiedler's contingency theory   matches leaders based on their preferred leadership style to specific situations and contexts, that is, leader effectiveness is contingent on the right match of a leader's style to an appropriate situation

full range leadership model (FRLM)   constituent dimensions that make up transformational, transactional and *laissez-faire* leadership

GLOBE   a research project across 62 societies looking to determine the extent to which the practices and values of business leadership are universal (that is, are similar globally), and the extent to which they are specific to just a few societies

identity from a psychological perspective   a unitary coherent construction produced by the individual

identity from a sociological perspective   self-identities are temporary, fluid and co-constructed within the social context

implicit leadership theory   cognitive models that individuals have developed over time and hold, and that drive their evaluation and understanding of their own and others' leadership behaviour

languaculture   language and meaning are inseparable from culture

language constitutes reality   a phenomenon only becomes 'real' through our naming of it and the meaning we attach to the phenomenon – how we think about it and describe it – will impact our behaviours in relation to it

leader behaviour description questionnaire (LBDQ)   a questionnaire for measuring leadership style.

leaderful moment   a methodology for investigating leadership that concentrates more on frames of leadership as an unfolding emergent process by using films and photographs.

linguistic-relativity hypothesis   speakers of different languages, that is, different language families/national languages, perceive and conceptualize the world and specific phenomena such as leadership systematically within each language but very differently across languages

leader substitutes theory   explores the situational variables that make a leader employing either instrumental or supportive leadership behaviour ineffective or redundant

LMX theory   explores the dyadic relationship between leader and follower and the impact on group performance

masculine   personal characteristics such as assertive, dominant, competent, competitive, agentic and authoritative

MLQ   a questionnaire used to measure the full range leadership model – transformational, transactional and *laissez-faire* leadership

multiple-linkage model   includes a complex list of leader behaviours, mediators and situational variables to provide a detailed insight into the complexity of the link between leader behaviour, context and performance

normative decision model   explores the decision-making procedures of participative leaders and their effectiveness

path-goal theory   explores how leaders can motivate followers to achieve set goals and improve their own and the organization's performance

performative effect of literature   it is through acts of speaking and writing that things come into existence

sensory knowledge tacit knowledge gained through reflection on felt meaning, lived experience, emotion and intuition

situational leadership theory explores the effectiveness of a leader who employs a mix of directive and supportive leader behaviours in relation to a subordinate's maturity

social constructivist perspective the reality an individual sees is truly subjective and fluid and it is continuously co-constructed through that individual's interaction with self and context

social identity theory how individuals self-categorize themselves into different social categories reflecting different levels of self-perception and belonging to social groups that dynamically relate to each other

stratified-systems theory (SST) a prescriptive model of organizational structure based on defining the hierarchical level according to the task complexity involved at each level

time span of discretion the maximum time for completing critical tasks within organizations

trait a distinguishing feature in character, appearance, habit or portrayal

transformational leadership questionnaire (TLQ) a questionnaire used to measure transformational leadership dimensions

triggers life events that have impacted on leadership development and learning

worldliness a new research stream encouraging emic research in non-western countries to explore the meaning and practice of leadership in local cultures

worldly mindset a manager's mindset focused particularly on his/her ability to manage the context through being aware of his/her own value set, ethical code, religious beliefs and those of others around him/her

References

Abrams, D., Randsley de Moura, G., Marques, J.M. and Hutchison, P. (2008) Innovation credit: When can leaders oppose their group's norms? *Journal of Personality and Social Psychology*, 95: 662–678.

Achua, C.F. and Lussier, R.N. (2010) *Effective Leadership*. Canada: Southwestern Cengage Learning.

Adair, J. (1973) *Action Centred Leadership*. New York: McGraw-Hill.

Adair, J. (2005) *How to Grow Leaders*. London: Kogan Page.

Agamben, G. (1993) *The Coming Community*. Minneapolis, MN: University of Minnesota Press.

Agar, M. (1994) *Language Shock: Understanding the Culture of Conversation*. New York: Morrow and Company.

Ailon, G. (2008) Mirror, mirror on the wall: Culture's consequences in a value-test of its own design. *Academy of Management Review*, 33(4): 885–904.

Ailon-Souday, G. and Kunda, G. (2003) The local selves of global workers: The social construction of national identity in the face of organizational globalization. *Organization Studies*, 24(7): 1073–1096.

Alban-Metcalfe, R.J. and Alimo-Metcalfe, B. (2000) An analysis of the convergent and discriminant validity of the transformational leadership questionnaire. *International Journal of Selection and Assessment*, 8(3): 158–175.

Alexander, L.D. (1979) The effect of level in the hierarchy and functional area have on the extent Mintzberg's roles are required by managerial jobs. *Academy of Management Proceedings*, 186–189.

Alford, C.F. (2008) Whistleblowing as responsible followership. In R. Riggio, I. Chaleff and J. Lipmen-Blumen (eds) *The Art of Followership*. San Francisco, CA: Jossey-Bass, 237–250.

Alimo-Metcalfe, B. (1996) The feedback revolution. *Health Services Journal*, 13: 26–28.

Alimo-Metcalfe, B. (1998) 360-degree feedback and leadership development. *International Journal of Selection and Assessment*, 6(1): 35–44.

Alimo-Metcalfe, B. and Alban-Metcalfe, R.J. (2001) The development of a new transformational leadership questionnaire. *Journal of Occupational and Organizational Psychology*, 74: 1–27.

Alvesson, M. (1993) *Cultural Perspectives on Organizations*. Cambridge: Cambridge University Press.

Alvesson, M. (1996) Leadership studies: From procedure and abstraction to reflexivity and situation. *The Leadership Quarterly*, 7(4): 455–485.

Alvesson, M. (2010) Leaders as saints: Leadership through moral peak performance. In M. Alvesson and A. Spicer (eds) *Metaphors We Lead By: Understanding Leadership in the Real World*. London: Routledge, 51–75.

Alvesson, M. (2011) Leadership and organizational culture. In A. Bryman, D. Collinson, K. Grint, B. Jackson and M. Uhl-Bien (eds) *The SAGE Handbook of Leadership*. London: Sage, 151–164.

Alvesson, M. and Karreman, D. (2000) Varieties of discourse: On the study of discourse analysis. *Human Relations*, 53(9): 1125–1149.

Alvesson, M. and Skoldberg, K. (2000) *Reflexive Methodology: New Vistas for Qualitative Research*. London: Sage.

Alvesson, M. and Spicer, A. (eds) (2010) *Metaphors We Lead By: Understanding Leadership in the Real World*. London: Routledge.

Alvesson, M. and Sveningsson, S. (2003a) The great disappearing act: difficulties in doing 'leadership'. *Leadership Quarterly*, 14(3): 359–381.

Alvesson, M. and Sveningsson, S. (2003b) Manager doing leadership: The extra-ordinization of the mundane. *Human Relations*, 56(12): 1435–1459.

Alvesson, M. and Willmott, H. (2002) Identity regulation as organizational control: Producing the appropriate individual. *Journal of Management Studies*, 39(5): 619–644.

Anand, S., Hu, J., Liden, R.C. and P.R. Vidyarthi (2011) Leader-member exchange: recent research findings and prospects for the future. In A. Bryman, D. Collinson, K. Grint, B. Jackson and M. Uhl-Bien (eds) *The SAGE Handbook of Leadership*. London: Sage, 311–325.

Andrews, J.O. and Field, R.H.G. (1998) Regrounding the concept of leadership. *Leadership and Organization Development Journal*, 19(3): 128–136.

Antonakis, J. (2001) The validity of the transformational, transactional, and laissez-faire leadership model as measured by the multifactor leadership questionnaire (5x). Unpublished doctoral dissertation, Walden University, Minneapolis, Minnesota.

Antonakis, J. and House, R. J. (2002) An analysis of the full-range leadership theory: The way forward. In B.J. Avolio and F.J. Yammarino (eds) *Transformational and Charismatic Leadership: The Road Ahead*. Amsterdam: JAI Press, 3–33.

Antonakis, J., Ashkanasy, N.M. and Dasborough, M.T. (2009) Does leadership need emotional intelligence? *Leadership Quarterly*, 20: 247–261.

Antonakis, J., Avolio, B.J. and Sivasubramaniam, N. (2003) Context and leadership: An examination of the nine-factor full-range leadership theory using the multifactor leadership questionnaire. *Leadership Quarterly*, 14: 261–295.

Argyris, C. (1964) *Integrating the Individual and the Organization*. New York: Wiley.

Arnold, K.A., Barling, J. and Kelloway, E.K. (2001) Transformational leadership or the iron cage: Which predicts trust, commitment and team efficacy? *Leadership and Organization Development Journal*, 22(7): 315–320.

Askling, B., Hofgaard Lycke, K. and Stave, O. (2004). Institutional leadership and leeway – important elements in a national system of quality assurance and accreditation: Experiences from a pilot study. *Tertiary Education and Management*, 10: 107–120.

Atwater, L.E. and Yammarino, F.J. (1992) Does self-other agreement on leadership perceptions moderate the validity of leadership and performance predictions? *Personnel Psychology*, 45: 141–164.

Avolio, B.J. (1999) *Full Leadership Development: Building the Vital Forces in Organizations*. Thousand Oaks, CA: Sage.

Avolio, B.J. and Bass, B.M. (1993) *Cross Generations: A Full Range Leadership Development Program*. Binghamton, NY: Center for Leadership Studies, Binghamton University.

Avolio, B.J. and Bass, B.M. (1994) *Evaluate the Impact of Transformational Leadership Training at Individual, Group, Organizational and Community Levels*. Final report to the W.K. Kellogg Foundation. Binghamton, NY: Binghamton University.

Avolio, B.J. and Bass, B.M. (1998) You can drag a horse to water, but you can't make it drink except when it's thirsty. *Journal of Leadership Studies*, 5: 1–17.

Avolio, B.J. and Bass, B.M. (eds) (2002) *Developing Potential across a Full Range of Leadership: Cases on Transactional and Transformational Leadership*. Mahwah, NJ: Lawrence Erlbaum.

Avolio, B.J. and Gardner, W.L. (2005) Authentic leadership development: getting to the root of positive forms of leadership. *Leadership Quarterly*, 16(3): 315–338.

Avolio, B.J. and Locke, E.E. (2002) Contrasting different philosophies of leader motivation: Altruism and egotistic. *Leadership Quarterly*, 13: 169–191.

Avolio, B.J. and Yammarino, F.J. (eds) (2002) *Transformational and Charismatic Leadership: The Road Ahead*. Oxford: UK Elsevier Science.

Avolio, B.J., Avey, J.B. and Quizenberry, D. (2010) Estimating the return on leadership development investment. *Leadership Quarterly*, 21: 633–644.

Avolio, B.J., Bass, B.M., and Jung, D.I. (1999) Re-examining the components of transformational and transactional leadership using the multifactor leadership questionnaire. *Journal of Occupational and Organizational Psychology*, 72: 441–462.

Avolio, B.J., Gardner, W.L., Walumbwa, F.O., Luthans, F. and May, D.R. (2004) Unlocking the mask: A look at the process by which authentic leaders impact follower attitudes and behaviours. *Leadership Quarterly*, 15: 801–823.

Avolio, B.J., Waldman, D.A. and Einstein, W.O. (1988) Transformational leadership in a management game simulation: Impacting the bottom line. *Group and Organization Studies*, 13(1): 59–80.

Baker, A.C., Jensen, P.J. and Kolb, D.A. (2005) Conversation as experiential learning. *Management Learning*, 36: 411–427.

Balkundi, P., and Kilduff, M. (2006) The ties that bind: A social network approach to leadership. *Leadership Quarterly*, 17: 419–439.

Bandura, A. (1977) *Social Learning Theory*. Englewood Cliffs, NJ: Prentice-Hall.

Barker, J.R. (1993) Tightening the iron cage: concertive control in self managed teams. *Administrative Science Quarterly*, 38: 408–437.

Barker, R.A. (2001) The nature of leadership. *Human Relations*, 54(4): 469–494.

Barling, J., Weber, T. and Kelloway, K.E. (1996) Effects of transformational leadership training on attitudinal and financial outcomes: A field experiment. *Journal of Applied Psychology*, 81: 827–832.

Barnard, C.I. (1950) *The Functions of the Executive*. Cambridge, MA: Harvard University Press.

Bartlett, C.A. and Ghoshal, S. (1997) The myth of the generic manager: New personal competencies for new management roles. *California Management Review*, 40(1): 92–116.

Baruch, Y. (2006) Role-play teaching: Acting in the classroom. *Management Learning*, 37: 43–61.

Bass, B.M. (1985a) *Leadership and Performance Beyond Expectations*. New York: Free Press.

Bass, B.M. (1985b) Leadership: good, better, best. *Organizational Dynamics*, 13: 26–4.

Bass, B.M. (1990) *Bass and Stogdill's Handbook of Leadership: Theory, Research, and Managerial Applications*, third edition. New York: Free Press.

Bass, B.M. (1992) Assessing the charismatic leaders. In M. Syrett and C. Hogg (eds) *Frontiers of Leadership*. Oxford: Blackwell, 414–418.

Bass, B.M. (1997) Does the transactional-transformational leadership paradigm transcend organizational and national boundaries? *American Psychologist*, 52: 130–139.

Bass, B.M. (1998) *Transformational Leadership: Industry, Military, and Educational Impact*. Mahwah, NJ: Lawrence Erlbaum Associates.

Bass, B.M. and Avolio, B.J. (1995) *MLQ Multifactor Leadership Questionnaire (MLQ FORM 5X-Short)*. Binghamton, NY: Center for Leadership Studies, Binghamton University.

Bass, B.M., and Avolio, B.J. (1990) Developing transformational leadership: 1992 and beyond. *Journal of European Industrial Training*, 14: 21–27.

Bass, B.M., and Avolio, B.J. (1993) Transformational leadership: A response to critiques. In M.M. Chemers and R. Ayman. (eds) *Leadership Theory and Research: Perspectives and Directions*. San Diego, CA: Academic Press, 49–79.

Bass, B.M., and Avolio, B.J. (1994) Introduction. In B.M. Bass and B.J. Avolio (eds) *Improving Organizational Effectiveness through Transformational Leadership*. Thousands Oaks, CA: Sage, 5–6.

Bass, B.M. and Riggio, R.E. (2006) *Transformational Leadership*, second edition. New York: Psychology Press.

Bass, B.M. and Steidlmeier, P. (1999) Ethics, character and authentic transformational leadership behavior. *Leadership Quarterly*, 10: 181–21.

Bass, B.M., Avolio, B.J., Jung, D.I. and Berson, Y. (2003) Predicting unit performance by assessing transformational and transactional leadership. *Journal of Applied Psychology*, 88(2): 207–218.

Bass, B.M., Valenzi, E.R., Farrow, D.L. and Solomon, R.J. (1975) Management styles associated with organizational, task, personal and interpersonal contingencies. *Journal of Applied Psychology*, 60(6): 720–729.

Bass, B.M., Waldman, D.A., Avolio, B.J. and Bebb, M. (1987) Transformational leadership and the falling dominoes effect. *Group and Organization Studies*, 12: 73–87.

Bateman Driskell, R. and Lyon, L. (2002) Are virtual communities true communities? Examining the environments and elements of community. *City and Community*, 1: 373–390.

Bathurst, R. (2008) Enlivening management practice through aesthetic engagement: Vico, Baumgarten and Kant. *Philosophy and Management*, 7(3): 87–102.

Bauman, Z. (2001) *Community: Seeking Safety in an Insecure World*. Cambridge: Polity Press.

Beechler, S. and Javidan, M. (2007) *Leading with a Global Mindset*. London: Emerald.

Beerel, A. (2009) *Leadership and Change Management*. London: Sage.

Benne, K.D. and Sheats, P. (1948) Functional roles of group members. *Journal of Social Issues*, 4(2): 41–49.

Bennett, N., Wise, C., Woods, P. A. and Harvey, J. A. (2003) *Distributed Leadership: A Review of Literature*. Nottingham: National College for School Leadership.

Bennis, W.G. (1984) The 4 competencies of leadership. *Training & Development Journal*, August: 17.

Bennis, W.G. (1989) *On Becoming a Leader*. Philadelphia, PA: Perseus Books.

Bennis, W.G. and Nanus, B. (1985) *Leaders: The Strategies for Taking Charge*. New York: Harper & Row.

Bennis, W.G. and Thomas, R.J. (2002) *Geeks and Geezers*. Boston, MA: Harvard Business School Press.

Bentley, J. and Turnbull, S. (2005) Stimulating leadership – The ten key triggers of leadership development. In R.W.T. Gill (ed.) *Leadership Under the Microscope*. Ross-on-Wye, Herefordshire: The Leadership Trust Foundation, 35–53.

Berry, A.J. and Cartwright, S. (2000) Leadership: A critical construction. *Leadership and Organization Development Journal*, 21(7): 342–349.

Beyer, J.M. (1999) Taming and promoting charisma in organisations. *Leadership Quarterly*, 10: 307–330.

Beyer, J.M. and Browning, L.D. (1999) Transfroming an industry in crisis: Charisma, routinization, and supportive cultural leadership. *Leadership Quarterly*, 10: 483–520.

Bieri, J. (1955) Cognitive complexity-simplicity and predictive behaviour. *Journal of Abnormal and Social Psychology*, 51: 263–268.

Billing, Y. and Alvesson, M. (2000) Questioning the notion of feminine leadership: A critical perspective on the gender labelling of leadership. *Gender, Work and Organization*, 7(3): 144–157.

Billsberry, J. and Edwards, G.P. (2008) Toxic celluloid: Representations of bad leadership on film and implications for leadership development. *Organisations and People*, 15(3): 104–110.

Bion, W.R. (1961) *Experiences in Groups*. London: Tavistock.

Black, J.S. and Mendenhall, M. (1990) Cross-cultural training effectiveness: A review and a theoretical framework for future research. *Academy of Management Review*, 15(1): 113–136.

Blake, R.R. and Mouton, J.S. (1964) *The Managerial Grid III*. Houston, TX: Gulf Publishing Company.

Blake, R.R. and Mouton, J.S. (1978) *The New Managerial Grid*. Houston, TX: Gulf Publishing Company.

Blanchard, K., Zigarmi, D. and Nelson, R. (1993) Situational leadership after 25 years: A retrospective. *Journal of Leadership Studies*, 1(1): 22–36.

Blanchard, K., Zigarmi, P. and Zigarmi, D. (1985) *Leadership and the One Minute Manager: Increasing Effectiveness Through Situational Leadership*. New York: William Morrow.

Blanchot, M. (1988) *The Unvowable Community*. Barrytown, NY: Station Hill Press.

Bligh, M.C. (2011) Followership and follower-centred approaches. In A. Bryman, D. Collinson, K. Grint, B. Jackson and M. Uhl-Bien (eds) *The SAGE Handbook of Leadership*. London: Sage, 425–436.

Bligh, M.C. and Kohles, J. (2008) The romance lives on: contemporary issues surrounding the romance of leadership. *Leadership*, 3(3): 343–360.

Bligh, M.C. and Schyns, B. (2007) Leading questions: the romance lives on: contemporary issues surrounding the romance of leadership. *Leadership*, 3(3): 343–360.

Bligh, M.C., Kohles, J.C. and Meindl, J.R. (2004a) Charisma under crisis: Presidential leadership, rhetoric, and media responses before and after the September 11th terrorists attacks. *Leadership Quarterly*, 15: 211–239.

Bligh, M.C., Kohles, J.C. and Meindl, J.R. (2004b) Charting the language of leadership: A methodological investigation of President Bush and the crisis of 9/11. *Journal of Applied Psychology*, 89: 562–574.

Bligh, M.C., Kohles, J.C. and Pillai, R. (2005) Charisma and crisis in the California recall election. *Leadership*, 1: 323–352.

Blumen, L.S. (2008) Bystanders to children's bullying: the importance of leadership by 'Innocent Bystanders'. In R. Riggio, I. Chaleff and J. Lipman-Blumen (eds) *The Art of Followership*. San Francisco, CA: Jossey-Bass, 219–236.

Boal, K.B. and Bryson, J.M. (1988) Charismatic leadership: A phenomenological and structural approach. In J.G. Hunt, B.R Baliga, H.P. Dachler and C.A. Schreisheim (eds) *Emerging Leadership Vistas*. Lexington, MA: Lexington Books, 11–28.

Boddy, C.R.P., Ladyshewsky, R. and Galvin, P. (2010) Leaders without ethics in global business: Corporate psychopaths. *Journal of Public Affairs*, 10: 121–138.

Bolden, R. (ed.) (2005) *What Is Leadership Development?* Exeter: Leadership South West and the University of Exeter.

Bolden, R. (ed.) (2006) *Leadership Development in Context*. Exeter: Leadership South West and the University of Exeter.

Bolden, R. (2011) Distributed leadership in organisations: A review of theory and research. *International Journal of Management Reviews*, 13(3): 251–269.

Bolden, R., Hawkins, B., Gosling, J. and Taylor, S. (2011) *Exploring Leadership: Individual, Organizational and Societal Perspectives*. Oxford: Oxford University Press.

Bolden, R., Petrov, G. and Gosling, J. (2008) *Developing Collective Leadership in Higher Education*. London: Leadership Foundation for Higher Education.

Bolt, P. (1999) *The Whole Manager: Achieving Success without Selling Your Soul*. Dublin: Oak Tree Press.

Book, E.W. (2000) *Why the Best Man for the Job is a Woman*. New York: HarperCollins.

Borman, W.C. (1974) The rating of individuals in organizations: An alternative approach. *Organizational Behaviour and Human Performance*, 12: 105–124.

Bowles, H.R. and McGinn, K.L. (2005) Claiming authority: Negotiating challenges for women leaders. In D.M. Messick and R.M. Kramer (eds) *The Psychology of Leadership: New Perspectives and Research*. Mahwah, NJ: Lawrence Erlbaum, 191–208.

Bowring, M.A. (2004) Resistance is not futile: liberating Captain Janeway from the masculine-feminine dualism of leadership. *Gender, Work and Organization*, 11(4): 381–405.

Bradbury, H. and Lichtenstein, B.M. (2000) Relationality in organisational research: Exploring the space between. *Organisation Science*, 11: 551–564.

Bradley, G.W. (1978) Self-serving bias in the attribution process: A re-examination of the fact of fiction question. *Journal of Personality and Social Psychology*, 36: 56–71.

Bratton, J., Grint, K. and Nelson, D. (2005) *Organizational Leadership*. London: Thomson Learning.

Brown, W. and Jaques, E. (1965) *Glacier Project Papers: Some Essays on Organization and Management from the Glacier Project Research*. London: Heinemann.

Brown, M.E. and Treviño, L.K. (2006) Ethical leadership: a review and future directions. *Leadership Quarterly*, 17: 595–616.

Brown, M.E., Treviño, L.K. and Harrison, D.A. (2005) Ethical leadership: A social learning perspective for construct development and testing. *Organisational Behaviour and Human Decision Processes*, 97: 117–134.

Bruhn, J.G. (2008) The functionality of gray area ethics in organisations. *Journal of Business Ethics*, 89(2): 204–214.

Bryman, A. (1992) *Charisma and Leadership in Organizations*. London: Sage.

Bryman, A. (2011) Research methods in the study of leadership. In A. Bryman, D. Collinson, K. Grint, B. Jackson and M. Uhl-Bien (eds) *The SAGE Handbook of Leadership*. London: Sage, 15–28.

Burgoyne, J. G. and Stewart, R. (1977) Implicit learning theories as determinants of the effect of management development programmes. *Personnel Review* 6(2): 5–14.

Burns, J.M. (1978) *Leadership*. New York: Harper & Row.

Burns, T. (1957) Management in action. *Operational Research Quarterly*, 8: 45–60.

Burr, V. (1995) *An Introduction to Social Constructionism*. London: Routledge.

Burrell, G. (1992) The organisation of pleasure. In M. Alvesson and H. Willmott (eds) *Critical Management Studies*, 66–89.

Bycio, P., Hackett, R.D. and Allen, J.S. (1995) Further assessments of Bass's (1985) conceptualisation of transactional and transformational leadership. *Journal of Applied Psychology*, 80: 468–478.

Cacioppe, R. (1998) An integrated model and approach for the design of effective leadership development programs. *Leadership and Organisation Development Journal*, 19(1): 44–53.

Cammock, P. (2002) *The Dance of Leadership*. Auckland: Prentice-Hall.

Cammock, P., Nilakant, V. and Dakin, S. (1995) Developing a lay model of managerial effectiveness: A social constructionist perspective. *Journal of Management Studies*, 32(4): 443–474.

Cannella, A.A. Jr. and Monroe, M.J. (1997) Contrasting perspectives on strategic leaders: Toward a more realistic view of top managers. *Journal of Management*, 23(3): 213–237.

Carless, S.A. (1998) Assessing the discriminant validity of transformational leader behaviours as measured by the MLQ. *Journal of Occupational and Organizational Psychology*, 71: 353–358.

Carless, S.A., Mann, L. and Wearing, A. (1995) An empirical test of the transformational leadership model. Leadership Symposium, Inaugural Australian Industrial and Organizational Psychology Conference, Sydney, Australia.

Carli L.L. and Eagly, A.H. (2011) Gender and leadership. In A. Bryman, D. Collinson, K. Grint, B. Jackson and M. Uhl-Bien (eds) *The SAGE Handbook of Leadership*. London: Sage, 103–117.

Carlson, S. (1951) *Executive Behaviour: A Study of the Work Load and the Working Methods of Managing Directors*. Stockholm: Strömbergs.

Carlyle, T. (1866) *On Heroes, Hero-Worship and the Heroic in History*. New York: John Wiley.

Carroll, B. and Levy, L. (2008) Defaulting to management: leadership defined by what it is not. *Organization*, 15(1): 75–96.

Carroll, B., Levy, L. and Richmond, D. (2008) Leadership as practice: challenging the competency paradigm. *Leadership*, 4(4): 363–379.

Carsten, M.K. and Bligh, M.C. (2007) Here today, gone tomorrow: follower perceptions of a departing leader and a lingering vision. In B. Shamir, R. Pillai, M.C. Bligh and M. Uhl-Bien (eds) *Follower-Centered Perspectives on Leadership: A Tribute to the Memory of James R. Meindl*. Charlotte, NC: Information Age Publishing, 211–242.

Carsten, M.K., Uhl-Bien, M., West, B.J., Patera, J.L. and McGregor, R. (2010) Exploring social constructions of followership: a qualitative study. *The Leadership Quarterly*, 21(3): 543–562.

Castells, M. (2001) *The Internet Galaxy: Reflections on the Internet, Business and Society*. Oxford: Oxford University Press.

Caza, A. and Jackson, B. (2011) Authentic leadership. In A. Bryman, D. Collinson, K. Grint, B. Jackson and M. Uhl-Bien (eds) *The SAGE Handbook of Leadership*. London: Sage, 353–364.

Chaleff, I. (2008) Creating new ways of following. In R. Riggio, I. Chaleff and J. Lipmen-Blumen (eds) *The Art of Followership*. San Francisco, CA: Jossey-Bass, 67–88.

Chang, H.V. (2008) *Authoethnography as Method*. Walnut Creek, CA: Left Coast Press.

Chapple, E.D. and Sayles, L.R. (1961) *The Measurement of Management*. New York: Macmillan.

Charan, R., Drotter, S. and Noel, J. (2001) *The Leadership Pipeline: How to Build the Leadership Powered Company*. San Francisco, CA: Jossey-Bass.

Chen, C.C., Belkin, L.Y. and Kurtzberg, T.R. (2007) Organizational Change. Member Emotion and Construction of charismatic leadership: a follower-centric contingency model. In B. Shamir, R. Pillai, M.C. Bligh and M. Uhl-Bien (eds) *Follower-Centered Perspectives on Leadership: A Tribute to the Memory of James R. Meindl*. Charlotte, NC: Information Age Publishing, 115–134.

Chhokar, J.S. (2007) *Culture and Leadership Across the World: The GLOBE Book of In-Depth Studies of 25 Societies*. Psychology Press.

Chia, R. (1996) The problem of reflexivity in organizational research: towards a postmodern science of organization. *Organization*, 3(1): 31–35.

Ciulla, J.B. (2004) Ethics and leadership effectiveness. In J. Antonakis, A.T. Cianciolo and R.J. Sternberg (eds) *The Nature of Leadership*. Thousand Oaks, CA: Sage, 302–327.

Ciulla, J.B. (2005) The state of leadership ethics and the work that lies before us. *Business Ethics: A European Review*, 14(4): 323–335.

Ciulla, J.B. (2012) Ethics and effectiveness: The nature of good leadership. In D.V. Day and J. Antonakis (eds) *The Nature of Leadership*, second edition. Los Angeles, CA: Sage.

Ciulla, J.B. and Forsyth, D.R. (2011) Leadership ethics. In A. Bryman, D. Collinson, K. Grint, B. Jackson, and M. Uhl Bien. (eds) *The SAGE Handbook of Leadership*. London: Sage, 229–241.

Clausen, L. (2010) Moving beyond stereotypes in managing cultural difference: Communication in Danish-Japanese corporate relationships. *Scandinavian Journal of Management*, 26: 57–66.

Cohen, A. (1985) *The Symbolic Construction of Community*. London: Tavistock.

Collins, D.B. (2001) Organisational performance: The future of leadership development programs. *Journal of Leadership and Organisation Studies*, 7: 43–54.

Collins, D.B. and Holton, E.F. (2004) The effectiveness of managerial leadership development programs: A meta-analysis of studies from 1982 to 2001. *Human Resource Development Quarterly*, 15(2): 217–248.

Collinson, D. (2003) Identities and insecurities: Selves at work. *Organization*, 10(3): 527–547.

Collinson, D. (2005) Dialectics of Leadership. *Human Relations*, 58(11): 1419–1442.

Collinson, D. (2006) Rethinking followership: A post-structuralist analysis of follower identities. *The Leadership Quarterly*, 17(2): 1419–1442.

Collinson, D. (2008) Conformist, resistant and disguised selves: A post-structuralist approach to identity and workplace followership. In R. Riggio, I. Chaleff and J. Lipmen-Blumen (eds) *The Art of Followership*. San Francisco, CA: Jossey-Bass, 309–324.

Collinson, D. (2009) Rethinking leadership and followership. In S.R. Clegg and C.L. Cooper (eds) *The Handbook of Organization Behavior*, volume 2. *Macro Approaches*. London: Sage, 251–264.

Collinson, D. (2011) Critical leadership studies. In A. Bryman, D. Collinson, K. Grint, B. Jackson and M. Uhl-Bien (eds) *The SAGE Handbook of Leadership*. London: Sage, 181–194.

Colvin, R.E. (2001) Leading from the middle: A challenge for middle managers. Paper presented at the Festschrift for Bernard Bass, SUNY Binghamton, Center for Leadership Studies, June.

Comer, D.R. (2000) Not just a mickey mouse exercise: using Disney's *The Lion King* to teach leadership. *Journal of Management Education*, 25(4): 430–436.

Conger, J.A. (1989) *The Charismatic Leader: Behind the Mystique of Exceptional Leadership*. San Francisco, CA: Jossey-Bass.

Conger, J.A. (1998) Qualitative research as the cornerstone methodology for understanding leadership. *Leadership Quarterly*, 9(1): 107–121.

Conger, J.A. (1992) *Learning to Lead*. San Francisco, CA: Jossey-Bass.

Conger, J.A. and Benjamin, B. (1999) *Building Leaders: How Successful Companies Develop the Next Generation*. San Francisco: Jossey-Bass.

Conger, J.A. and Kanungo, R.N. (1987) Toward a behavioral theory charismatic leadership in organizational settings. *Academy of Management Review*, 12: 637–647.

Conger, J.A. and Kanungo, R.N. (1998) *Chariamtic Leadership in Organisations*. Thousand Oaks, CA: Sage.

Connor, D.R. (1995) *Managing at the Speed of Change: How Resilient Managers Succeed and Prosper Where Others Fail*. New York: Villard Books.

Contractor, N.S., DeChurch, L.A., Carson, J., Carter, D.R. and Keegan, B. (2012) The topology of collective leadership. *Leadership Quarterly*, 23: 994–1011.

Cooper, C.D., Scandura, T.A. and Schriesheim, C.A. (2005) Looking forward but learning from our past: potential challenges to developing authentic leadership theory and authentic leaders. *Leadership Quarterly,* 16(3): 475–493.

Cope, J., Kempster, S. and Parry, K. (2011) Exploring distributed leadership in a small business context. *International Journal of Management Reviews*, 13(3): 270–285.

Corlett, W. (1989) *Community Without Unity: A Politics of Derridan Extravagance*. Durham, NC: Duke University Press.

Corley, K.G. (2004) Defined by our strategy or our culture? Hierarchical differences in perceptions of organizational identity and change. *Human Relations*, 57(9): 1145–1177.

Cunha, M.P., Guimarães-Costa, N., Rego, A. and Clegg, S.R. (2010) Leading and following (un) ethically in *Limen. Journal of Business Ethics*, 97: 189–206.

Cunliffe, A.L. (2009) The philosopher leader: on relationalism, ethics and reflexivity – A critical perspective to teaching leadership. *Management Learning*, 40(1): 87–101.

Cunliffe, A.L. and Eriksen, M. (2011) Relational leadership. *Human Relations*, 64(11): 1425–1449.

Cunliffe, A.L. and Linstead, S.A. (2009) Introduction: teaching from critical perspectives. *Management Learning*, 40(1): 5–9.

Curphy, G.J. (1992) An empirical investigation of the effects of transformational and transactional leadership on organizational climate, attrition and performance. In K.E. Clark, M.B. Clark and D.R. Campbell (eds) *Impact of Leadership*. Greensboro, NC: The Center for Creative Leadership, 177–188.

Currie, G. and Lockett, A. (2011) Distributing leadership in health and social care: Concertive, conjoint or collective? *International Journal of Management Reviews*, 13(3): 286–300.

Currie, G., Lockett, A. and Suhomlinova, O. (2009) The institutionalzation of distributed leadership: A 'Catch-22' in English public services. *Human Relations*, 62 (11): 1735–1761.

Dachler, H.P. (1988) Constraints on the emergence of new vistas in leadership and management research: an epistemological overview. In J.G. Hunt, B.R. Baliga, H.P. Dachler and C.A. Schriesheim (eds) *Emerging Leadership Vistas*. Lexington, MA: Lexington Books, 267–286.

Dahl, R.A. (1957) The concept of power. *Behavioural Science*, 2: 201–205.

Dansereau, F., Graen, G. and Haga, W.J. (1975) A vertical dyad linkage approach to leadership within formal organizations: A longitudinal investigation of the role making process. *Organizational Behavior and Human Performance*, 13(1): 46–78.

Dansereau, F., Yammarino, F.J. and Kohles, J. (1999) Multiple levels of analysis from a longitudinal perspective: Some implications for theory building. *Academy of Management Review*, 24(2): 346–357.

Davis, K.M. and Gardner, W.L. (2012) Charisma under crisis revisited: Presidential leadership, perceived leader effectiveness, and contextual influences. *Leadership Quarterly*, 23: 918–933.

Day, D.V. (2000) Leadership development: A review in context. *Leadership Quarterly*, 11(4): 581–613.

Delanty, G. (2003) *Community*. Abingdon: Routledge.

Den Hartog, D.N., Van Muijen, J.J. and Koopman, P.L. (1997) Transactional versus transformational leadership: An observational field study. *Journal of Occupational and Organizational Psychology*, 70: 19–34.

Denis, J., Kisfalvi, V., Langley, A. and Rouleau, L. (2011) Perspectives on strategic leadership. In A. Bryman, D. Collinson, K. Grint, B. Jackson, and M. Uhl Bien (eds) *The SAGE Handbook of Leadership*. London: Sage, 71–85.

Derossi, F. (1974) A profile of Italian managers in large firms. *International Studies of Management and Organization*, 4(1–2): 138–202.

Derossi, F. (1978) The crisis in managerial roles in Italy. *International Studies of Management and Organization*, 8(3): 64–99.

Dobbins, G.H. and Platz, S.J. (1986) Sex differences in leadership: How real are they? *Academy of Management Review*, 11: 118–127.

Donaldson, T. and Dunfee, T.W. (1994) Toward a unified conception of business ethics: Integrative social contracts theory. *Academy of Management Review*, 19(2): 252–284.

Dorfman, P.W. (2004) International and cross-cultural leadership research. In B.J. Punnett and O. Shenkar (eds) *Handbook for International Management Research*, second edition. Ann Arbor, MI: University of Michigan, 265–335.

Downton, J.V. (1973) *Rebel Leadership: Commitment and Charisma in the Revolutionary Process*. New York: Free Press.

Druskat, V.U. (1994) Gender and leadership style: transformational and transactional leadership in the Roman Catholic Church. *Leadership Quarterly*, 5: 99–119.

Dubin, R. (1979) Metaphors of leadership: An overview. In J.G. Hunt and L.L. Larson (eds) *Cross Currents in Leadership*. Carbondale, IL: Southern Illinois University Press, 225–238.

DuBrin, A.J. (2010) *Principles of Leadership,* sixth edition. Canada: Southwestern Cengage Learning.

Durkheim, E. (1951) *Suicide*. New York: Free Press

Durkheim, E. (1965) *The Elemental Forms of Religious Life*. New York: Free Press

Dvir, T. (1998) The impact of transformational leadership training on follower development and performance: a field experiment. Doctoral dissertation, Tel Aviv University, Ramat, Aviv, Israel.

Eagly, A.H. (1987) *Sex Differences in Social Behaviour: A Social-Role Interaction*. Hillsdale, NJ: Lawrence Erlbaum Associates.

Eagly, A.H. and Carli, L.L. (2003) The female leadership advantage: an evaluation of the evidence. *The Leadership Quarterly*, 14: 807–834.

Eagly, A.H. and Carli, L.L. (2004) Women and men as leaders. In J. Antonakis, R.J. Sternberg and A.T. Cianciolo (eds) *The Nature of Leadership*. Thousand Oaks, CA: Sage, 279–301.

Eagly, A.H. and Johnson, B.T. (1990) Gender and leadership style: a meta-analysis. *Psychological Bulletin*, 108(2): 233–256.

Eagly, A.H., Makhijani, M.G. and Klonsky, B. (1992) Gender and the evaluation of leaders: a meta-analysis. *Psychological Bulletin*, 111: 3–22.

Eagly, A.H., Karau, S.J. and Makhijani, M.G. (1995) Gender and the effectiveness of leaders: a meta-analysis. *Psychological Bulletin*, 117: 125–145.

Eagly, A.H., Johannesen-Schmidt, M.C. and van Engen, M. (2003) Transformational, transactional and laissez-faire leadership styles: A meta-analysis. *Psychological Bulletin*, 129: 569–591.

Edwards, G.P. and Jepson, D. (2008) Departmental affiliation, leadership and leadership development. In K. Turnbull-James and J. Collins (eds) *Leadership Perspectives: Knowledge into Action*. Basingstoke: Palgrave Macmillan.

Edwards, G.P. (2005) An investigation of transformational, transactional and laissez-faire leadership at different hierarchical levels in uk manufacturing companies using multiple ratings. PhD Dissertation, Strathclyde Graduate School of Business, Strathclyde University, UK.

Edwards, G.P. (2011) Concepts of community: A framework for contextualising distributed leadership. *International Journal of Management Reviews*, 13(3): 301–312.

Edwards, G.P. and Gill, R. (2012) Transformational leadership across hierarchical levels in UK manufacturing organizations. *Leadership and Organisation Development Journal*, 33(1): 25–50.

Edwards, G.P. and Turnbull, S. (2013a) Special issue on new paradigms in evaluating leadership development. *Advances in Developing Human Resources*, 15(1): 3–9.

Edwards, G.P. and Turnbull, S. (2013b) A cultural approach to leadership development evaluation. *Advances in Developing Human Resources*, 15(1): 46–60.

Edwards, G.P. and Gill, R. (2012) Transformational leadership across hierarchical levels in UK manufacturing organizations. *Leadership and Organisation Development Journal*, 33(1): 25–50.

Edwards, G.P., Elliott, C., Iszatt-White, M. and Schedlitzki, D. (2013) Critical and alternative approaches to leadership learning and development. *Management Learning*, 44(1): 3–10.

Edwards, G.P., Schyns, B., Gill, R. and Higgs, M. (2012) The MLQ factor structure in a UK context. *Leadership and Organization Development Journal*, 33(4): 369–382.

Edwards, G.P., Ward, J., Schedlitzki, D. and Wood, M. (2010) Toxic leadership: Representations and critical reflections from *Batman – The Dark Knight* (2008). 9th International Conference on Studying Leadership, Lund University, Sweden, December.

Edwards, G.P., Winter, P.K. and Bailey, J. (2002) *Leadership in Management*. Ross-on-Wye: The Leadership Trust Foundation.

Eisenbeiß, S.A. and Boerner, S. (2013) A double-edged sword: transformational leadership and individual creativity. *British Journal of Management*, 24: 54–68.

Eisenhardt, K.K. and Bourgeois III, L.J. (1988) Politics of strategic decision-making in high-velocity environments: Towards a midrange theory. *Academy of Management Journal*, 31(4): 737–770.

Ellemers, N., de Gilder, D. and Haslam, S.A. (2004) Motivating individuals and groups at work: A social identity perspective on leadership and group performance. *Academy of Management Reviews*, 29(3): 459–478.

Elliott, C. and Stead, V. (2008) Learning from leading women's experience: Towards a socio-logical understanding. *Leadership*, 4(2): 159–180.

Ely, K., Boyce, L.A., Nelson, J.K., Zaccaro, S.J., Hernez-Broome, G. and Whyman, W. (2010) Evaluating leadership coaching: A review and integrated framework. *Leadership Quarterly*, 21: 585–599.

Ely, R. and Padavic, I. (2007) A feminist analysis of organizational research on sex differences. *Academy of Management Review*, 32(4): 1121–1143.

Engen, M.L. van, Leeden, R. van der and Willemsen, T.M. (2001) Gender, context and leadership styles: A field study. *Journal of Occupational and Organizational Psychology*, 74: 581–598.

Ensaria, N. and Murphy, S.E. (2003) Cross-cultural variations in leadership perceptions and attribution of charisma to the leader. *Organizational Behavior and Human Decision Processes*, 92: 52–66.

Epitropaki, O. and Martin, R. (2005) From ideal to real: A longitudinal study of the role of implicit leadership theories on leader-member exchanged and employee outcomes. *Journal of Applied Psychology*, 89: 293–310.

Erez, A., Lepine, J.A. and Elms, H. (2002) Effects of rotated leadership and peer evaluation on the functioning and effectiveness of self-managed teams: a quasi-experiment. *Personnel Psychology*, 55(4): 929–948.

Etzioni, A. (1961) *A Comparative Analysis of Complex Organizations*. New York: Free Press.

Etzioni, A. (1964) *Modern Organizations*. New York: Prentice-Hall.

Evans, M.G. (1970) The effects of supervisory behaviour on the path-goal relationship. *Organizational Behaviour and Human Performance*, 5: 277–298.

Evans, M.G. (1974) Extensions of a path-goal theory of motivation. *Journal of Applied Psychology*, 59: 172–178.

Fairclough, N. (2003) *Analysing Discourse: Textual Analysis for Social Research*. Abingdon: Routledge.

Fairhurst, G.T. (2007) *Discursive Leadership: In Conversation with Leadership Psychology*. London: Sage.

Fairhurst, G.T. (2009) Considering context in discursive leadership research. *Human Relations*, 62(11): 1607–1633.

Fairhurst, G.T. (2011a) Discursive approaches to leadership. In A. Bryman, D. Collinson, K. Grint, B. Jackson and M. Uhl-Bien (eds) *The SAGE Handbook of Leadership*. London: Sage, 495–507.

Fairhurst, G.T. (2011b) *The Power of Framing: Creating the Language of Leadership*. San Francisco, CA: Jossey-Bass.

Fairhurst, G.T. and Cooren, F. (2004) Organizational language in use: interaction analysis, conversation analysis, and speech act schematics. In D. Grant, C. Hardy, C. Oswick, N. Phillips and L. Putnam (eds) *The Sage Handbook of Organizational Discourse*. London: Sage, 131–152.

Fiedler, F.E. (1964) A contingency model of leadership effectiveness. In L. Berkowitz (ed.) *Advances in Experimental Social Psychology*, Vol 1. New York: Academic Press, 149–190.

Fiedler, F.E. (1967) *A Theory of Leadership Effectiveness*. New York: McGraw-Hill.

Fiedler, F.E. (1995) Reflections by an accidental theorist. *Leadership Quarterly*, 6(4): 453–461.

Fiedler, F.E. and Garcia, J.E. (1987) *New Approaches to Leadership: Cognitive Resources and Organizational Performance*. New York: Wiley.

Finkelstein, S. and Hambrick, D.C. (1996) *Strategic Leadership: Top Executives and Their Effects on Organisations*. St Paul, MN: West.

Fitzsimons, D., Turnbull James, K. and Denyer, D. (2011) Alternative approaches to studying shared and distributed leadership. *International Journal of Management Reviews*, 13(3): 313–328.

Ford, J. (2010) Studying leadership critically: a psychosocial lens on leadership identities. *Leadership*, 6(1): 47–65.

Ford, J. and Harding, N. (2007) Move over management: We are all leaders now. *Management Learning*, 38(5): 475–493.

Ford, J., Harding, N. and Learmonth, M. (2008) *Leadership as Identity: Constructions and Deconstructions*. Basingstoke: Palgrave Macmillan.

Foucault, M. (1977) *Discipline and Punish*. London: Allen and Unwin.

French, J. and Raven, B.H. (1959) The bases of social power. In D. Cartwright (ed.) *Studies of Social Power*. Ann Arbor, MI: Institute for Social Research, 150–167.

French, R. (1997) The teacher as container of anxiety: psychoanalysis and the role of the teacher. *Journal of Management Education*, 21(4): 483–495.

Freud, S. (1921/1985) Group psychology and the analysis of the ego. *Civilization, Society and Religion*, Vol. 12. Harmondsworth: Pelican Freud Library, 91–178.

Fry, L. and Kriger, M. (2009) Towards a theory of being-centered leadership: Multiple levels of being as context for effective leadership. *Human Relations*, 62: 1667–1696.

Fulmer, R.M. (1997) The evolving paradigm of leadership development. *Organizational Dynamics*, 25(4): 59–72.

Furnham, A. (2010) Six learning experiences that shape all top people. *The Sunday Times*, 10 October: Appointments, 2.

Gabriel, Y. (1997) Meeting god: When organizational members come face to face with the supreme leader. *Human Relation*, 50(4): 315–342.

Gabriel, Y. (1999) *Organizations in Depth: The Psychoanalysis of Organizations*. London: Sage.

Gabriel, Y. (2011) Psychoanalytic approaches to leadership. In A. Bryman, D. Collinson, K. Grint, B. Jackson and M. Uhl-Bien (eds) *The SAGE Handbook of Leadership*. London: Sage, 393–404.

Garcia, E.L. (1995) Transformational leadership processes and salesperson performance effectiveness: A theoretical model and partial empirical examination. Unpublished doctoral dissertation, Santa Barbara, CA: Fielding Graduate Institute, Fielding Graduate University.

Gardner, H. (1999) *Intelligence Reframed: Multiple Intelligences for the Twenty-First Century*. New York: Basic Books.

Gardner, H. (2000) *Intelligence Reframed: Multiple Intelligences for the Twenty-First Century*. New York: Basic Books.

Gardner, W.I. and Avolio, B. (1998) The charismatic relationship: A dramaturgical perspective. *Academy of Management Review*, 23: 32–58.

Gardner, W.L., Avolio, B.J., Luthans, F., May, D.R. and Walumbwa, F. (2005) Can you see the real me? A Self based model of authentic leader and follower development. *Leadership Quarterly*, 16(3): 343–372.

Gardner, W.L., Cogliser, C.C., Davis, K.M. and Dickens, M.P. (2011) Authentic leadership: A review of the literature and research agenda. *Leadership Quarterly*, 22: 1120–1145.

Gayá Wicks, P. and Rippin. A. (2010) Art as experience: An inquiry into art and leadership using dolls and doll-making. *Leadership*, 6: 259–278.

Geertz, C. (1973) *The Interpretation of Cultures: Selected Essays*. New York: Basic Books.

Gentry, W.A. and Martineau, J.W. (2010) Hierarchical linear modelling as an example for measuring change over time in a leadership development evaluation context. *Leadership Quarterly*, 21: 645–656.

George, B. (2003) *Authentic Leadership: Rediscovering the Secrets of Creating Lasting Value*. San Francisco, CA: Jossey-Bass.

Gergen, K.J. (1985) The social constructionist movement in modern psychology. *American Psychologist*, 40: 266–275.

Geyer, A.L.J. and Steyrer, J.M. (1998) Transformational leadership and objective performance in banks. *Applied Psychology: An International Review*, 47: 397–420.

Ghoshal, S. (2005) Bad management theories are destroying good management practices. *Academy of Management Learning and Education*, 4(1): 75–91.

Gibb, C.A. (1954) Leadership. In G. Lindzey and E. Aronson. (eds) *The Handbook of Social Psychology*, second edition, Vol. 4. Reading, MA: Addison-Wesley, 205–283.

Gill, R. (1985) Leadership styles in Southeast Asia and the U.S.A.: A comparative study. Unpublished paper, Ross-on-Wye, Herefordshire: Leadership Trust Foundation.

Gill, R. (1997) Cross-cultural similarities and differences in leadership styles and behaviour: A comparison between UK and Southeast Asian managers. Working Paper No. LT-RG-97–8. Ross-on-Wye: Leadership Trust Foundation.

Gill, R. (1999) Think globally, act locally: What does it mean for leadership in Britain and Southeast Asia? Working Paper No. LT-RG-99–14. Ross-on-Wye: Leadership Trust Foundation.

Gill, R. (2003) Towards a general theory of leadership. Working paper No. LT-RG-03–20. Ross-on-Wye: Leadership Trust Foundation.

Gill, R. (2006) *Theory and Practice of Leadership*. London: Sage.

Gill R. (2011) *Theory and Practice of Leadership*, second edition. London: Sage.

Gill, R, Levine, N. and Pitt, D.C. (1998) Leadership and organizations for the new millennium. *The Journal of Leadership Studies*, 5(4): 46–59.

Gillespie, R. (1991) *Manufacturing Knowledge: A History of the Hawthorne Experiments*. Cambridge: Cambridge University Press.

Goethals, G.R. and Sorenson, G.L.J. (2006) *The Quest for a General Theory of Leadership*. Cheltenham: Edwards Elgar.

Goleman, D. (1995) *Emotional Intelligence*. New York: Bantam Books.

Goleman, D. (2001) What makes a leader? In J. Henry (ed.) *Creative Management*. London: Sage, 125–139.

Goodman, P.S. (1967) An empirical examination of Elliot Jaques' concept of time span. *Human Relations*, 20: 155–170.

Goodwin, V.L., Wofford, J.C. and Whittington, J.L. (2001) A theoretical and empirical extension to the transformational leadership construct. *Journal of Organizational Behavior*, 22: 759–775.

Gordon, R.D. (2002) Conceptualising leadership with respect to its historical-contextual antecedents to power. *The Leadership Quarterly*, 13(2): 151–167.

Gordon, R.D. (2011) Leadership and power. In A. Bryman, D. Collinson, K. Grint, B. Jackson and M. Uhl-Bien (eds) *The SAGE Handbook of Leadership*. London: Sage, 195–202.

Gordon, R.D. (2010) Dispersed leadership: exploring the impact of antecedent forms of power using a communicative framework. *Management Communication Quarterly*, 24: 260–287.

Gosling, J. and Mintzberg, H. (2003) The five minds of a manager. *Harvard Business Review*, 81(11): 54–63.

Gosling, J., Bolden, R. and Petrov, G. (2009) Distributed leadership in higher education: What does it accomplish? *Leadership*, 5(3): 299–310.

Graeff, C.L. (1997) Evolution of situational leadership theory: A critical review. *Leadership Quarterly*, 8(2): 153–170.

Graen, G.B. (1976) Role-making processes within complex organizations. In M.D. Dunnette (ed.) *Handbook of Industrial and Organizational Psychology*. Chicago: Rand McNally, 1202–1245.

Graen, G.B. (2006) In the eye of the beholder: cross-cultural lesson in leadership from project GLOBE: A response viewed from the third culture bonding (TCB) model of cross-cultural leadership. *Academy of Management Perspectives*, 20(4): 95–101.

Graen, G.B. and Cashman, J.F. (1975) A role making model in formal organizations: A developmental approach. In J.G. Hunt and L.L. Larson (eds) *Leadership Frontiers*. Kent, OH: Kent State Press, 143–165.

Graen, G.B. and Uhl-Bien, M. (1991) The transformation of professionals into self-managing and partially self-designing contributions: Toward a theory of leadership making. *Journal of Management Systems*, 3(3): 33–48.

Graen, G.B. and Uhl-Bien, M. (1995) Relationship-based approach to leadership: Development of leader-member exchange (LMX) theory of leadership over 25 years: applying a multi-level multi-domain perspective. *The Leadership Quarterly*, 6(2): 219–247.

Grandy, G. and Holton, J. (2013) Evaluating leadership development needs in a health care setting through a partnership approach. *Advances in Developing Human Resources*, 15(1): 61–82.

Greenleaf, R.K. (1977) *Servant Leadership: A Journey into the Nature of Legitimate Power and Greatness*. Mahwah, NJ: Paulist Press.

Griffey, E. and Jackson, B. (2010) The portrait as leader: Commissioned portraits and the power of tradition. *Leadership*, 6(2): 1–25.

Grint, K. (1995) *Management: A Sociological Introduction*. Cambridge: Polity.

Grint, K. (1997) *Leadership: Classical, Contemporary and Critical Approaches*. Oxford: Oxford University Press.

Grint, K. (2000) *The Arts of Leadership*. Oxford: Oxford University Press.

Grint, K. (2001) *The Arts of Leadership*. Oxford: Oxford University Press.

Grint, K. (2005a) *Leadership: Limits and Possibilities*. Basingstoke: Palgrave Macmillan.

Grint, K. (2005b) Problems, problems, problems: The social construction of 'leadership'. *Human Relations*, 58(11): 1467–1494.

Grint, K. (2008) *Leadership, Management and Command: Re-thinking D-Day*. Basingstoke: Palgrave.

Grint, K. (2010) The sacred in leadership: separation: Sacrifice and silence. *Organizations Studies*, 31(1): 89–107.

Grint, K. (2011) A history of leadership. In A. Bryman, D. Collinson, K. Grint, B. Jackson and M. Uhl-Bien (eds) *The SAGE Handbook of Leadership*. London: Sage, 3–14.

Gronn, P. (2002) Distributed leadership as a unit of analysis. *Leadership Quarterly*, 13(4): 423–451.

Gronn, P. (2003) Leadership: Who needs it? *School Leadership and Management*, 23(3): 267–290.

Gronn, P. (2008) The future of distributed leadership. *Journal of Educational Administration*, 46(2): 141–158.

Gronn, P. (2009a) Leadership configurations. *Leadership*, 5(3): 381–394.

Gronn, P. (2009b) Hybrid leadership. In K. Leithwood, B. Mascall and T. Strauss (eds) *Distributed Leadership According to the Evidence*. New York: Routledge, 17–40.

Gronn, P. (2011) Hybrid configurations of leadership. In A. Bryman, D. Collinson, K. Grint, B. Jackson, and M. Uhl Bien (eds) *The SAGE Handbook of Leadership*. London: Sage, 437–454.

Gross, R. (2010) *Psychology: The Science of Mind and Behaviour*, sixth edition. Hodder Education.

Guest, R.H. (1955–6) Of time and the foremen. *Personnel*, 32: 478–486.

Guthey, E. and Jackson, B. (2005) CEO portraits and the authenticity paradox. *Journal of Management Studies*, 42(5): 1057–1082.

Guthey, E. and Jackson, B. (2011) Cross-cultural leadership revisited. In A. Bryman, D. Collinson, K. Grint, B. Jackson and M. Uhl-Bien (eds) *The SAGE Handbook of Leadership*. London: Sage, 165–178.

Habermas, J. (1984) *The Theory of Communicative Action Vol. 1: Reason and Rationalization in Society*. Boston, NA: Beacon Press.

Habermas, J. (1987) *The Theory of Communicative Action, Vol. 2: Lifeworld and System: A Critique of Functionalist Reason*. Boston, NA: Beacon Press..

Hailey, J. (1996) The expatriate myth: Cross-cultural perceptions of expatriate managers. *The International Executive*, 38(20): 255–271.

Hales, C. (1986) What do managers do? A critical review of the evidence. *Journal of Management Studies*, 23(1): 88–115.

Hales, C. (1999) Why do managers do what they do? Reconciling evidence and theory in accounts of managerial work. *British Journal of Management*, 10: 335–350.

Halpin, A.W. and Winter, B.J. (1957) A factorial study of the leader behaviour descriptions. In R.M. Stogdill and A.E. Coons (eds) *Leader Behaviour: Its Description and Measurement*. Columbus, OH: Bureau of Business Research, Ohio State University.

Halverston, S.K., Murphy, S.E. and Riggio, R. (2004) Charismatic leadership in crisis situations: A laboratory investigation of stress and crisis. *Small Group Research*, 35: 495–514.

Hambrick, D.C. (1989) Guest editor's introduction: Putting top managers back in the strategy picture. *Strategic Management Journal*, 10(1): 5–15.

Hambrick, D.C. (2007) Upper echelons theory: An update. *Academy of Management Review*, 32(3): 334–343.

Hambrick, D.C. and Mason, P.A. (1984) Upper echelons: The organisation as a reflection of its top managers. *Academy of Management Review*, 9(2): 193–206.

Hannan, M. and Freeman, J. (1984) Structural inertia and organisational change. *American Sociological Review*, 49: 149–164.

Hannum, K.M. and Craig, S.B. (2010) Introduction to the special issue on leadership development evaluation. *Leadership Quarterly*, 21: 581–582.

Hansen, H. and Bathurst, R. (2011) Aesthetics and leadership. In A. Bryman, D. Collinson, K. Grint, B. Jackson and M. Uhl-Bien (eds) *The SAGE Handbook of Leadership*. London: Sage, 255–266.

Hansen, H., Ropo, A. and Sauer, E. (2007) Aesthetic leadership. *The Leadership Quarterly*, 18(6): 544–560.

Hanson, B. (2013) The leadership development interface: Aligning leaders and organizations toward more effective leadership learning. *Advances in Developing Human Resources*, 15(1): 106–120.

Harding, N., Lee, H., Ford, J. and Learmonth, M. (2011) Leadership and charisma: A desire that cannot speak its name? *Human Relations*, 64(7): 927–949.

Hardy, C. (2001) Researching organizational discourse. *International Studies of Management and Organization*, 31(3): 25–47.

Harrington, K.V. and Griffin, R.W. (1990) Ripley, Burke, Gorman and friends: Using the film *Aliens* to teach leadership and power. *Journal of Management Education*, 14(3): 79–86

Harris, A.(2004) Distributed leadership: leading or misleading. *Educational Management and Administration*, 32: 11–24.

Harris, A. (2008) *Distributed School Leadership: Developing Tomorrow's Leaders*. London: Routledge.

Harris, A. (ed.) (2009a) *Distributed Leadership: Different Perspectives*. London: Routledge.

Harris, A. (2009b) Distributed leadership and knowledge creation. In K. Leithwood, B. Mascall and T. Strauss (eds) *Distributed Leadership According to the Evidence*. New York: Routledge, 253–266.

Harter, S. (2002) Authenticity. In C.R. Synder and S.J. Lopez. (eds) *Handbook of Positive Psychology*. New York: Oxford University Press, 382–394.

Hartley, P. and Bruckmann, C.G. (2002) *Business Communication*. London: Routledge.

Haslam, S.A. (2004), *Psychology in Organisations: The Social Identity Approach*, second edition. Sage, London.

Haslam, S.A. and Ryan, M. (2008) The road to the glass cliff: differences in the perceived suitability of men and women for leadership positions in succeeding and failing organizations. *The Leadership Quarterly*, 19: 530–546.

Hatch, M. J., Kostera, M. and Kozminski, A. J. (2005) *The Three Faces of Leadership: Manager, Artist, Priest*. Malden, MA: Blackwell Publishing.

Hater, J.J. and Bass, B.M. (1988) Superiors' evaluations and subordinates' perceptions of transformational and transactional leadership. *Journal of Applied Psychology*, 73(4): 695–702.

Heenan, D.A. and Bennis, W. (2000) *Co-leaders: The Power of Great Partnerships*. Chichester: Wiley & Sons.

Helgesen, M.E. (1990) *The Female Advantage: Women's Ways of Leadership*. New York: Doubleday.

Hemphill, J.K. (1958) Administration as problem solving. In A.W. Halpin (ed.) *Administrative Theory in Education*. New York: Macmillan, 89–118.

Hemphill, J.K. and Coons, A.E. (1957) Development of the leader behaviour description questionnaire. In R.M. Stogdill and A.E. Coons (eds) *Leader Behaviour: Its Description and Measurement*. Columbus, OH: Bureau of Business Research, Ohio State University, 6–38.

Henry, E. and Pene, H. (2001) Kaupapa Maori: Locating indigenous ontology, epistemology and methodology in the academy. *Organization*, 8(2): 234–242.

Hersey, P. and Blanchard, K.H. (1971) *The Management of Organizational Behaviour*, third edition. Englewood Cliffs, NJ: Prentice Hall.

Hersey, P. and Blanchard, K.H. (1988) *Management of Organisational Behaviour*, fifth edition. Englewood Cliffs, NJ: Prentice-Hall.

Hickman, C.R. (1990) *Mind of a Manager, Soul of a Leader*. New York: Wiley.

Hinkin, T.R. and Schriesheim, C.A. (2008) A theoretical and empirical examination of the transactional and non-leadership dimensions of the multifactor leadership questionnaire (MLQ). *Leadership Quarterly*, 19: 501–513.

Hinkin, T.R. and Tracy, J.B. (1999) The relevance of charisma for transformational leadership in stable organizations. *Journal of Organizational Change Management*, 12: 105–119.

Hofstede, G. (1980) *Culture's Consequences: International Differences in Work-Related Values*. Beverly Hills, CA: Sage.

Hofstede, G. (2002) Dimensions do not exist: a reply to Brendan McSweeney. *Human Relations*, 55(11): 1–7.

Hofstede, G. (2009) Who is the fairest of them all? Galit Ailon's Mirror. *Academy of Management Review*, 34(3): 570–572.

Hogg, M.A. (2001) A social identity theory of leadership. *Personality and Social Psychological Review*, 5(3): 184–200.

Hogg, M.A. (2008) Social identity processes and the empowerment of followers. In R. Riggio, I. Chaleff and J. Lipmen-Blumen (eds) *The Art of Followership*. San Francisco, CA: Jossey-Bass, 267–276.

Hogg, M.A. and van Knippenberg, D. (2003) Social identity and leadership processes in groups. In M.P. Zanna (ed.) *Experimental Social Psychology*, Vol. 35. San Diego, CA: Academic Press, 1–52.

Hogg, M.A., Martin, R. and Weeden, K. (2003) Leader-member relations and social identity. In D. Van Knippenberg and M. Hogg (eds) *Leadership And Power: Identity Processes In Groups and Organizations*. London: Sage, 18–33.

Hollander, E.P. (1995) Ethical challenges in the leader-follower relationship. *Business Ethics Quarterly*, 5(1): 55–65.

Honey, P. and Mumford, A. (1989) *Manual of Learning Opportunities*. Maidenhead: Honey.

Hoover, N.R. (1987) Transformational and transactional leadership: A test of the model. Doctoral dissertation, University of Louisville, Louisville, KY.

Hoppe, B. and Reinelt, C. (2010) Social network analysis and the evaluation of leadership networks. *Leadership Quarterly*, 21: 600–619.

Hosking, D.M. (1988) Organizing, leadership and skilful processes. *Journal of Managements Studies*, 25(2): 147–166.

Hosking, D.M. (2007) Not leaders, not followers: A postmodern discourse of leadership processes. In B. Shamir, R. Pillai, M.C. Bligh and M. Uhl-Bien (eds) *Follower-centered Perspectives on Leadership: A Tribute to the Memory of James R. Meindl*. Charlotte, NC: Information Age Publishing, 243–264.

Hosking, D.M. (2011) Moving relationality: meditations on a relational approach to leadership. In A. Bryman, D. Collinson, K. Grint, B. Jackson and M. Uhl-Bien (eds) *The SAGE Handbook of Leadership*. London: Sage, 455–467.

Hosking, D.M. and Morley, I.E. (1988) The skills of leadership. In J.G. Hunt, R. Baliga and C. Schriesheim (eds) *Emerging Leadership Vistas*. Lexington, MA: Lexington Press.

Hosking, D.M. and Morley, I.E. (1991) *A Social Psychology of Organising*. London: Harvester Wheatsheaf.

House, R.J. (1971) A path-goal theory of leader effectiveness. *Administrative Science Quarterly*, 16: 321–328.

House, R.J. (1977) A 1976 theory of charismatic leadership. In J.G. Hunt and L.L. Larson (eds) *Leadership: The Cutting Edge*. Carbondale, IL: Southern Illinois University Press, 189–207.

House, R.J. (1996) Path-goal theory of leadership: Lessons, legacy and a reformulated theory. *Leadership Quarterly*, 7(3): 323–352.

House, R.J. and Dessler, G. (1974) The path-goal theory of leadership: Some post hoc and a priori tests. In J. Hunt and L. Larson (eds) *Contingency Approaches in Leadership*. Carbondale, IL: Southern Illinois University Press, 29–55.

House, R.J. and Mitchell, R.R. (1974) Path-goal theory of leadership. *Journal of Contemporary Business*, 3: 81–97.

House, R.J., Spangler, W. and Woycke, J. (1991) Personality and charisma in the U.S. Presidency: A psychological theory of leader effectiveness. *Administrative Science Quarterly*, 36: 364–396.

House, R.J., Hanges, P.J., Javidan, M., Dorfman, P.W. and Gupta, V. (eds) (2004) *Leadership, Culture and Organizations: The GLOBE Study of 62 Societies*. London: Sage.

Howard, A. and Bray, D.W. (1988) *Managerial Lives in Transition: Advancing Age and Changing Times*. New York: Guilford Press.

Howell, J.M. and Avolio, B.J. (1993) Predicting consolidated unit performance: Leadership behavior, locus of control, and support for innovation. *Journal of Applied Psychology*, 78: 891–902.

Howell, J.M. and Frost, P.J. (1989) A laboratory study of charismatic leadership. *Organizational Behavior and Human Decision Processes*, 43: 243–269.

Howell, J.M. and Higgins, C.A. (1990) Champions of technological innovations. *Administrative Science Quarterly*, 35: 317–341.

Howell, J.P. and Mendez, M.J. (2008) Three perspectives on followership. In R. Riggio, I. Chaleff and J. Lipmen-Blumen (eds) *The Art of Followership*. San Francisco, CA: Jossey-Bass, 25–40.

Hoyt, C. (2007) Women and Leadership. In P.G. Northouse (ed.) *Leadership: Theory and Practice*. Thousand Oaks, CA: Sage, 265–299.

Hughes, L.W. and Avey, J.B. (2009) Transforming with levity: Humour, leadership and follower attitudes. *Leadership and Organization Development Journal*, 30(6): 540–562.

Hughes, R.L., Ginnett, R.C. and Curphy, G.J. (1999) *Leadership: Enhancing Lessons of Experience*. Singapore: Irwin-McGraw-Hill.

Hunt, J.G. (1991) *Leadership: A New Synthesis*. Thousand Oaks, CA: Sage.

Hunt, J.G. (1999) Transformational/charismatic leadership's transformation of the field: An historical essay. *Leadership Quarterly*, 10(2): 129–144.

Hunt, J.G. and Ropo, A. (1998) Multi-level leadership: Grounded theory and mainstream theory applied to the case of General Motors. In F. Dansereau and F.J. Yammarino (eds) *Leadership: The Multiple-level Approaches*. Stamford, CT: JAI Press, 289–327.

Hunt, J.G., Boal, K.B. and Dodge, G.E. (1999) The effects of visionary and crisis-responsive charisma on followers: an experimental examination of two kinds of charismatic leadership. *Leadership Quarterly*, 10: 423–448.

Hyde, M. and Chavis, D.M. (2007) Sense of community and community building. In R.A. Cnaan and C. Milofsky (eds) *Handbook of Community Movements and Local Organisations*. New York: Springer, 179–192.

Ilgen, D.R. and Feldman, J.M. (1983) Performance appraisal: A process focus. In L.L. Cummings and B.M. Staw (eds) *Research in Organizational Behavior*, Vol.5. Greenwich, CT: JAI Press, 141–197.

Islam, G. (2009) Animating leadership: Crisis and renewal of governance in four mythic narratives. *The Leadership Quarterly*, 20: 828–836.

Jackson, B. and Guthey, E. (2007) Putting the visual into the social construction of leadership. In B. Shamir, R. Pillai, M.C. Bligh and M. Uhl-Bien (eds) *Follower-centered Perspectives on Leadership: A Tribute to the Memory of James R. Meindl*. Information Age Publishing, 167–186.

Jackson, B. and Parry, K. (2008) *A Very Short, Fairly Interesting And Reasonably Cheap Book About Studying Leadership*. London: Sage.

Jackson, B. and Parry, K. (2011) *A Very Short, Fairly Interesting And Reasonably Cheap Book About Studying Leadership*, second edition. London: Sage.

Jacobs, T.O. and Jaques, E. (1987) Leadership in complex systems. In J.A. Zeidner (ed.) *Human Productivity Enhancement*, Vol. 2. New York: Praeger, 7–65.

Janson, A. (2008) Extracting leadership knowledge from formative experiences. *Leadership*, 4(1): 73–94.

Jaques, E. (1976) *A General Theory of Bureaucracy*. London: Heinemann.

Jaques, E. (1989) *Requisite Organization*. Arlington, VA: Cason Hall.

Jaques, E. (1990) In praize of hierarchy. *Harvard Business Review*, 68: 127–133.

Jaques, E. and Clement, S.D. (1991) *Executive Leadership: A Practical Guide to Managing Complexity*. Malden, MA: Blackwell.

Jarvis, C., Gulati, A., McCririck, V. and Simpson, P. (2013) Leadership matters: Tensions in evaluating leadership development. *Advances in Developing Human Resources*, 15(1): 27–45.

Jaworski, J. (1996) *Synchronicity*. San Francisco. CA: Berett-Koehler.

Jepson (now Schedlitzki), D. (2009a) Leadership context: The importance of departments. *Leadership and Organisation Development Journal*, 30(1): 36–52.

Jepson, D. (2009b) Studying leadership at cross-country level: A critical analysis. *Leadership*, 5(1), 61–80.

Jepson, D. (2009b) Leadership context: the importance of departments. *Leadership and Organization Development Journal*, 30(1): 36–52.

Jepson, D. (2010) The importance of national language as a level of discourse within individuals' theorising of leadership – A qualitative study of German and English employees. *Leadership*, 6(4): 425–445.

Jones, A.M. (2005) The anthropology of leadership: Culture and corporate leadership in the American South. *Leadership*, 9(1): 259–278.

Jones, S. (ed.) (1995) *Cybersociety: Computer Mediated Communication and Community.* London: Sage.

Judge, T.A., Bono, J.E., Ilies, R. and Gerhardt, M.W. (2002) Personality and leadership: A qualitative and quantitative review. *Journal of Applied Psychology*, 87: 765–780.

Kabacoff, R.I. (1999) Management level, job function and leadership style: A large sample study. Paper presented at the 107th Annual Convention of the American Psychological Association, Boston, MA, US.

Kane, T.D. and Tremble, T.R., Jr (1998) Transformational leadership effects at different levels of the army. Unpublished manuscript, Arlington, VA: U.S. Army Research Institute for the Behavioural and Social Sciences.

Kanste, O., Miettunen, J. and Kyngäs, H. (2007) Psychometric properties of the multifactor leadership questionnaire among nurses. *Journal of Advanced Nursing*, 57: 201–212.

Kanter, R.M. (1984) *The Change Masters: Innovation And Entrepreneurship in the American Corporation.* New York: Simon and Schuster.

Kanungo, R.N. and Mendonca, M. (1996) *Ethical Dimensions of Leadership.* Thousand Oaks, CA: Sage.

Katz, R.L. (1974) Skills of an effective administrator. *Harvard Business Review*, 52(5): 90–102. (Originally published in *Harvard Business Review* in 1955.)

Katz, D. and Kahn, R.L. (1951) Human organization and worker motivation. In L.R. Tripp (ed.) *Industrial Productivity*. Madison, WI: Industrial Relations Research Association.

Katz, D. and Kahn, R.L. (1966) *The Social Psychology of Organizations.* New York: John Wiley.

Katz, D. and Kahn, R.L. (1978) *The Social Psychology of Organizations*, second edition. New York: John Wiley.

Kelan, E.K. (2013) The becoming of business bodies: gender, appearance, and leadership development. *Management Learning*, 44(1): 45–62.

Keller, R.T. (1992) Transformational leadership and the performance of research and development project groups. *Journal of Management*, 18: 489–501.

Kellerman, B. (2004) *Bad Leadership: What It Is, How It Happens, Why It Matters.* Boston, MA: Harvard Business School Press.

Kellerman, B. (2008) *Followership: How Followers are Creating Change and Changing Leader.* Boston, MA: Harvard Business School Press.

Kelley, R.E. (1988) In praise of followers. *Harvard Business Review*, 66(6): 141–148.

Kelley, R.E. (1992) *The Power of Followership.* New York: Doubleday.

Kelley, R.E. (2008) Rethinking followership. In Riggio, R. Chaleff, I. and Lipmen-Blumen, J. (eds) *The Art of Followership*. San Francisco, CA: Jossey-Bass, 5–16.

Kelloway, E.K. and Barling, J. (1993) Members' participation in local union activities: Measurement, prediction, and replication. *Journal of Applied Psychology*, 78: 262–279.

Kelloway, E.K. and Barling, J. (2000) What we have learned about developing transformational leaders. *Leadership and Organization Development Journal*, 21(7): 355–362.

Kelloway, E.K., Barling, J., Kelley, E., Comtois, J. and Gatien, B. (2003) Remote transformational leadership. *Leadership and Organization Development Journal*, 24(3): 163–171.

Kempster, S. (2006) Leadership learning through lived experience: A process of apprenticeship? *Journal of Management and Organization*, 12(1): 4–22.

Kempster, S. (2009a) *How Managers have Learnt to Lead: Exploring the Development of Leadership Practice*. Basingstoke: Palgrave.

Kempster, S. (2009b) Observing the invisible: Examining the role of observational learning in the development of leadership practice. *Journal of Management Development*, 28(5): 439–456.

Kempster, S. and Stewart, J. (2010) Becoming a leader: A co-produced auto-ethnographic exploration of situated learning of leadership practice. *Management Learning*, 41(2): 205–219.

Kempster, S. and Stewart, J. (2010) Becoming a leader: A co-produced autoethnographic exploration of situated learning of leadership practice. *Management Learning*, 41(2): 205–219.

Kennedy, F., Carroll, B. and Francoeur, J. (2013) Mindset not skill set: Evaluating in new paradigms of leadership development. *Advances in Developing Human Resources*, 15(1): 10–26.

Kenney, R.A., Schwartz-Kenney, B.M. and Blascovich, J. (1996) Implicit leadership theories: Defining leaders described as worthy of influence. *Personality and Social Psychology Bulletin*, 22: 1128–1143.

Kernis, M.H. (2003) Toward a conceptualization of optimal self-esteem. *Psychological Inquiry*, 14(1): 1–26.

Kerr, S. and Jermier, J.M. (1978) Substitutes for leadership: their meaning and measurement. *Organizational Behavior and Human Performance*, 22: 375–403.

Kets de Vries, M. (2003) *Leaders, Fools and Imposters: Essays on the Psychology of Leadership*. Bloomington, IN: iUniverse.com.

Khaleelee, O. and Woolf, R. (1996) Personality, life experience and leadership capability. *Leadership and Organization Development Journal*, 17(6): 5–11.

Kirkpatrick, S.A. and Locke, E.A. (1991) Leadership: Do traits matter? *The Executive*, 5: 48–60.

Kirkpatrick, S.A. and Locke, E.A. (1996) Direct and indirect effects of three core charismatic leadership components on performance and attitudes. *Journal of Applied Psychology*, 81: 36–51.

Kleiner, A. (2001) Elliot Jaques levels with you. *Strategy and Business*, 1st Quarter.

Knights, D. and O'Leary, M. (2006) Leadership, ethics and responsibility to the other. *Journal of Business Ethics*, 67: 125–137.

Knights, D. and Willmott, H. (1992) Conceptualising leadership processes: A study of senior managers in a financial services company. *Journal of Management Studies*, 29: 761–782.

Knights, D. and Willmott, H. (1999) *Management Lives: Power and Identity in Work Organizations*. London: Sage.

Kochan, T. Bezrukova, K., Ely, R., Jackson, S., Joshi, A., Jehn, K., Leonard, J., Levine, D. and Thomas, D. (2003) The effects of diversity on business performance: report of the diversity research network. *Human Resource Management*, 42(1): 3–21.

Koene, B.A.S., Vogelaar, L.W. and Soeters, J.L. (2002) Leadership effects on organizational climate and financial performance: Local leadership effect in chain organizations. *Leadership Quarterly*, 13: 193–215.

Koh, W.L. (1990) An empirical validation of the theory of transformational leadership in secondary schools in Singapore. Doctoral dissertation, University of Oregon, Eugene.

Koh, W.L., Steers, R.M. and Terborg, J.R. (1995) The effects of transformational leadership on teacher attitudes and student performance in Singapore. *Journal of Organizational Behavior*, 16: 319–333.

Koivunen, N. (2007) The processual nature of leadership discourses. *Scandinavian Journal of Management*, 23: 285–305.

Kolb, D.A. (1984) *Experiential Learning*. Englewood Cliffs, NJ: Prentice Hall.

Komaki, J.K. (1998) *Leadership from an Operant Perspective*. New York: Routledge.

Korukonda, A.R. and Hunt, J.G. (1987) Management and leadership: Towards conceptual clarity. Paper presented at ORSA/TIMS Joint National Meeting, St Louis, MO.

Kotter, J.P. (1988) *The Leadership Factor*. New York: Free Press.

Kotter, J.P. (1990) *A Force for Change: How Leadership Differs From Management*. New York: The Free Press.

Kotter, J.P. (1996) *Leading Change*. Boston, MA: Harvard Business School Press.

Kotter, J.P. (2002) *The Heart of Change*. Boston, MA: Harvard Business School Press.

Kotter, J.P. (2007) Leading change: Why transformation efforts fail. *Harvard Business Review*, 85(1): 96–103. (Originally published in 1995,)

Kotter, J.P. and Schlesinger, L.A. (1979) Choosing strategies for change. *Harvard Business Review*, March–April: 106–114.

Krishnan, V.R. (2004) Impact of transformational leadership on followers' influence strategies. *Leadership and Organization Development Journal*, 25(1): 58–72.

Kubler-Ross, E. (1969) *On Death and Dying*. New York: Routledge.

Kurke, L.B. and Aldrich, H.E. (1983) Mintzberg was right! A replication and extension of 'The nature of managerial work'. *Management Science*, 29(8): 975–984.

Ladkin, D. (2006) The enchantment of the charismatic leader: charisma reconsidered as aesthetic encounter. *Leadership*, 2(2): 165–179.

Ladkin, D. (2008) Leading beautifully: How mastery, congruence and purpose create the aesthetic of embodied leadership practice. *The Leadership Quarterly*, 19(1): 31–41.

Ladkin, D. (2010) *Rethinking Leadership: A New Look at Old Leadership Questions*. Cheltenham: Edgar Elgar.

Lancaster, K. (1997) When spectators become performers: contemporary performance-entertainments meet the needs of an 'unsettled' audience. *Journal of Popular Culture*, 30(4): 75–88.

Lau, A.W., Newman, A.R. and Broedling, L.A. (1980) The nature of managerial work in the public sector. *Public Administration Review*, 40: 513–520.

Leavy, B. and McKiernan, P. (2009) *Strategic Leadership: Governance and Renewal*. Basingstoke: Routledge.

Leduc, R.F. and Block, S.R. (1985) Conjoint directorship: Clarifying management roles between the board of directors and the executive director. *Journal of Voluntary Action Research*, 14(4): 67–76.

Leithwood, K. and Jantzi, D. (1990) Transformational leadership: How principals can help reform cultures. *School Effectiveness and School Improvement*, 1: 249–280.

Leithwood, K., Mascall, B. and Strauss, T. (2009) *Distributed Leadership According to the Evidence*. New York: Routledge.

Levay, C. (2010) Charismatic Leadership in resistance to change. *Leadership Quarterly*, 21: 127–143.

Levy, D.L., Alvesson, M., and Willmott, H. (2003) Critical approaches to strategic management. In M. Alvesson and H. Willmott (eds) *Studying Management Critically*. London: Sage, 92–110.

Lewin, K. (1951) *Field Theory in Social Science*. New York: Harper and Row.

Lewin, K., Lippitt, R. and White, R.K. (1939) Patterns of aggressive behaviour in experimentally created social climates. *Journal of Social Psychology*, 10: 271–301.

Lewis, P. and Jacobs, T.O. (1992) Individual differences in strategic leadership capacity: A constructive/developmental view. In R.L. Phillips and J.G. Hunt (eds) *Strategic Leadership: A Multi-organizational-level Perspective*. Westport, CT: Quorum Books, 121–137.

Lichterman, P. (1996) *The Search for Political Community: American Activists Reinventing Commitment*. Cambridge: Cambridge University Press.

Liden, R.C. and Antonakis, J. (2009) Considering context in psychological leadership research. *Human Relations*, 62(11): 1587–1605.

Liden, R.C., Wayne, S.J. and Stilwell, D. (1993) A longitudinal study on the early development of leader-member exchange. *Journal of Applied Psychology*, 78: 662–674.

Likert, R. (1961) *New Patterns of Management*. New York: McGraw-Hill.

Lindebaum, D. and Cartwright, S. (2010) A critical examination of the relationship between emotional intelligence and transformational leadership. *Journal of Management Studies*, 47(7): 1317–1342.

Lindebaum, D. and Cassell, C. (2012) A contradiction in terms? Making sense of emotional intelligence in a construction management environment. *British Journal of Management*, 23(1): 65–79.

Lipman-Blumen, J. (2005) *The Allure of Toxic Leaders: Why we Follow Destructive Bosses and Corrupt Politicians – And how we can Survive Them*. New York: Oxford University Press.

London, M. and Tornow, W.W. (1998) Introduction: 360-degree feedback – more than a tool. In M. London and W. Tornow (eds) *Maximising the Value of 360-Degree Feedback*. Greensboro, NC: Center for Creative Leadership, 1–8.

Lord, R.G. and Maher, K.J. (1993) *Leadership and Information Processing*. London: Routledge.

Lord, R.G., Foti, R.J. and De Vader, C.L. (1984) A test of leadership categorization theory: Internal structure, information processing and leadership perceptions. *Organizational Behavior and Human Performance*, 34: 343–378.

Low, S.M. and Lawrence-Zúñiga, D. (eds) (2003). *The Anthropology of Space and Place: Locating Culture*. Malden, MA: Blackwell.

Lowe, K.B. and Gardner, W. (2000) Ten years of the leadership quarterly: Contributions and challenges for the future. *Leadership Quarterly*, 11(4): 459–514.

Lukes, S. (2005) *Power: A Radical View*. Basingstoke: Palgrave Macmillan.

Luthans, F. and Avolio, B.J. (2003) Authentic leadership: A positive development approach. In K.S. Cameron, J.E. Dutton and R.E. Quinn (eds) *Positive Organizational Scholarship*. San Francisco, CA: Berrett-Koehler, 241–258.

Maccoby, M. (2000) Narcissistic leaders: The incredible pros, the inevitable cons. *Harvard Business Review*, 78(1): 69–77.

MacIntyre, A. (1991) *After Virtue*. Notre Dame Press, IN: University of Notre Dame.

Mackenzie, R.A. (1969) The management process in 3-D. *Harvard Business Review*, 47(6): 80–87.

Maffesoli, M. (1996) *The Time of Tribes: The Decline of Individualism in Mass Society*. London: Sage.

Mahoney, T.A. (1961) *Building the Executive Team*. Englewood Cliffs, NJ: Prentice-Hall.

Mahoney, T.A., Jerdee, J.H. and Carroll, S.I. (1965) The job(s) of management. *Industrial Relations*, 4: 97–110.

Mainemelis, C., Boyatzis, R.E. and Kolb, D.A. (2002) Learning styles and adaptive felxibilty: Testing experiential learning theory. *Management Learning*, 33: 5–33.

Mann, F.C. (1965) Toward an understanding of the leadership role in formal organizations. In R. Dubin, G.C. Homans, F.C. Mann and D.C. Miller (eds) *Leadership and Productivity*. San Francisco, CA: Chandler, 68–103.

Mann, R.D. (1959) A review of the relationship between personality and performance in small groups. *Psychological Bulletin*, 56: 241–270.

Markus, H. and Wurf, E. (1987) The dynamic self-concept: A social psychological perspective. *Annual Review of Psychology*, 38: 299–337.

Martin, J. and Siehl, C. (1983) Organizational culture and counterculture: An uneasy symbiosis. *Organizational Dynamics*, 122: 52–64.

Martin, J. and Meyerson, D. (1988) Organizational cultures and the denial, channeling, and acknowledgement of ambiguity. In L.R. Pondy, R.J. Boland and H. Thomas (eds) *Managing Ambiguity and Change*. New York: Wiley, 93–125.

Martin, N.H. (1956) Differential decisions in the management of an industrial plant. *Journal of Business*, 29: 249–260.

Martin, N.H. (1959) The levels of management and their mental demands. In W.L. Warner and N.H. Martin (eds) *Industrial Man*. New York: Harper & Row.

Marturano, A. and Arsenault, P. (2008) Charisma. In A. Marturano and J. Gosling (eds) *Leadership: The Key Concepts*. Routledge, 18–22.

Masi, R.J. (1994) Transformational leadership and its role in empowerment, productivity, and commitment to quality. Unpublished doctoral dissertation, Chicago, IL: University of Illinois.

Maslow, A.H. (1954) *Motivation and Personality*. New York: Harper.

Maslow, A.H. (1968) *Toward a Psychology of Being*. New York: Van Nostrand.

McCall, M.W. (1998) *High Flyers: Developing the Next Generation of Leaders*. Boston, MA: Harvard Business School Press.

McCall, M.W. (2004) Leadership development through experience. *Academy of Management Executive*, 18(3): 127–130.

McCall, M.W. (2009) Recasting leadership development. *Industrial and Organisational Psychology: perspectives of Science and Practice*, 3(1): 3–19.

McCall, M.W. and Segrist, C.A. (1980) In pursuit of the manager's job: Building on Mintzberg. Technical Report No.14, Greensboro, CA: Center for Creative Leadership.

McCauley-Smith, C., Williams, S., Gillon, Braganza, A. and Ward, C. (2013) Individual leader to interdependent leadership: A case study in leadership development and tripartite evaluation. *Advances in Developing Human Resources*, 15(1): 83–105.

McMillan, D. and Chavis, D.M. (1986) Sense of community: A definition and a theory. *Journal of Community Psychology*, 14: 6–23.

McSweeney, B. (2002) Hofstede's model of national cultural differences and their consequences: A triumph of faith – A failure of analysis. *Human Relations*, 55(1): 89–118.

Meindl, J.R., Ehrlich, S.B. and Dukerich, J.M. (1985) The romance of leadership. *Administrative Science Quarterly*, 30(1): 78–102.

Mendonca, M. and Kanungo, R.N. (2007) *Ethical Leadership*. New York: McGraw Hill.

Menzies Lyth, I. (1988) *Containing Anxiety in Institutions: Selected Essays*. London: Free Association Books.

Militello, M. and Benham, M.K.P. (2010) 'Sorting out' collective leadership: How Q-methodology can be used to evaluate leadership development. *Leadership Quarterly*, 21: 620–632.

Ming-Wang, Z. and Satow, T. (1994) Leadership styles and organizational effectiveness in Chinese-Japanese joint ventures. *Journal of Managerial Psychology*, 9(4): 31–36.

Mintzberg, H. (1980) *The Nature of Managerial Work*. Englewood Cliffs, NJ: Prentice – Hall. (Original work published in 1973.)

Nancy, J.-L. (1991) *The Inoperative Community*. Minneapolis, MN: University of Minnesota Press.

Nel, D., Pitt, L. and Watson, R. (1989) Business ethics: Defining the twilight zone. *Journal of Business Ethics*, 8: 781–791.

Nicholls, J. (1994) The 'heart, head and hands' of transforming leadership. *Leadership and Organization Development Journal*, 15(6): 8–15.

Nilakant, V. (1991) Dynamics of middle managerial roles: A study in 4 Indian organizations. *Journal of Managerial Psychology*, 6(1): 17–24.

Niles, M.C. (1949) *Middle Management: The Job of the Junior Administrator*. New York: Harper.

Niles, M.C. (1958) *The Essence of Management*. New York: Harper.

Northouse, P.G. (2006) *Leadership: Theory and Practice, 4th edn*. Thousand Oaks: Sage.

Northouse, P.G. (2007) *Leadership: Theory and Practice*, fourth edition. Thousand Oaks, CA: Sage.

Northouse, P.G. (2009) *Leadership: Theory and Practice*, fifth edition. Thousand Oaks, CA: Sage.

O'Sullivan, S. (2006) *Art Encounters Deleuze and Guattari: Thought Beyond Representation*. New York: Palgrave Macmillan.

Oborn, E., Barrett, M. and Dawson, S. (2013) Distributed leadership in policy formulation: A socio-material perspective. *Organization Studies*, 34: 253–276.

Offermann, L.R., Kennedy, J.K. and Wirtz, P.W. (1994) Implicit leadership theories: Content, structure and generalizability. *Leadership Quarterly*, 5: 43–58.

Onmen, M.K. (1987) The relationship of clergy leadership characteristics to growing or declining churches. Unpublished doctoral dissertation, University of Louisville, Louisville, KY.

Orvis, K.A. and Langkamer Ratwani, K. (2010) Leader self-development: A contemporary context for leader development evaluation. *Leadership Quarterly*, 21: 657–674.

Osborn, R.N. and Marion, R. (2009) Contextual leadership, transformational leadership and the performance of international innovation seeking alliances. *Leadership Quarterly*, 20: 191–206.

Osborn, R.N., Hunt, J.G. and Jauch, L.R. (2002) Toward a contextual theory of leadership. *Leadership Quarterly*, 13(6): 797–837.

Oshagbemi, T. and Gill, R.W.T. (2004) Differences in leadership styles and behaviour across hierarchical levels in UK organizations. *Leadership and Organization Development Journal*, 25(1): 93–106.

Paolillo, J.G. (1981) Role profiles for managers at different hierarchical levels. *Academy of Management Proceedings*, 91–94.

Parker, M. (2004) Becoming manager: Or, the werewolf looks anxiously in the mirror, checking for unusual facial hair. *Management Learning*, 35: 45–59.

Parry, K. and Jackson, B. (2008) *A very short, fairly interesting and reasonably cheap book about studying leadership*. London: Sage.

Pasternack, B.A., Williams, T.D. and Anderson, P.F. (2001) Beyond the cult of the CEO: Building institutional leadership. *Strategy and Business*, January.

Pavett, C.M. and Lau, A. (1983) Managerial work: The influence of hierarchical level and functional speciality. *Academy of Management Journal*, 26: 170–7.

Pawar, B.S. and Eastman, K.K. (1997) The nature and implications of contextual influences on transformational leadership: A conceptual examination. *Academy of Management Review*, 22: 90–109.

Pearce, C.L. and Conger, J.A. (2003) *Shared Leadership: Reframing the Hows and Whys of Leadership*. Thousand Oaks, CA: Sage.

Pearce, C.L. and Manz, C.C. (2005) The new silver bullets of leadership: the importance of self and shared leadership in knowledge work. *Organizational Dynamics*, 34: 130–140.

Pearce, C.L. and Sims, H.P. (2000) Shared leadership: toward a multi-level theory of leadership. In M.M. Beyerlein, D.A. Johnson and S.T. Beyerlein (eds) *Advances in Interdisciplinary Studies of Work Teams: Team Development*, Vol. 7. Greenwich, CT: JAI Press, 115–139.

Pearce, C.L. and Sims, H.P. (2002) The relative influence of vertical vs. shared leadership on the longitudinal effectiveness of change management teams. *Group Dynamics: Theory, Research and Practice*, 6: 172–197.

Pearce, C.L., Conger, J.A. and Locke, E.A. (2008a) Shared leadership theory. *Leadership Quarterly*, 19: 622–628.

Pearce, C.L., Manz, C.C. and Sims, H.P., Jr (2008b) The roles of vertical and shared leadership in the enactment of executive corruption: implications for research and practice. *Leadership Quarterly*, 19: 353–359.

Pearce, C.L., Manz, C.C. and Sims, H.P., Jr (2009) Where do we go from here? Is shared leadership the key to team success? *Organizational Dynamics*, 38: 234–238.

Peters, L.H., Hartke, D.D. and Pohlmann, J.T. (1985) Fiedler's contingency theory of leadership: and application of the meta-analysis procedures of Schmidt and Hunter. *Psychological Bulletin*, 97: 273–285.

Pfeffer, J. (1977) The ambiguity of leadership. *Academy of Management Review*, 2: 104–112.

Pfeffer, J. (1992a) *Managing with Power.* Boston, MA: Harvard Business School Press.

Pfeffer, J. (1992b) Understanding power in organisations. *California Management Review*, 34(2): 29–50.

Pfiffner, J.M. and Sherwood, F.P. (1960) *Administrative Organization*. Englewood Cliffs, NJ: Prentice-Hall.

Phal, R. (2001) *On Friendship*. Cambridge: Polity Press.

Phillips, J.S. and Lord, R.G. (1986) Notes on the practical and theoretical consequences of implicit leadership theories for the future of leadership measurement. *Journal of Management*, 12: 31–41.

Phillips, R.L. and Hunt, J.G. (eds) (1992) *Strategic Leadership: A Multi-organizational Level Perspective*. Westport, CT: Quorum.

Pillai, R. (1996) Crisis and the emergence of charismatic leadership in groups: An experimental investigation. *Journal of Applied Social Psychology*, 26: 543–562.

Pillai, R. and Meindl, J.R. (1998) Context and charisma: a 'meso' level examination of the relationship of organic structure, collectivism, and crisis to charismatic leadership. *Journal of Management*, 24: 643–671.

Pillai, R. and Williams, E.A. (1998) Does leadership matter in the political arena? Voter perceptions of candidates' transformational and charismatic leadership and the 1996 U.S. presidential vote. *Leadership Quarterly*, 9: 397–416.

Pillai, R., Kohles, J.C. and Bligh, M.C. (2007) Through thick and thin?: Follower constructions of presidential leadership amidst crisis, 2001–2005. In B. Shamir, R. Pillai, M.C. Bligh and M. Uhl-Bien (eds) *Follower-centered Perspectives on Leadership: A Tribute to the Memory of James R. Meindl*. Charlotte, NC: Information Age Publishing, 135–166.

Pillai, R., Schreisheim, C.A. and Williams, E.A. (1995) Fairness perceptions and trust as mediators for transformational and transactional leadership: A two-sample study. *Journal of Management*, 25: 897–933.

Pillai, R., Williams, E.A., Lowe, K.B. and Jung, D.I. (2003) Personality, transformational leadership, trust and the 2000 U.S. presidential vote. *Leadership Quarterly*, 14: 161–192.

Pitman, B., III (1993) The relationship between charismatic leadership behaviors and organizational commitment among white collar workers. Unpublished doctoral dissertation, Georgia State University, Atlanta, GA.

Podsakoff, P.M. and Organ, D.W. (1986) Self-reports in organizational research: Problems and prospects. *Journal of Management*, 12(4): 69–82.

Podsakoff, P.M., MacKenzie, S.B. and Bommer, W.H. (1996) Transformational leader behaviors and substitutes for leadership as determinants of employee satisfaction, commitment, trust and organizational citizenship behaviours. *Journal of Management*, 22: 259–298.

Podsakoff, P.M., MacKenzie, S.B., Moorman, R.H. and Fetter, R. (1990) Transfromational leader behaviours and their effects on followers' trust in leader, satisfaction, and organisational citizenship behaviours. *Leadership Quarterly*, 1(2): 107–142.

Podsakoff, P.M. Mackenzie, S.B., Lee, J. and Podsakoff, N.P. (2003) Common method biases in behavioural research: A critical review of the literature and recommended remedies. *Journal of Applied Psychology*, 88(5): 879–903.

Porter, L.W. and McLaughlin, G.B. (2006) Leadership and the organizational context: Like the weather? *Leadership Quarterly*, 17: 559–576.

Powell, G.N. (1990) One more time: Do female and male managers differ? *Academy of Management Executive*, 4: 68–75.

Powell, G.N. and Graves, L.M. (2003) *Women and Men in Management*, third edition. Thousand Oaks, CA: Sage.

Price, T.L. (2003) The ethics of authentic transformational leadership. *Leadership Quarterly*, 14: 67–81.

Prince, L. (2006) Eating the menu rather than the dinner: Tao and leadership. *Leadership*, 1(1): 105–126.

Pye, A. (2005) Leadership and organizing: Sense-making in action. *Leadership*, 1(1): 31–50.

Quinn, R.E. (1984) Applying the competing values approach to leadership: Toward an integrative framework. In J.G. Hunt, D.M. Hosking, C.A. Schriesheim and R. Stewart (eds) *Leaders and Managers: International Perspectives on Managerial Behavior and Leadership*. New York: Pergamon, 227.

Raelin, J. (2004) Preparing for leaderful practice. *Training and Development*, March: 65–70.

Rafferty, A.E. and Griffin, M.A. (2004) Dimensions of transformational leadership: Conceptual and empirical extensions. *Leadership Quarterly*, 5: 329–354.

Rajan, A. (2000) Does management development fail to produce leaders? In K. W. Parry and J.R. Meindl (eds) *Grounding Leadership Theory and Research: Issues and Perspectives*. Greenwich, CT: Information Age Publishing, 21–38.

Rast, D.E., Gaffney, A.M., Hogg, M.A. and Crisp, R.J. (2012) Leadership under uncertainty: When leaders who are non-prototypical group members can gain support. *Journal of Experimental Social Psychology*, 48: 646–653.

Rheingold, H. (1993) *The Virtual Community: Homesteading on the Electronic Frontier*. Reading, MA: Addison-Wesley.

Richards, D. (1996) Strangers in a strange land: Expatriate paranoia and the dynamics of exclusion. *The International Journal of Human Resource Management*, 7(2): 553–571.

Rickards, T. (2012) *Dilemmas of Leadership*, second edition. Abingdon: Routledge.

Riggio, R. Chaleff, I. and Lipmen-Blumen, J. (eds) (2008) *The Art of Followership*. San Francisco, CA: Jossey–Bass

Ropo, A. and Eriksson, M. (1997) Managing a theatre production: Conflict, communication and competence. In M. Fitzgibbon and A. Kelly (eds) *From Maestro to Manager: Critical Issues in Arts and Culture Management*. Dublin: Oak Tree Press.

Ropo, A., Parviainen, J. and Koivunen, N. (2002) Aesthetics in leadership: From absent bodies to social bodily presence. In K.W. Parry and J.R. Meindl (eds) *Grounding Leadership Theory and Research: Issues, Perspectives and Methods*. Greenwich, CT: Information Age Publishing, 21–38.

Rosch, E. (1978) Principles of categorization. In E. Rosch and B. Lloyd (eds) *Cognition and Categorization*. Hillsdale, NJ: Lawrence Erlbaum, 27–48.

Rost, J.C. (1991) *Leadership for the Twenty-first Century*. Westport, CT: Praeger.

Rost, J.C. (2008) Followership: an outmoded concept. In R. Riggio, I. Chaleff and J. Lipmen-Blumen (eds) *The Art of Followership*. San Francisco, CA: Jossey-Bass, 53.

Rowe, W.G. (2001) Creating wealth in organizations: The role of strategic leadership. *Academy of Management Executive*, 15(1): 81–94.

Sadler, P. (1997) *Leadership*. London: Kogan Page.

Salam, S., Cox, J.F. and Sims, H.P., Jr (1997) In the eye of the beholder: How leadership relates to 360-degree performance ratings. *Group and Organization Management*, 22(2): 185–209.

Salovey, P. and Mayer, J. (1990) Emotional Intelligence. *Imagination, Cognition, and Personality*, 9: 185–211.

Saskin, M. (1988) The visionary leader. In J.A. Conger and R.A. Kanungo (eds) *Charismatic Leadership: The Elusive Factor in Organizational Effectiveness*. San Francisco, CA: Jossey-Bass, 122–160.

Sayles, L.R. (1964) *Managerial Behavior*. New York: McGraw-Hill.

Schama, S. (2006) *The Power of Art*. New York: HarperCollins.

Schedlitzki, D., Kempster, S. and Edwards, G. (2011) Anxiety and desire in leader becoming. Paper presented at the Developing Leadership Capacity Conference (DLCC), July, Bristol Business School.

Schein, E.H. (1992) *Organisational Culture and Leadership*, second edition. San Francisco, CA: Jossey Bass.

Schein, E.H. (2004) *Organizational Culture and Leadership*, third edition. San Francisco: John Wiley & Sons.

Schein, V.E. (1975) Relationships between sex role stereotypes and requisite management characteristics among female managers. *Journal of Applied Psychology*, 60: 340–344.

Schneider, B. (1989) Thoughts on leadership and management. In L. Atwater and R. Penn (eds) *Military Leadership: Traditions and Future Trends*. Annapolis, MD: U.S. Naval Academy.

Schyns, B. and Schilling, J. (2011) Implicit leadership theories: Think leader, think effective? *Journal of Management Inquiry*, 20(2): 141–150.

Schyns, B., Tymon, A., Kiefer, T. and Kerschreiter, R. (2013) New ways of leadership development: A picture paints a thousand words. *Management Learning*, 44(1): 11–24.

Sczesny, S. (2003) A closer look beneath the surface: Various facets of the think-manager-think-male stereotype. *Sex Roles*, 49: 353–363.

Selznick, P. (1957) *Leadership in Administration: A Sociological Interpretation*. Evanston, IL: Row, Peterson.

Shamir, B. (2007) From passive recipients to active co-producers: Followers' roles in the leadership process. In B. Shamir, R. Pillai, M.C. Bligh and M. Uhl-Bien (eds) *Follower-centered Perspectives on Leadership: A Tribute to the Memory of James R. Meindl*. Charlotte, NC: Information Age Publishing, ix–xxix.

Shamir, B. and Eilam, G. (2005) What's your story? A life-stories approach to authentic leadership development. The Leadership Quarterly, 16: 395–417.

Shamir, B., Arthur, M.B. and House, R.J. (1994) The rhetoric of charismatic leadership: A theoretical extension, a case study, and implications for research. *Leadership Quarterly*, 5(1): 25–42.

Shamir, B., House, R.J. and Arthur, M.B. (1993) The motivational effect of charismatic leadership: A self-concept based theory. *Organization Science*, 4(4): 577–594.

Shamir, B., Pillai, R., Bligh, M.C. and Uhl-Bien, M. (eds) (2007) *Follower-centered Perspectives on Leadership: A Tribute to the Memory of James R. Meindl*. Charlotte, NC: Information Age Publishing.

Sheep, M.L. (2006) When categories collide: A discursive psychology approach to the elasticity of multiple identities. ProQuest dissertations and theses, University of Cincinnati, Cincinnati, OH.

Shields, R. (ed.) (1996) *Cultures of the Internet*. London: Sage.

Shiba, S. (1998) Leadership and breakthrough. *Centre for Quality Management Journal*, 7(2): 10–22.

Sinclair, A. (2007a) *Leadership for the Disillusioned: Moving Beyond Myths and Heroes to Leading that Liberates*. Crows Nest, Australia: Allen and Unwin.

Sinclair, A. (2007b) Teaching leadership critically to MBAs: Experiences form heaven and hell. *Management Learning*, 38(4): 458–471.

Sinclair, A. (2009) Seducing leadership: Stories of leadership development. *Gender, Work and Organization*, 16(2): 266–284.

Sinclair, A. (2011) Being leaders. In A. Bryman, D. Collinson, K. Grint, B. Jackson and M. Uhl-Bien (eds) *The SAGE Handbook of Leadership*. London: Sage, 508–517.

Singer, A.E. (2003) *Aesthetic Reason: Artworks and the Deliberative Ethos*. University Park, PA: Pennsylvania State University Press.

Sinha, J.B.P. (1995) *The Cultural Context of Leadership and Power*. New Delhi: Sage.

Sivanathan, N. and Fekken, G.C. (2002) Emotional intelligence, moral reasoning and transformational leadership. *Leadership and Organization Development Journal*, 23(4): 198–204.

Sivasubramaniam, N., Murry, W.D., Avolio, B.J. and Jung, D.I. (1997) A longitudinal model of the effects of team leadership and group potency on performance. Unpublished manuscript, Binghamton University, Center for Leadership Studies.

Slobin, D. I. (2000) Verbalized events: A dynamic approach to linguistic relativity and determinism. In S. Niemeier and R. Dirven (eds) *Evidence for Linguistic Relativity*. Philadelphia, PA: John Benjamins Publisher, 107–138.

Small, D.A., Gelfand, M., Babcock, L. and Gettman, H. (2007) Who goes to the bargaining table? The influence of gender and framing on the initiation of negotiation. *Journal of Personality and Social Psychology*, 93(4): 600–613.

Smircich, L. (1983) Concept of culture and organizational analysis. *Aministrative Science Quarterly*, 28: 339–358.

Smircich, L. and Morgan, G. (1982) Leadership: The management of meaning. *Journal of Applied Behavioural Science*, 18: 257–273.

Smith, M. and Kollock, P. (eds) (1999) *Communities in Cyberspace*. London: Routledge.

Smither, R.D. (1988) The psychology of work and human performance. New York: Harper & Row.

Solansky, S.T. (2010) The evaluation of two key leadership development program components: Leadership skills assessment and leadership mentoring. *The Leadership Quarterly*, 21: 675–681.

Sosik, J.J. (1997) Effect of transformational leadership and anonymity on idea generation in computer-mediated groups. *Group and Organization Management*, 22(4): 460–487.

Sosik, J.J. and Godshalk, V.M. (2000) Leadership styles, mentoring functions and job-related stress: A conceptual model and preliminary study. *Journal of Organizational Behavior*, 21: 365–390.

Sosik, J.J., Avolio, B.J. and Kahai, S.S. (1997) Effects of leadership style and anonymity on group potency and effectiveness in a group decision support system environment. *Journal of Applied Psychology*, 82(1): 89–103.

Spillane, J.P. (2006) *Distributed Leadership*. San Francisco, CA: Jossey-Bass.

Stamp, G. (1988) *Longitudinal Research into Methods of Assessing Managerial Potential*. Alexandria, VA: US Army Research Institute.

Stead, V. (2013) Learning to deploy (in)visibility: an examination of women leaders' lived experiences. *Management Learning*, 44(1): 63–80.

Stead, V. and Elliott C. J. (2009) *Women's Leadership*. Basingstoke: Palgrave Macmillan.

Stech, E.L. (1983) *Leadership Communication*. Chicago, IL: Nelson-Hall.

Stech, E.L. (2004) Psychodynamic approach. In P.G. Northouse (ed.) *Leadership Theory and Practice*. Thousand Oaks, CA: Sage, 235–263.

Stech, E.L. (2008) A new leadership-followership paradigm. In R. Riggio, I. Chaleff and J. Lipmen-Blumen (eds) *The Art of Followership*. San Francisco, CA: Jossey-Bass, 41–52.

Stieglitz, H. (1969) *The Chief Executive – And His Job*. Personnel Policy Study No. 214. New York: National Industrial Conference Board.

Stogdill, R.M. (1948) Personal factors associated with leadership: A survey of the literature. *Journal of Psychology*, 25: 35–71.

Stogdill, R.M. and Coons. A.E. (eds) (1957) *Leader Behaviour: Its Description and Measurement*. Columbus, OH: Bureau of Business Research, Ohio State University.

Stogdill, R.M. (1974) *Handbook of leadership: A survey of the theory and research*. New York: Free Press.

Storey, J. (2005) What next for strategic-level leadership research? *Leadership*, 1(1): 89–104.

Strati, A. (1992) Aesthetic understanding of organizational life. *Academy of Management Review*, 17(3): 568–581.

Streyer, J. (1998) Charisma and the archetypes of leadership. *Organization Studies*, 19(5): 807–828.

Sutherland, I. (2013) Arts-based methods in leadership development: Affording aesthetic workplaces, reflexivity and memories with momentum. *Management Learning*, 44(1): 25–44.

Sveningsson, S.F. and Larsson, M. (2006) Fantasies of leadership: Identity work. *Leadership*, 2(2): 203–224.

Sy, T. (2010) What do you think of followers? Examining the content, structure, and consequences of implicit followership theories. *Organizational Behaviour and Human Decision Processes*, 113(2): 73–84.

Tajfel, H. (1978) *Differentiation Between Social Groups*. London: Academic.

Takala, T., Tanttu, S., Lamsa, A.M. and Virtanen, A. (2013) Discourses of charisma: Barack Obama's first 6 months as the president of the USA. *Journal of Business Ethics*, 115(1): 149–166.

Tayeb, M. (2001) Conducting research across cultures: overcoming drawbacks and obstacles. *International Journal of Cross Cultural Management*, 1(1): 91–108.

Taylor, S. and Ladkin, D. (2009) Understanding arts-based methods in managerial development. *Academy of Management Learning & Education*, 8(1): 55–69.

Taylor, S.S., Fisher, D. and Dufresne, R.L. (2002) The aesthetics of management storytelling: A key to organisational learning. *Management Learning*, 33: 313–330.

Tejeda, M.J., Scandura, T.A. and Pillai, R. (2001) The MLQ revisited: Psychometric properties and recommendations. *Leadership Quarterly*, 12: 31–52.

Tepper, B.T. and Percy, P.M. (1994) Structural validity of the multifactor leadership questionnaire. *Educational and Psychological Measurement*, 54: 734–744.

Thite, M. (1997) Relationship between leadership and information technology project sources. Unpublished doctoral dissertation, Swinbourne University of Technology, Melbourne, Australia.

Thomason, G.F. (1966) Managerial work roles and relationships: Part I. *Journal of Management Studies*, 3: 270–284.

Thomason, G.F. (1967) Managerial work roles and relationships: Part II. *Journal of Management Studies*, 4: 17–30.

Thorpe, R., Gold, J. and Lawler, J. (2011) Locating distributed leadership. *International Journal of Management Reviews*, 13(3): 239–250.

Thurston, P.W. and Clift, R.T. (1996) *Distributed Leadership: School Improvement through Collaboration*. Greenwich, CT: JAI Press.

Tichy, N.M. (1997) *The Leadership Engine: How Winning Companies Build Leaders at Every Level*. New York: Harper Collins.

Tichy, N.M. and Devanna, M.A. (1986) *The Transformational Leader*. New York: Wiley.

Tichy, N.M. and Devanna, M.A. (1990) *The Transformational Leader*, second edition. New York: Wiley.

Tietze, S. Cohen, L. and Musson, G. (2003) *Understanding Organizations Through Language.* London: Sage.

Tikhomirov, A.A. and Spangler, W.D. (2010). Neo-charismatic leadership and the fate of mergers and acquisitions: An institutional model of CEO leadership. *Journal of Leadership and Organisational Studies,* 17(1): 44–60.

Toh, S.M. and Denisi, A.S. (2003) Host country national (HNC) reactions to expatriate pay policies: A proposed model and implications. *Academy of Management Review,* 28(4): 606–621.

Tomlinson, M., O'Reilly, D. and Wallace, M. (2013) Developing leaders as symbolic violence: Reproducing public service leadership through the (misrecognised) development of leaders' capitals. *Management Learning,* 44(1): 81–97.

Touraine, A. (1995) *Critique of Modernity.* Oxford: Blackwell.

Touraine, A. (1997) *What is Democracy?* Oxford: Westview Press.

Tourish, D. and Pinnington, A. (2002) Transformational leadership, corporate cultism and the spirituality paradigm: An unholy trinity in the workplace? *Human Relations,* 55(2): 147–172.

Treviño, L.K., Hartman, L.P. and Brown, M.E. (2000) Moral person and moral manager: How executives develop a reputation for ethical leadership. *California Management Review,* 42: 128–142.

Treviño, L.K., Brown, M.E. and Hartman, L.P. (2003) A qualitative investigation of perceived executive ethical leadership: Perceptions from inside and outside the executive suite. *Human Relations,* 55: 5–37.

Triandis, H.C., Kurowski, L.L. and Gelfand, M.J. (1994) Workplace diversity. In H.C. Triandis, M.D. Dunette and L.M. Hough (eds) *Handbook of Industrial and Organizational Psychology,* vol. 4. Palo-Alto, CA: Consulting Psychologists Press, 769–827.

Trice, H.M. and Beyer, J.M. (1986) Charisma and its routinization in two social movement organizations. *Research in Organizational Behavior,* 8: 113–164.

Trice, H.M. and Beyer, J.M. (1993) *The Culture of Work Organizations.* Englewood Cliffs, NJ: Prentice Hall.

Tsoukas, H. and Chia, R. (2002) On organisational becoming: Rethinking organisational change. *Organisation Science,* 13: 567–582.

Turnbull James, K. and Burgoyne, J. (2001) *Leadership Development: Best Practice Guide for Organisations.* London: Council for Excellence in Management and Leadership.

Turnbull, S., Case, P., Edwards, G., Jepson, D. and Simpson, P. (2011) *Worldly Leadership.* London: Palgrave.

Turner, J.C. (1985) Social categorization and the self-concept. In H. Tajfel (ed.) *Advances in Group Processes.* Greenwich, CT: JAI Press, 77–122.

Turner, J.C. (1987) Introducing the problem: individual and group. In J.C. Turner, M.A. Hogg, P.J. Oakes, S.D. Reicher and M.S. Wetherell (eds) *Rediscovering the Social Group: A Self-categorization Theory.* Oxford: Blackwell, 1–18.

Turner, J.C. (1991) *Social Influence.* Milton Keynes: Open University Press.

Turner, N., Barling, J., Epitropaki, O., Butcher, V. and Milner, C. (2002) Transformational leadership and moral reasoning. *Journal of Applied Psychology,* 87(2): 304–311.

Turner, V. (1969) *The Ritual Process: Structure and Anti-Structure.* London: Routledge.

Twenge, J.M. (1997) Changes in masculine and feminine traits over time: a meta-analysis. *Sex Roles,* 36: 305–325.

Twenge, J.M. (2001) Changes in women's assertiveness in response to status and roles: a cross-temporal meta-analysis, 1931–1993. *Journal of Personality and Social Psychology,* 81: 133–145.

Uhl-Bien, M. (2004) Relational leadership approaches. In G.R. Goethals, G.J. Sorenson and J.M. Burns (eds) *Encyclopedia of Leadership.* Thousand Oask, CA: Sage.

Uhl-Bien, M. (2006) Relational leadership theory: exploring social processes of leadership and organizing. *The Leadership Quarterly*, 17: 654–676.

Uhl-Bien, M. and Pillai, R. (2007) The romance of leadership and the social construction of followership. In B. Shamir, R. Pillai, M.C. Bligh and M. Uhl-Bien (eds) *Follower-centered Perspectives on Leadership: A Tribute to the Memory of James R. Meindl*. Charlotte, NC: Information Age Publishing, 187–210.

Van Engen, M.L. (2001) Gender and leadership: a contextual perspective. Doctoral dissertation, Tilburg University, the Netherlands.

Van Gennep, A. (1960) *The Rites of Passage*. London: Routledge.

Van Maanen, J. (1979) The fact of fiction in organizational ethnography. *Administrative Science Quarterly*, 24(4): 539–550.

Vecchio, R.P. (1987) Situational leadership theory: An examination of a prescriptive theory. *Journal of Applied Psychology*, 72(3): 444–451.

Vecchio, R.P. (2002) Leadership and gender advantage. *The Leadership Quarterly*, 13: 674–671.

Vecchio, R.P. (2003) In search of the gender advantage. *The Leadership Quarterly*, 14: 835–850.

Vecchio, R.P. and Boatwright, K.J. (2002) Preferences for idealized style of supervision. *Leadership Quarterly*, 13: 327–342.

Vicere, A.A. and Fulmer, R.M. (1998) *Leadership By Design*. Boston, MA: Harvard Business School Press.

Vine, B., Holmes, J., Marra, M., Pfeifer, D. and Jackson, B. (2008) Exploring co-leadership talk through interactional sociolinguistics. *Leadership*, 4(3): 339–360.

Von Cranach, M. (1986) Leadership as a function of group action. In C.F. Graumann and S. Moscovici (eds) *Changing Conceptions of Leadership*. New York: Springer Verlag, 115–134.

Vroom, V.H. and Yetton, P.W. (1973) *Leadership and Decision Making*. Pittsburgh, PA: University of Pittsburgh Press.

Waldman, D.A., Bass, B.M. and Einstein, W.O. (1987) Leadership and outcomes of the performance appraisal process. *Journal of Occupational Psychology*, 60: 177–186.

Waldman, D.A., Bass, B.M. and Yammarino, F.J. (1990) Adding to contingent-reward behavior: The augmenting effect of charismatic leadership. *Group and Organization Studies,* 15: 381–394.

Waldman, D.A., Javidan, M. and Varella, P. (2004) Charismatic leadership at the strategic level: A new application of upper echelons theory. *Leadership Quarterly*, 15: 355–380.

Waldman, D.A., Keller, R. T. and Berson, Y. (2006) Leadership and organizational learning: A multiple levels perspective. *Leadership Quarterly*, 17(1): 110–11.

Walumbwa, F.O., Wang, P., Lawler, J.J. and Shi, K. (2004) The role of collective efficacy in the relations between transformational leadership and work outcomes. *Journal of Occupational and Organizational Psychology*, 77: 515–530.

Walumbwa, F.O., Avolio, B.J., Gardner, W.L., Wernsing, T.S. and Peterson, S.J. (2008) Authentic leadership: Development and validation of a theory based measure. *Journal of Management*, 34(1): 89–126.

Warner, L.S. and Grint, K. (2006) American Indian ways of leading and knowing. *Leadership*, 2(2): 225–244.

Warner, N. (2007) Screening leadership through Shakespeare: Paradoxes of leader-follower relations in Henry V on film. *The Leadership Quarterly*, 18: 1–15.

Washington, M., Boal, K.B. and Davis, J.N. (2008) Institutional leadership: Past, present and future. In R. Greenwood, C. Oliver, K. Sahlin and R. Suddaby (eds) *The Sage Handbook of Organisational Institutionalism*. London: Sage, 721–736.

Wasserstein, A.G., Brennan, P.J. and Rubenstein, A.H. (2007) Institutional leadership and faculty response: Fostering professionalism at the University of Pennsylvania School of Medicine. *Academic Medicine*, 82(11): 1049–1055.

Weber, M. (1947) *The Theory of Social and Economic Organisations*, trans. T. Parsons. New York: Free Press.

Weber, M. (1968). In S. Eisenstadt (ed.) *Max Weber on Charisma and Institution Building, Selected papers*. Chicago, IL: Univeristy of Chicago Press.

Weick, K.E. (1993) The collapse of sensemaking in organizations: The Mann Gulch disaster. *Administrative Science Quarterly*, 38: 628–652.

Weierter, S. (1994) Substitutes for transactional leadership: the impact of transactional leader behaviors on workgroup perceptions and first line supervisor level. Unpublished doctoral dissertation, Griffith University, Brisbane, Australia.

Wenger, E. (1998) *Communities of Practice: Learning, Meaning, and Identity*. Cambridge: Cambridge University Press.

Western, S. (2008) *Leadership: A Critical Text*. Thousand Oaks, CA: Sage.

Wheatley, M. J. (1994) *Leadership and the New Science: Learning About Organizations from an Orderly Universe*. San Francisco, CA: Berrett Koehler.

Whitely, W.T. (1978) Nature of managerial work revisited. *Academy of Management Proceedings*, 195–199.

Whyte, W.F. (1943) *Street Corner Society: The Social Structure of an Italian Slum*. Chicago, IL: University of Chicago Press.

Williams, B.A.O. (1982) *Moral Luck*. Cambridge: Cambridge University Press.

Williams, E.A., Pillai, R., Lowe, K.B., Jung, D. and Herst, D. (2009) Crisis, charisma, values, and voting in the 2004 presidential election. *Leadership Quarterly*, 20: 70–86.

Willner, A.R. (1984) *The Spellbinders*. New Haven, CT: Yale University Press.

Wittgenstein, L. (1953) *Philosophical Investigations*. Oxford: Blackwells.

Witz, A., Warhurst, C. and Nickson, D. (2003) The labour of aesthetics and the aesthetics of organization. *Organization*, 10(1): 33–54.

Wood, M. and Ladkin, D. (2008) The event's the thing: Brief encounters with the leaderful moment. In K. Turnbull-James and J. Collins (eds) *Leadership Perspectives: Knowledge into Action*. Basingstoke: Palgrave Macmillan, 15–28.

Wright, P.L. (1996) *Managerial Leadership*. London: Routledge.

Yammarino, F.J. and Bass, B.M. (1990) Long-term forecasting of transformational leadership and its effects among naval officers: some preliminary findings. In K.E. Clark and M.R. Clark (eds) *Measures of Leadership*. Greenboro, NC: Center for Creative Leadership. West Orange, NJ: Leadership Library of America, 151–170.

Yammarino, F.J. and Dubinsky, A.J. (1994) Transformational leadership theory: using levels of analysis to determine boundary conditions. *Personnel Psychology*, 47: 787–811.

Yammarino, F.J., Spangler, W.D. and Bass, B.M.(1993) Transformational leadership and performance: A longitudinal investigation. *Leadership Quarterly*, 4(1): 81–102.

Yammarino, F.J., Dionne, S.D., Chun, J.U. and Dansereau, F. (2005) Leadership and levels of analysis: A state-of-the-science review. *The Leadership Quarterly*, 16(6): 879–919.

Yammarino, F.J., Dionne, S.D., Schriesheim, C.A. and Dansereau, F. (2008) Authentic leadership and positive leadership behaviour: A meso, multi-level perspective. *The Leadership Quarterly*, 19(6): 697–707.

Yokochi, N. (1989) Leadership styles of Japanese business executives and managers: Transformational and transactional. Doctoral dissertation, United States International University, San Diego, CA.

Young, M. and Dulewicz, V. (2008) Similarities and differences between leadership and management: High performance competencies in the British Royal Navy. *British Journal of Management*, 19: 17–32.

Yukl, G. (1971) Toward a behavioural theory of leadership. *Organizational Behavior and Human Performance*, 6: 414–440.

Yukl, G. (1989) *Leadership in Organizations*, second edition. Englewood Cliffs, NJ: Prentice Hall.

Yukl, G. (1994) *Leadership in Organizations*, third edition. Englewood Cliffs, NJ: Prentice Hall.

Yukl, G.A. (1999) An evaluation of conceptual weaknesses in transformational and charismatic leadership theories. *Leadership Quarterly*, 10(2): 285–307.

Yukl, G.A. (2002) *Leadership in Organizations*, fifth edition. Englewood Cliffs, NJ: Prentice-Hall International.

Yukl, G.A. (2010) *Leadership in Organizations*, seventh edition. Englewood Cliffs, NJ: Prentice-Hall International.

Yukl, G. (2011) Contingency theories of effective leadership. In A. Bryman, D. Collinson, K. Grint, B. Jackson and M. Uhl-Bien (eds) *The SAGE Handbook of Leadership*. London: Sage, 286–298.

Zaccaro, S.J. and Horn, Z. (2003) Leadership theory and practice: Fostering an effective symbiosis. *Leadership Quarterly*, 14: 769–806.

Zaccaro, S.J. and Klimoski, R.J. (2001) The nature of organizational leadership: An introduction. In S.J. Zaccaro and R.J. Klimoski (eds) *The Nature of Organizational Leadership: Understanding the Performance Imperatives Confronting Today's Leaders*. Jossey-Bass, San Francisco, CA, 3–41.

Zaccaro, S.J., Kemp, C. and Bader, P. (2004) Leader traits and attributes. In J. Antonakis, A.T. Cianciolo and R.J. Sternberg (eds) *The Nature of Leadership*. Thousand Oaks, CA: Sage, 101–124.

Zaleznik, A. (1977) Managers and leaders: are they different? *Harvard Business Review*, 55: 67–78.

Zaleznik, A. (1989) *The Managerial Mystique: Restoring Leadership in Business*. New York: Harper & Row.

Zaleznik, A. and Kets de Vries, M.F.R. (1975) *Power and the Corporate Mind*. Boston, MA: Houghton-Mifflin.

Zohar, D. and Marshall, I. (2001) *Spiritual Intelligence*. London: Bloomsbury.

Zoller, H. M. and Fairhurst, G. T. (2007) Resistance leadership: The overlooked potential in critical organization and leadership studies. *Human Relations*, 60(9): 1331–1360.

Index